volume

3

THE LEGEND OF
DORORO AND
HYAKKIMARU

Created by
OSAMU TEZUKA

Adaptation by
SATOSHI SHIKI

どろろと百鬼丸伝

THE LEGEND OF DORORO AND HYAKKIMARU

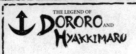

CONTENTS

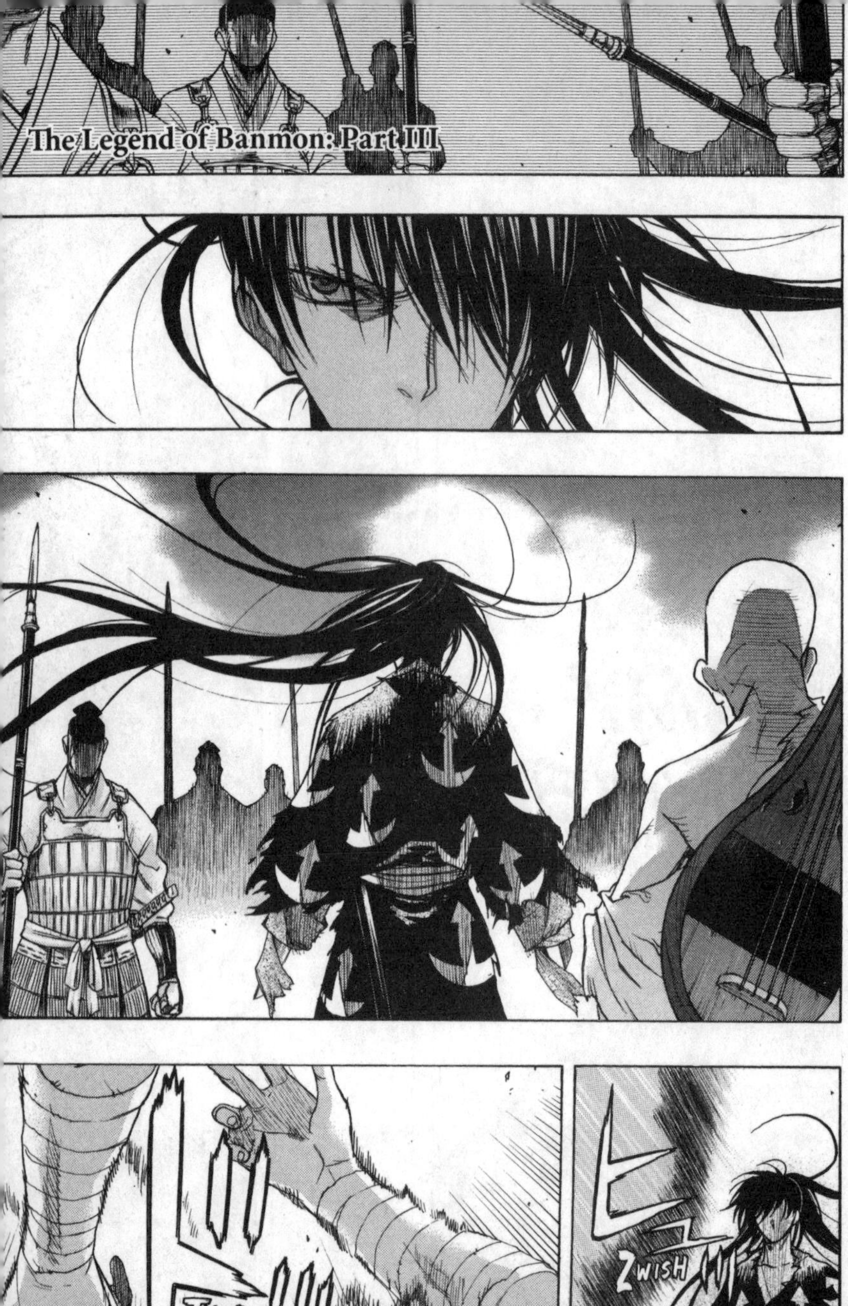
The Legend of Banmon: Part III
ZWISH
THUD

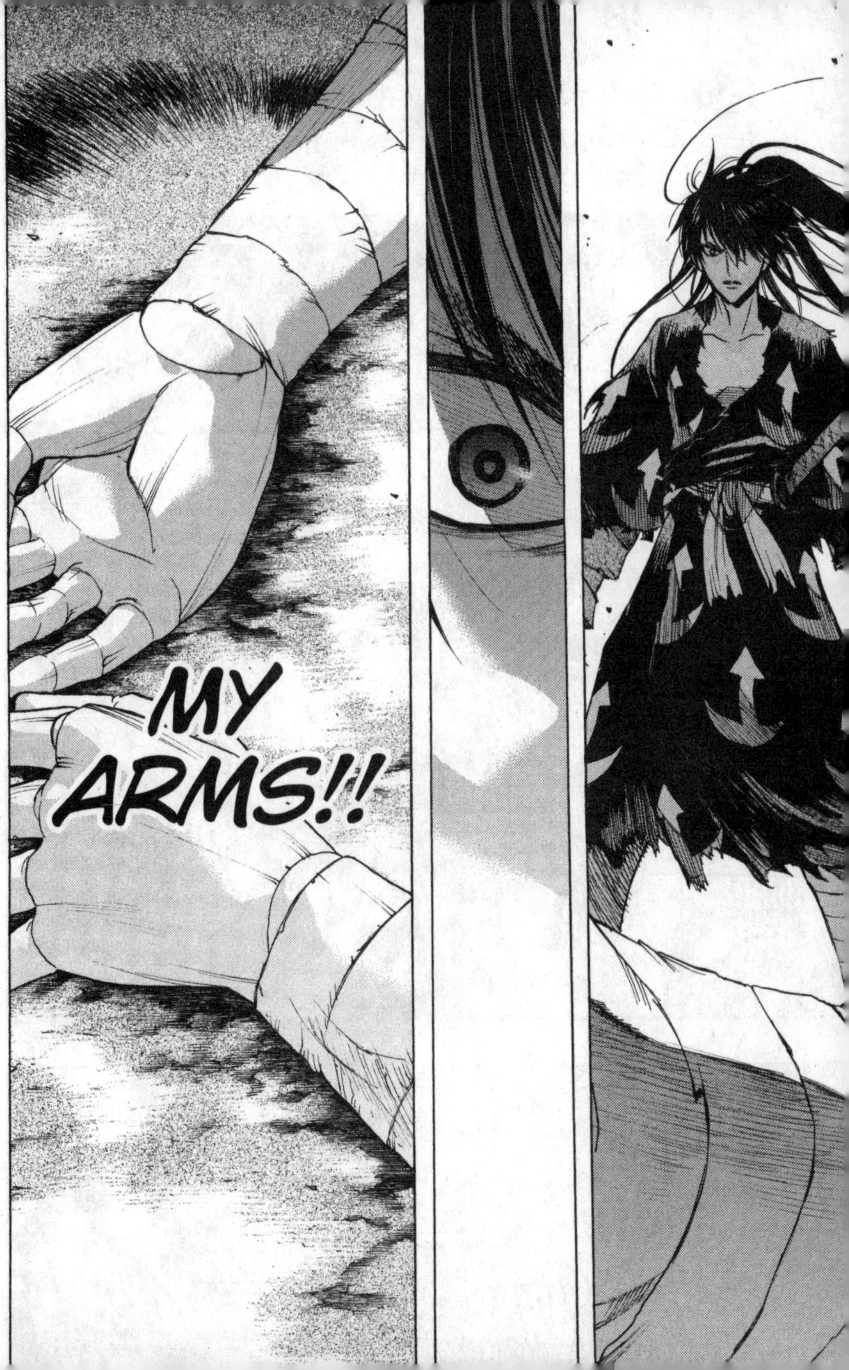
MY ARMS!!

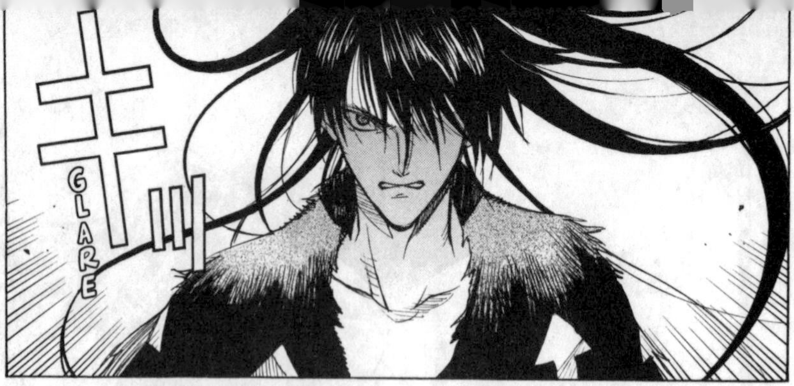
GLARE
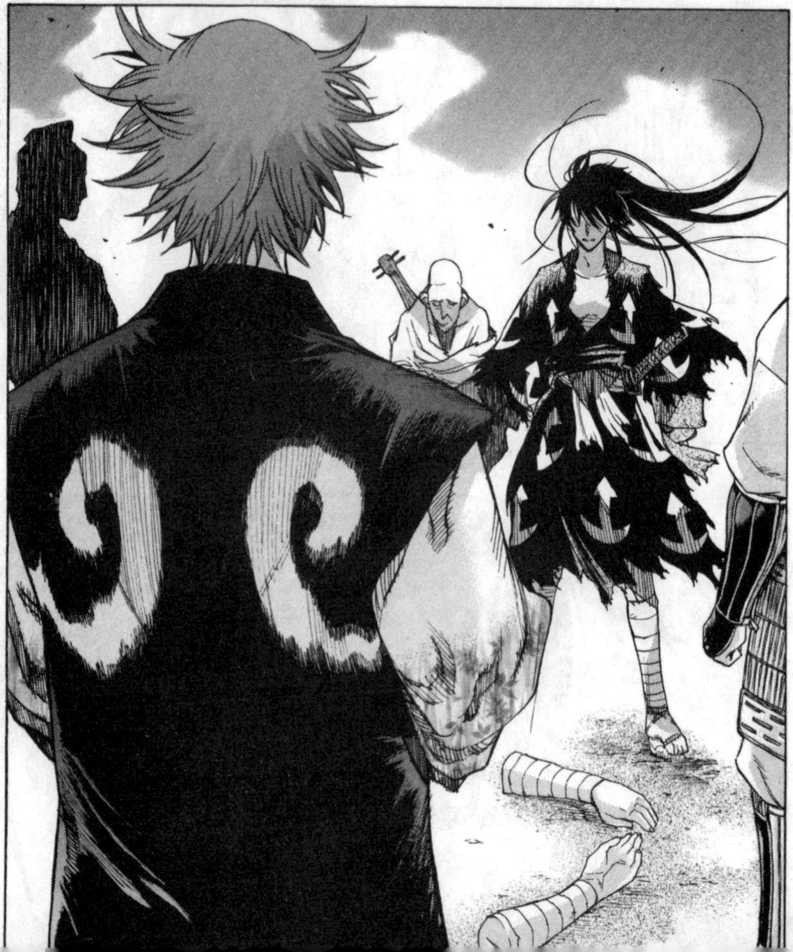

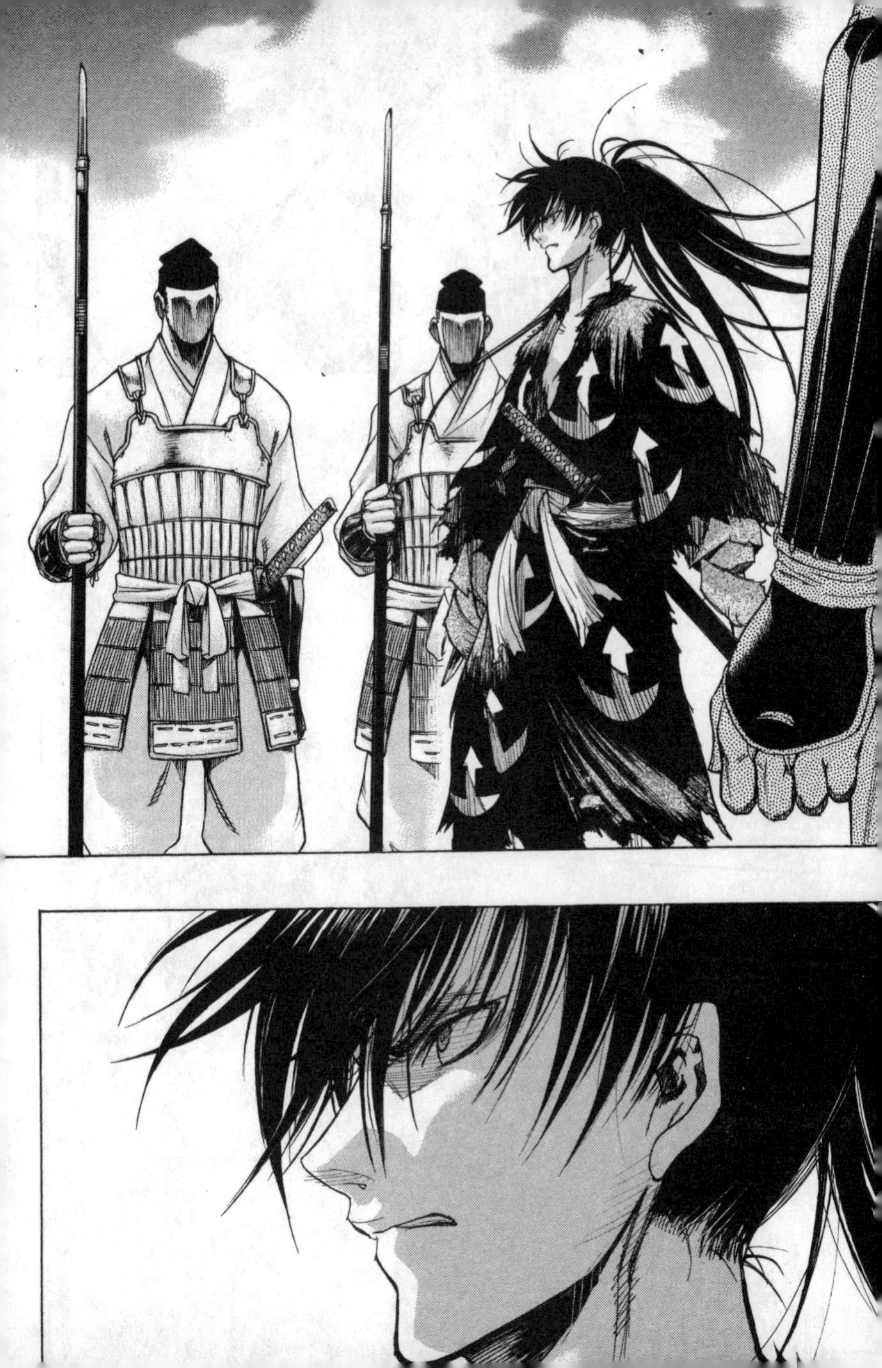

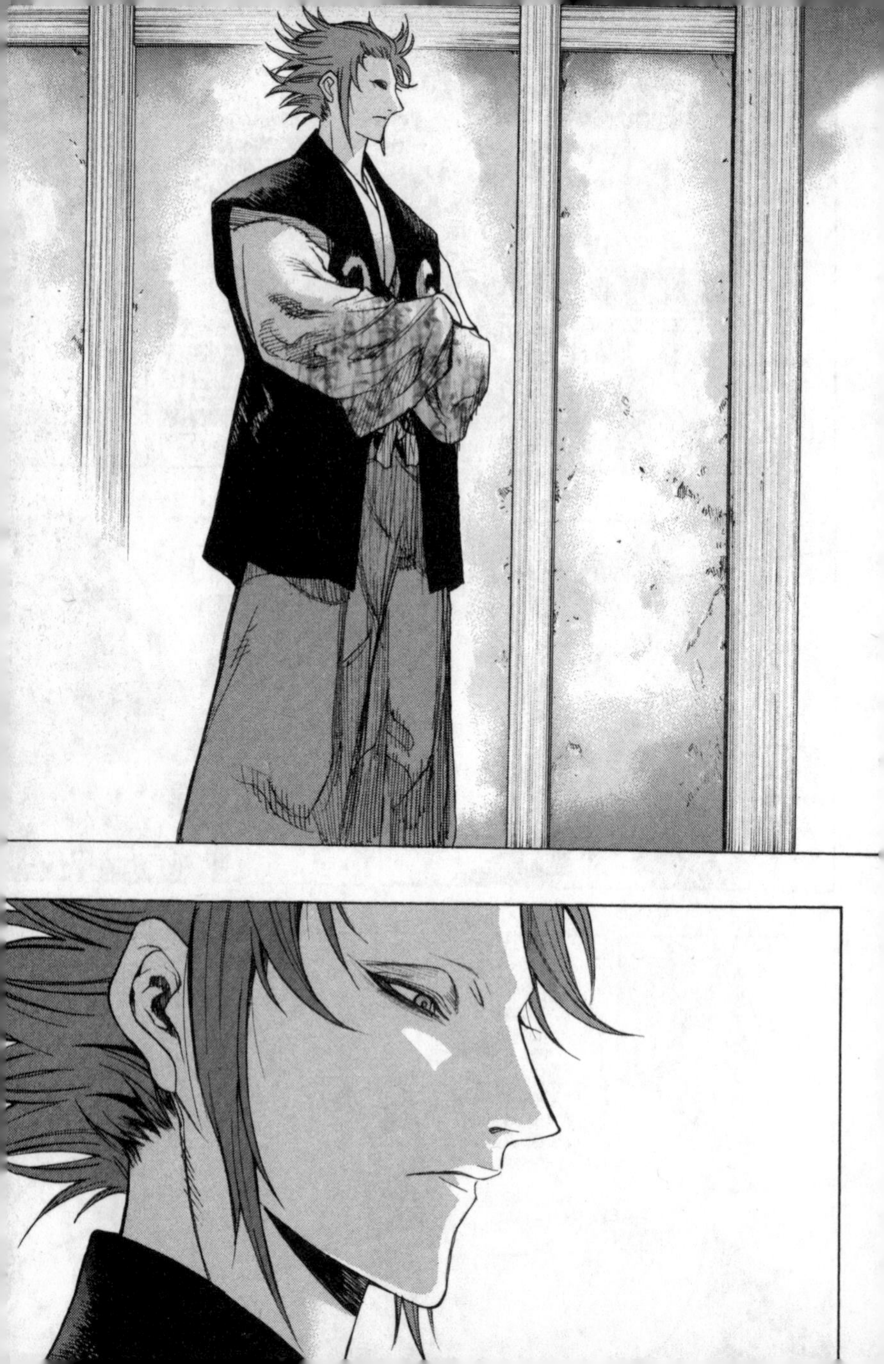

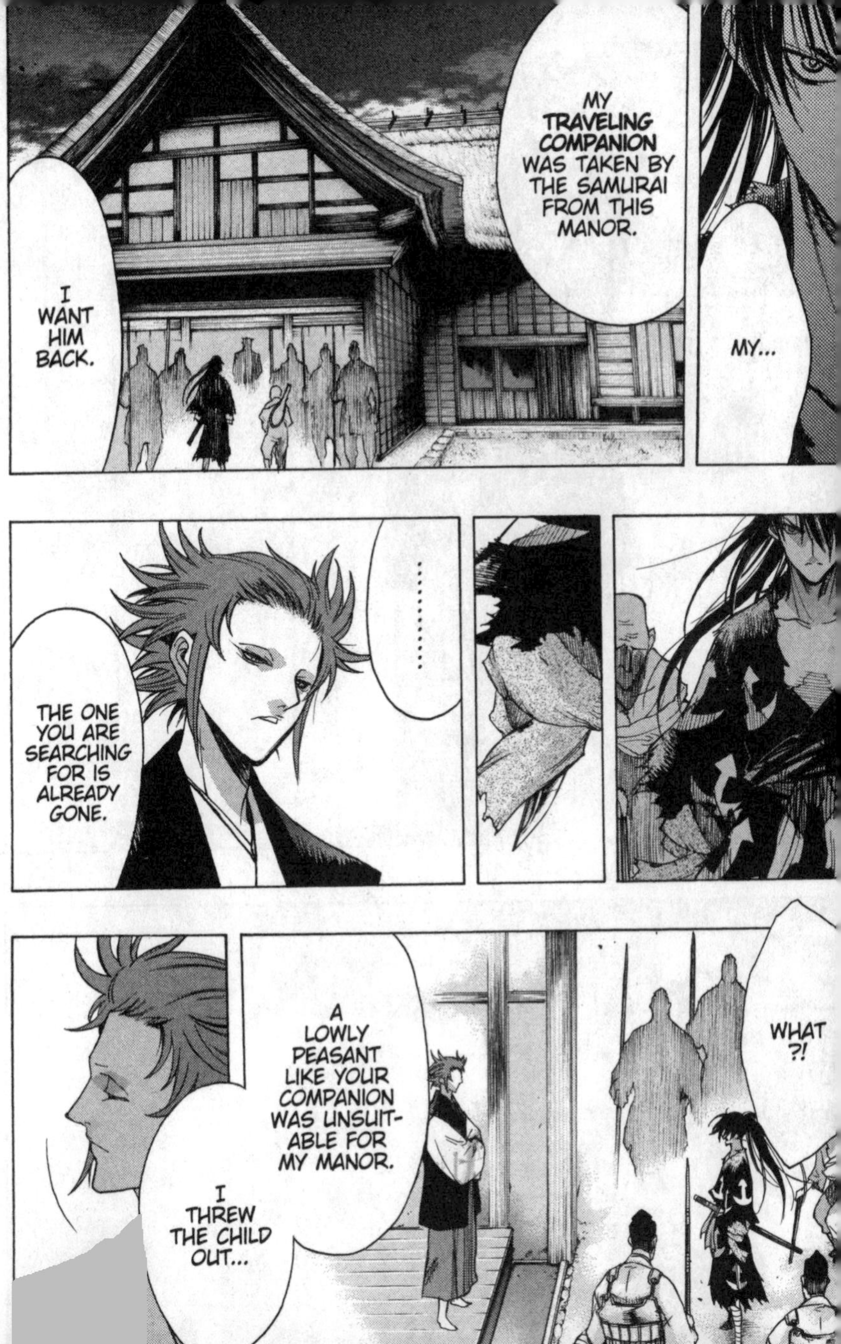
MY...
MY TRAVELING COMPANION WAS TAKEN BY THE SAMURAI FROM THIS MANOR.
I WANT HIM BACK.
......
THE ONE YOU ARE SEARCHING FOR IS ALREADY GONE.
WHAT?!
A LOWLY PEASANT LIKE YOUR COMPANION WAS UNSUIT-ABLE FOR MY MANOR.
I THREW THE CHILD OUT...

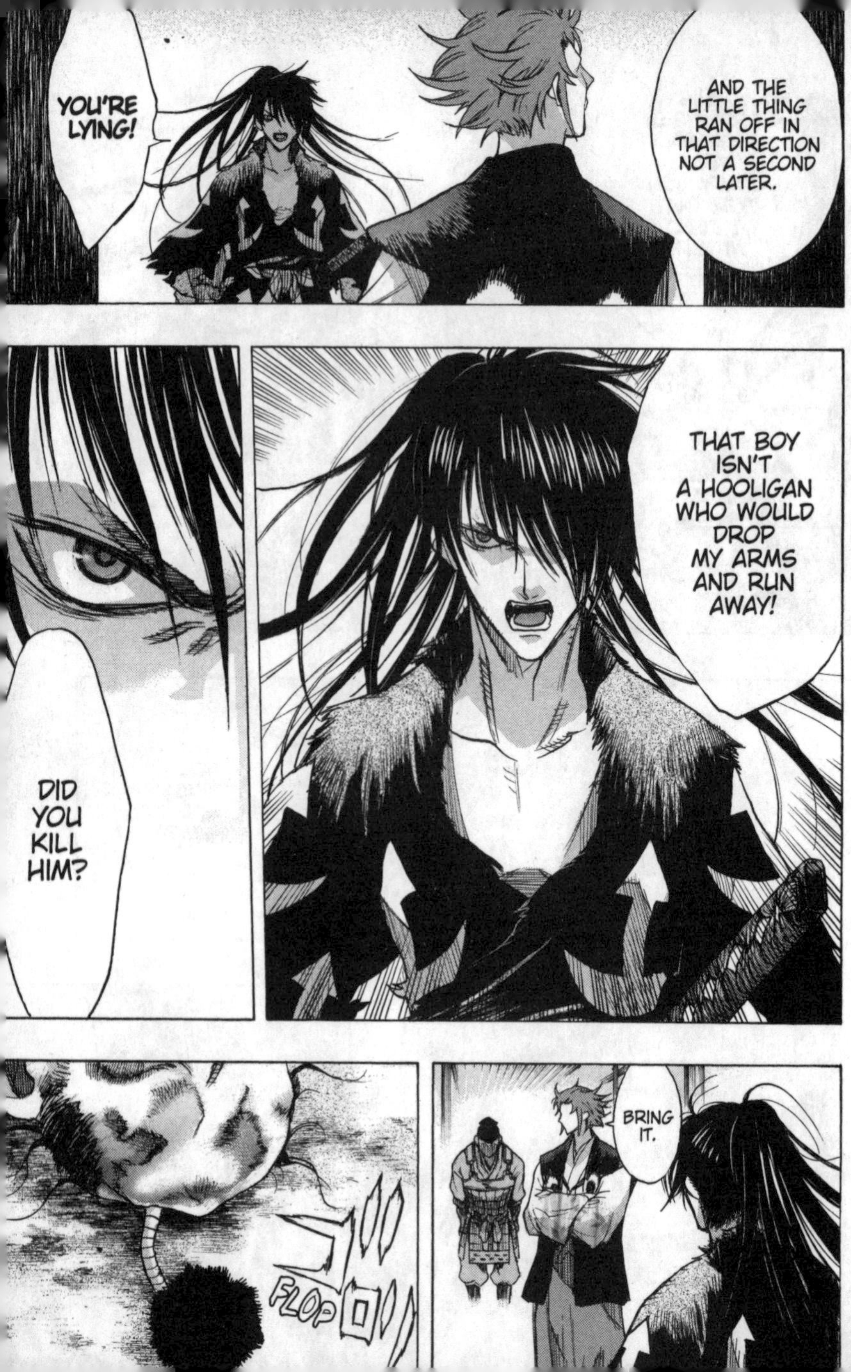
AND THE LITTLE THING RAN OFF IN THAT DIRECTION NOT A SECOND LATER.
YOU'RE LYING!
THAT BOY ISN'T A HOOLIGAN WHO WOULD DROP MY ARMS AND RUN AWAY!
DID YOU KILL HIM?
BRING IT.
FLOP

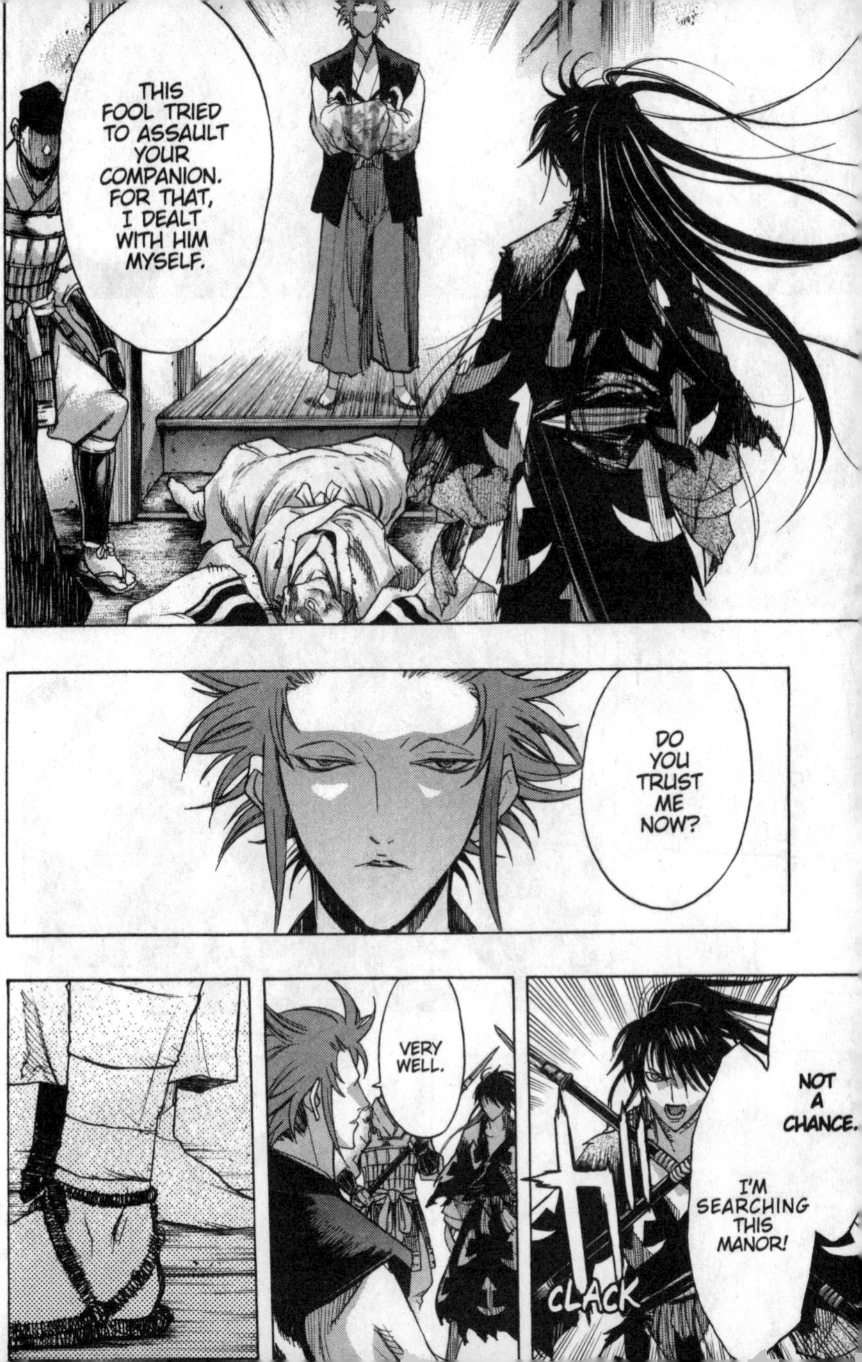
THIS FOOL TRIED TO ASSAULT YOUR COMPANION. FOR THAT, I DEALT WITH HIM MYSELF.
DO YOU TRUST ME NOW?
NOT A CHANCE.
I'M SEARCHING THIS MANOR!
CLACK
VERY WELL.

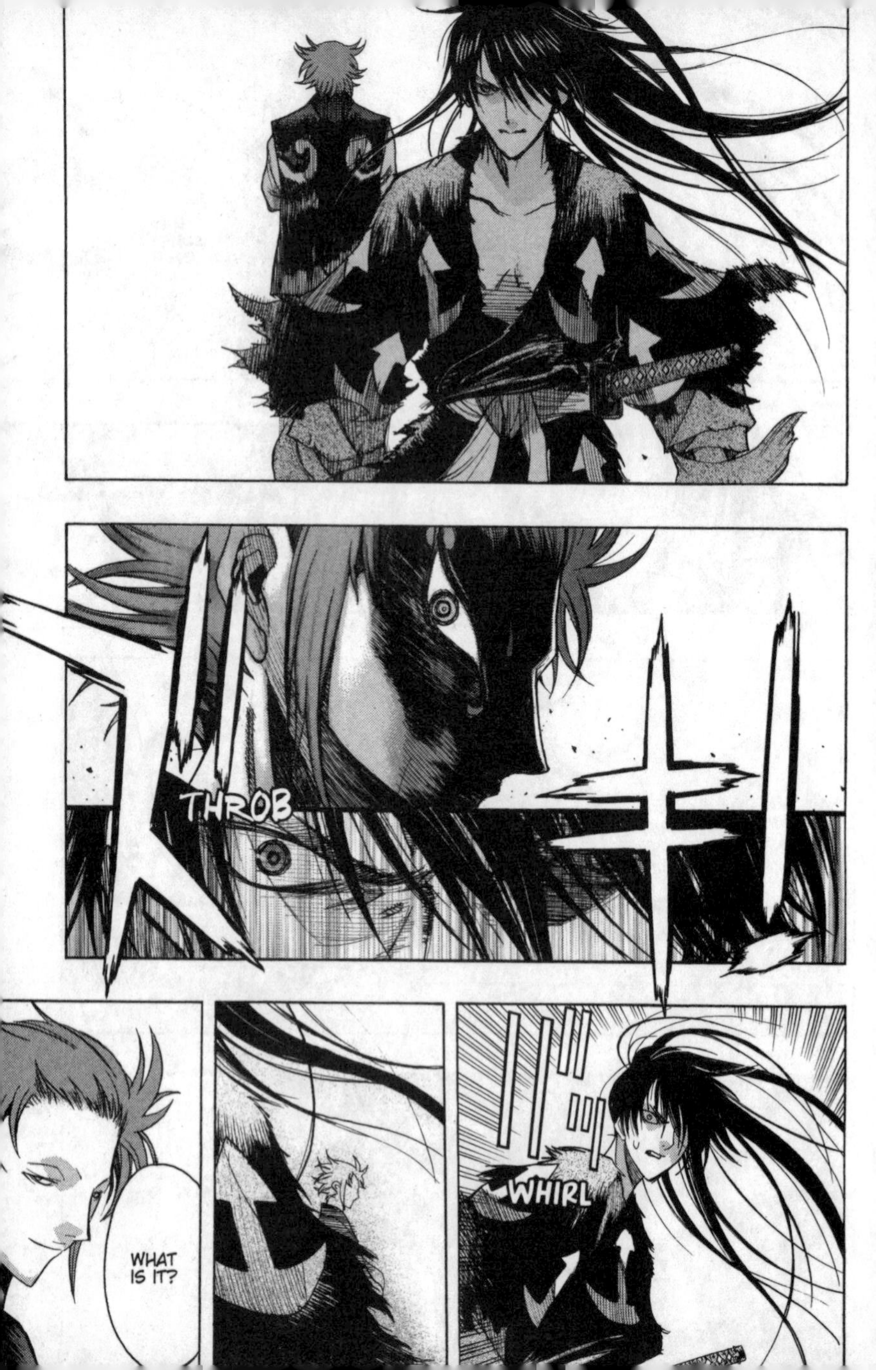
THROB
WHIRL
WHAT IS IT?

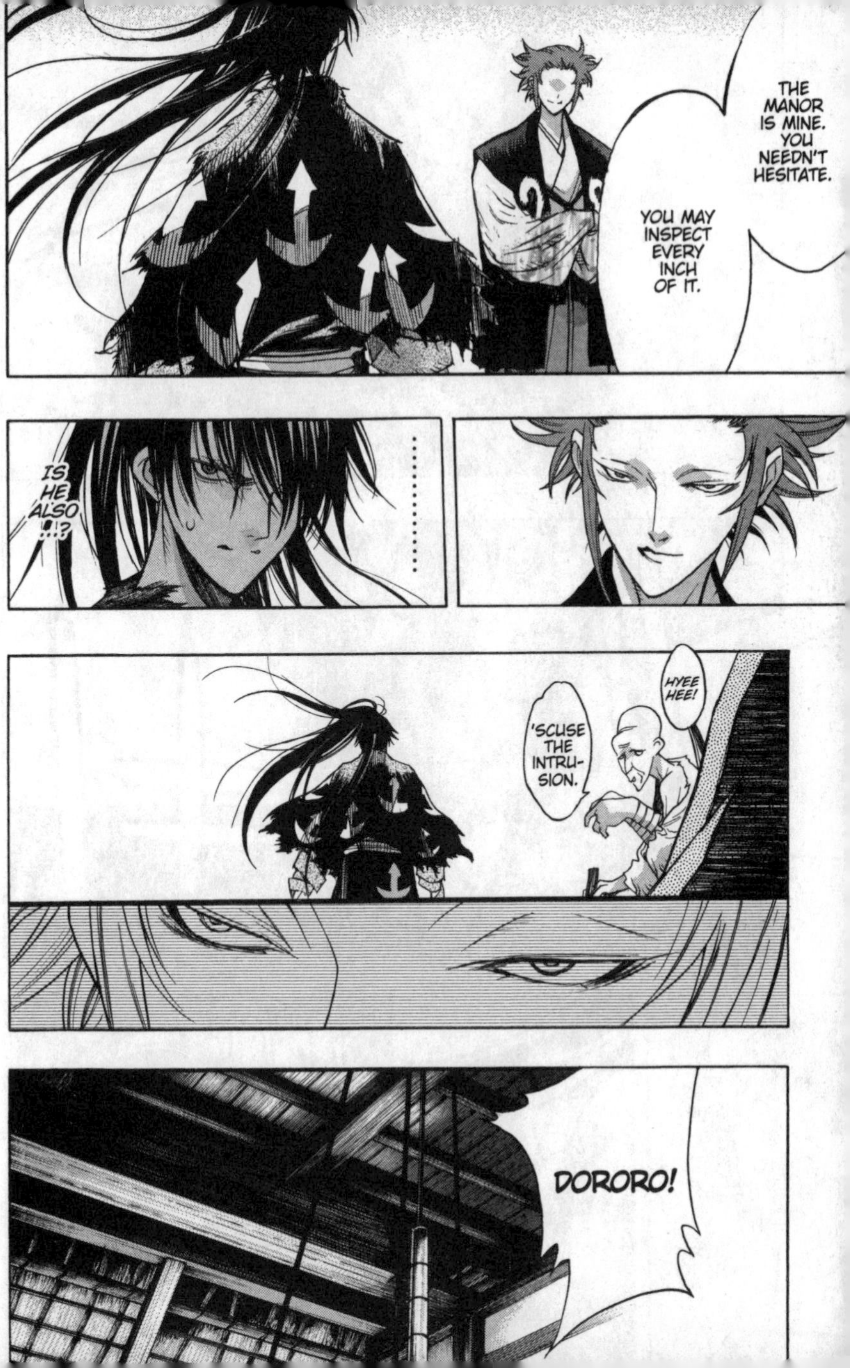
THE MANOR IS MINE. YOU NEEDN'T HESITATE.
YOU MAY INSPECT EVERY INCH OF IT.
....
IS HE ALSO ...?
HYEE HEE!
'SCUSE THE INTRUSION.
DORORO!

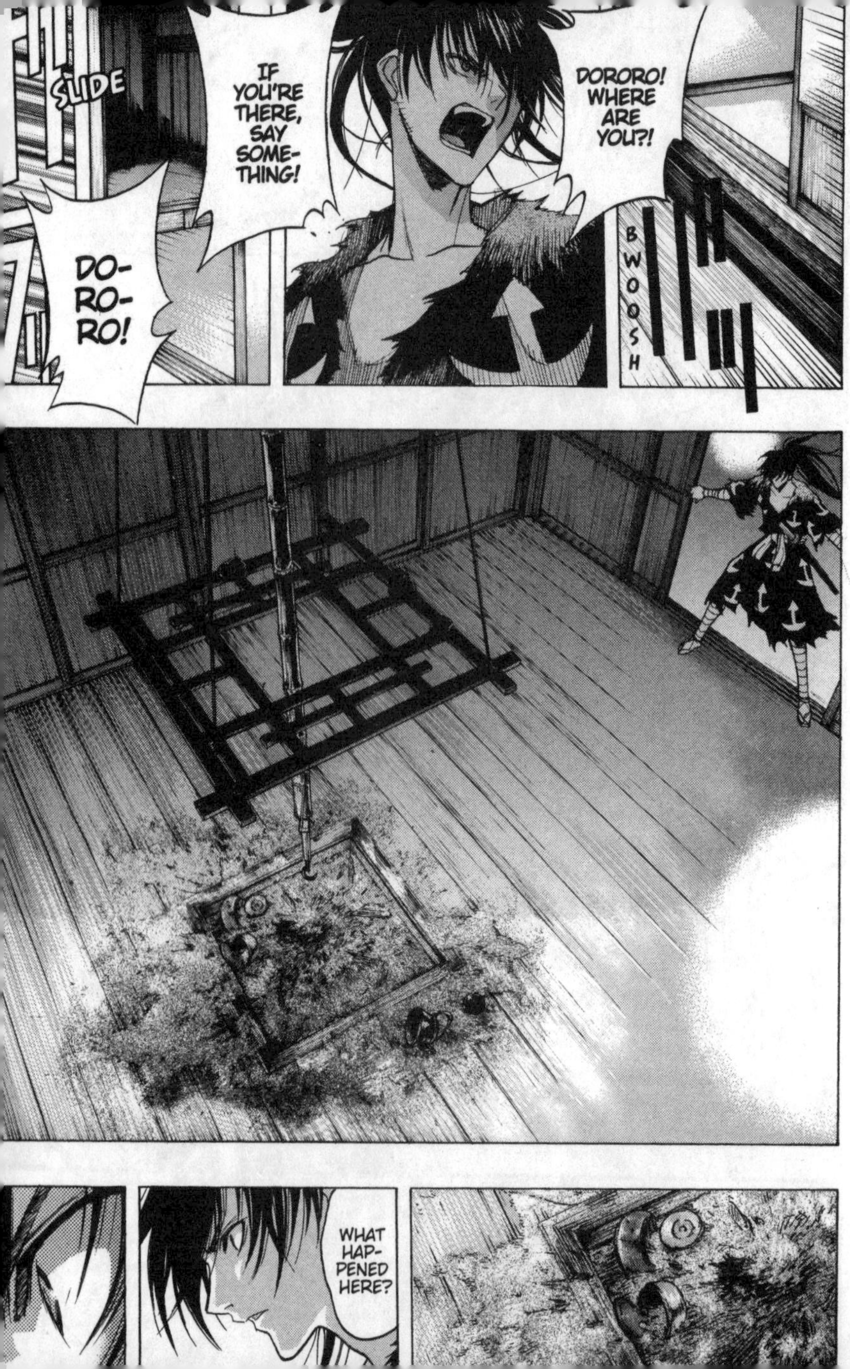
DORORO! WHERE ARE YOU?!
BWOOSH
IF YOU'RE THERE, SAY SOME-THING!
SLIDE
DO-RO-RO!
WHAT HAP-PENED HERE?

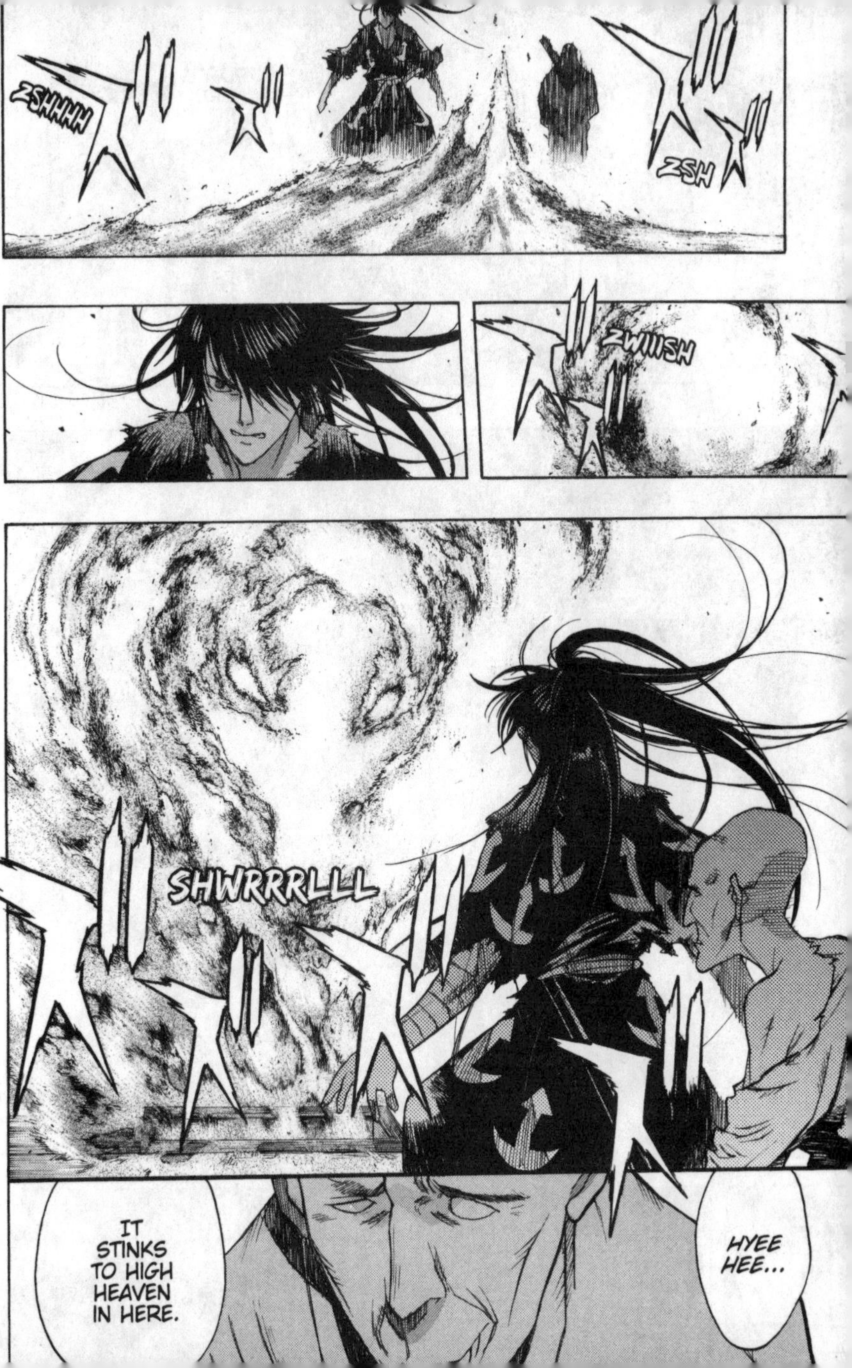
ZSH
ZSHHHH
ZWIIISH
SHWRRRLLL
HYEE HEE...
IT STINKS TO HIGH HEAVEN IN HERE.

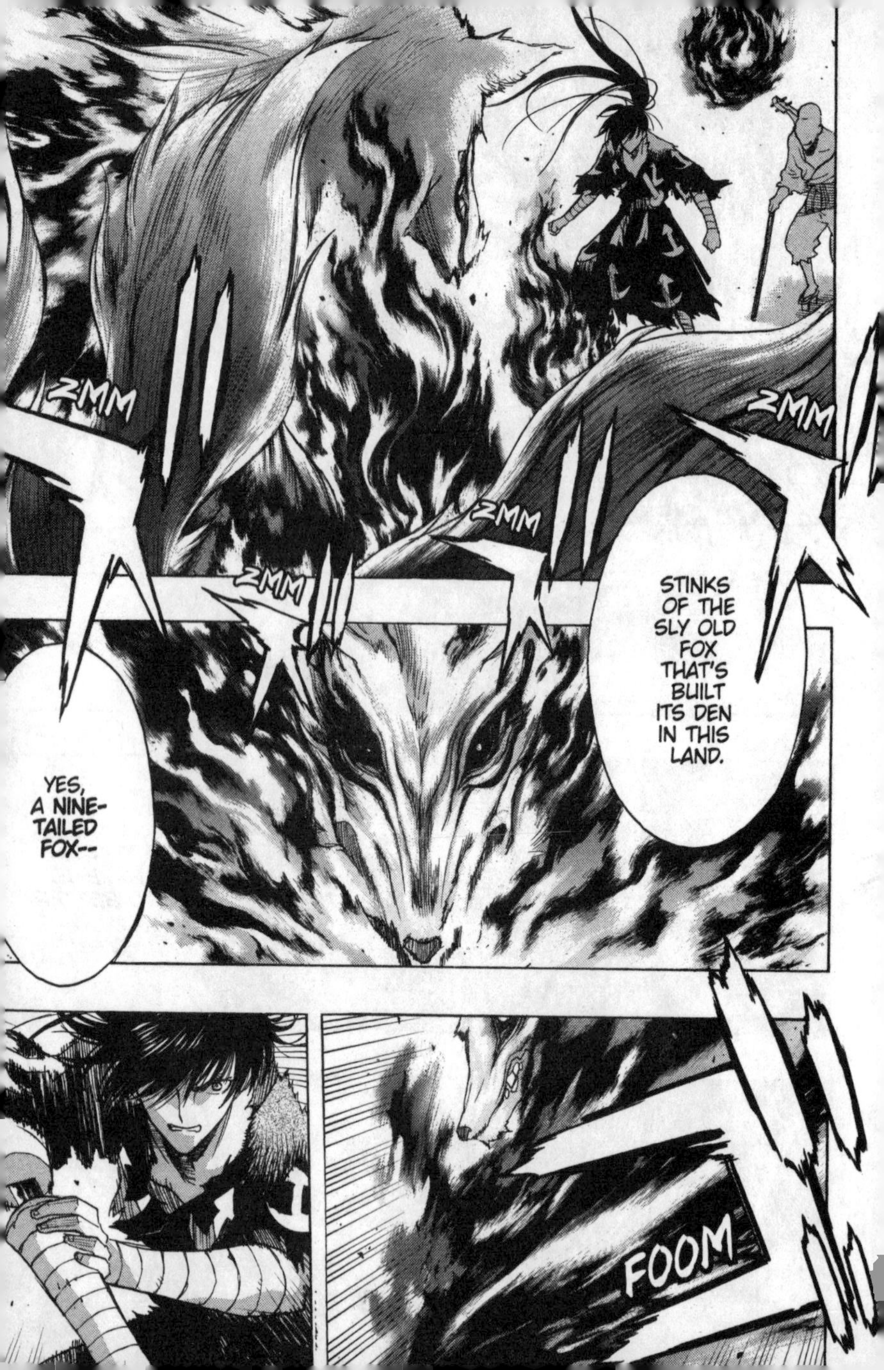
ZMM
ZMM
ZMM
ZMM
STINKS OF THE SLY OLD FOX THAT'S BUILT ITS DEN IN THIS LAND.
YES, A NINE-TAILED FOX--
FOOM

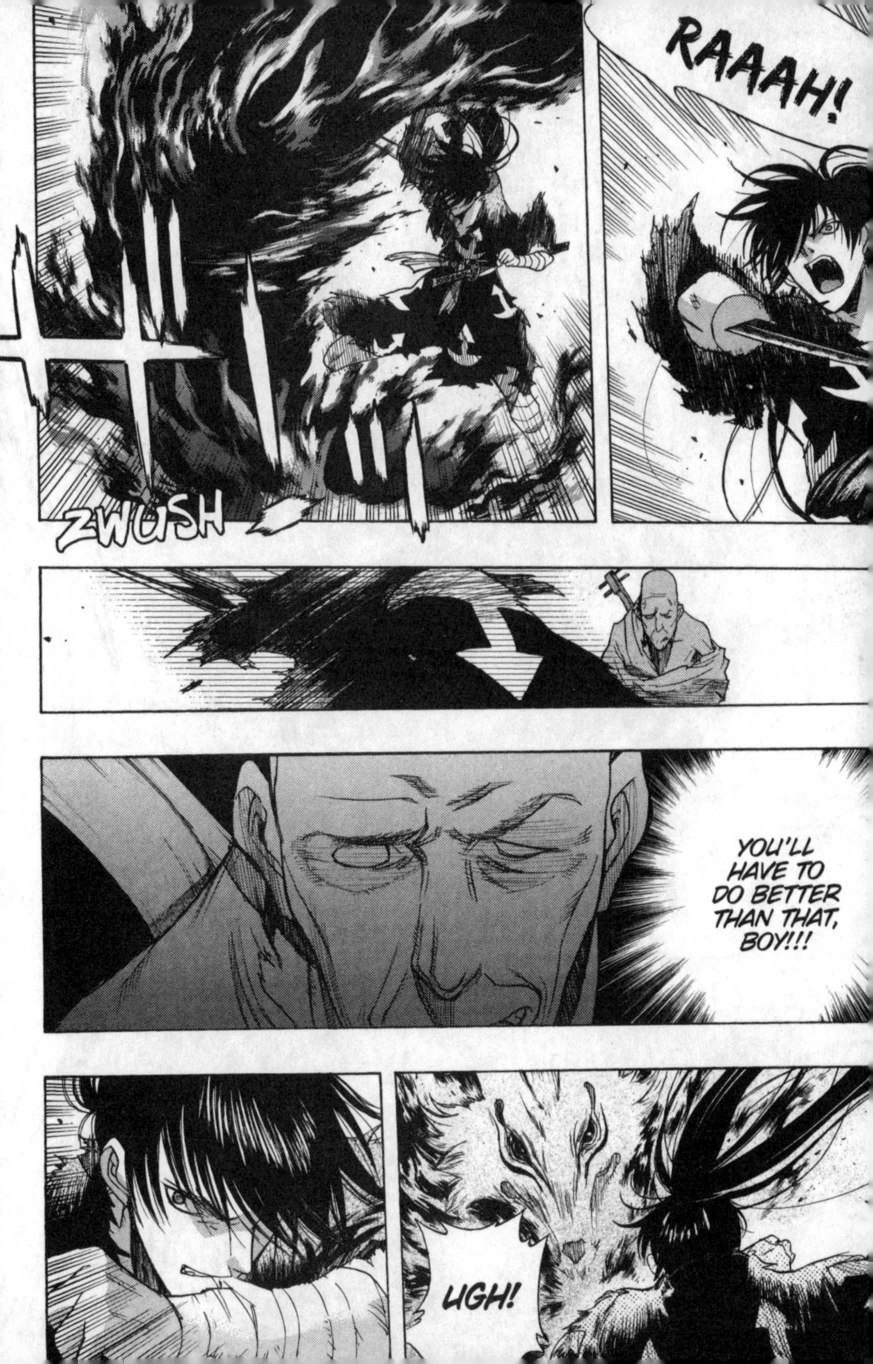
RAAAH!
ZWUSH
YOU'LL HAVE TO DO BETTER THAN THAT, BOY!!!
UGH!

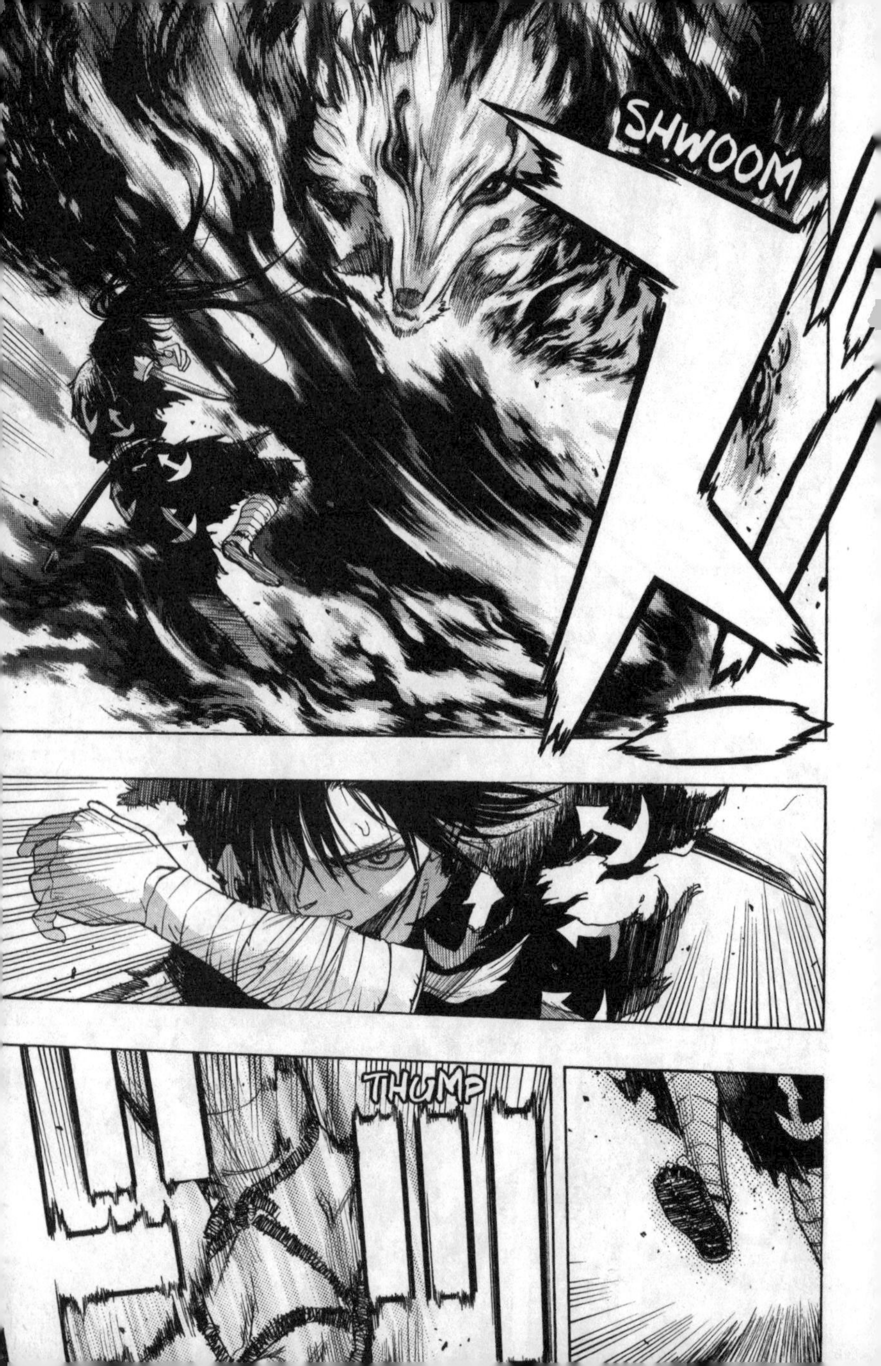
SHWOOM
THUMP

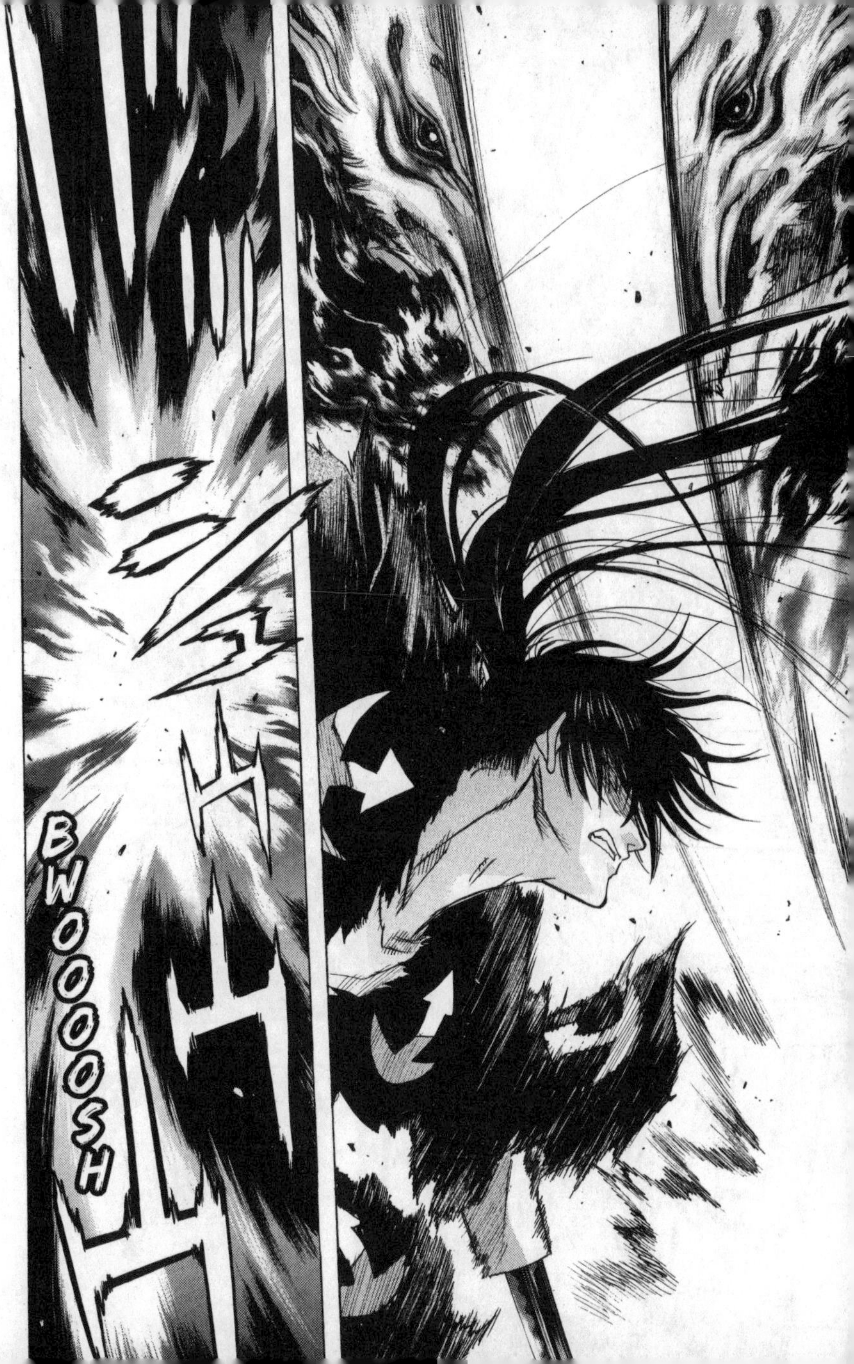
BWOOOOOSH

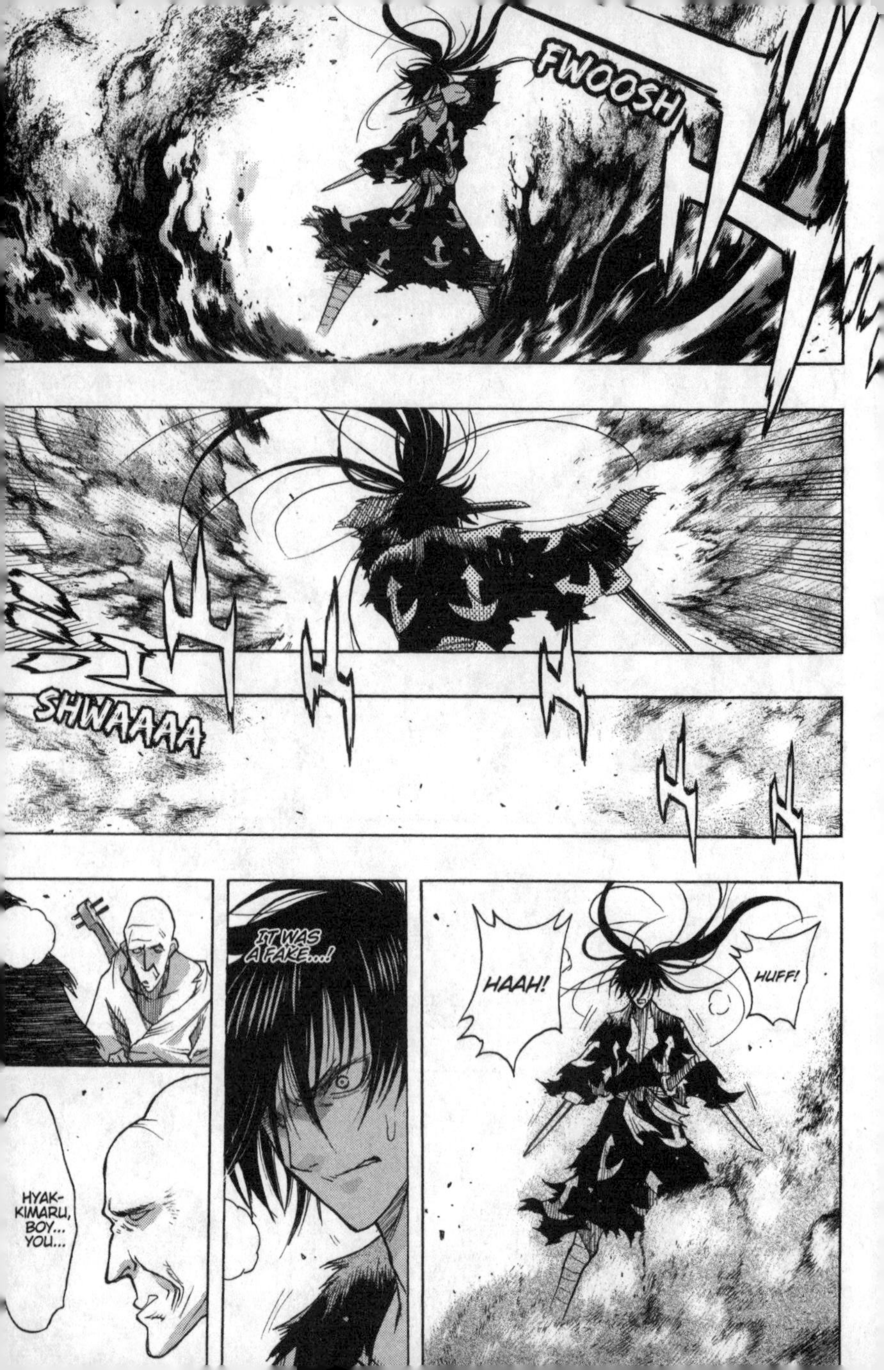
FWOOSH
SHWAAAA
HUFF!
HAAH!
IT WAS A FAKE...!
HYAK-KIMARU, BOY... YOU...

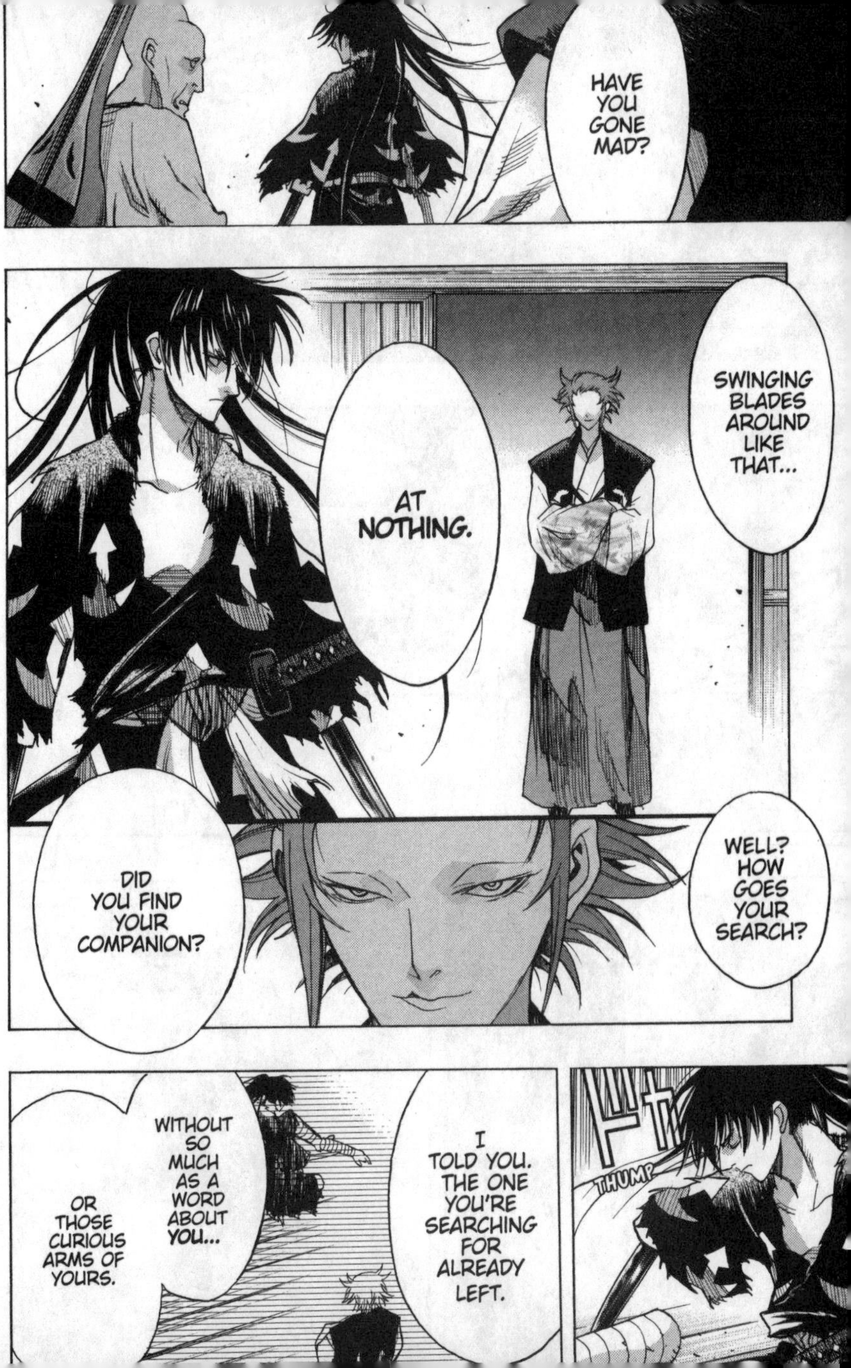
HAVE YOU GONE MAD?
SWINGING BLADES AROUND LIKE THAT...
AT NOTHING.
WELL? HOW GOES YOUR SEARCH?
DID YOU FIND YOUR COMPANION?
THUMP
I TOLD YOU. THE ONE YOU'RE SEARCHING FOR ALREADY LEFT.
WITHOUT SO MUCH AS A WORD ABOUT YOU...
OR THOSE CURIOUS ARMS OF YOURS.

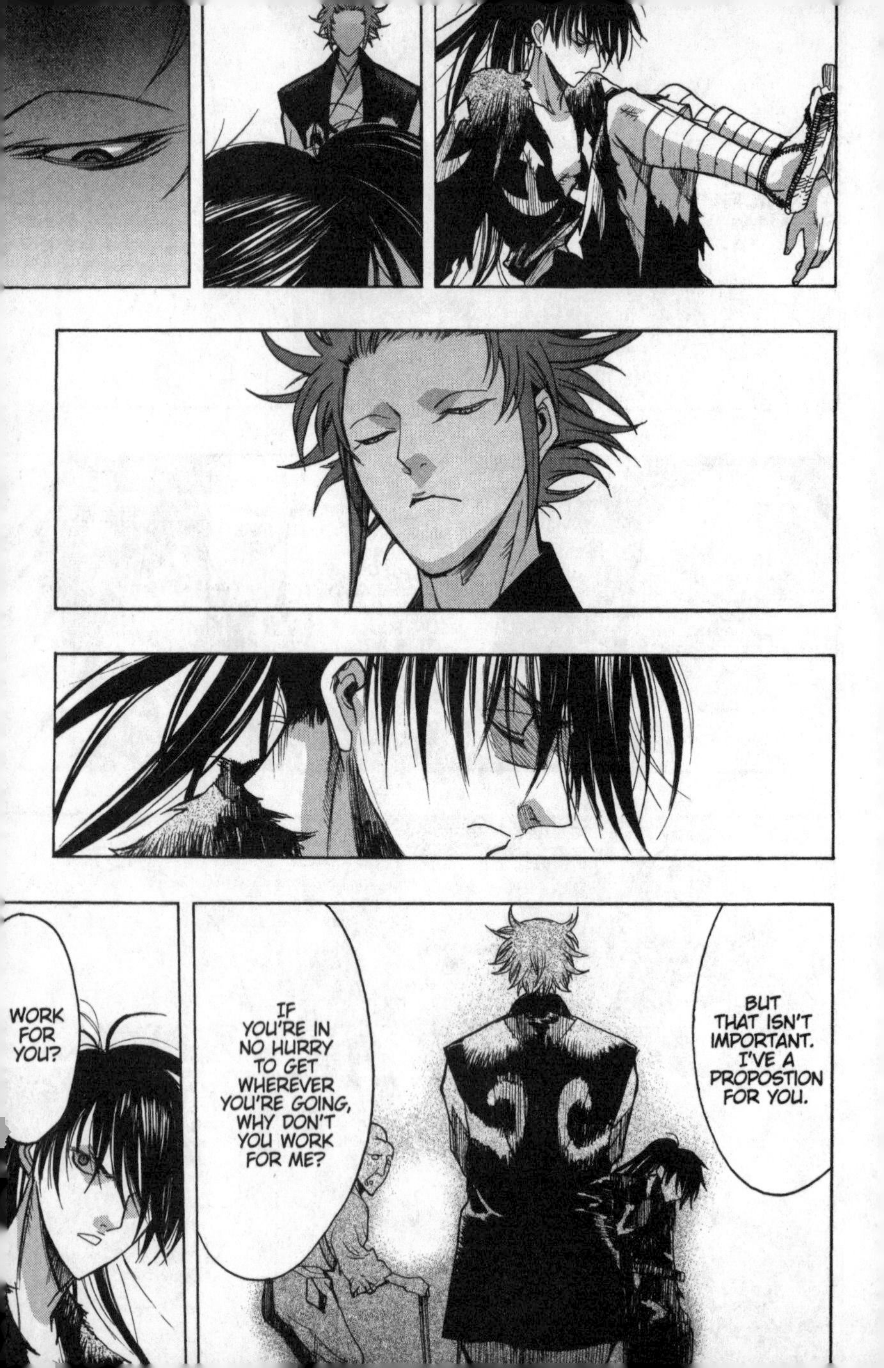
BUT THAT ISN'T IMPORTANT. I'VE A PROPOSTION FOR YOU.
IF YOU'RE IN NO HURRY TO GET WHEREVER YOU'RE GOING, WHY DON'T YOU WORK FOR ME?
WORK FOR YOU?

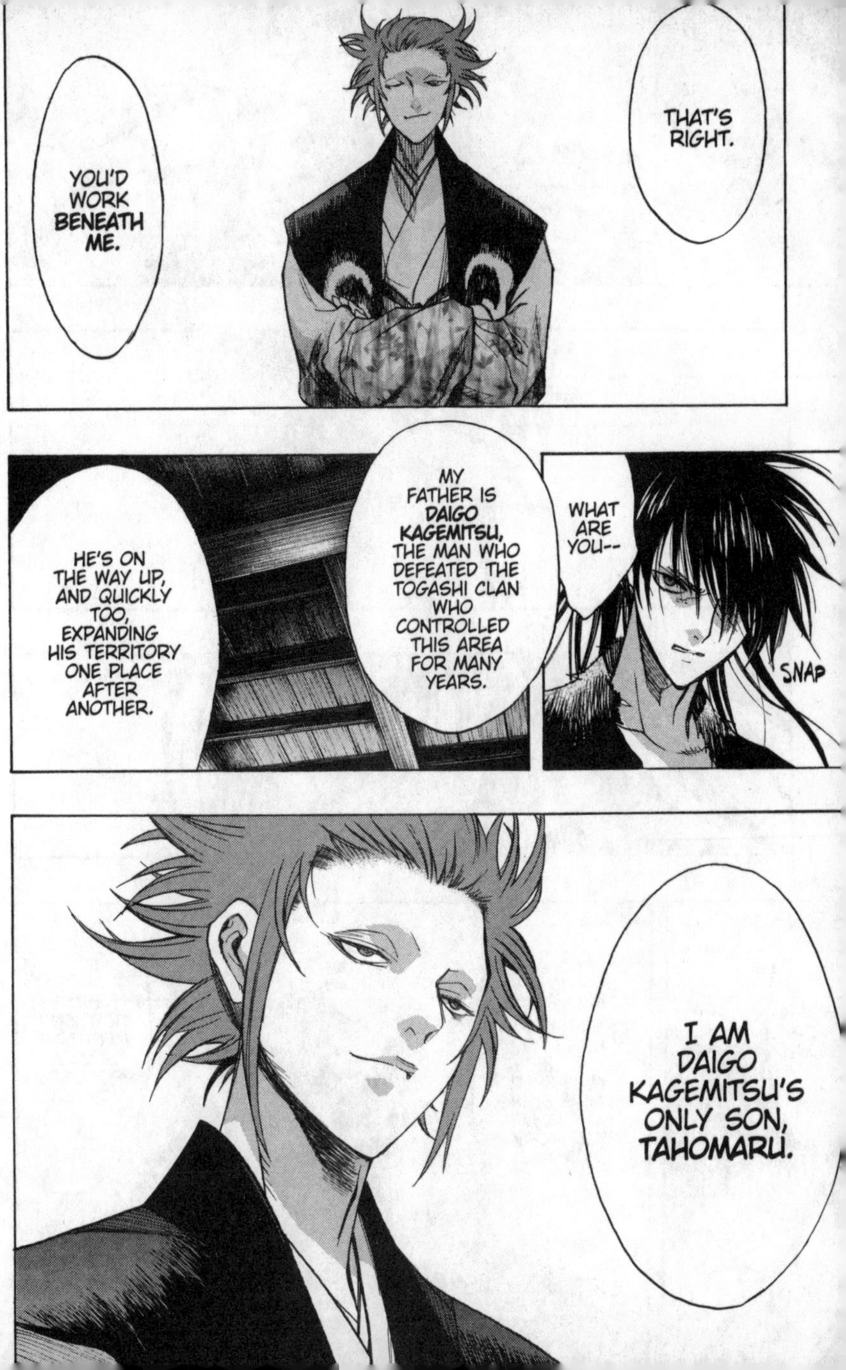
THAT'S RIGHT.
YOU'D WORK BENEATH ME.
WHAT ARE YOU--
SNAP
MY FATHER IS DAIGO KAGEMITSU, THE MAN WHO DEFEATED THE TOGASHI CLAN WHO CONTROLLED THIS AREA FOR MANY YEARS.
HE'S ON THE WAY UP, AND QUICKLY TOO, EXPANDING HIS TERRITORY ONE PLACE AFTER ANOTHER.
I AM DAIGO KAGEMITSU'S ONLY SON, TAHOMARU.

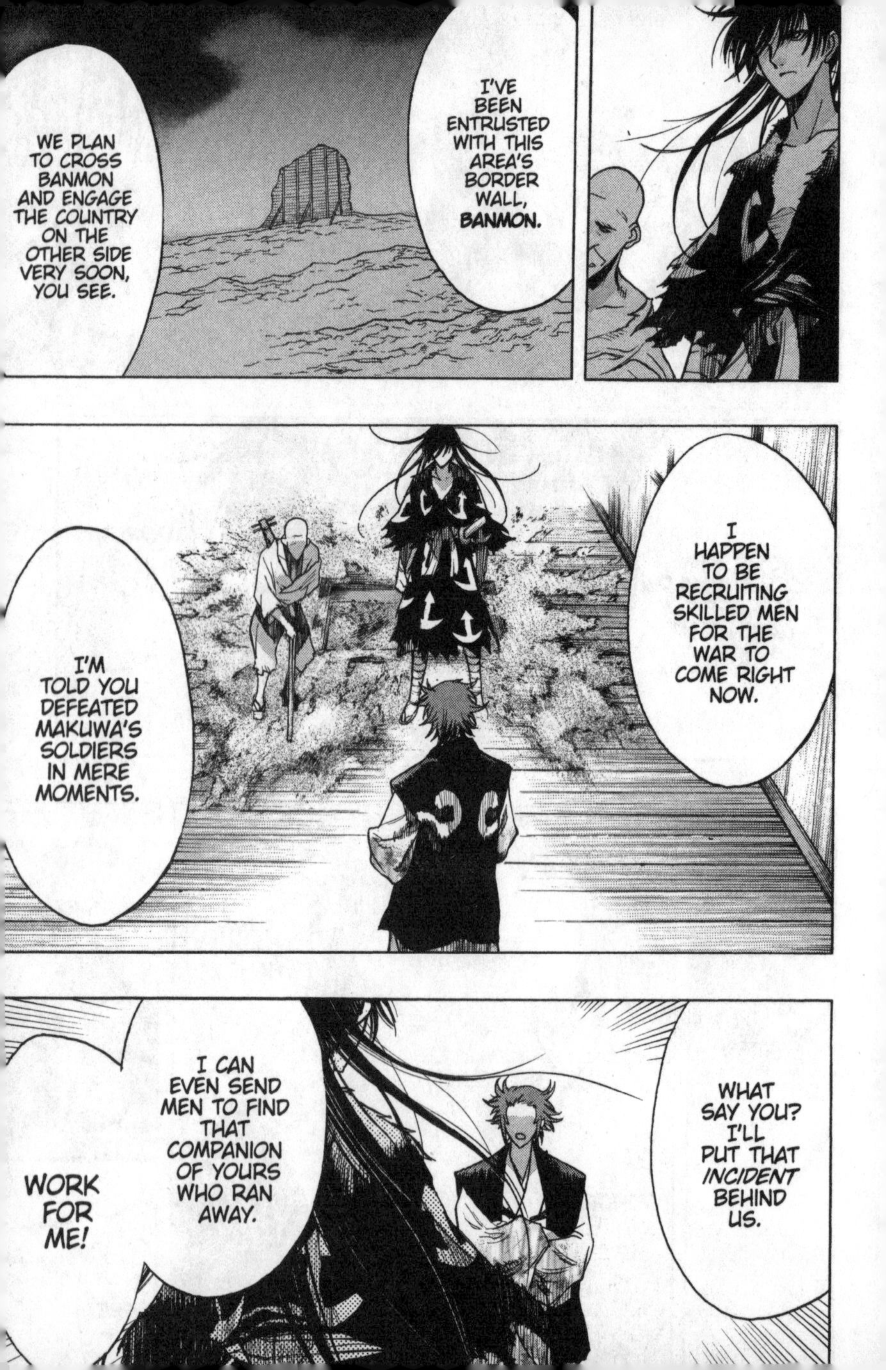
I'VE BEEN ENTRUSTED WITH THIS AREA'S BORDER WALL, **BANMON.**
WE PLAN TO CROSS BANMON AND ENGAGE THE COUNTRY ON THE OTHER SIDE VERY SOON, YOU SEE.
I HAPPEN TO BE RECRUITING SKILLED MEN FOR THE WAR TO COME RIGHT NOW.
I'M TOLD YOU DEFEATED MAKUWA'S SOLDIERS IN MERE MOMENTS.
WHAT SAY YOU? I'LL PUT THAT *INCIDENT* BEHIND US.
I CAN EVEN SEND MEN TO FIND THAT COMPANION OF YOURS WHO RAN AWAY.
WORK FOR ME!

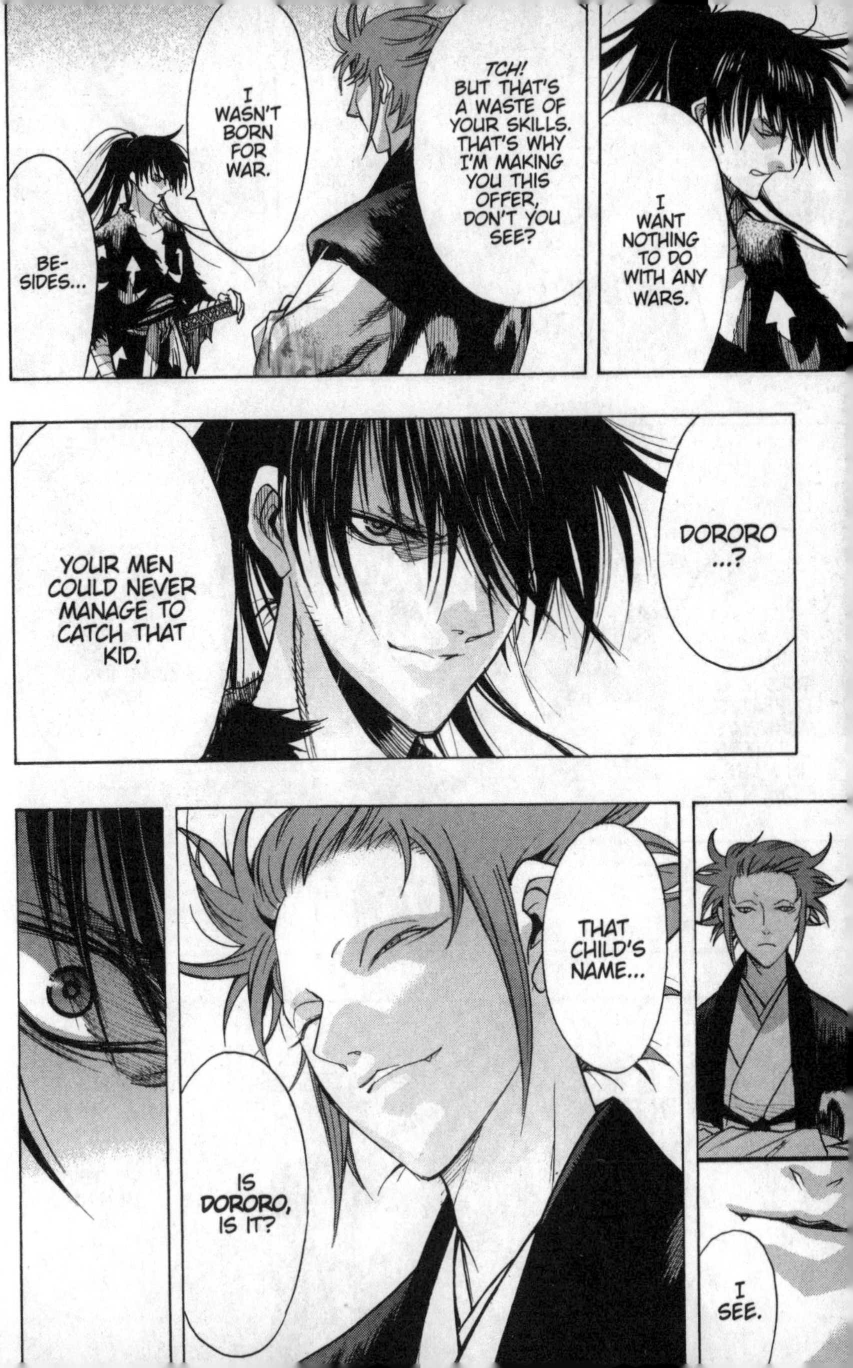
I WANT NOTHING TO DO WITH ANY WARS.
TCH! BUT THAT'S A WASTE OF YOUR SKILLS. THAT'S WHY I'M MAKING YOU THIS OFFER, DON'T YOU SEE?
I WASN'T BORN FOR WAR.
BE-SIDES...
DORORO ...?
YOUR MEN COULD NEVER MANAGE TO CATCH THAT KID.
I SEE.
THAT CHILD'S NAME...
IS DORORO, IS IT?

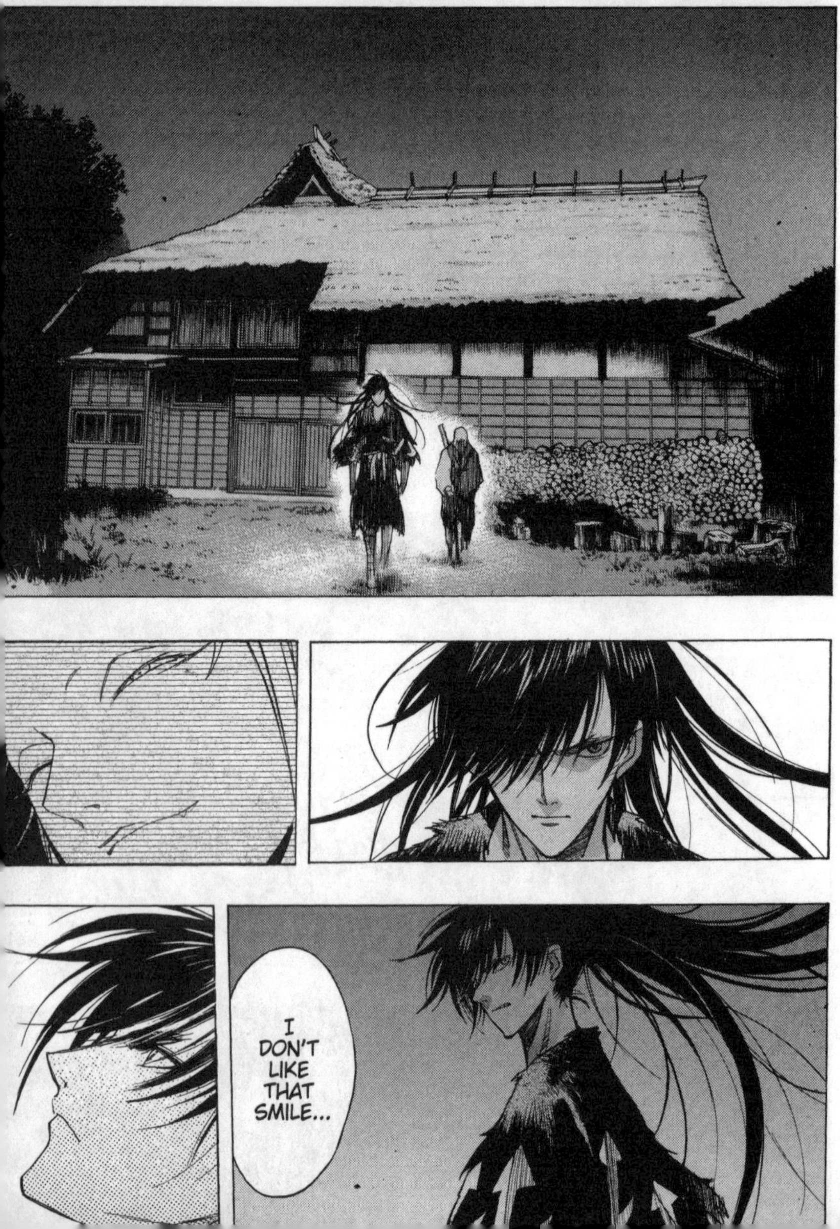
I DON'T LIKE THAT SMILE...

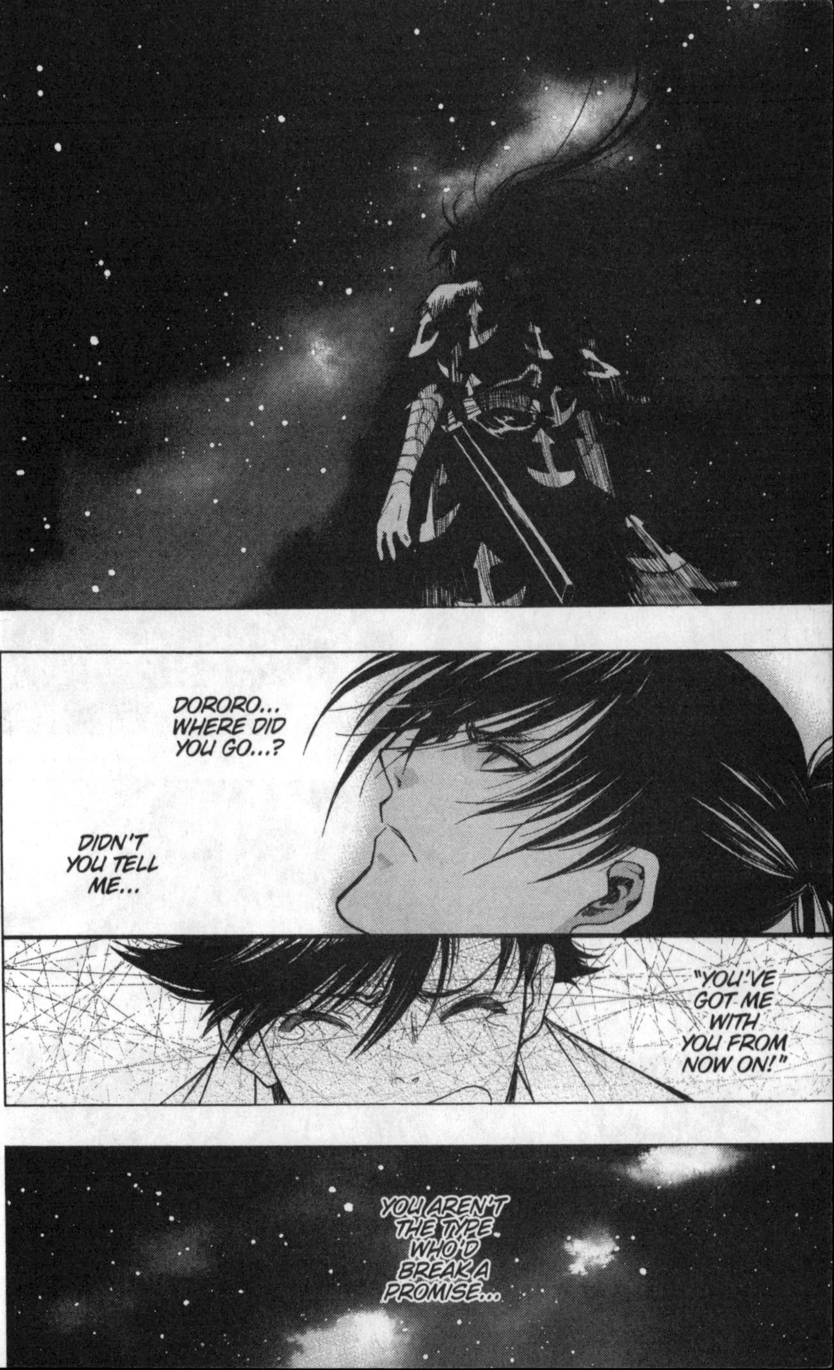
DORORO... WHERE DID YOU GO...?
DIDN'T YOU TELL ME...
"YOU'VE GOT ME WITH YOU FROM NOW ON!"
YOU AREN'T THE TYPE WHO'D BREAK A PROMISE...

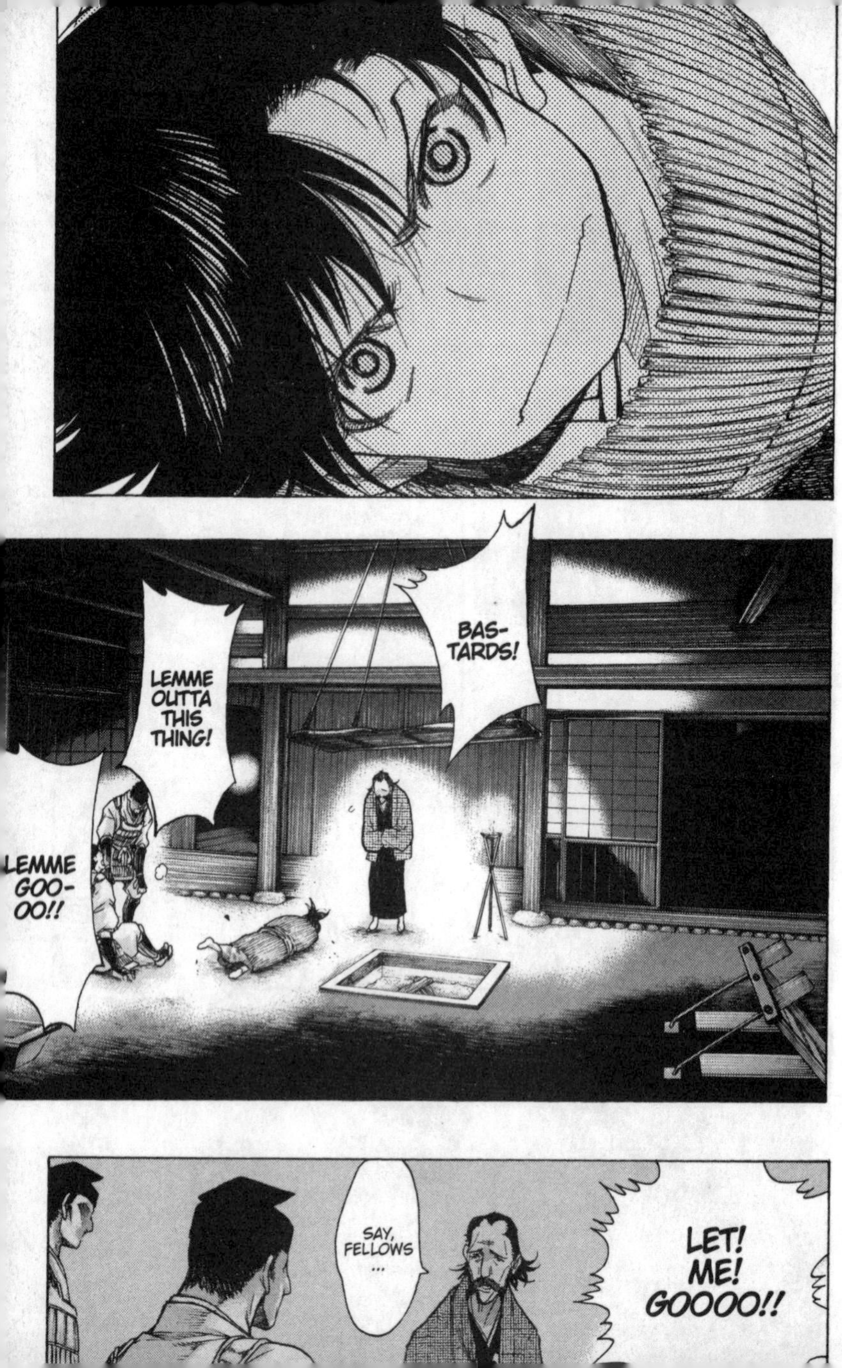
BAS-
TARDS!
LEMME OUTTA THIS THING!
LEMME GOO-OO!!
LET! ME! GOOOO!!
SAY, FELLOWS ...

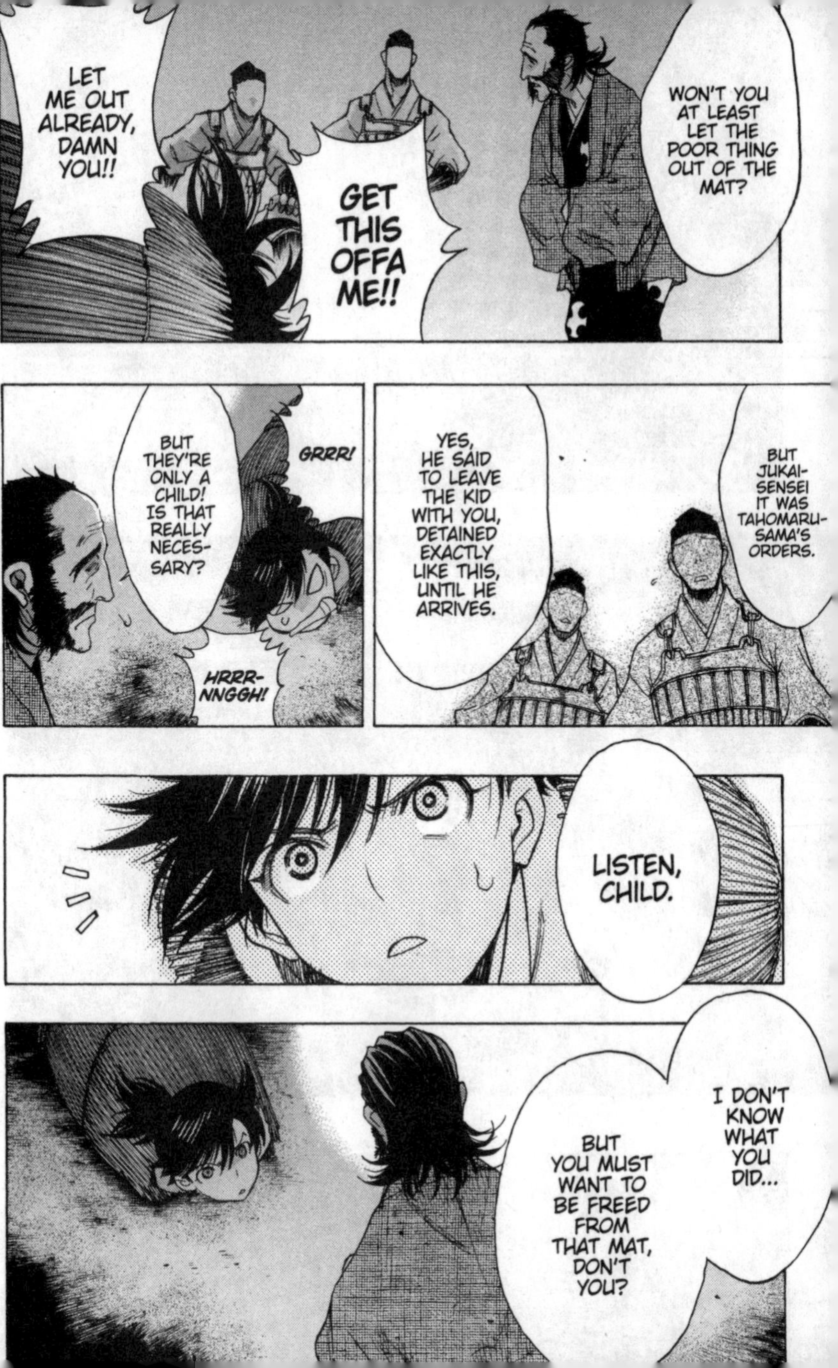
WON'T YOU AT LEAST LET THE POOR THING OUT OF THE MAT?
GET THIS OFFA ME!!
LET ME OUT ALREADY, DAMN YOU!!
BUT JUKAI-SENSEI IT WAS TAHOMARU-SAMA'S ORDERS.
YES, HE SAID TO LEAVE THE KID WITH YOU, DETAINED EXACTLY LIKE THIS, UNTIL HE ARRIVES.
BUT THEY'RE ONLY A CHILD! IS THAT REALLY NECES-SARY?
GRRR!
HRRR-NNGGH!
LISTEN, CHILD.
I DON'T KNOW WHAT YOU DID...
BUT YOU MUST WANT TO BE FREED FROM THAT MAT, DON'T YOU?

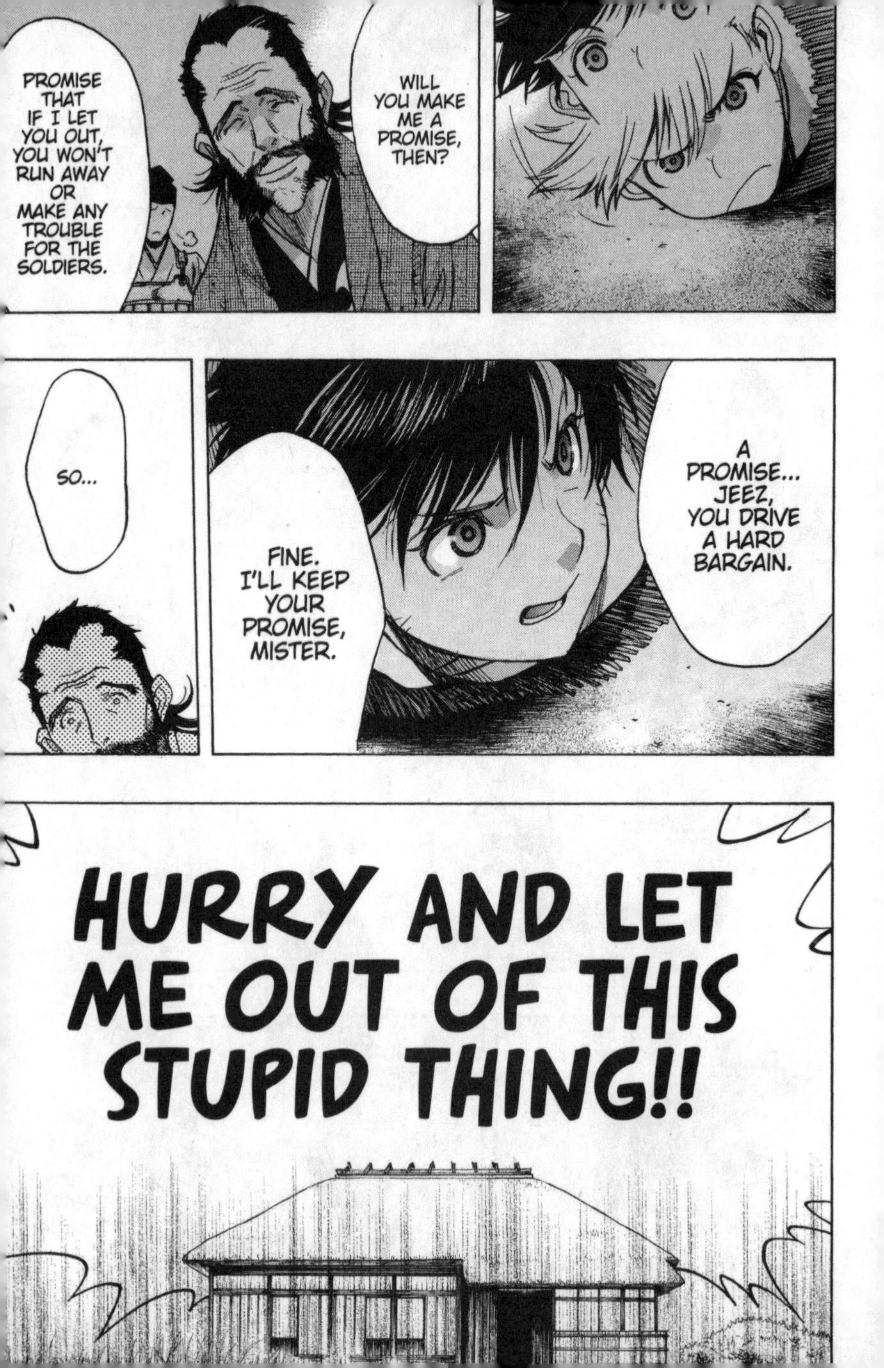
WILL YOU MAKE ME A PROMISE, THEN?
PROMISE THAT IF I LET YOU OUT, YOU WON'T RUN AWAY OR MAKE ANY TROUBLE FOR THE SOLDIERS.
A PROMISE... JEEZ, YOU DRIVE A HARD BARGAIN.
FINE. I'LL KEEP YOUR PROMISE, MISTER.
SO...
HURRY AND LET ME OUT OF THIS STUPID THING!!

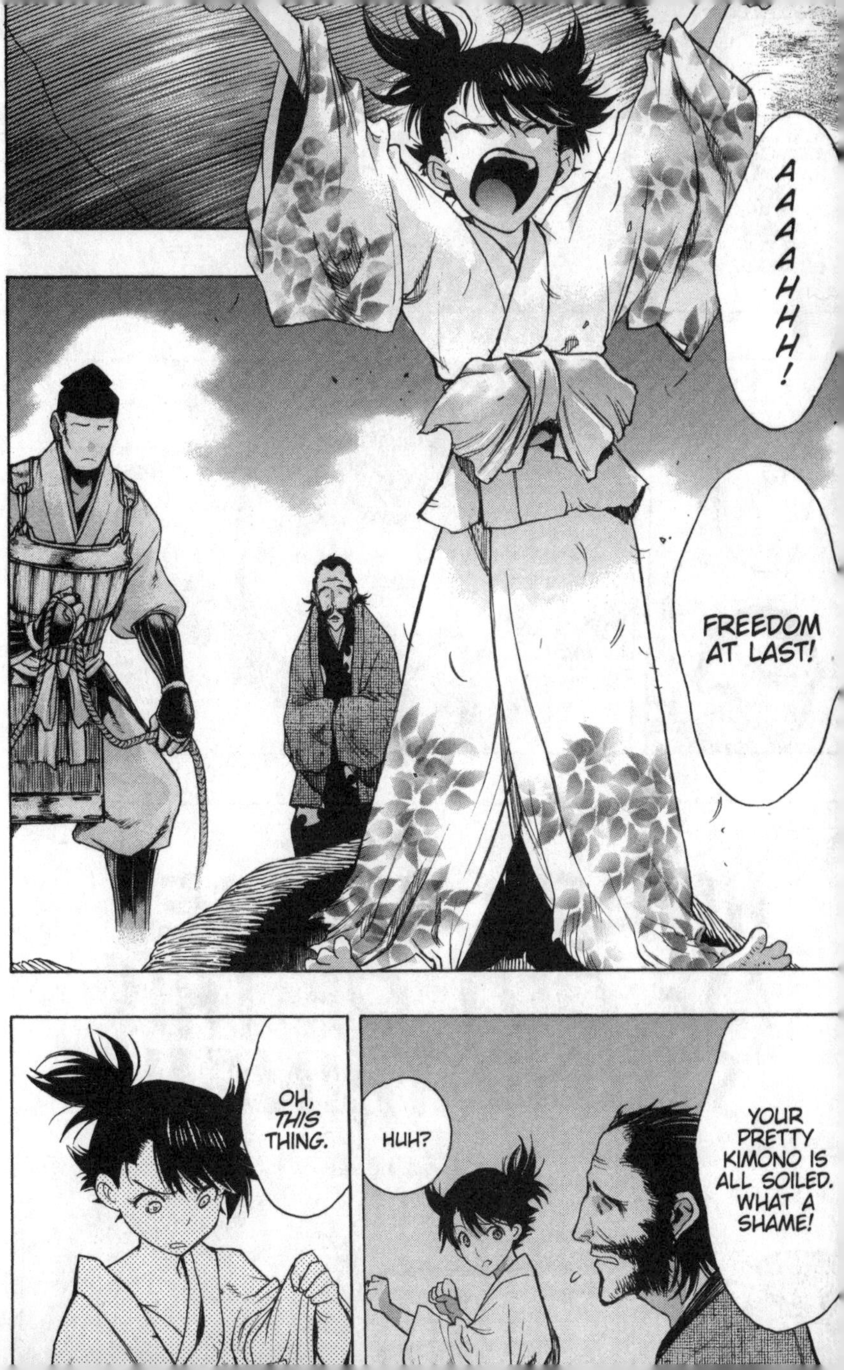
AAAAHHH!
FREEDOM AT LAST!
YOUR PRETTY KIMONO IS ALL SOILED. WHAT A SHAME!
HUH?
OH, *THIS* THING.

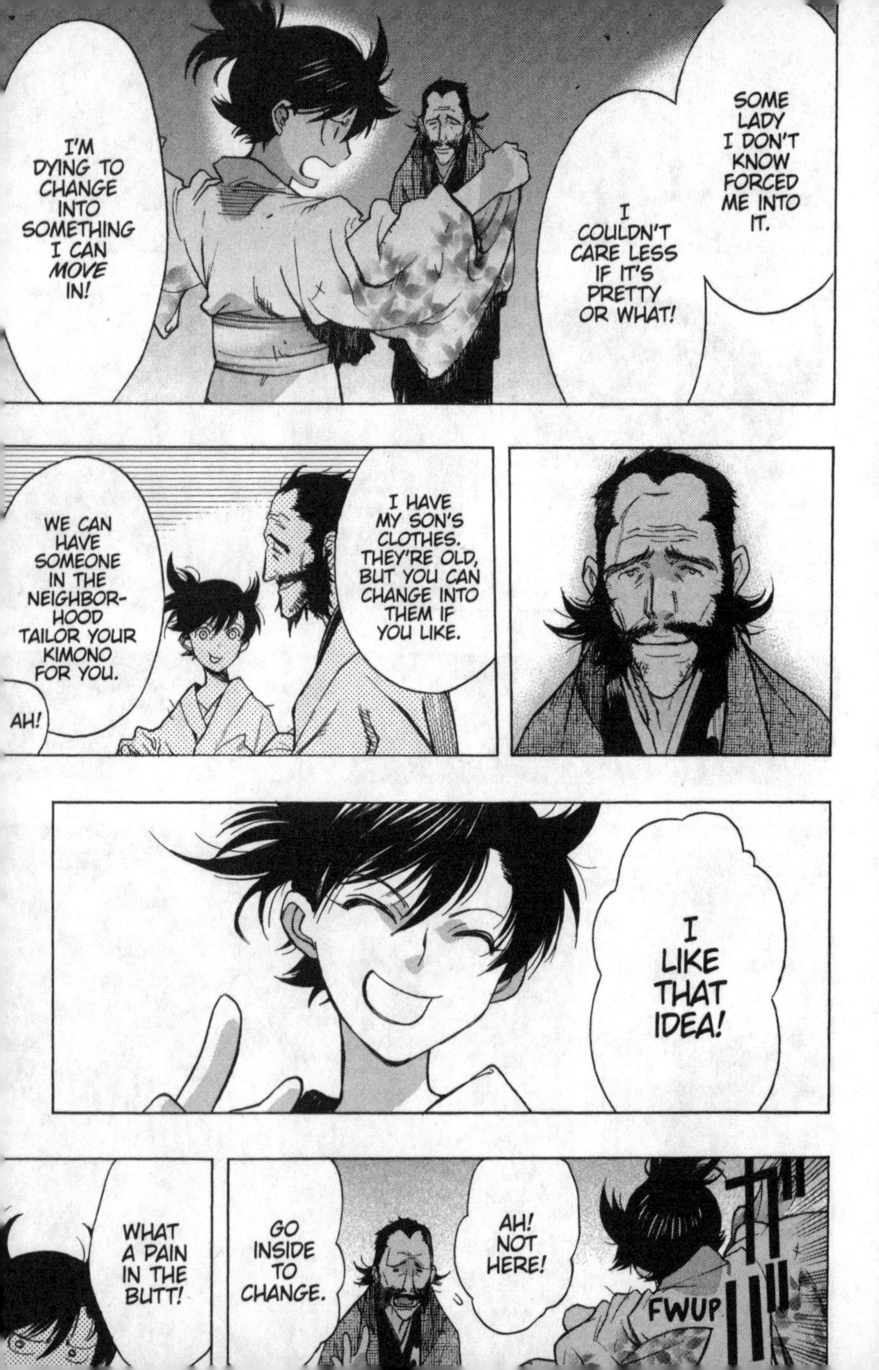
SOME LADY I DON'T KNOW FORCED ME INTO IT.
I COULDN'T CARE LESS IF IT'S PRETTY OR WHAT!
I'M DYING TO CHANGE INTO SOMETHING I CAN *MOVE* IN!
I HAVE MY SON'S CLOTHES. THEY'RE OLD, BUT YOU CAN CHANGE INTO THEM IF YOU LIKE.
WE CAN HAVE SOMEONE IN THE NEIGHBOR-HOOD TAILOR YOUR KIMONO FOR YOU.
AH!
I LIKE THAT IDEA!
FWUP
AH! NOT HERE!
GO INSIDE TO CHANGE.
WHAT A PAIN IN THE BUTT!

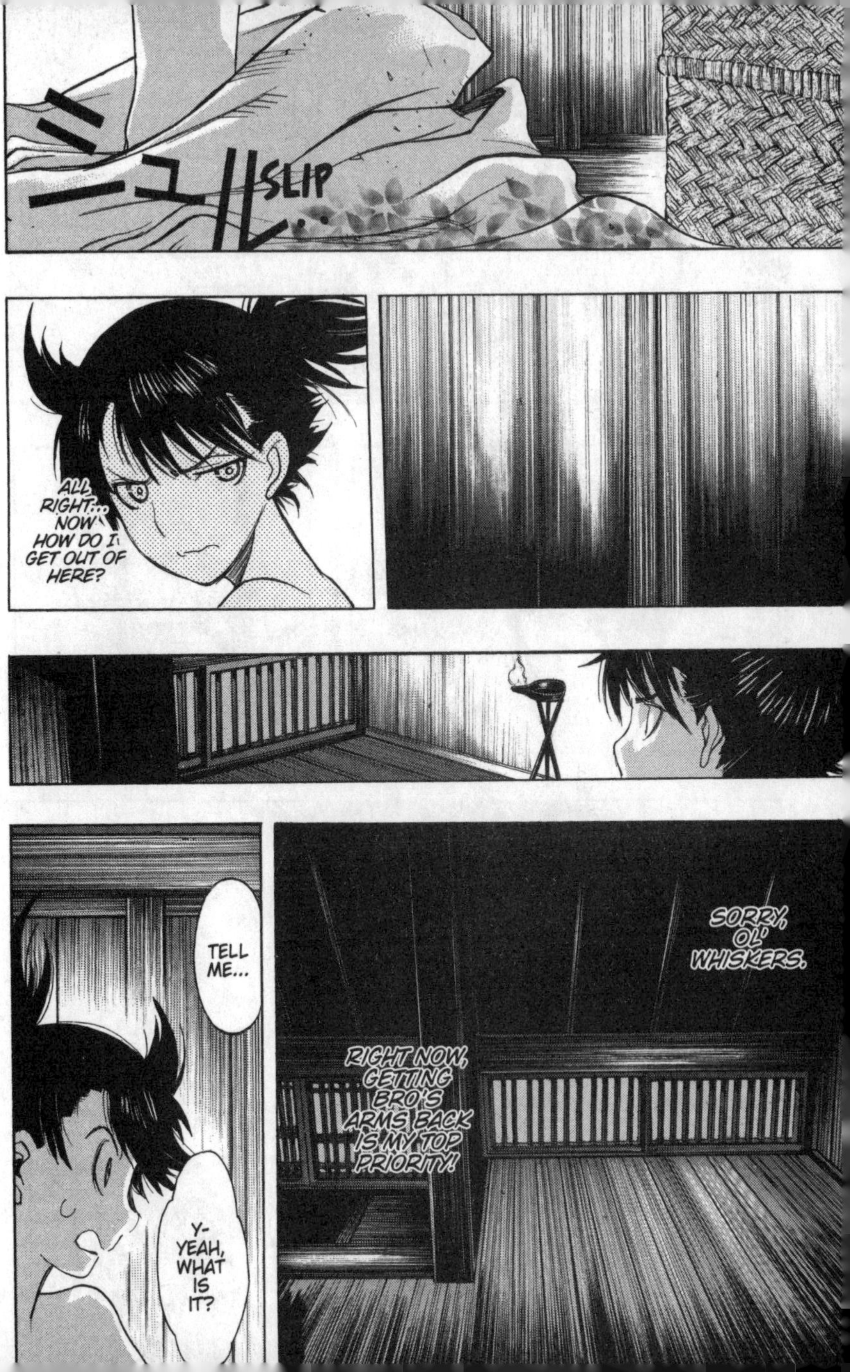
SLIP
ALL RIGHT... NOW HOW DO I GET OUT OF HERE?
SORRY, OL' WHISKERS.
RIGHT NOW, GETTING BRO'S ARMS BACK IS MY TOP PRIORITY!
TELL ME...
Y-YEAH, WHAT IS IT?

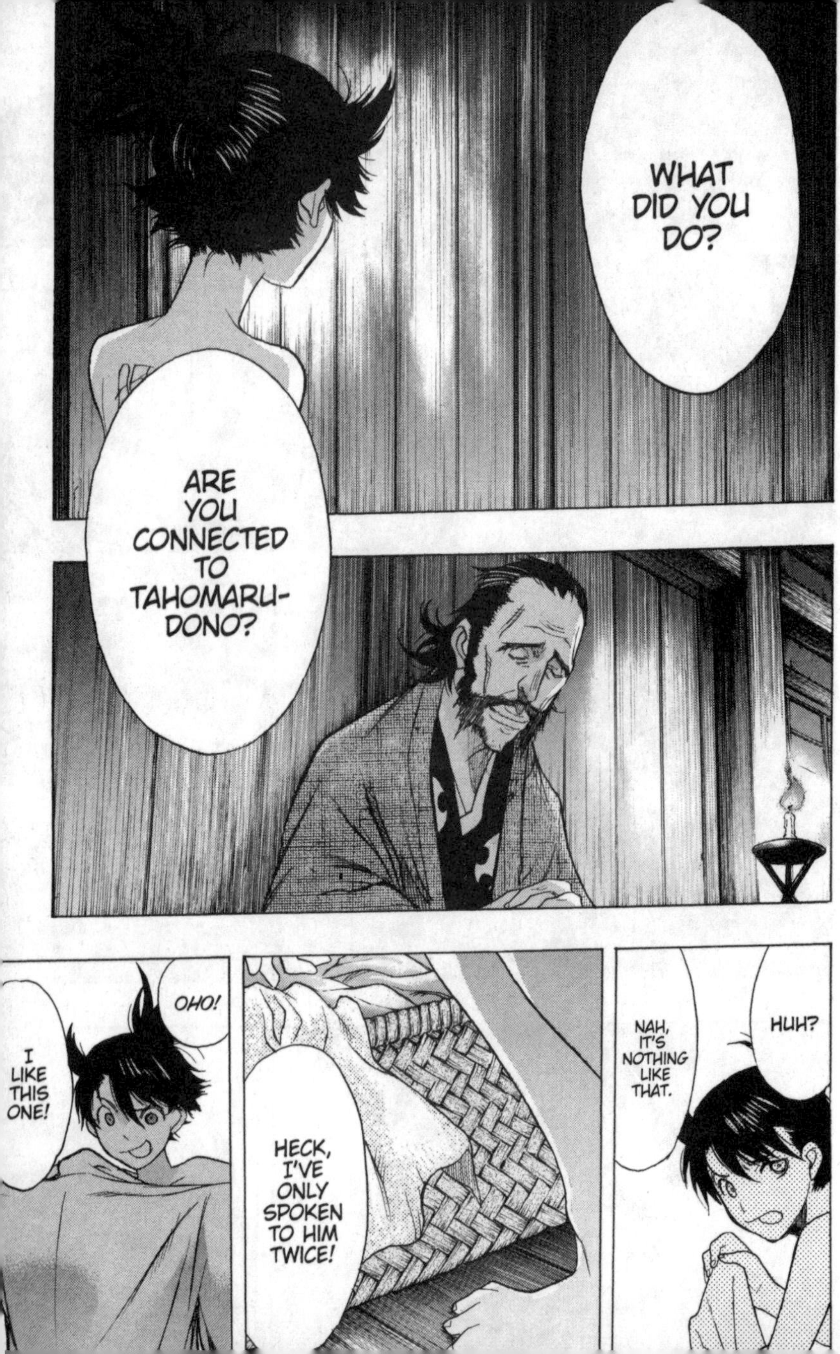
WHAT DID YOU DO?
ARE YOU CONNECTED TO TAHOMARU-DONO?
HUH?
NAH, IT'S NOTHING LIKE THAT.
HECK, I'VE ONLY SPOKEN TO HIM TWICE!
OHO!
I LIKE THIS ONE!

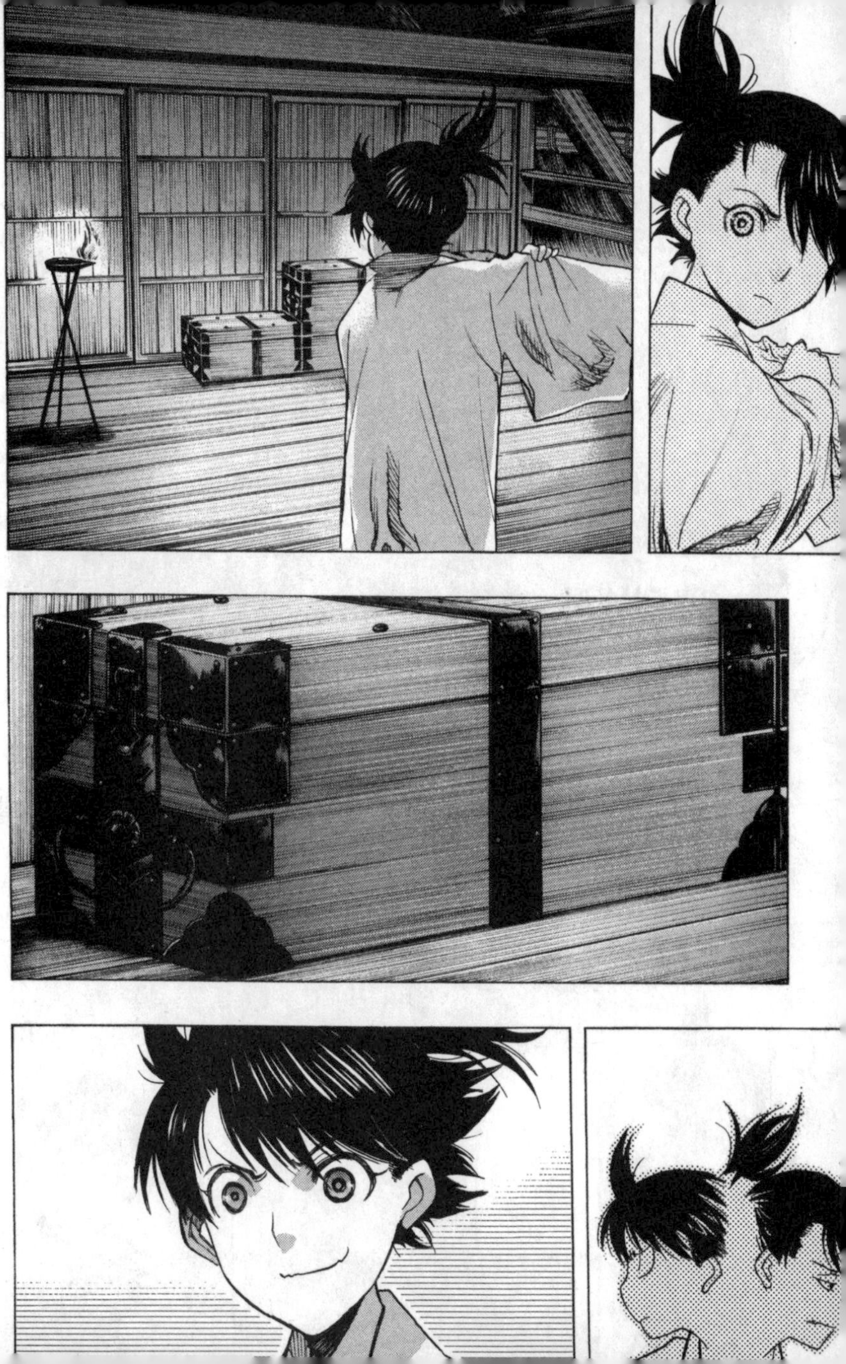

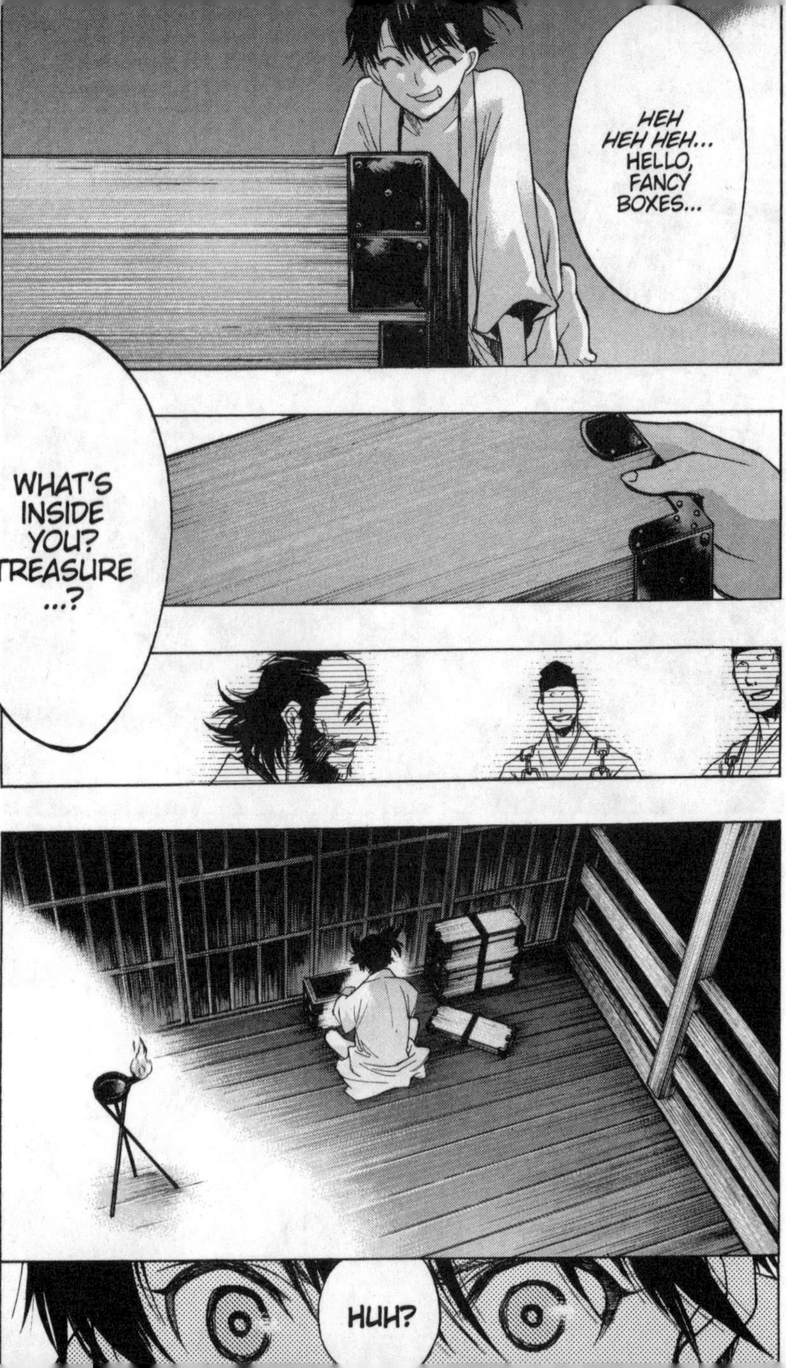
HEH HEH HEH... HELLO, FANCY BOXES...
WHAT'S INSIDE YOU? TREASURE ...?
HUH?

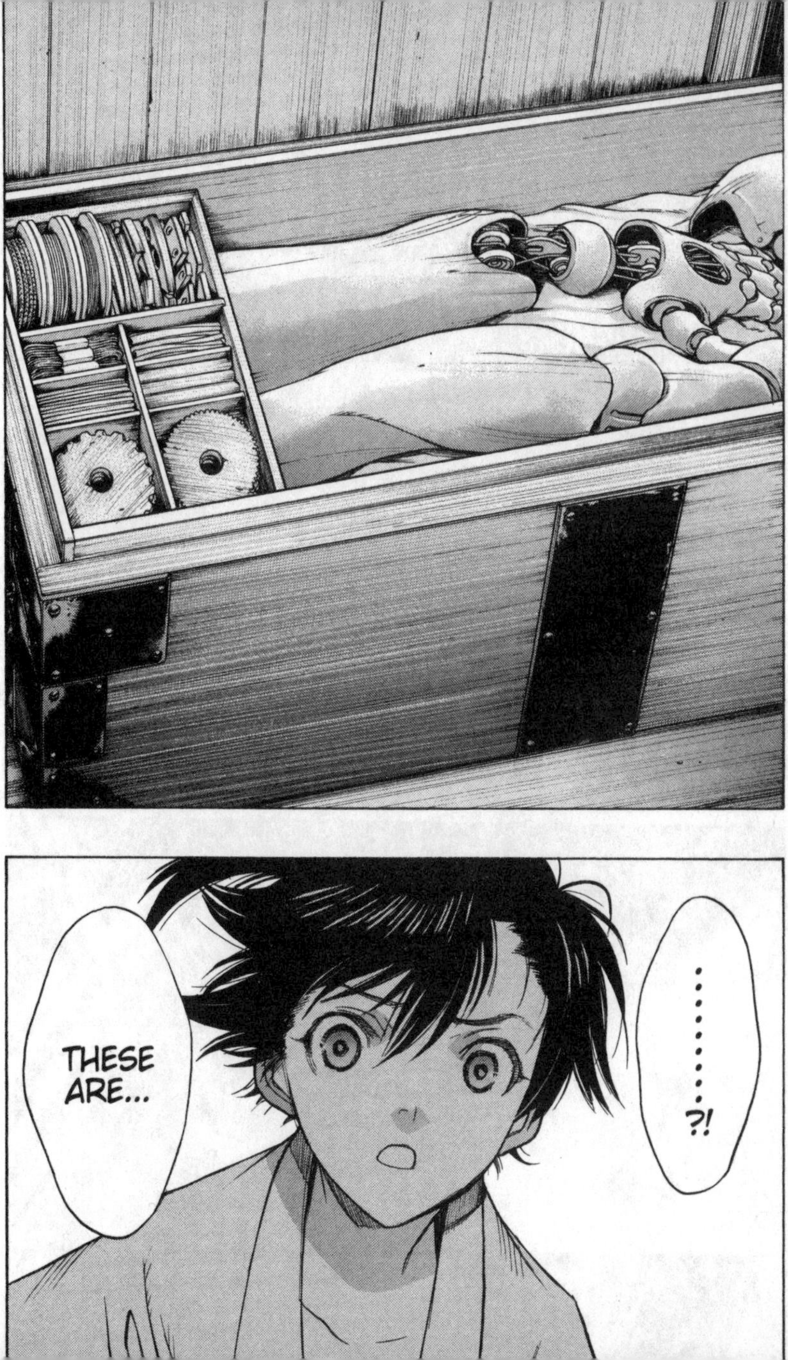
........?!
THESE ARE...

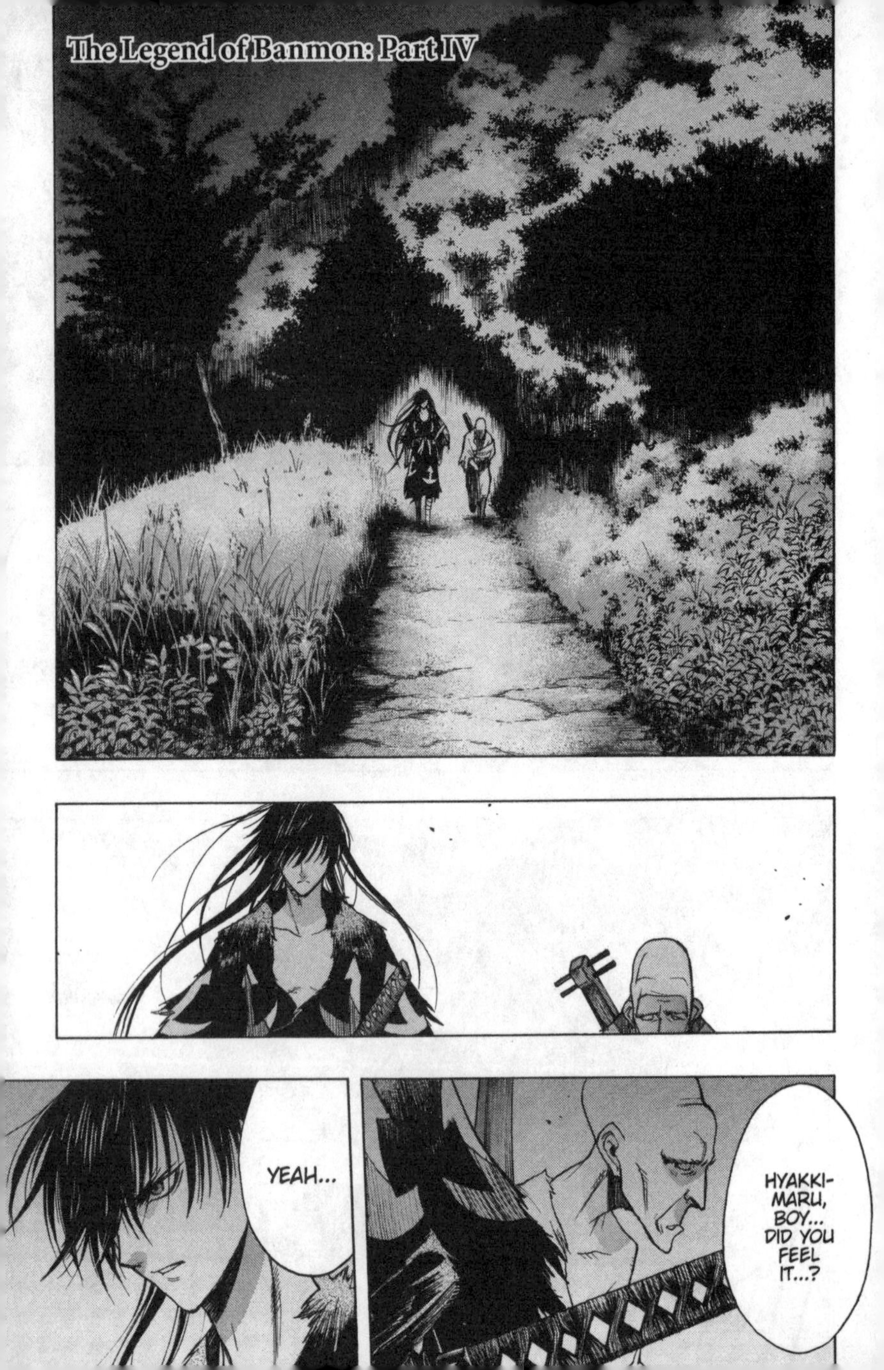
The Legend of Banmon: Part IV
HYAKKI-MARU, BOY... DID YOU FEEL IT...?
YEAH...

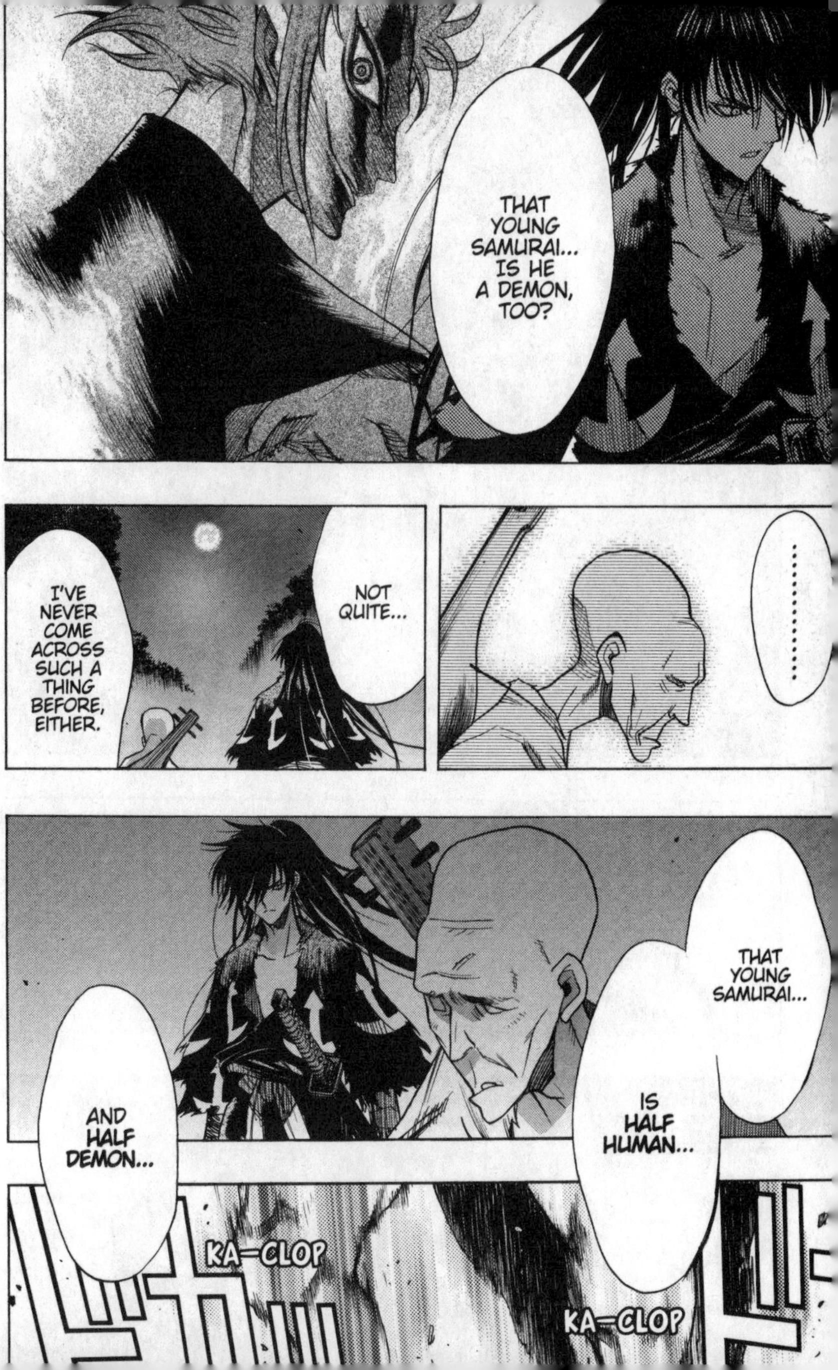
THAT YOUNG SAMURAI... IS HE A DEMON, TOO?
......
NOT QUITE...
I'VE NEVER COME ACROSS SUCH A THING BEFORE, EITHER.
THAT YOUNG SAMURAI...
IS HALF HUMAN...
AND HALF DEMON...
KA-CLOP
KA-CLOP

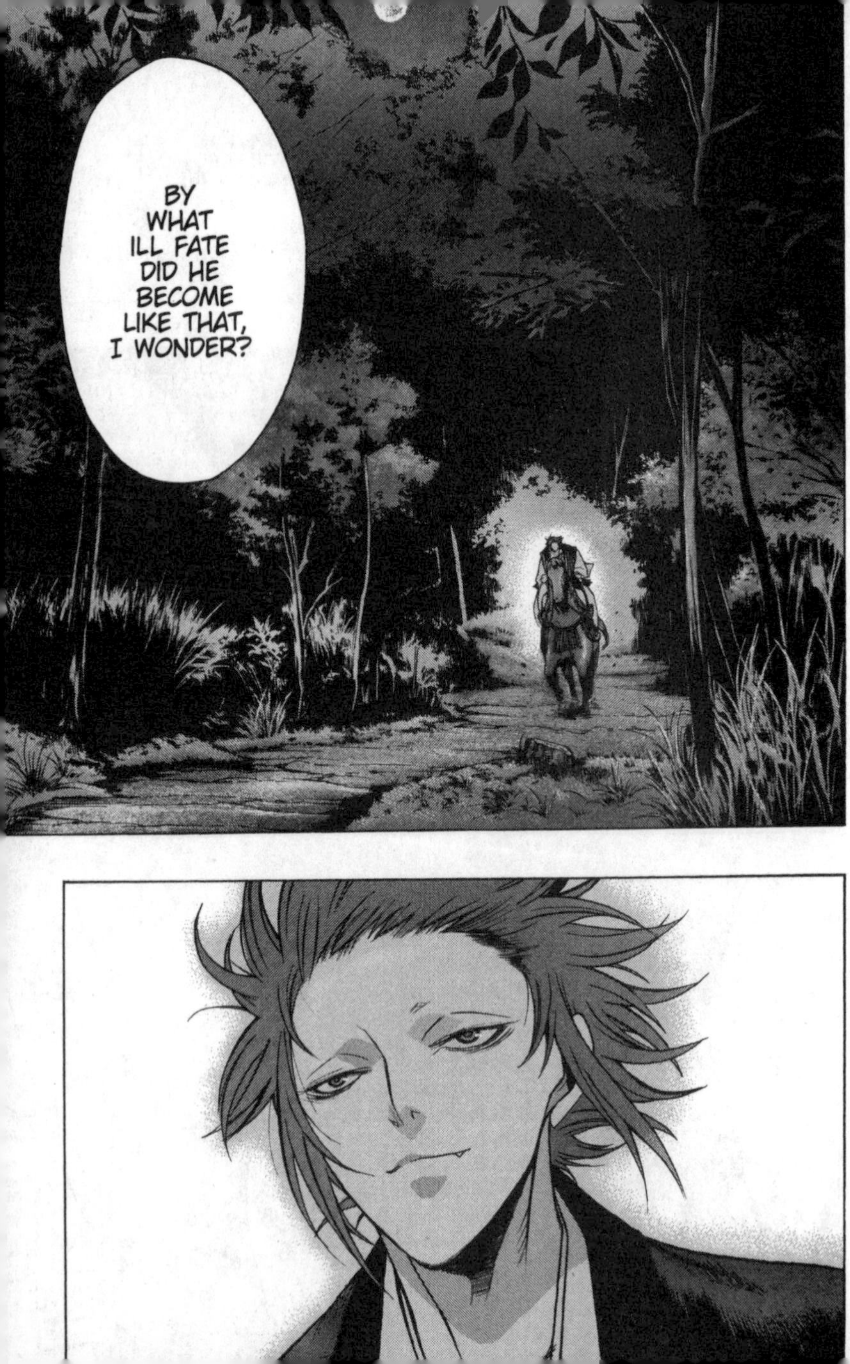
BY WHAT ILL FATE DID HE BECOME LIKE THAT, I WONDER?

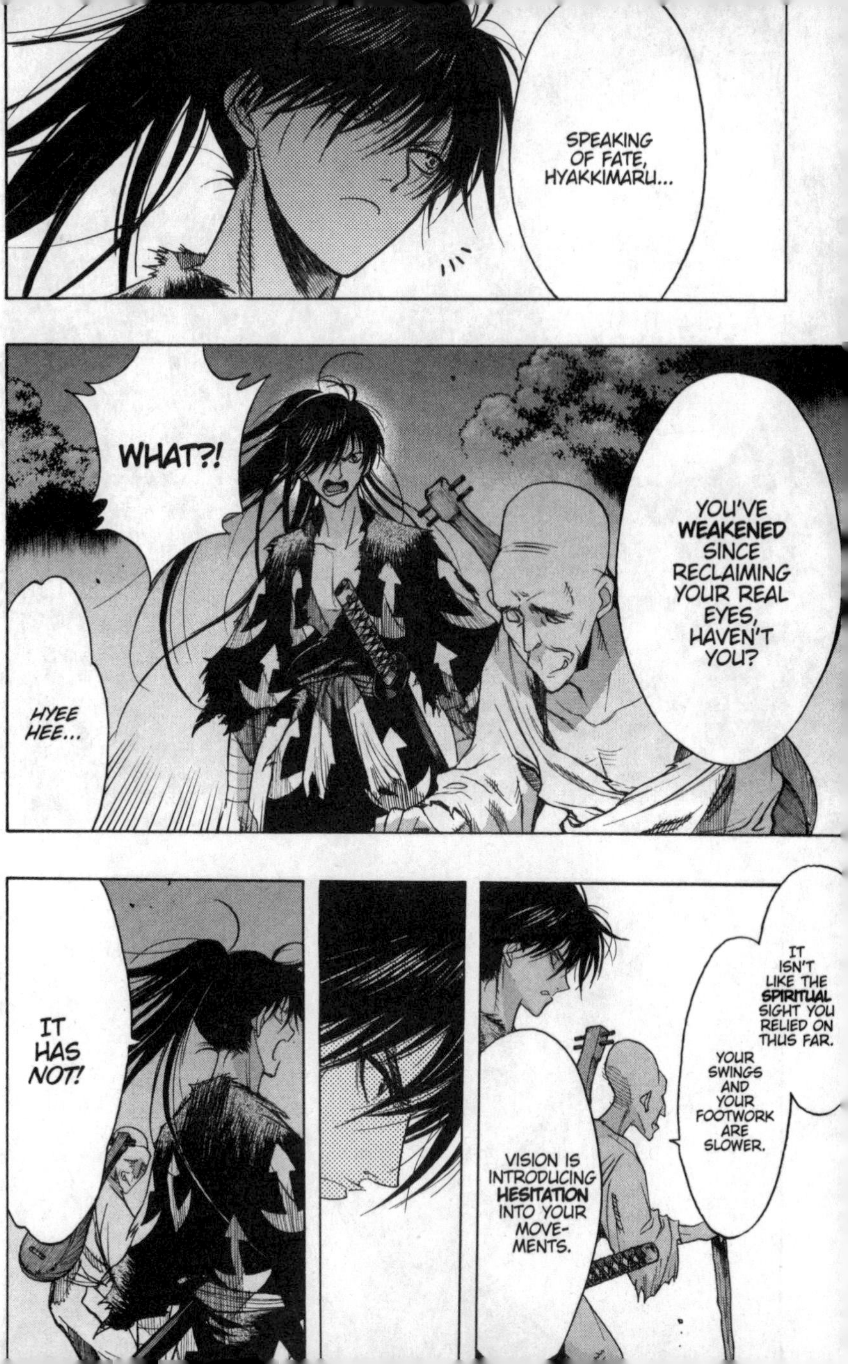
SPEAKING OF FATE, HYAKKIMARU...
YOU'VE WEAKENED SINCE RECLAIMING YOUR REAL EYES, HAVEN'T YOU?
WHAT?!
HYEE HEE...
IT ISN'T LIKE THE SPIRITUAL SIGHT YOU RELIED ON THUS FAR.
YOUR SWINGS AND YOUR FOOTWORK ARE SLOWER.
VISION IS INTRODUCING HESITATION INTO YOUR MOVE-MENTS.
IT HAS NOT!

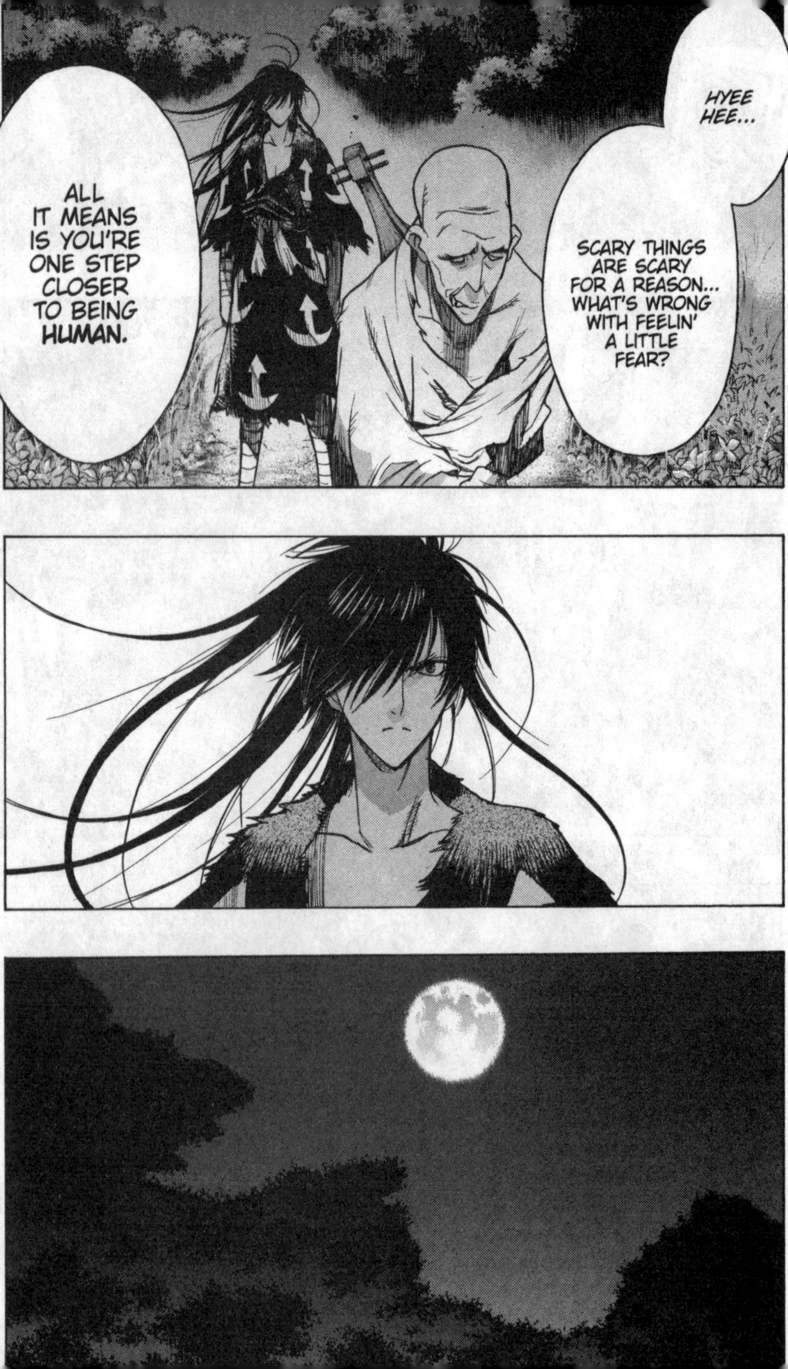
HYEE HEE...
SCARY THINGS ARE SCARY FOR A REASON... WHAT'S WRONG WITH FEELIN' A LITTLE FEAR?
ALL IT MEANS IS YOU'RE ONE STEP CLOSER TO BEING **HUMAN.**

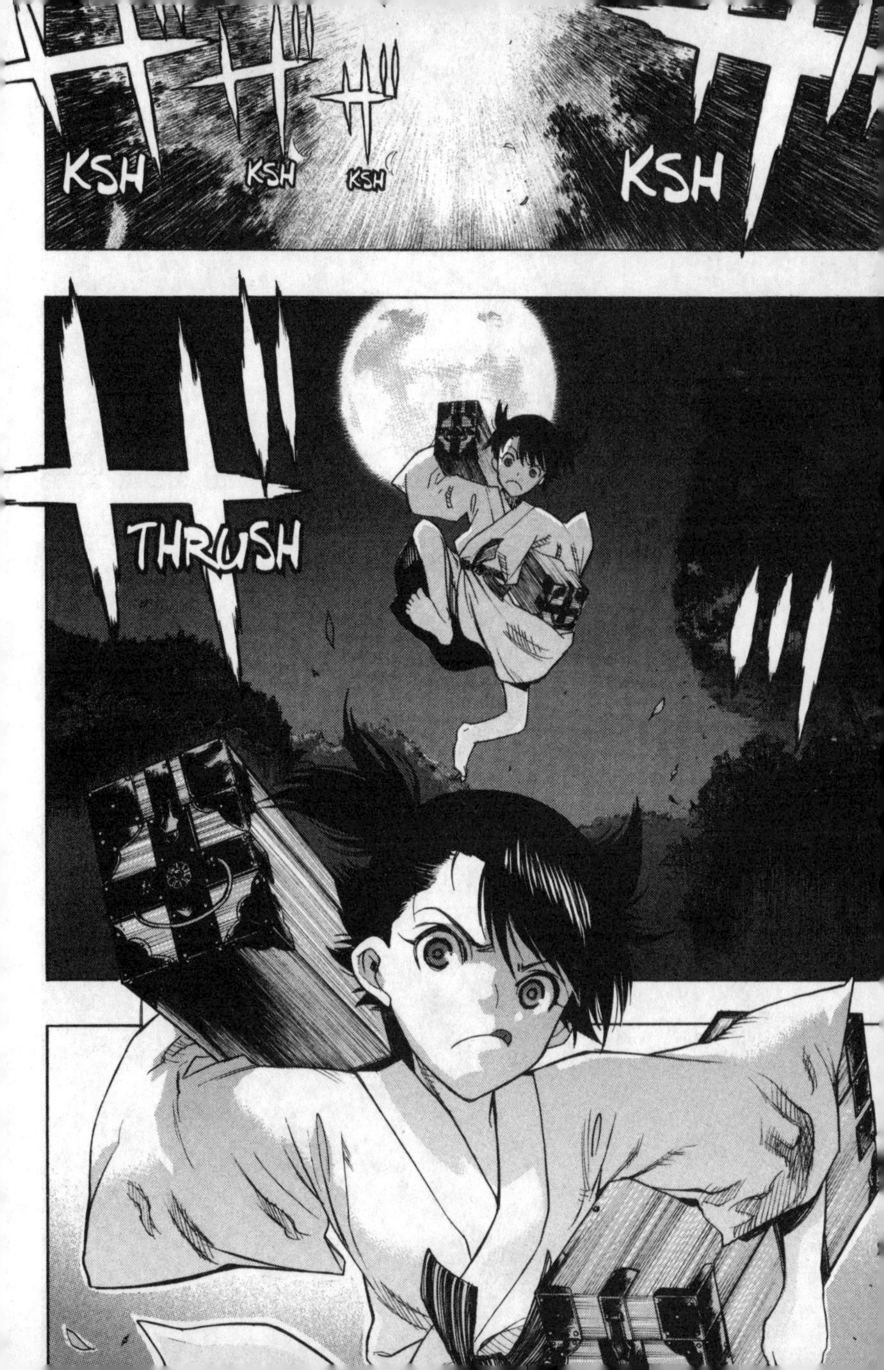
KSH
KSH
KSH
KSH
THRUSH

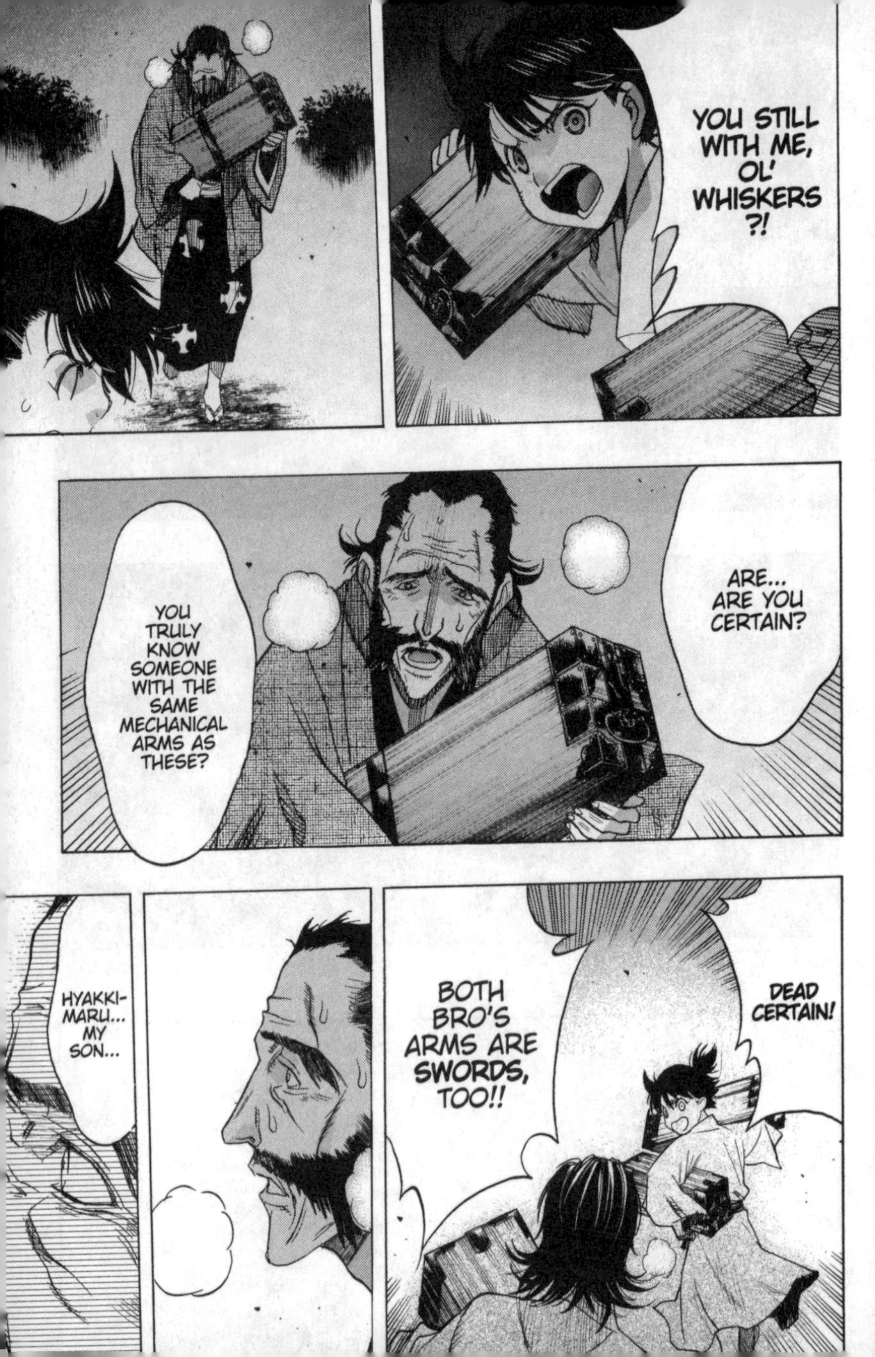
YOU STILL WITH ME, OL' WHISKERS?!
ARE... ARE YOU CERTAIN?
YOU TRULY KNOW SOMEONE WITH THE SAME MECHANICAL ARMS AS THESE?
DEAD CERTAIN!
BOTH BRO'S ARMS ARE SWORDS, TOO!!
HYAKKIMARU... MY SON...

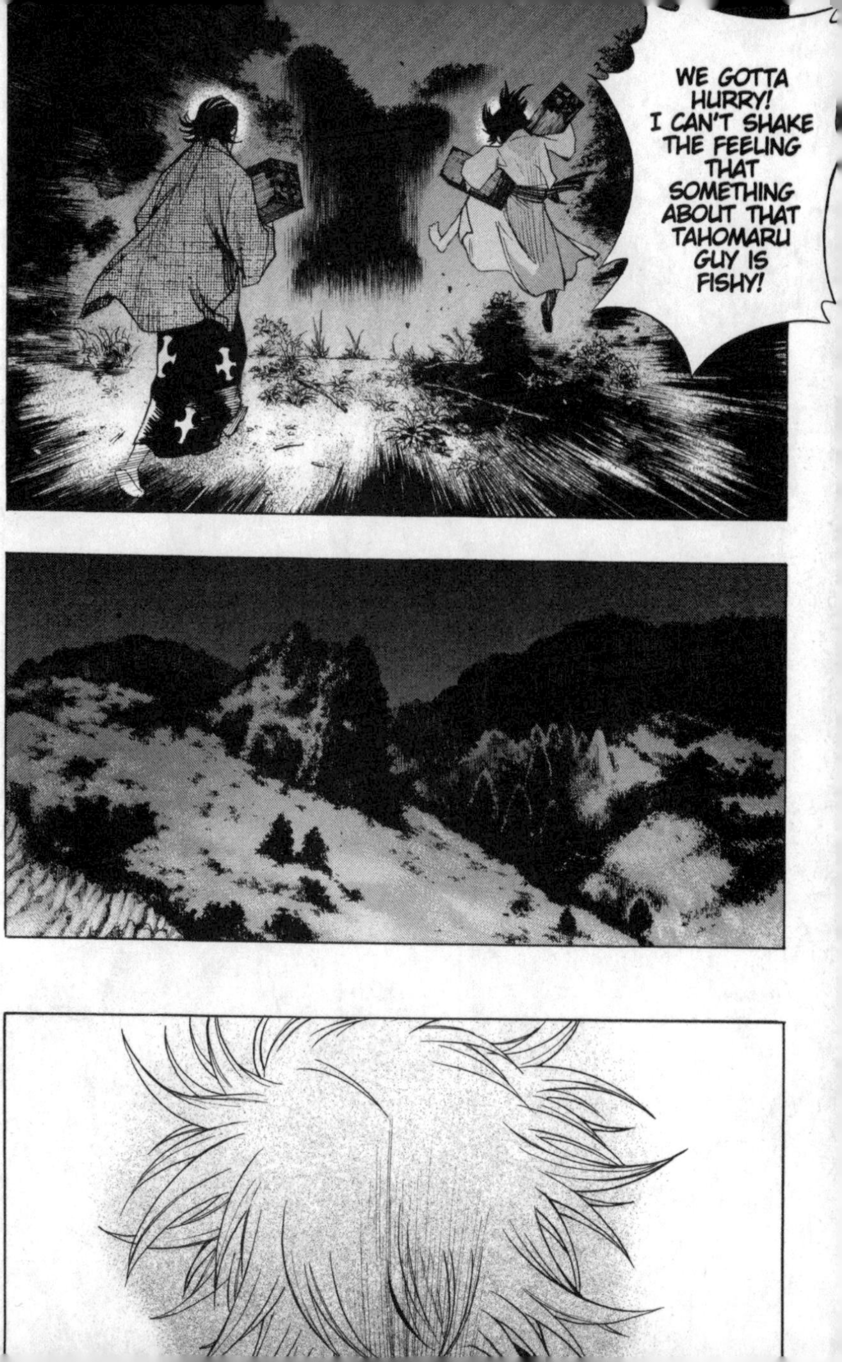
WE GOTTA HURRY! I CAN'T SHAKE THE FEELING THAT SOMETHING ABOUT THAT TAHOMARU GUY IS FISHY!

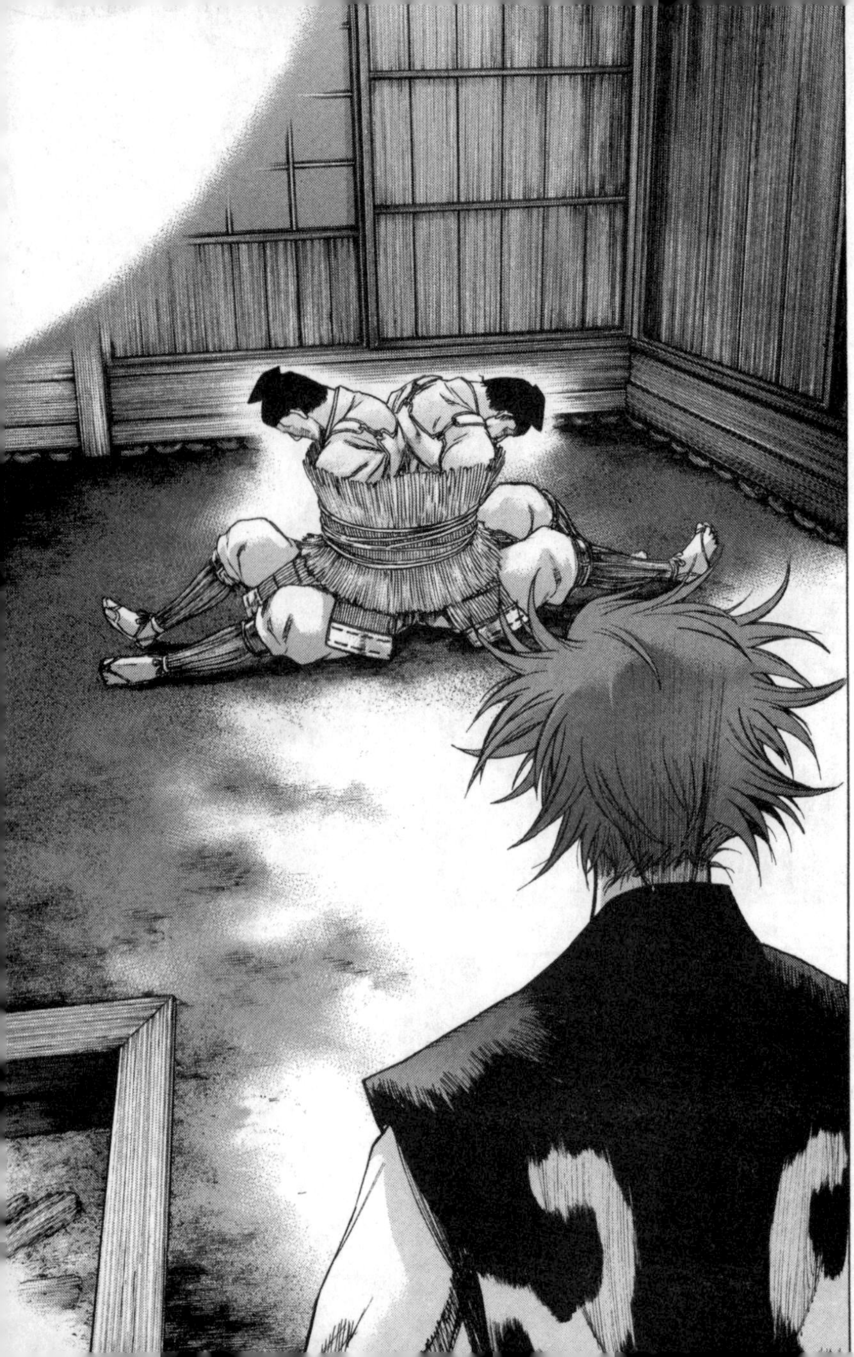

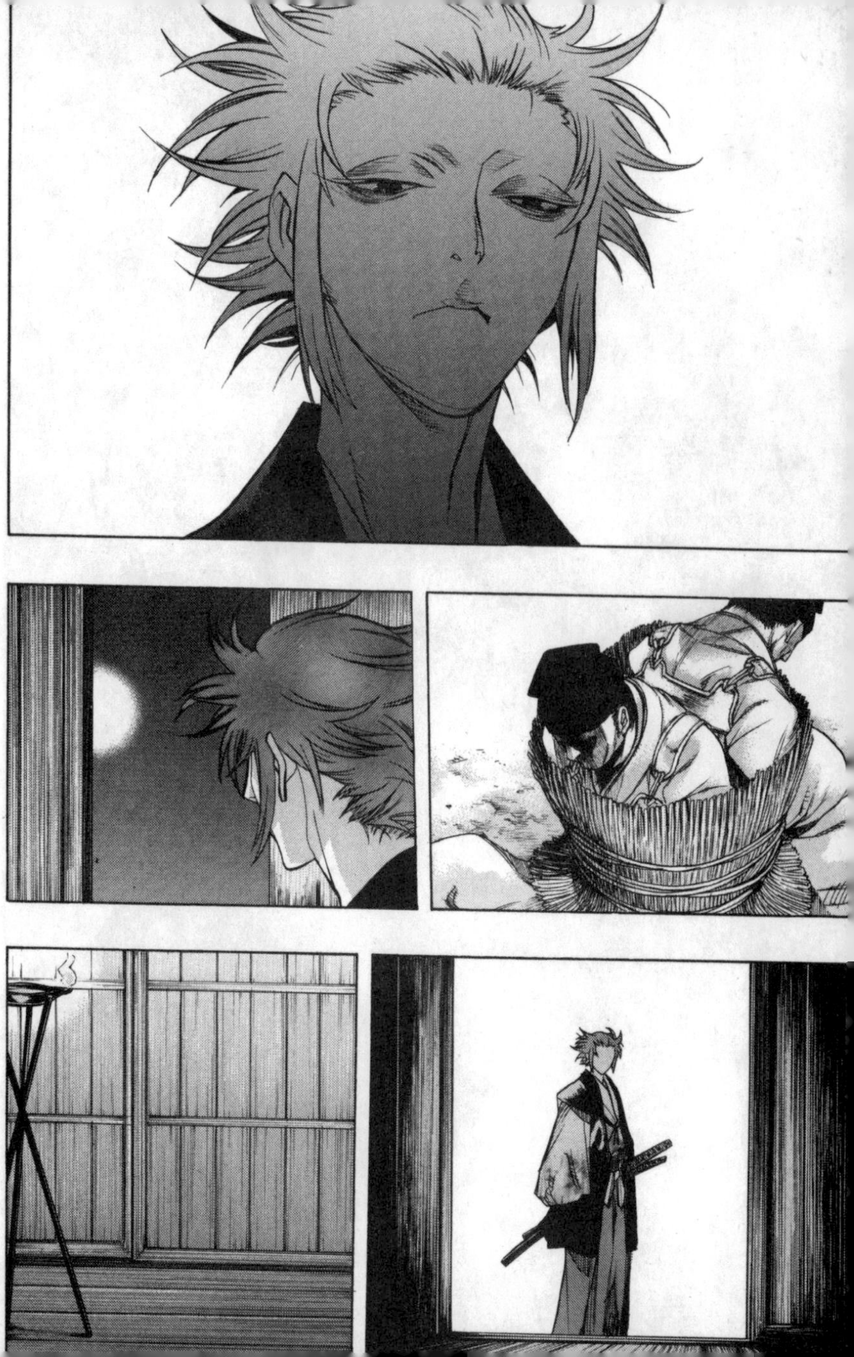

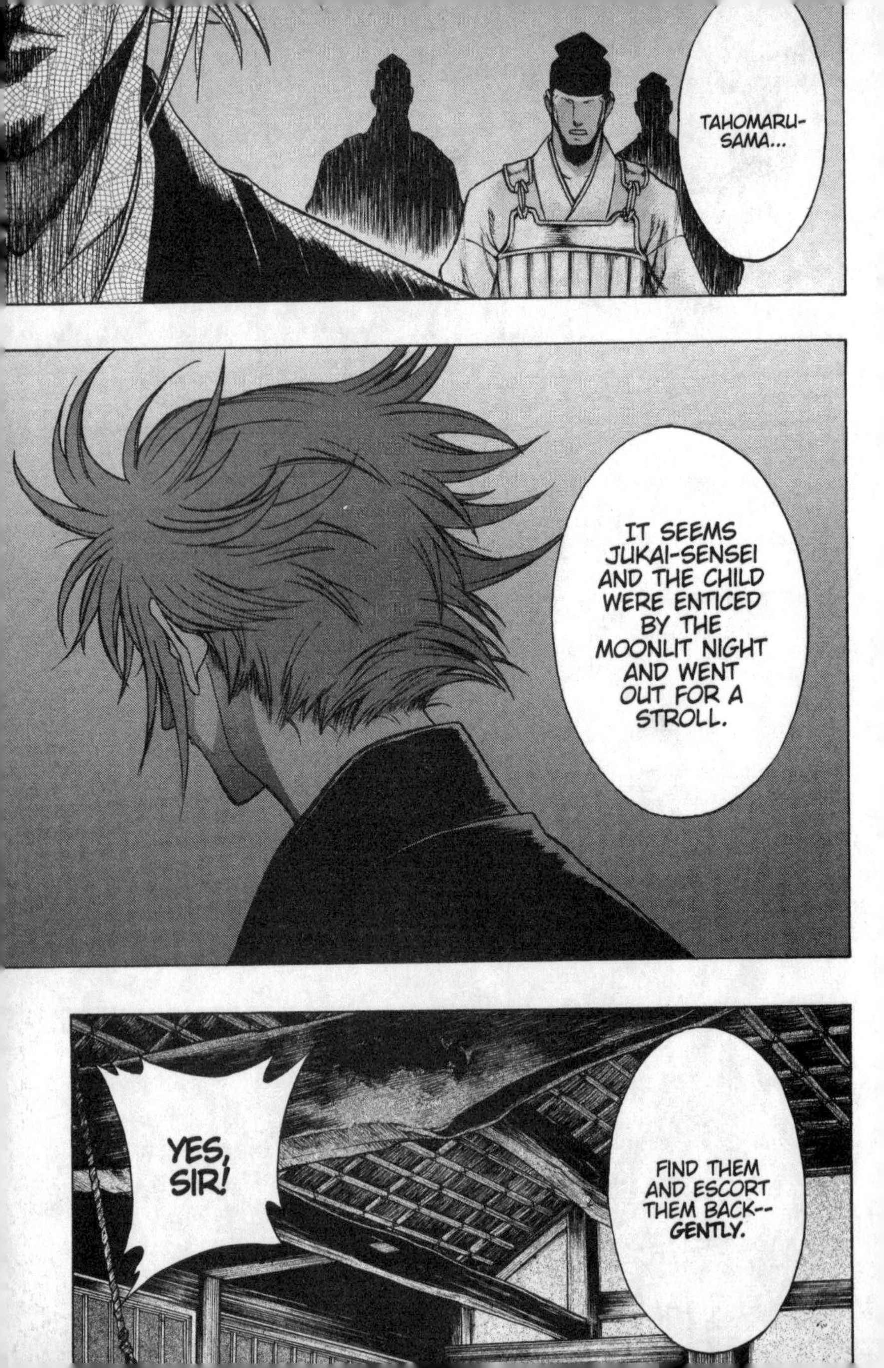
TAHOMARU-SAMA...
IT SEEMS JUKAI-SENSEI AND THE CHILD WERE ENTICED BY THE MOONLIT NIGHT AND WENT OUT FOR A STROLL.
FIND THEM AND ESCORT THEM BACK-- GENTLY.
YES, SIR!

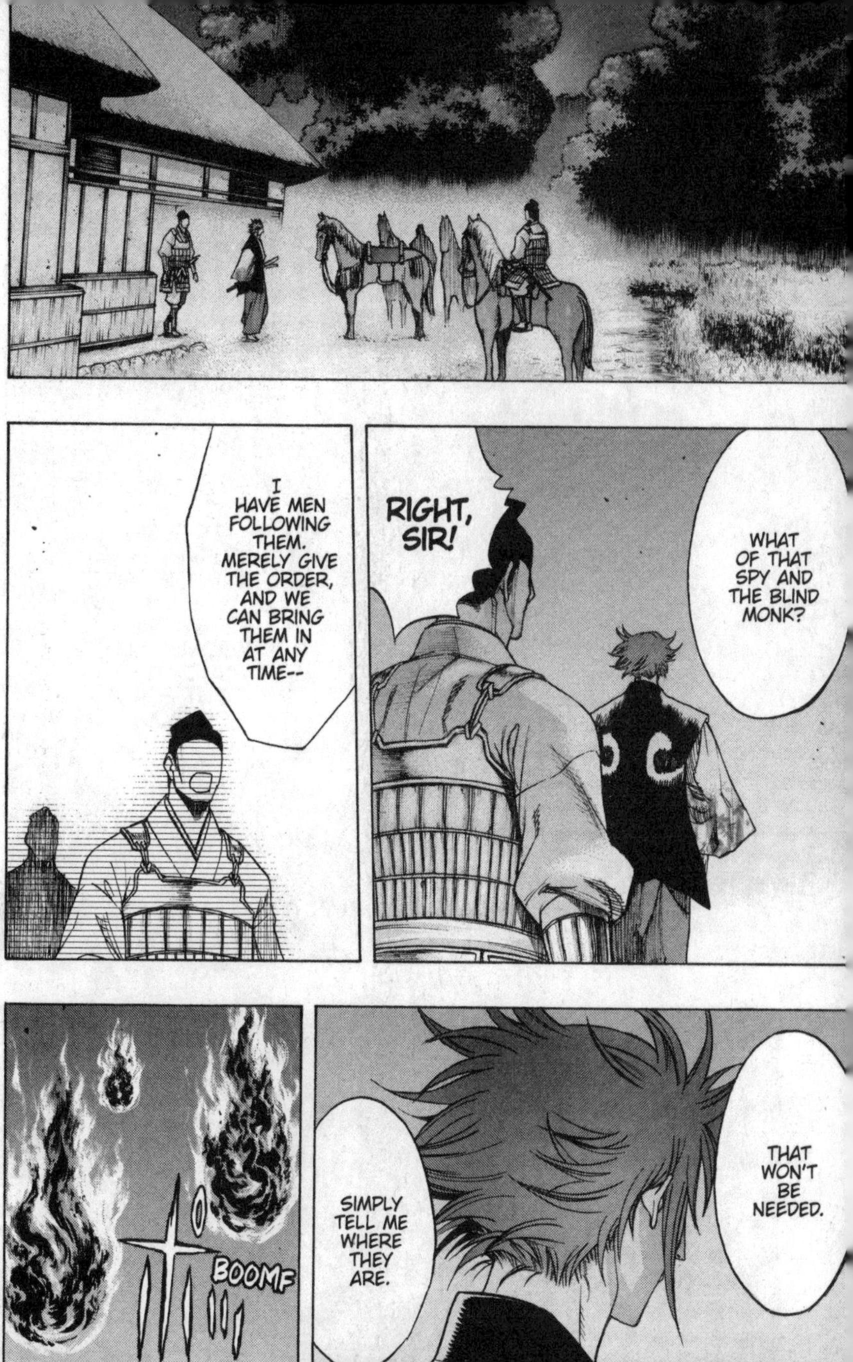
WHAT OF THAT SPY AND THE BLIND MONK?
RIGHT, SIR!
I HAVE MEN FOLLOWING THEM. MERELY GIVE THE ORDER, AND WE CAN BRING THEM IN AT ANY TIME--
THAT WON'T BE NEEDED.
SIMPLY TELL ME WHERE THEY ARE.
BOOMF

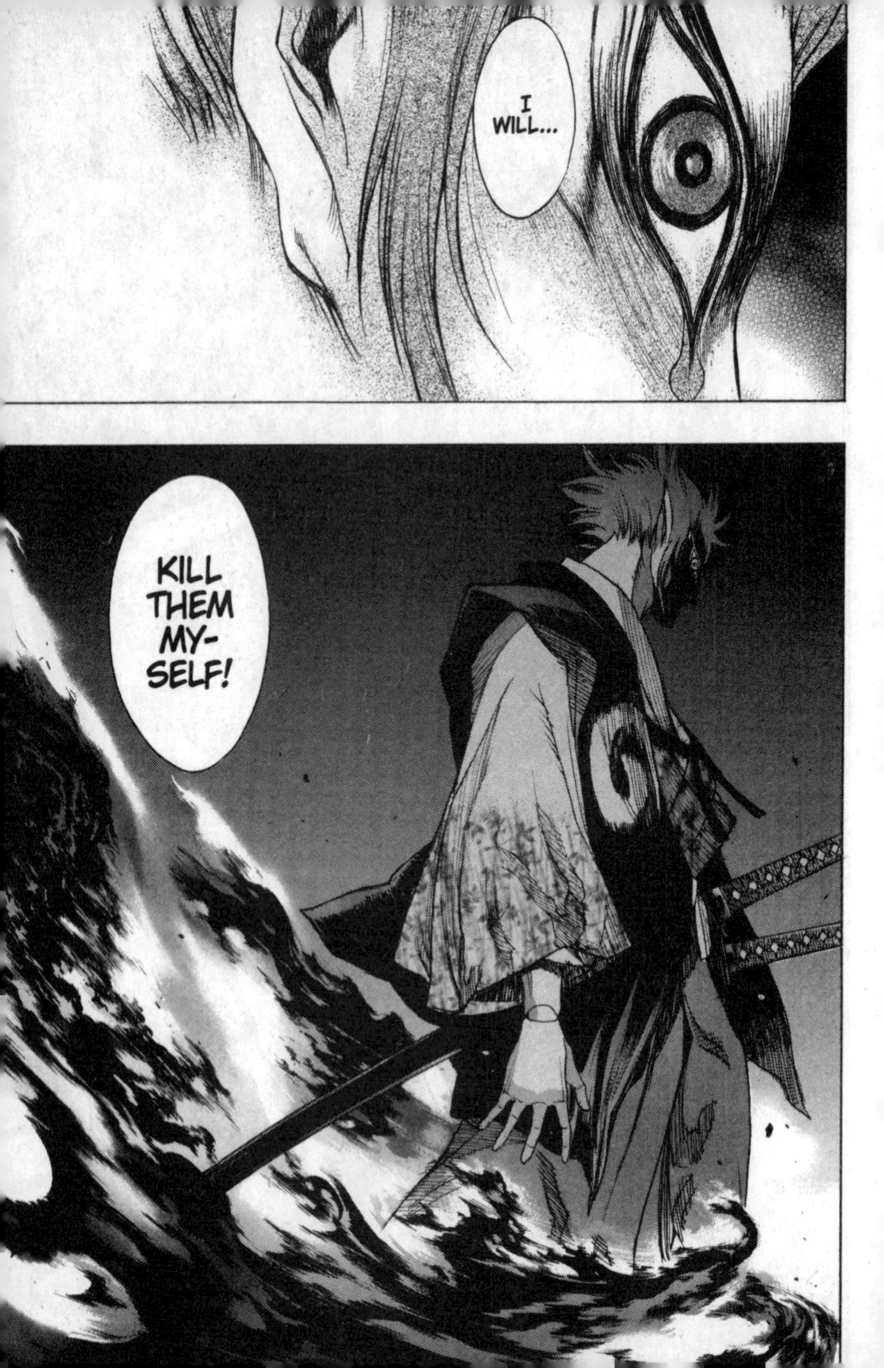
I WILL...
KILL THEM MY-SELF!

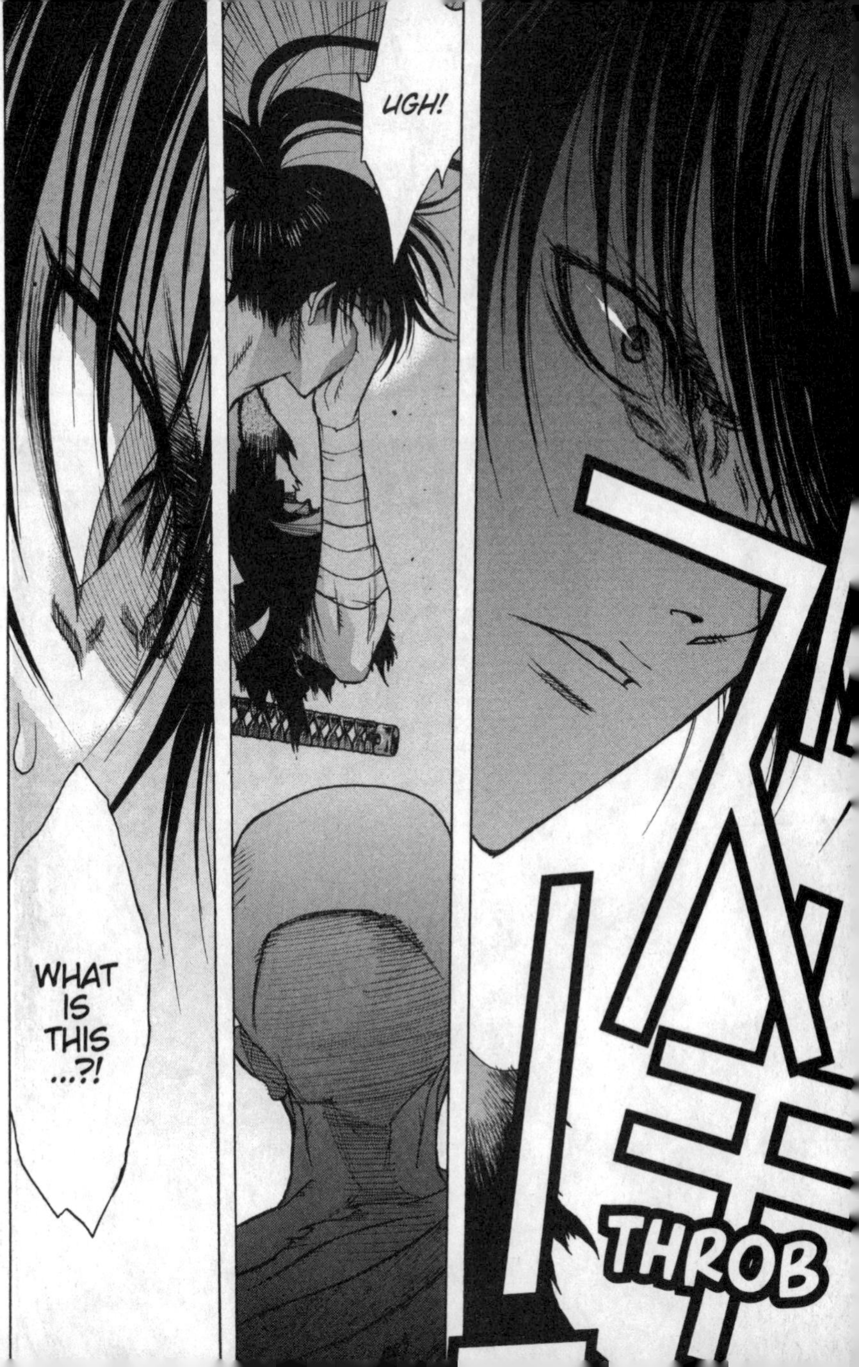
THROB
UGH!
WHAT IS THIS ...?!

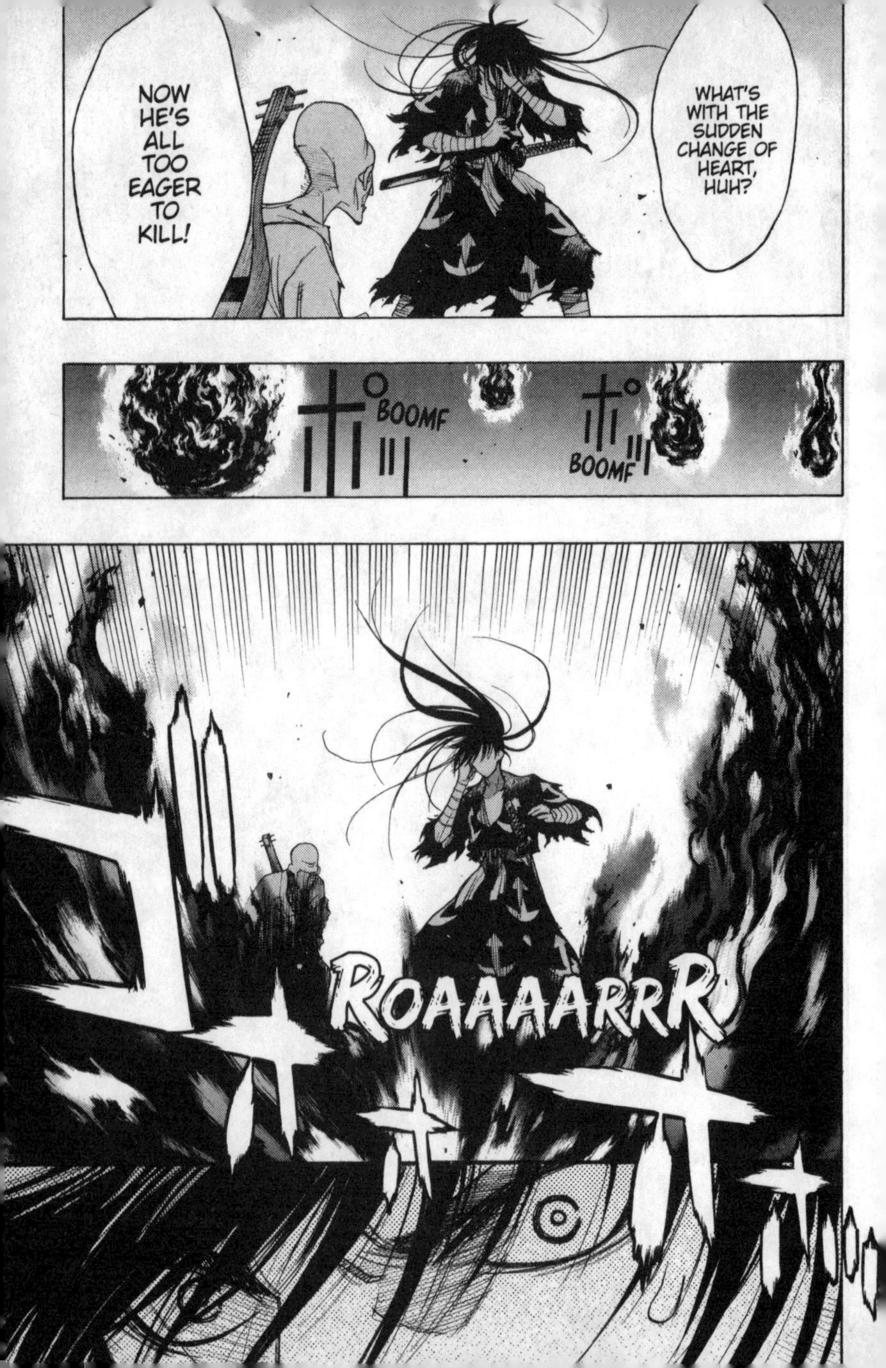
WHAT'S WITH THE SUDDEN CHANGE OF HEART, HUH?
NOW HE'S ALL TOO EAGER TO KILL!
BOOMF
BOOMF
ROAAAARRR

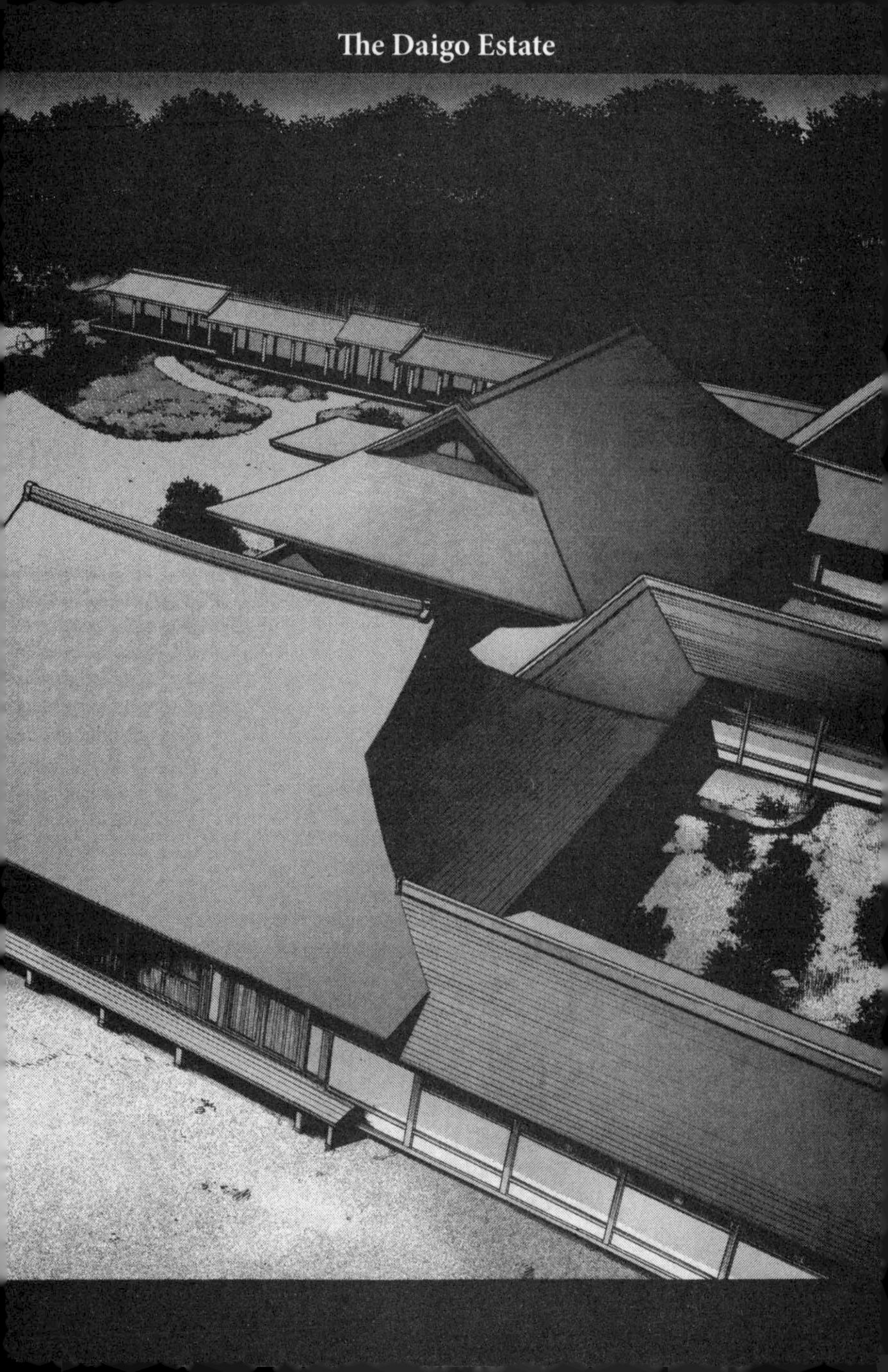
The Daigo Estate

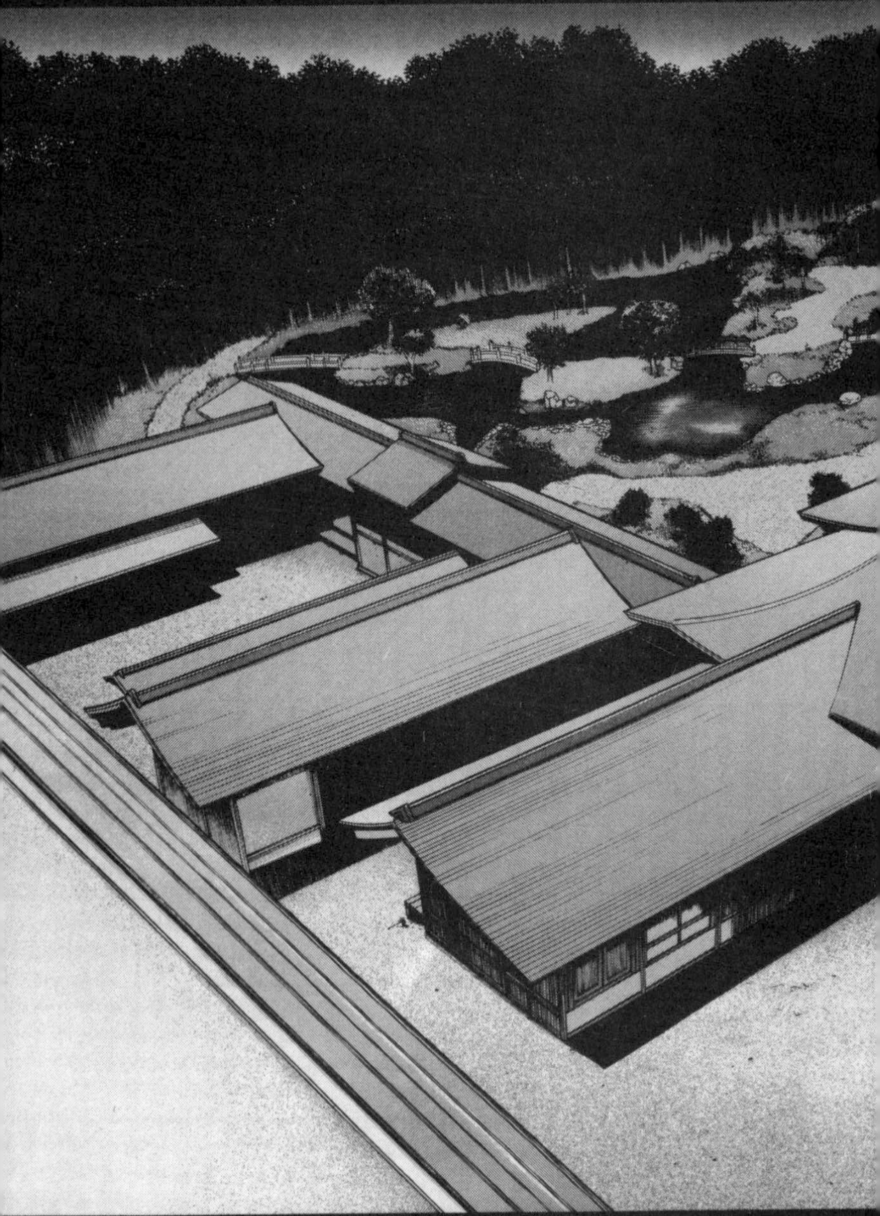

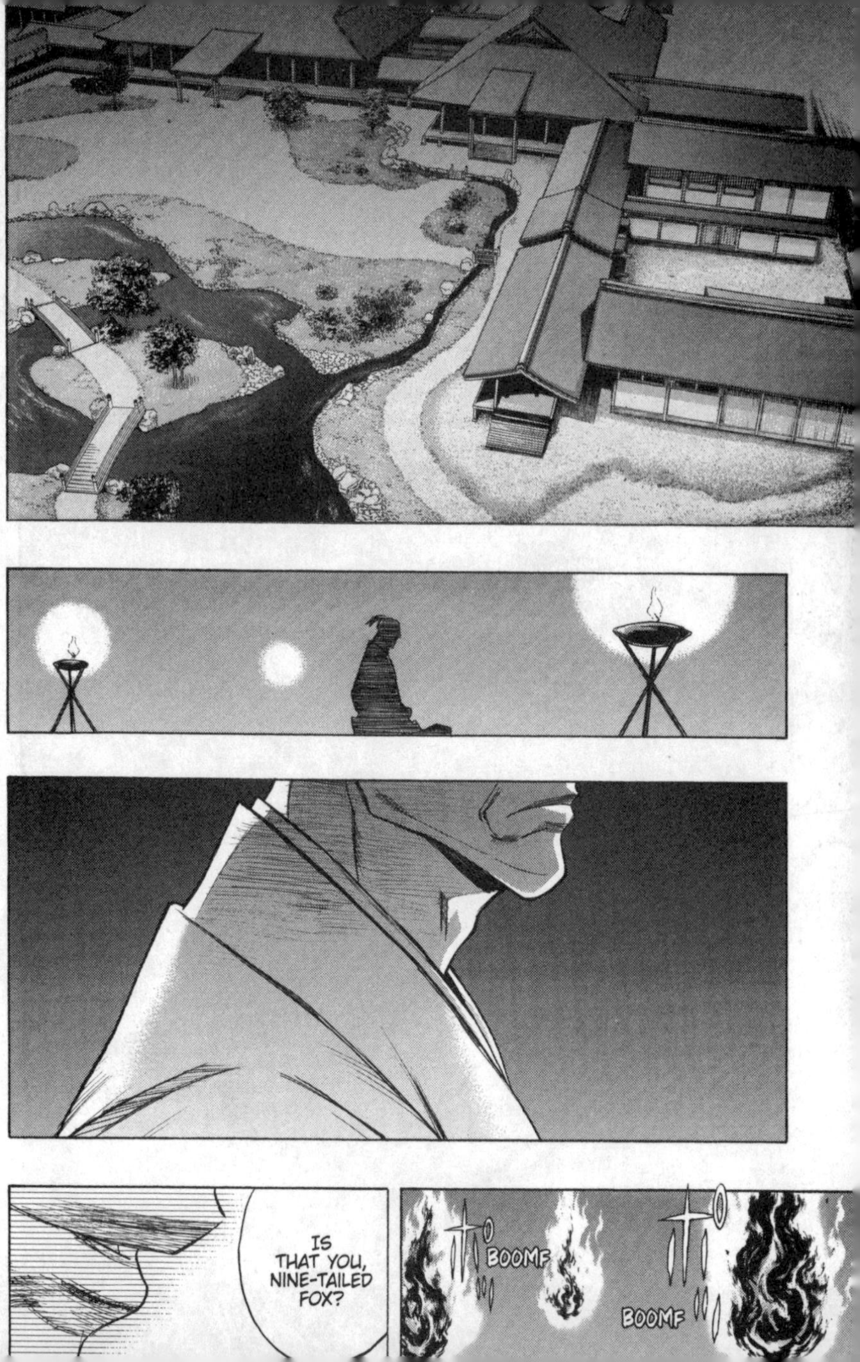
BOOMF
BOOMF
IS THAT YOU, NINE-TAILED FOX?

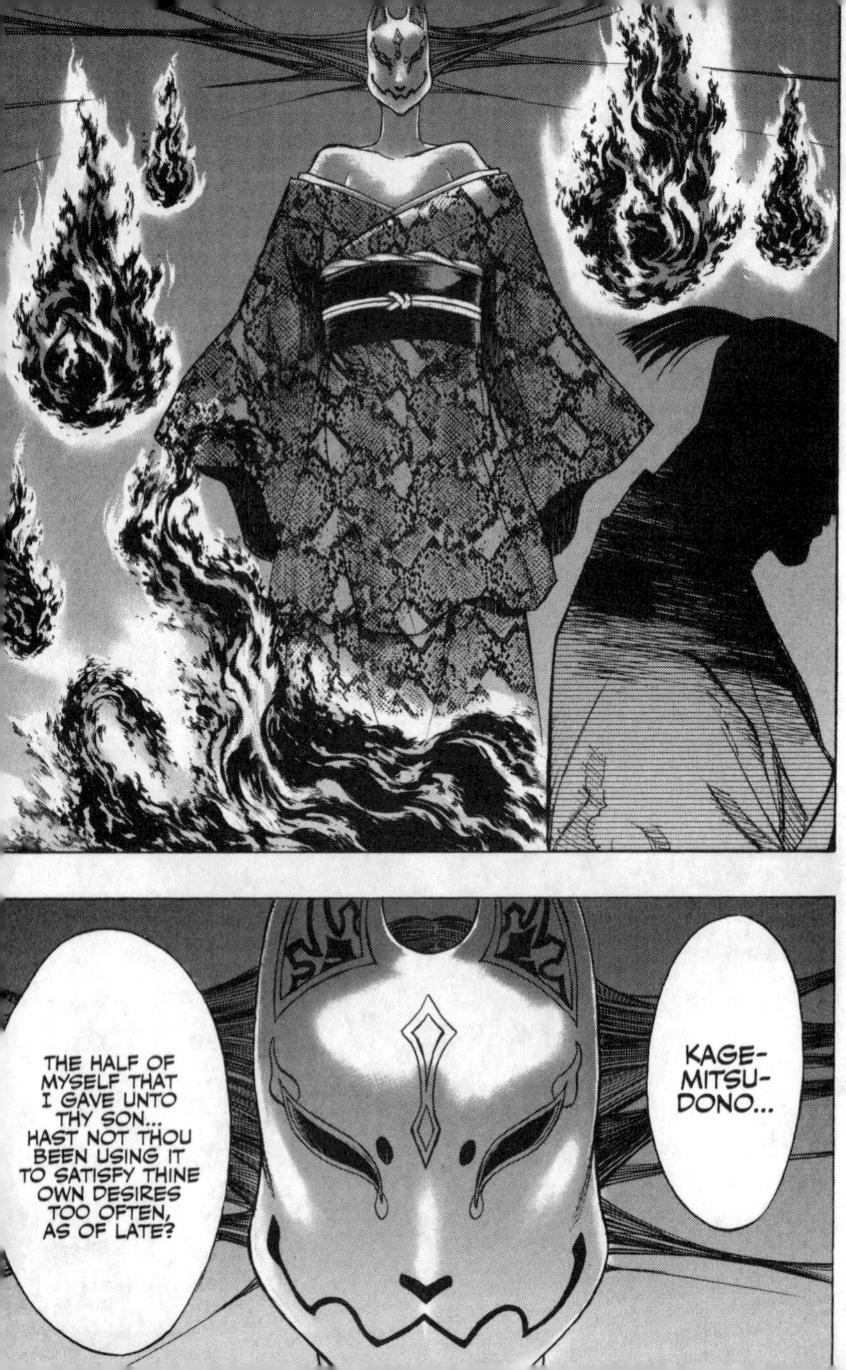
KAGE-MITSU-DONO...
THE HALF OF MYSELF THAT I GAVE UNTO THY SON... HAST NOT THOU BEEN USING IT TO SATISFY THINE OWN DESIRES TOO OFTEN, AS OF LATE?

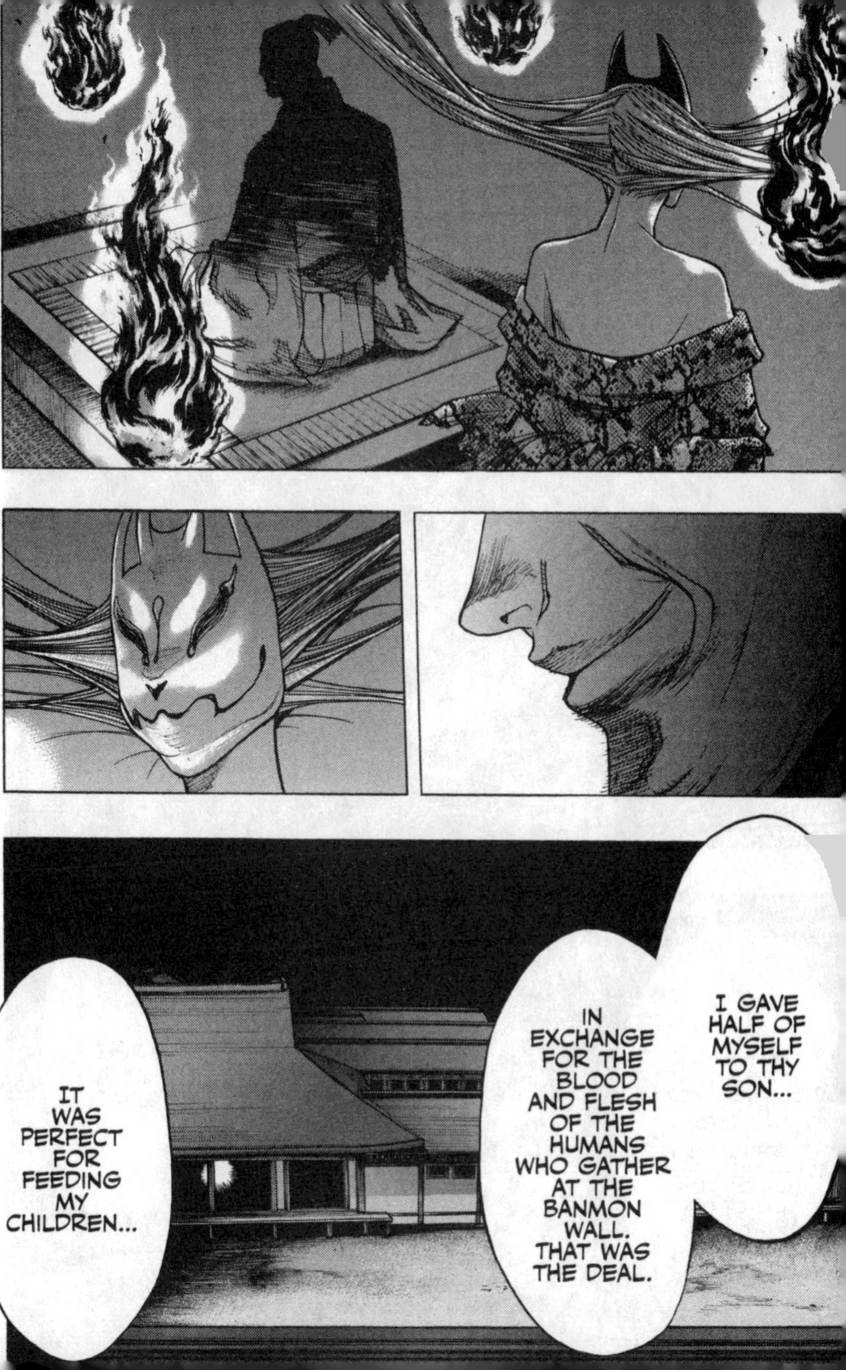
I GAVE HALF OF MYSELF TO THY SON...
IN EXCHANGE FOR THE BLOOD AND FLESH OF THE HUMANS WHO GATHER AT THE BANMON WALL. THAT WAS THE DEAL.
IT WAS PERFECT FOR FEEDING MY CHILDREN...

BUT THY SON TENDS TO OVERUSE OUR POWER.

RELAX.

I'LL HAVE TAHOMARU COMMAND THE CAMPAIGN TO CROSS BANMON AND INVADE ASAKURA TERRITORY.

WITH THAT POWER...

WE'LL HAVE YOU **FEASTING** ON BLOOD AND FLESH.

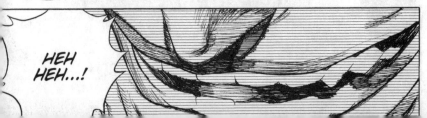

HEH HEH...!

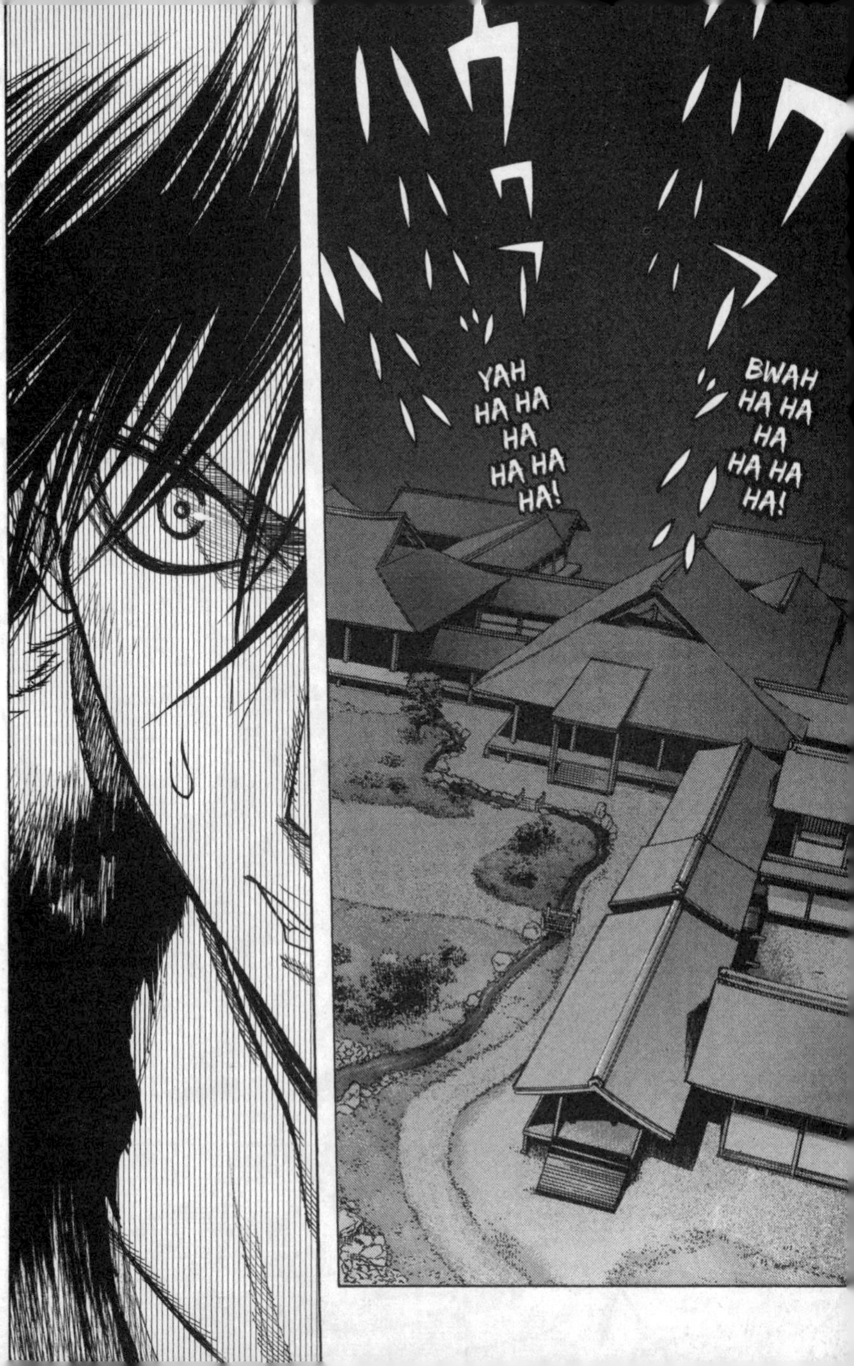
BWAH HA HA HA HA HA HA!
YAH HA HA HA HA HA HA!

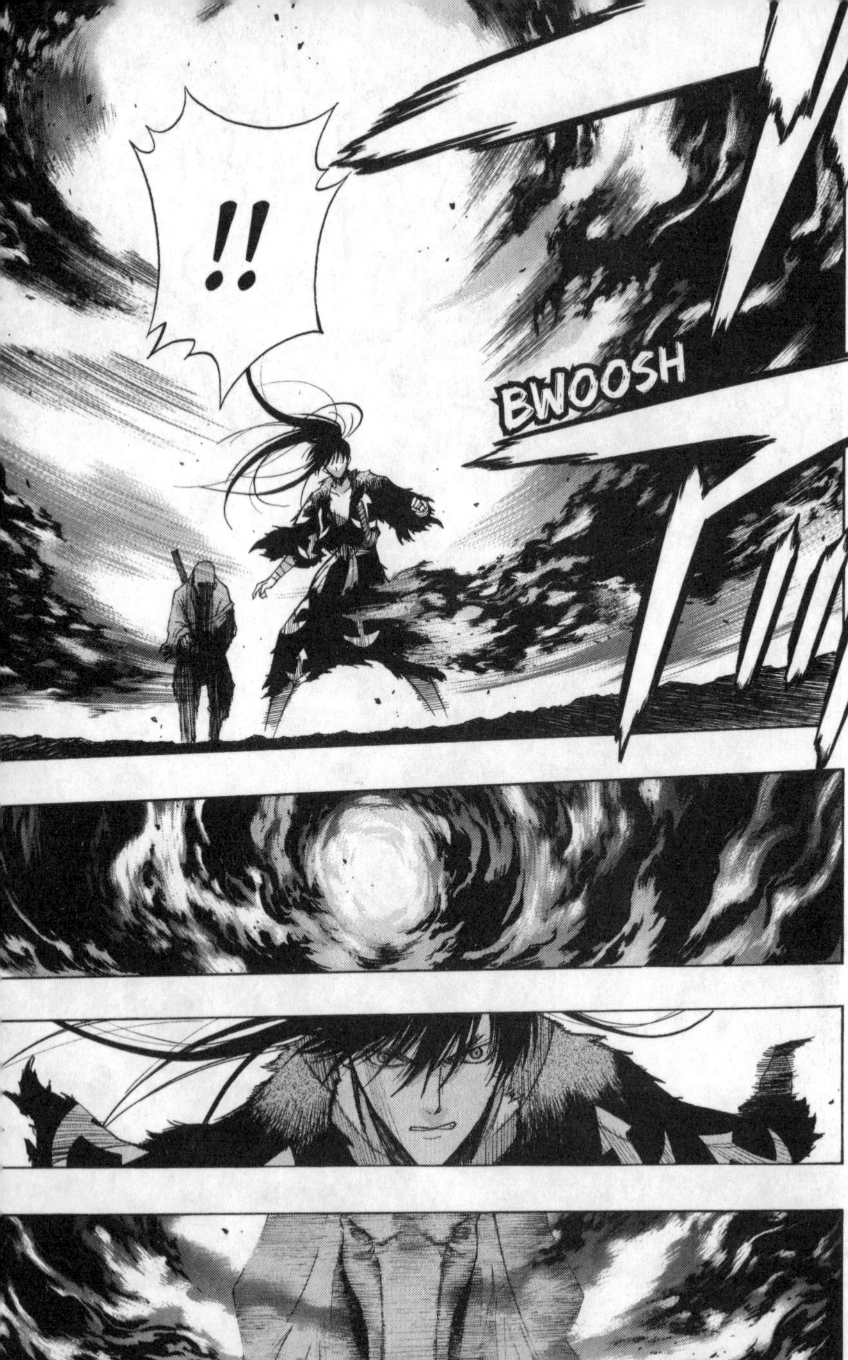

BWOOSH
!!

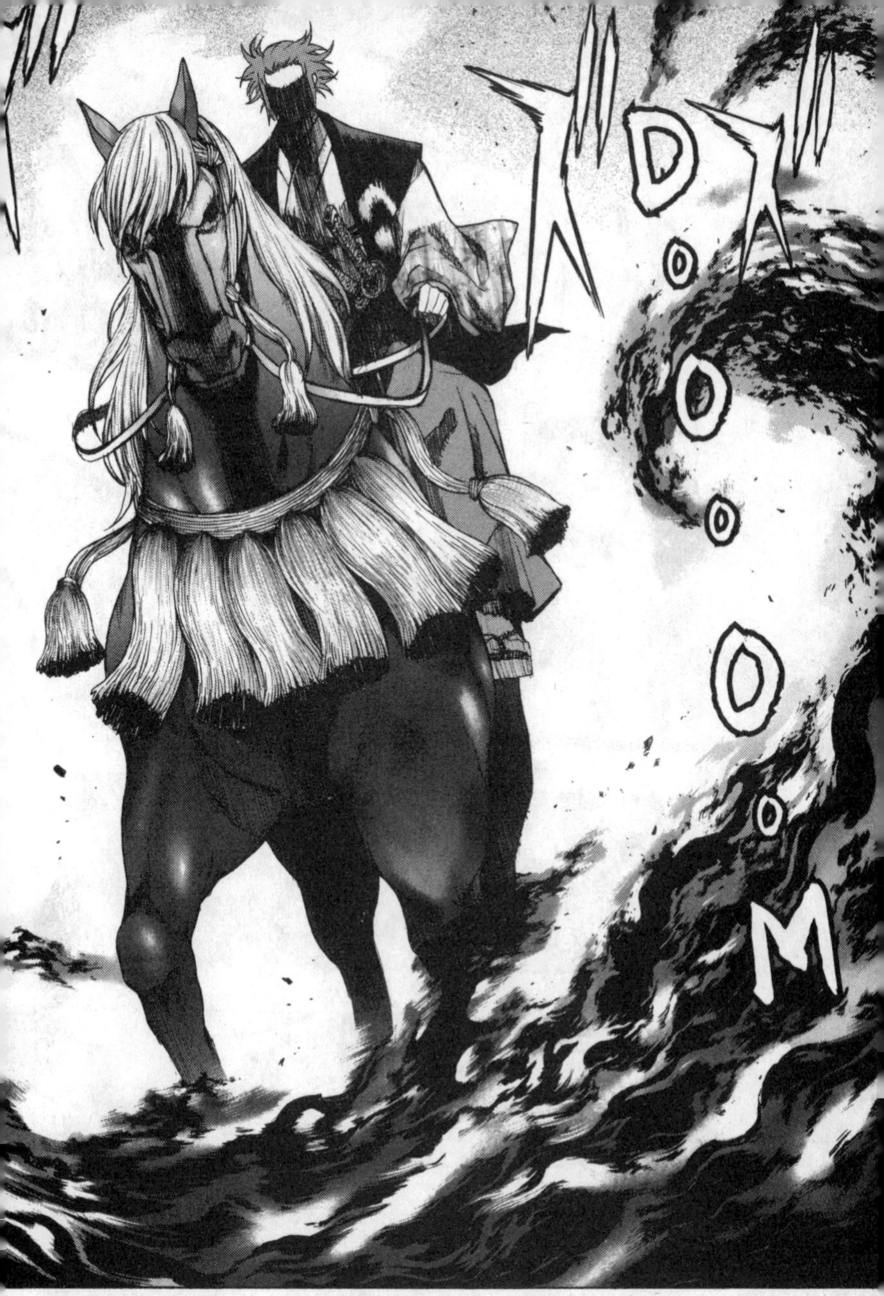
DOOOOOM

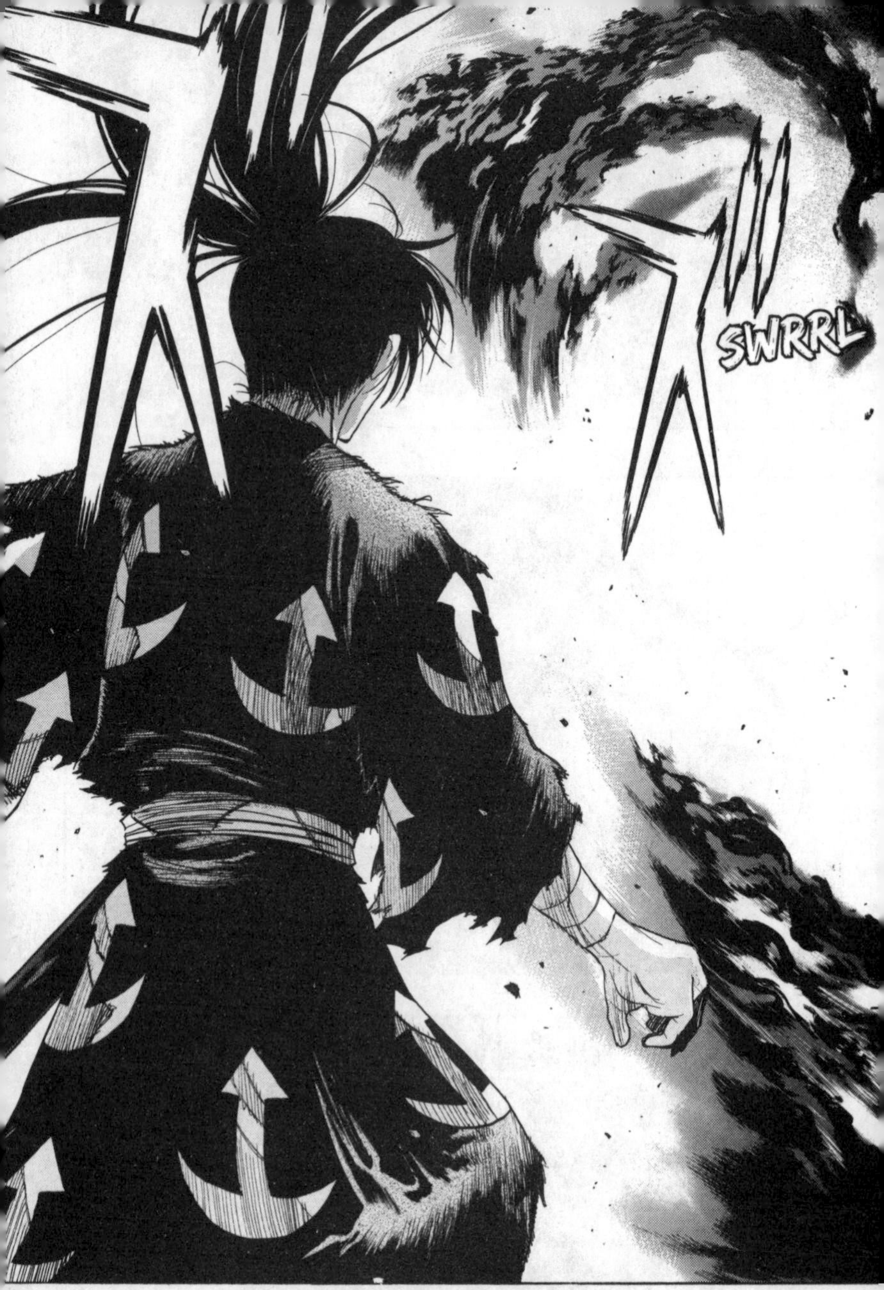
SWRRL

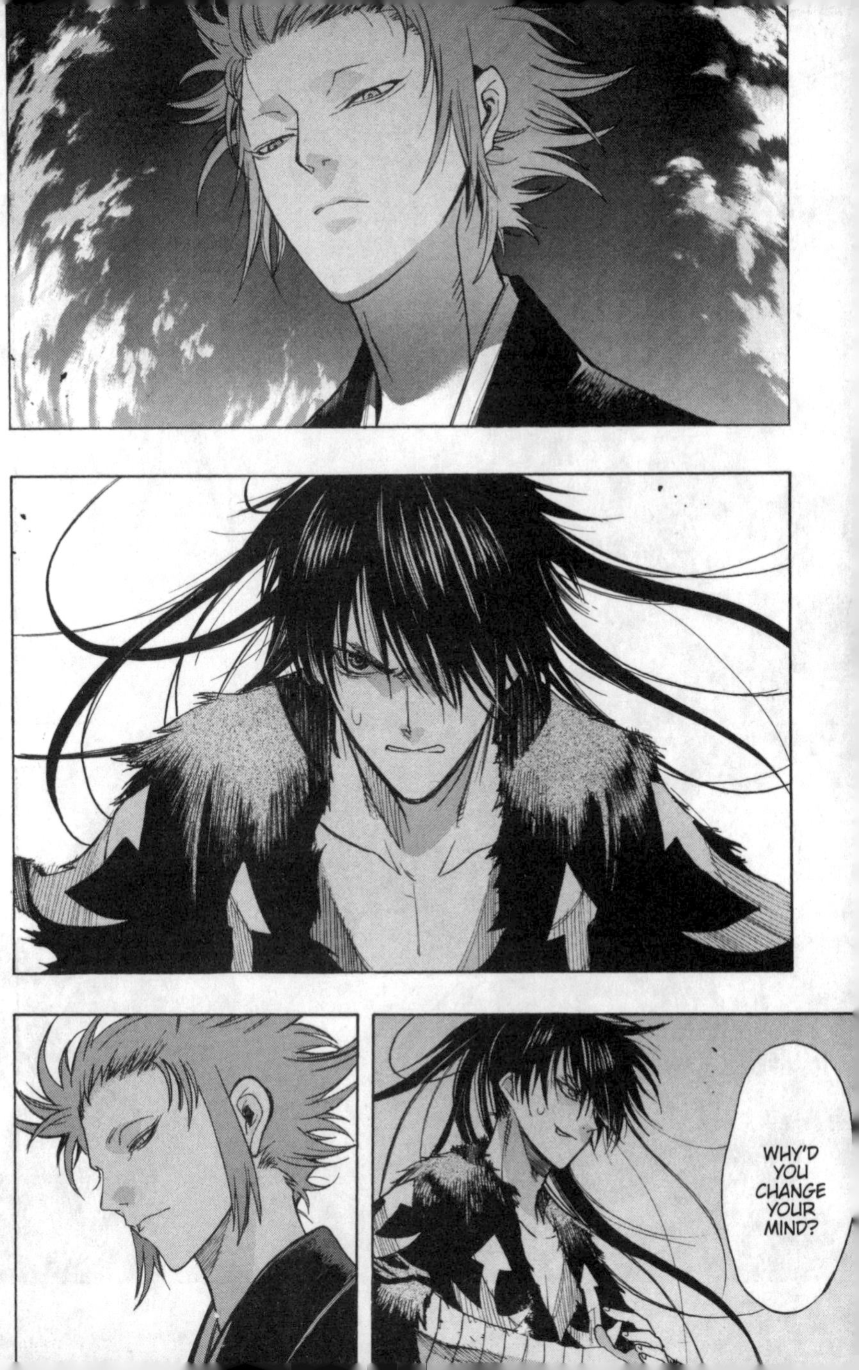
WHY'D YOU CHANGE YOUR MIND?

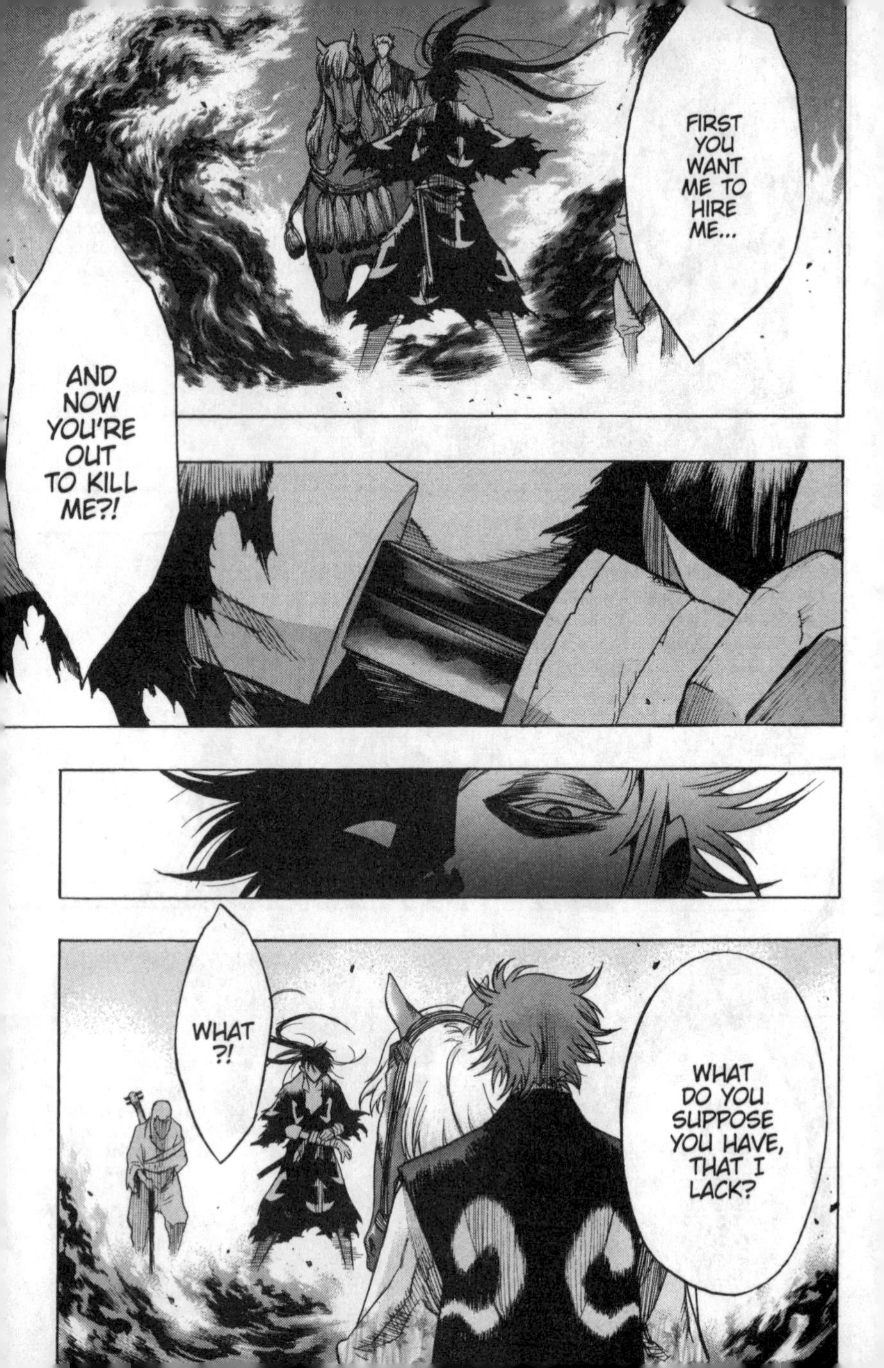
FIRST YOU WANT ME TO HIRE ME...
AND NOW YOU'RE OUT TO KILL ME?!
WHAT DO YOU SUPPOSE YOU HAVE, THAT I LACK?
WHAT ?!

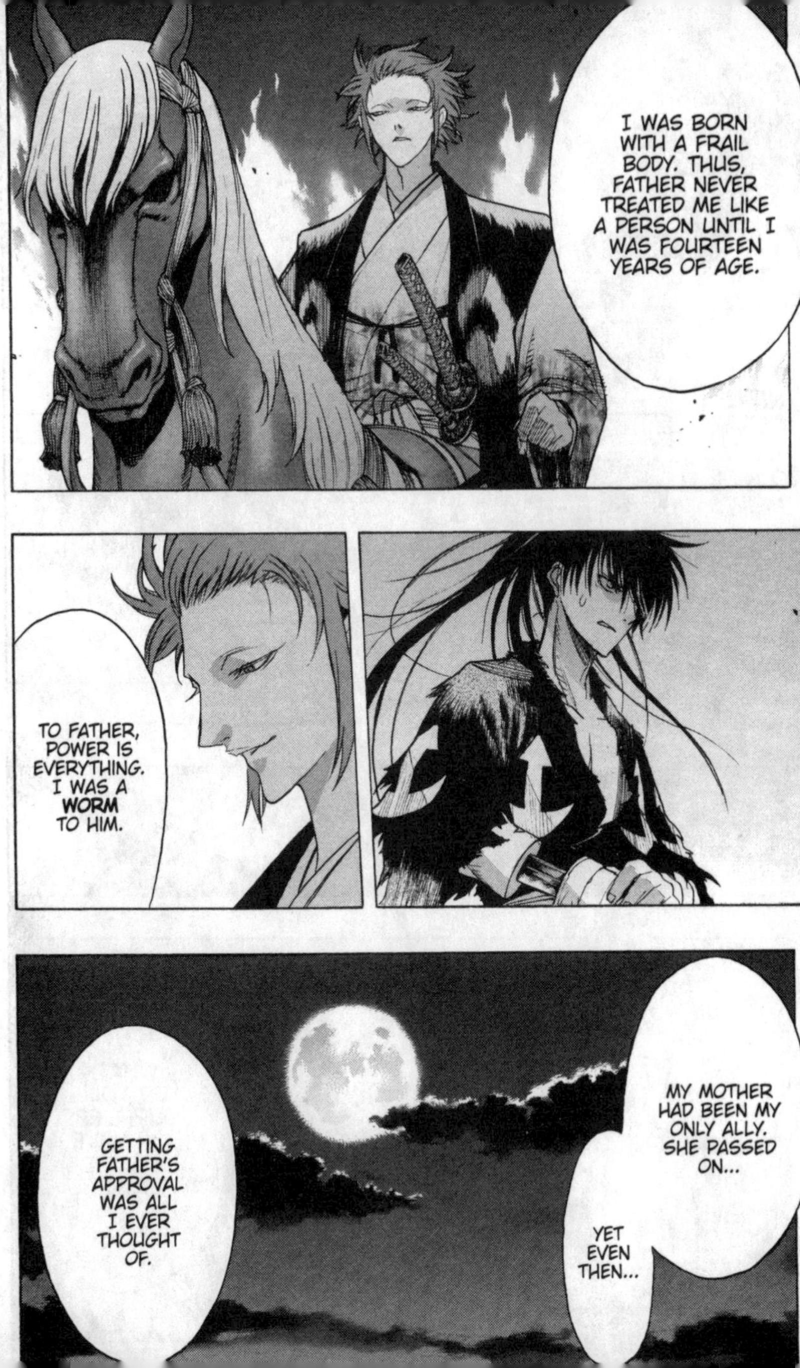
I WAS BORN WITH A FRAIL BODY. THUS, FATHER NEVER TREATED ME LIKE A PERSON UNTIL I WAS FOURTEEN YEARS OF AGE.
TO FATHER, POWER IS EVERYTHING. I WAS A **WORM** TO HIM.
MY MOTHER HAD BEEN MY ONLY ALLY. SHE PASSED ON...
YET EVEN THEN...
GETTING FATHER'S APPROVAL WAS ALL I EVER THOUGHT OF.

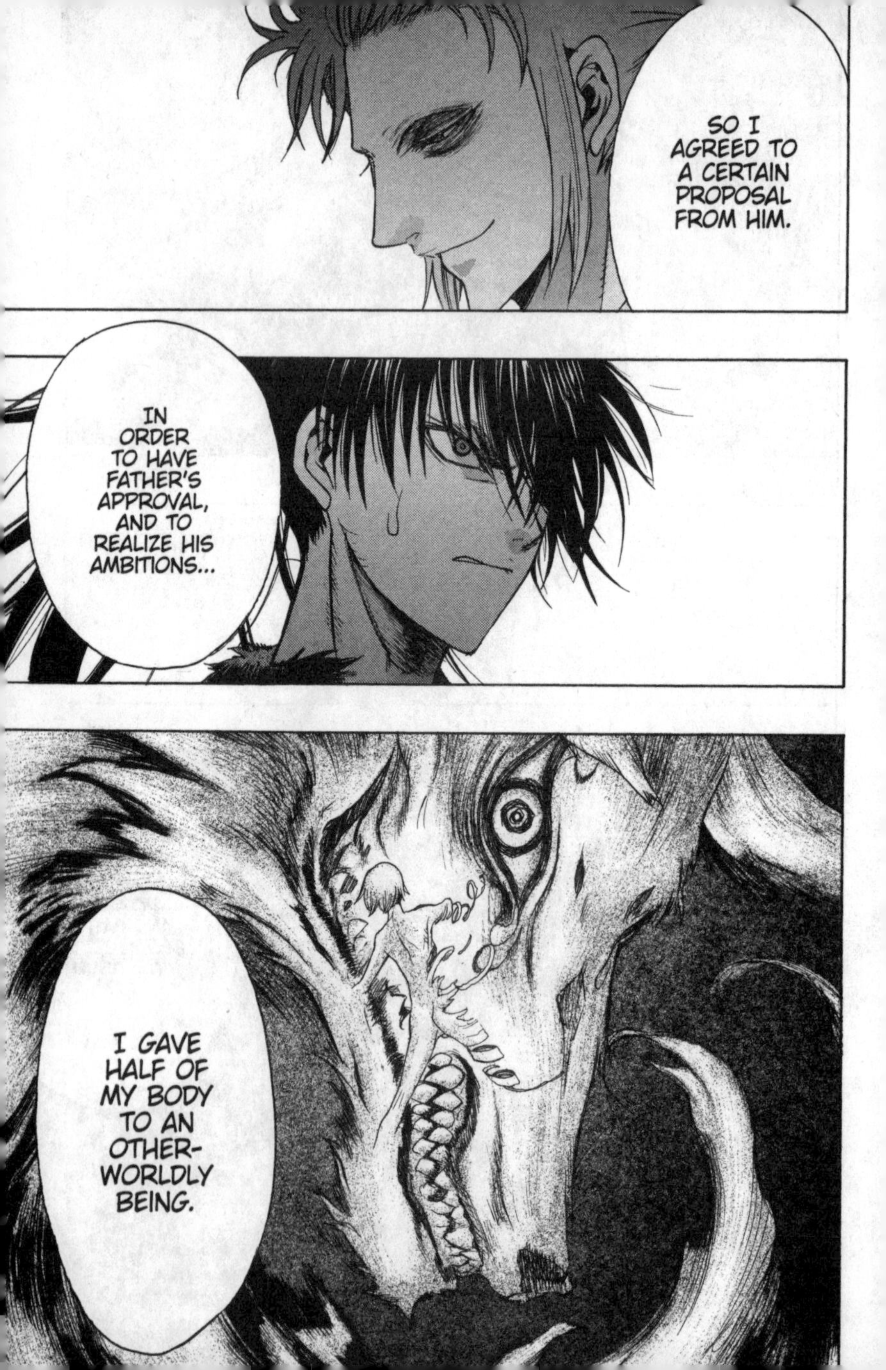
SO I AGREED TO A CERTAIN PROPOSAL FROM HIM.
IN ORDER TO HAVE FATHER'S APPROVAL, AND TO REALIZE HIS AMBITIONS...
I GAVE HALF OF MY BODY TO AN OTHER-WORLDLY BEING.

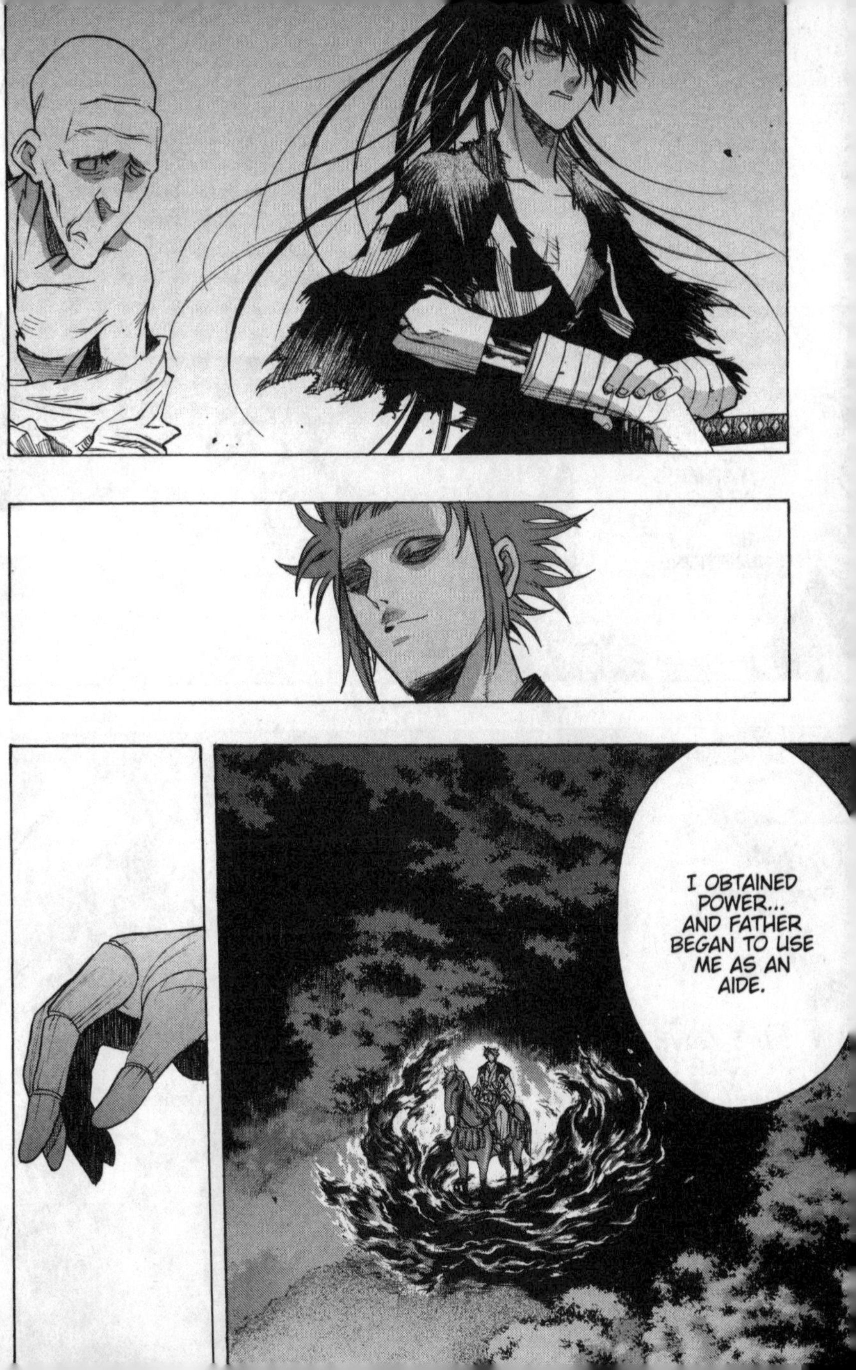
I OBTAINED POWER... AND FATHER BEGAN TO USE ME AS AN AIDE.

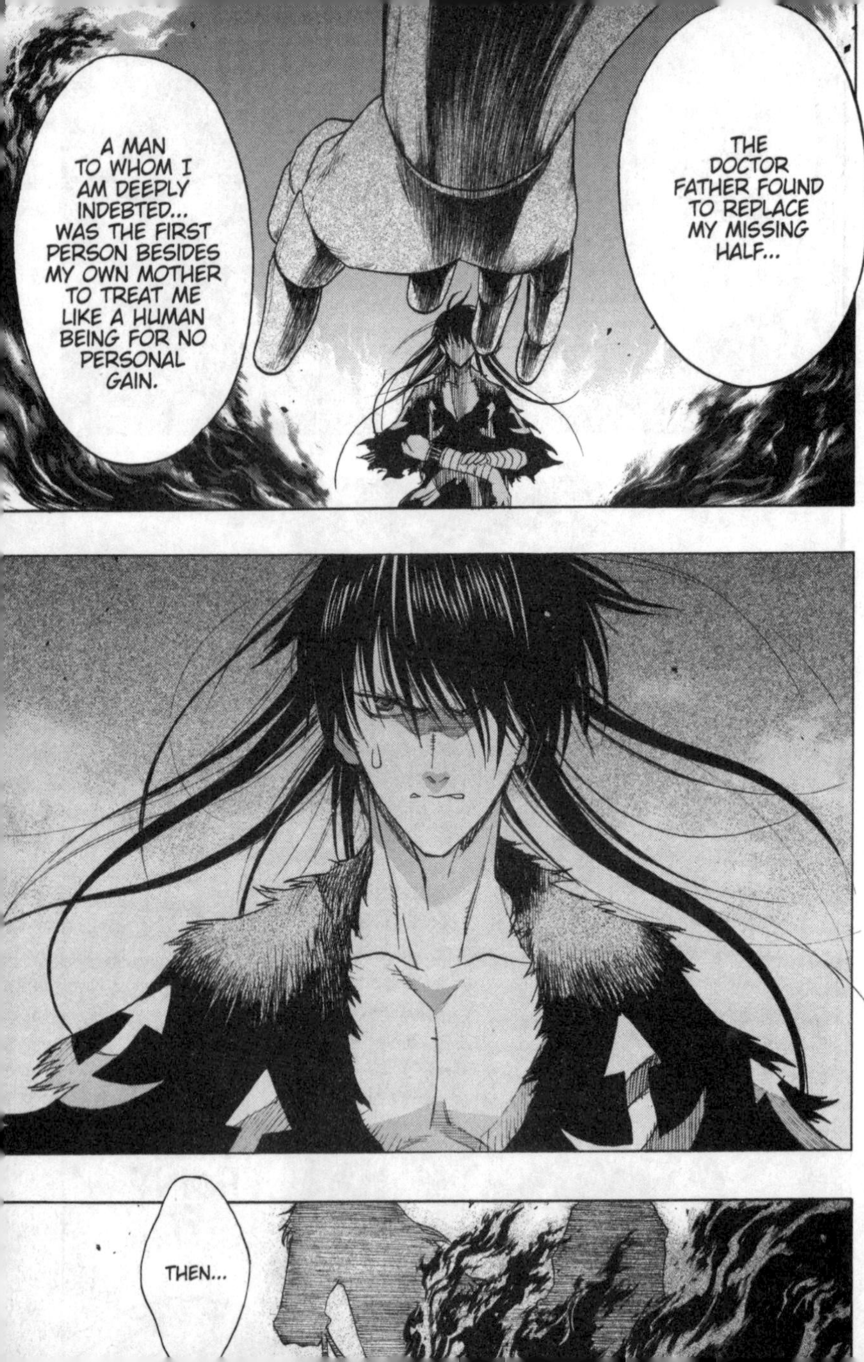
THE DOCTOR FATHER FOUND TO REPLACE MY MISSING HALF...
A MAN TO WHOM I AM DEEPLY INDEBTED... WAS THE FIRST PERSON BESIDES MY OWN MOTHER TO TREAT ME LIKE A HUMAN BEING FOR NO PERSONAL GAIN.
THEN...

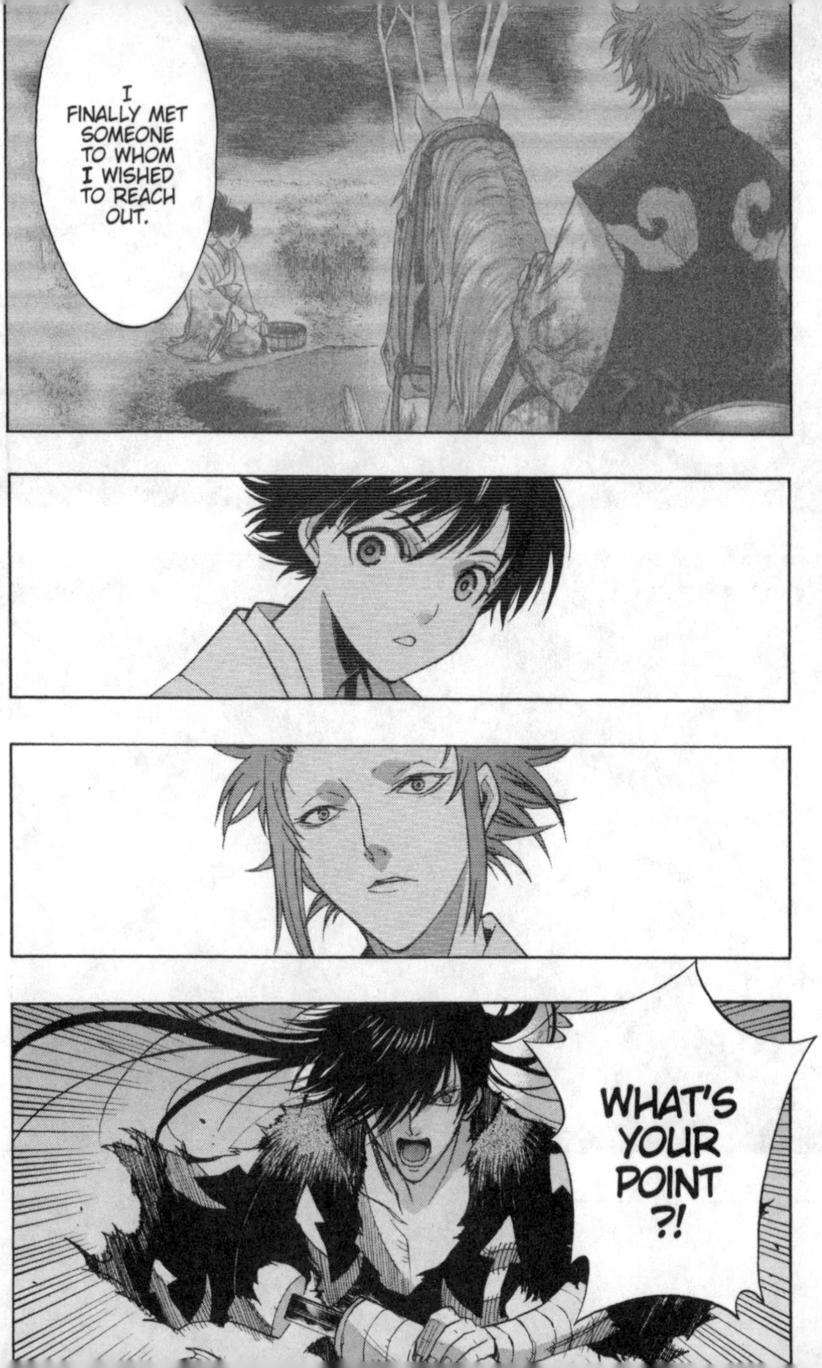
I FINALLY MET SOMEONE TO WHOM I WISHED TO REACH OUT.
WHAT'S YOUR POINT ?!

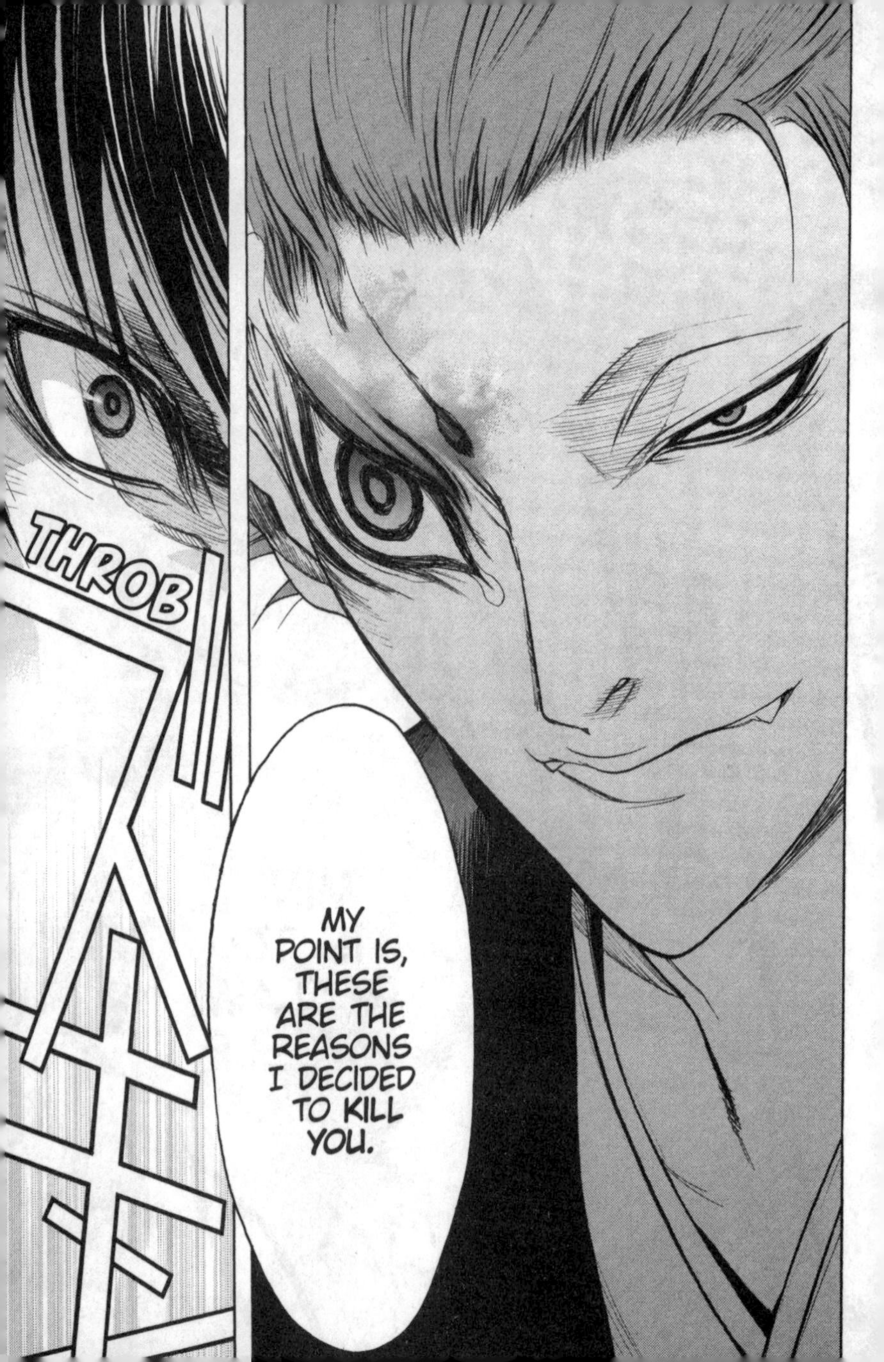
MY POINT IS, THESE ARE THE REASONS I DECIDED TO KILL YOU.
THROB

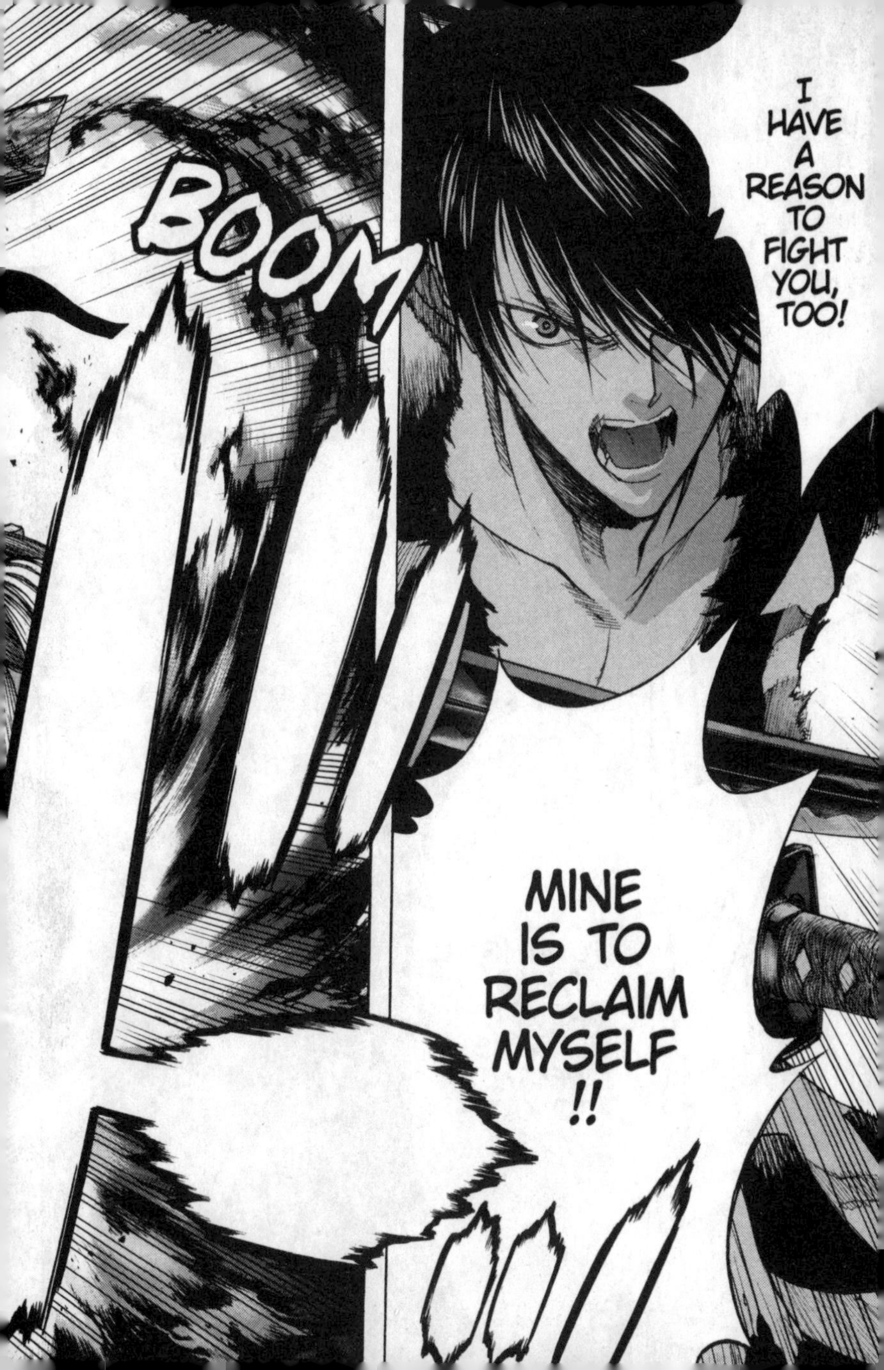
I HAVE A REASON TO FIGHT YOU, TOO!
BOOM
MINE IS TO RECLAIM MYSELF!!

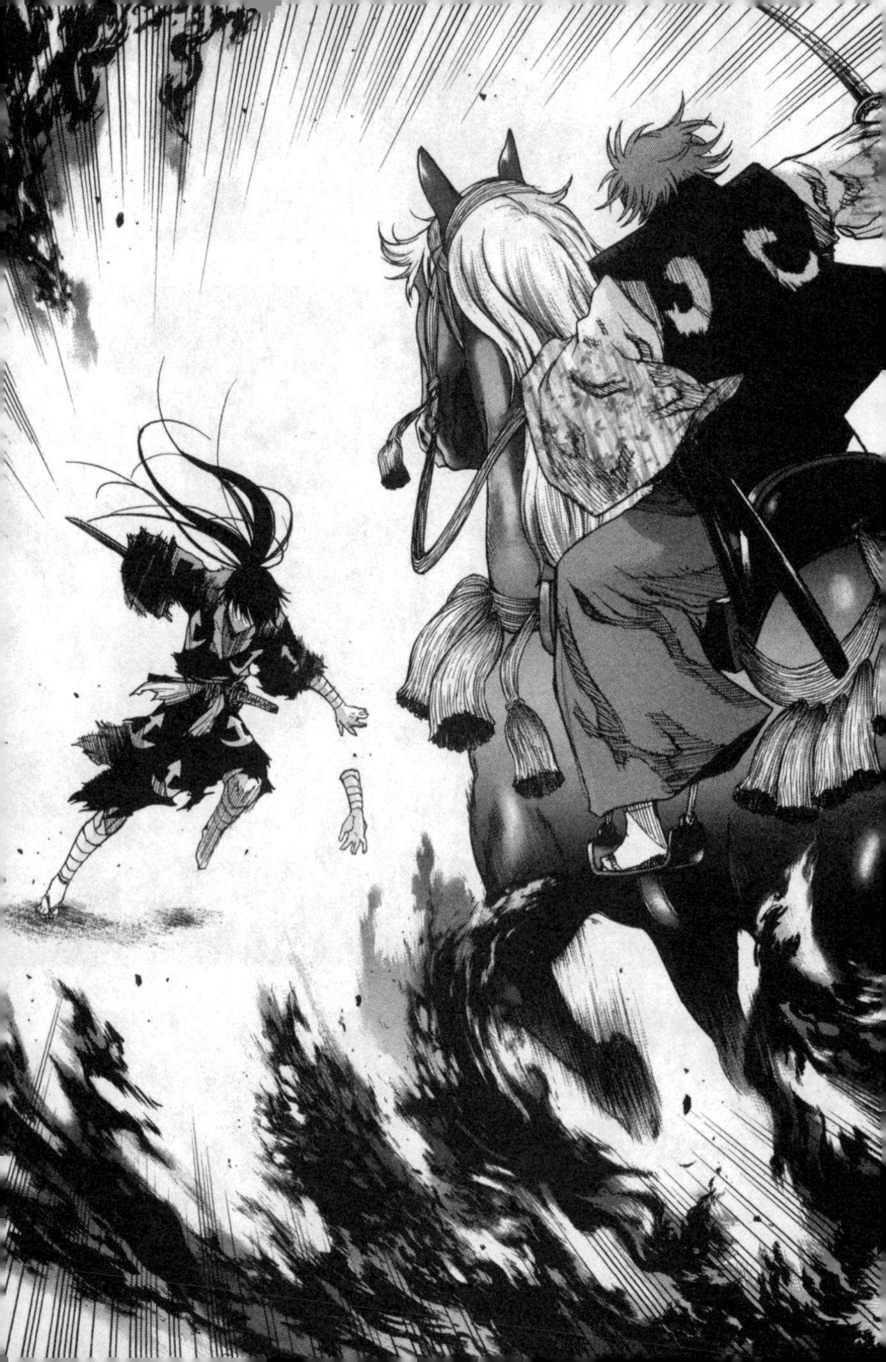

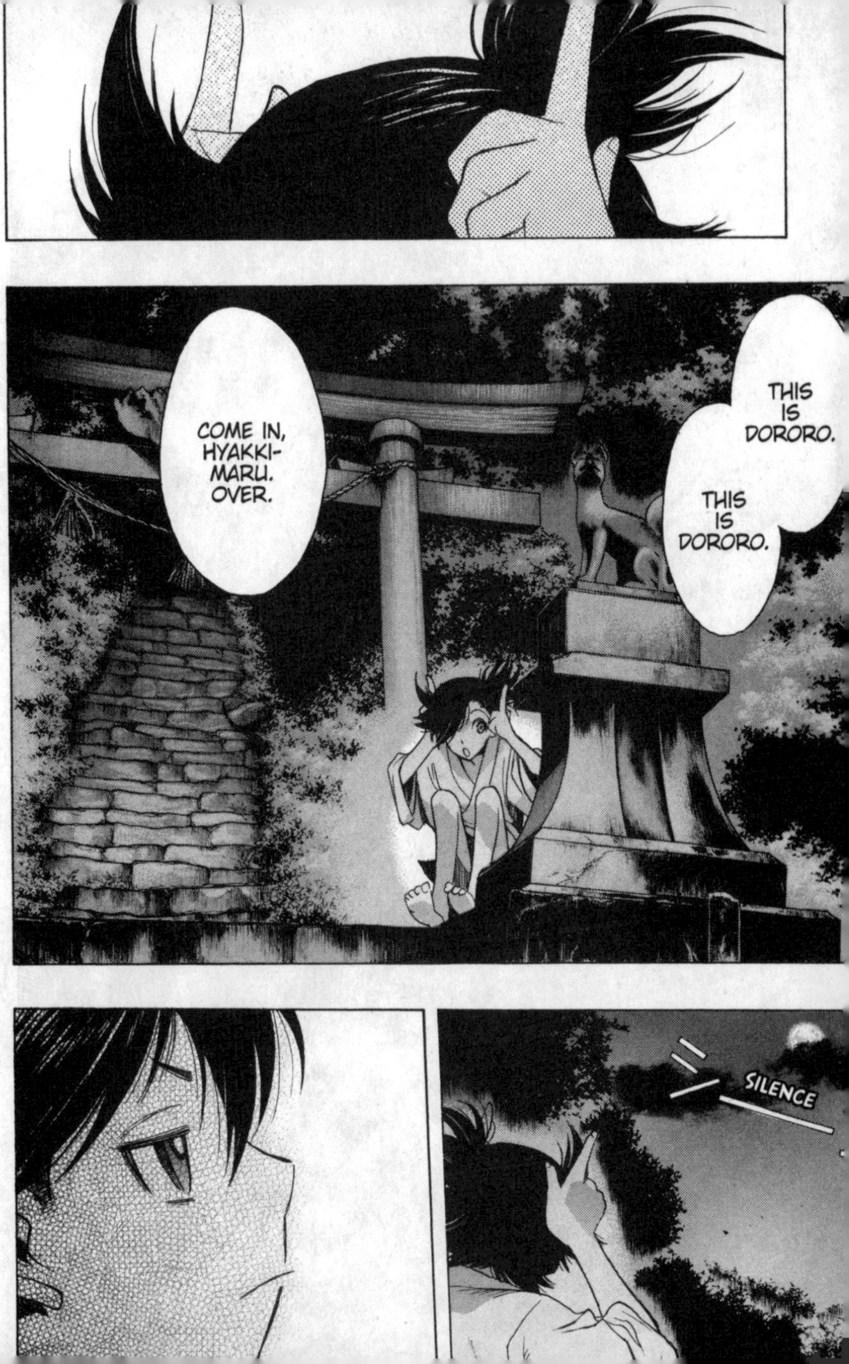
THIS IS DORORO.
THIS IS DORORO.
COME IN, HYAKKI-MARU. OVER.
SILENCE

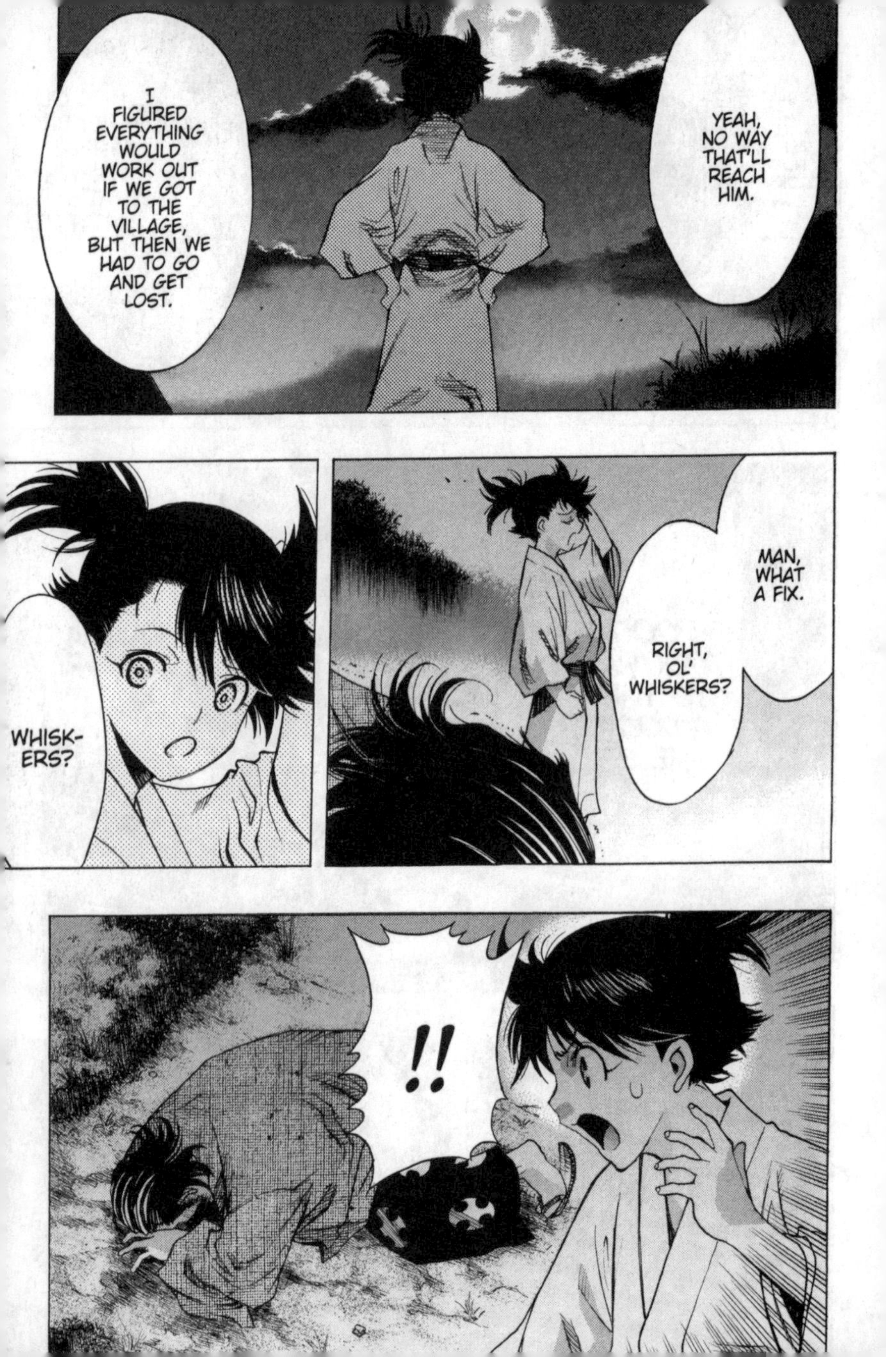
YEAH, NO WAY THAT'LL REACH HIM.
I FIGURED EVERYTHING WOULD WORK OUT IF WE GOT TO THE VILLAGE, BUT THEN WE HAD TO GO AND GET LOST.
MAN, WHAT A FIX.
RIGHT, OL' WHISKERS?
WHISK-ERS?
!!

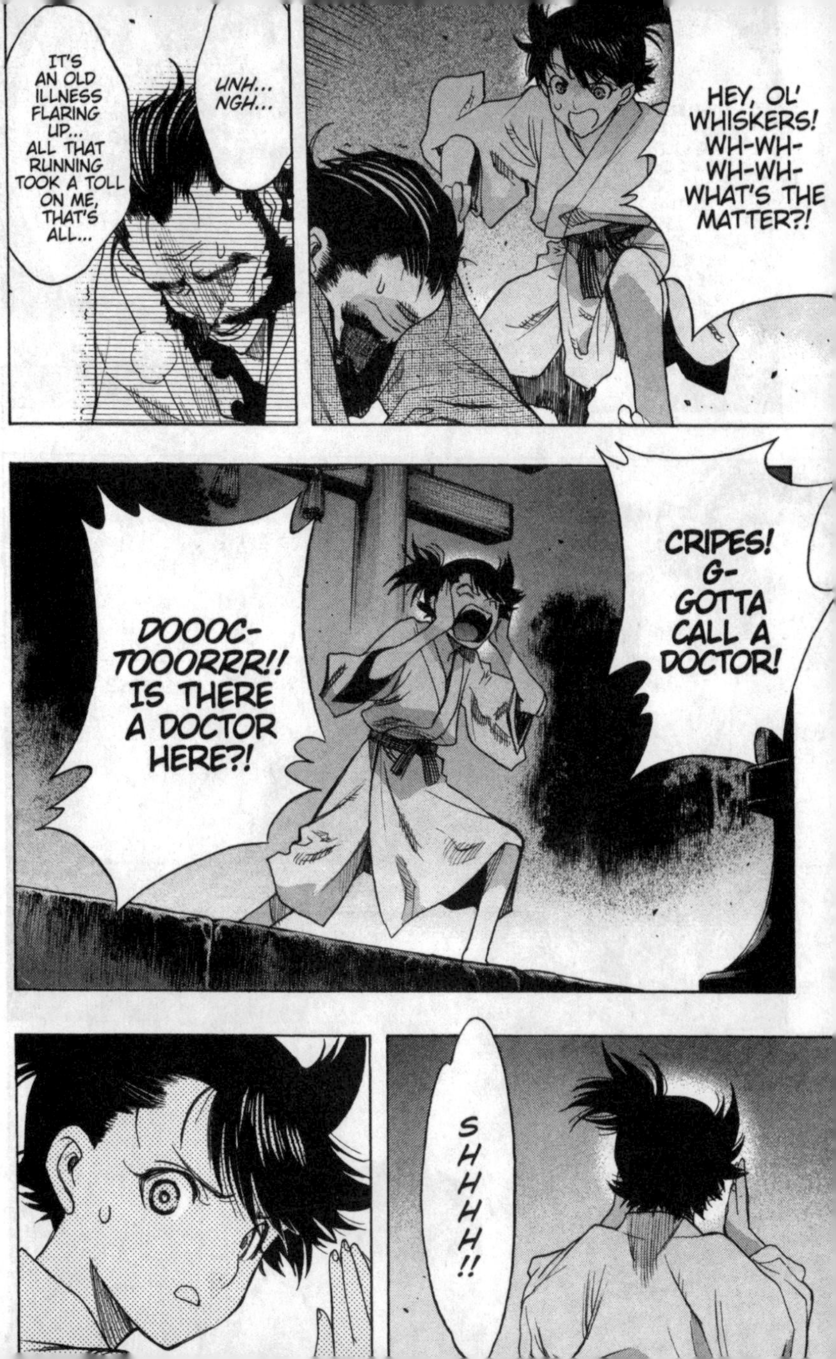
HEY, OL' WHISKERS! WH-WH-WH-WH-WHAT'S THE MATTER?!
UNH... NGH...
IT'S AN OLD ILLNESS FLARING UP... ALL THAT RUNNING TOOK A TOLL ON ME, THAT'S ALL...
CRIPES! G-GOTTA CALL A DOCTOR!
DOOOC-TOOORRR!! IS THERE A DOCTOR HERE?!
SHHHH!!

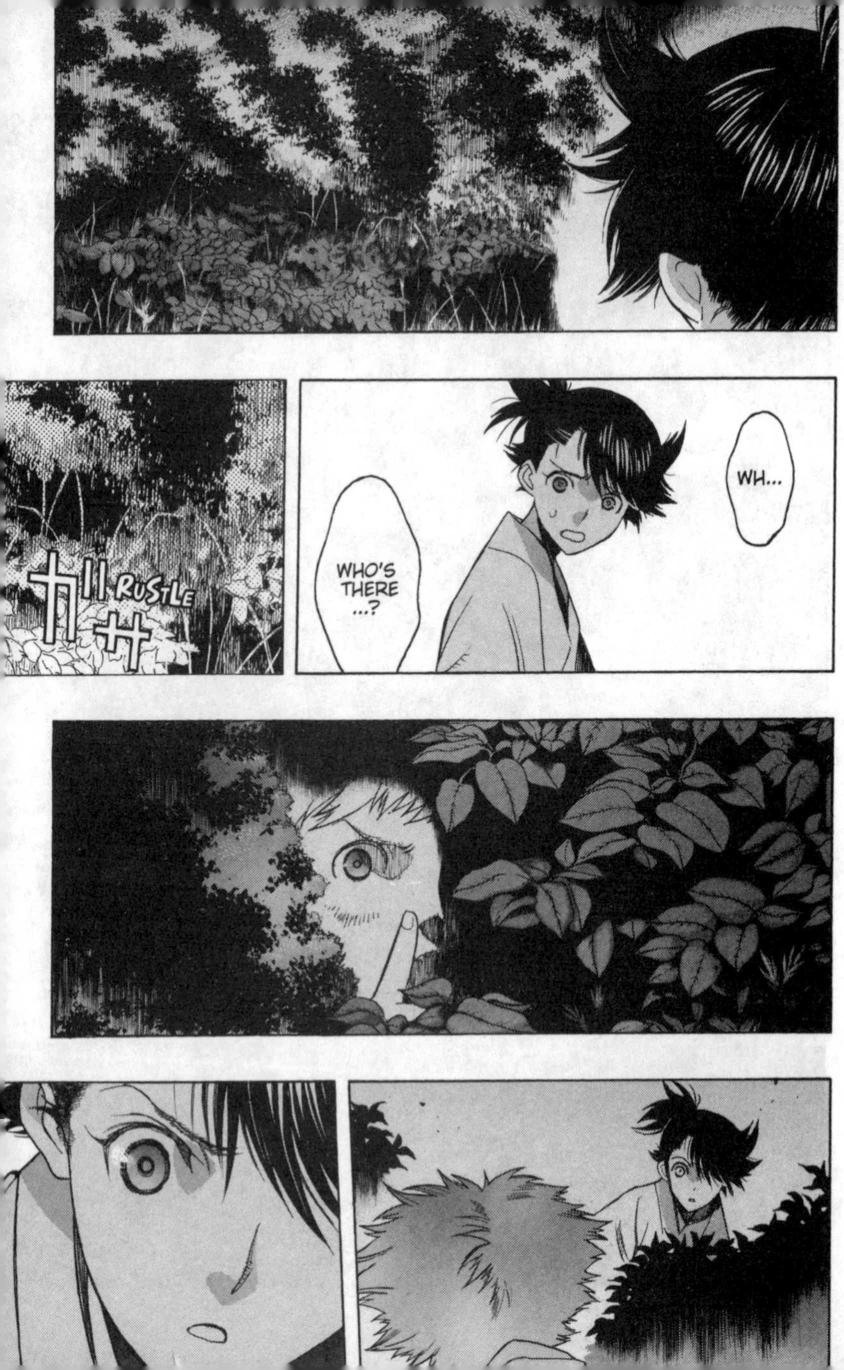
WH...
WHO'S THERE ...?
RUSTLE

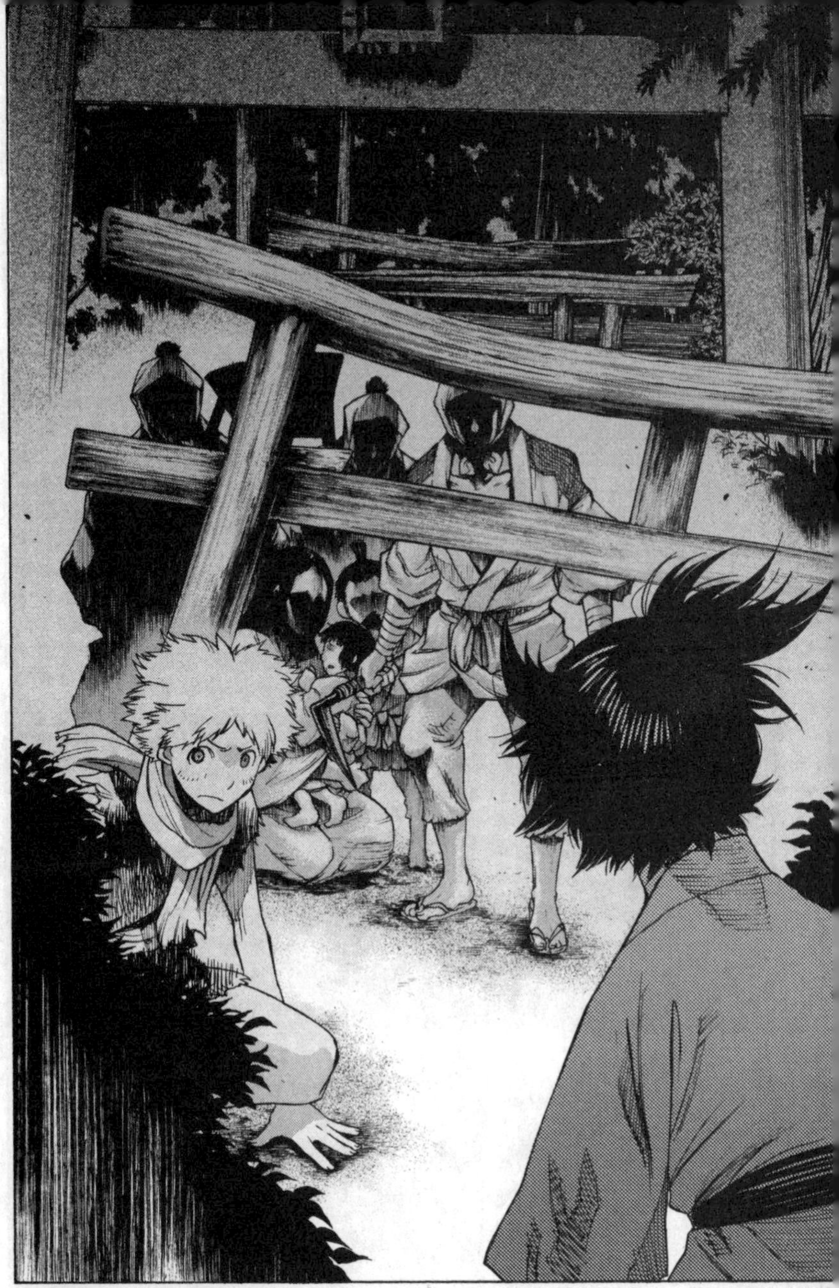

どろろと百鬼丸伝

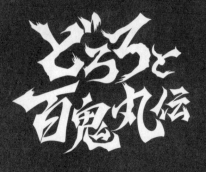

THE LEGEND OF
DORORO AND HYAKKIMARU

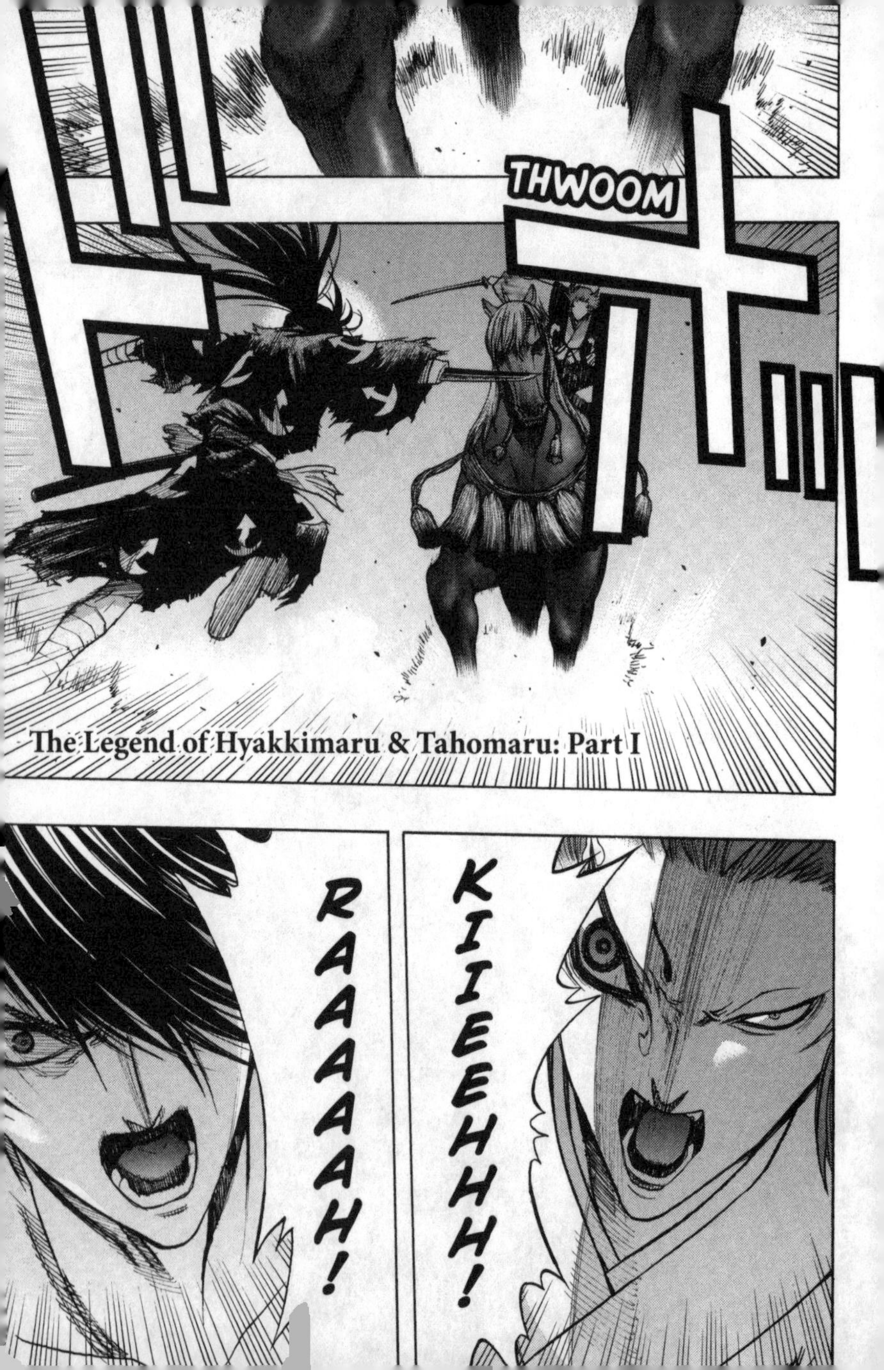
THWOOM
The Legend of Hyakkimaru & Tahomaru: Part I
KIIEEHHH!
RAAAAAH!

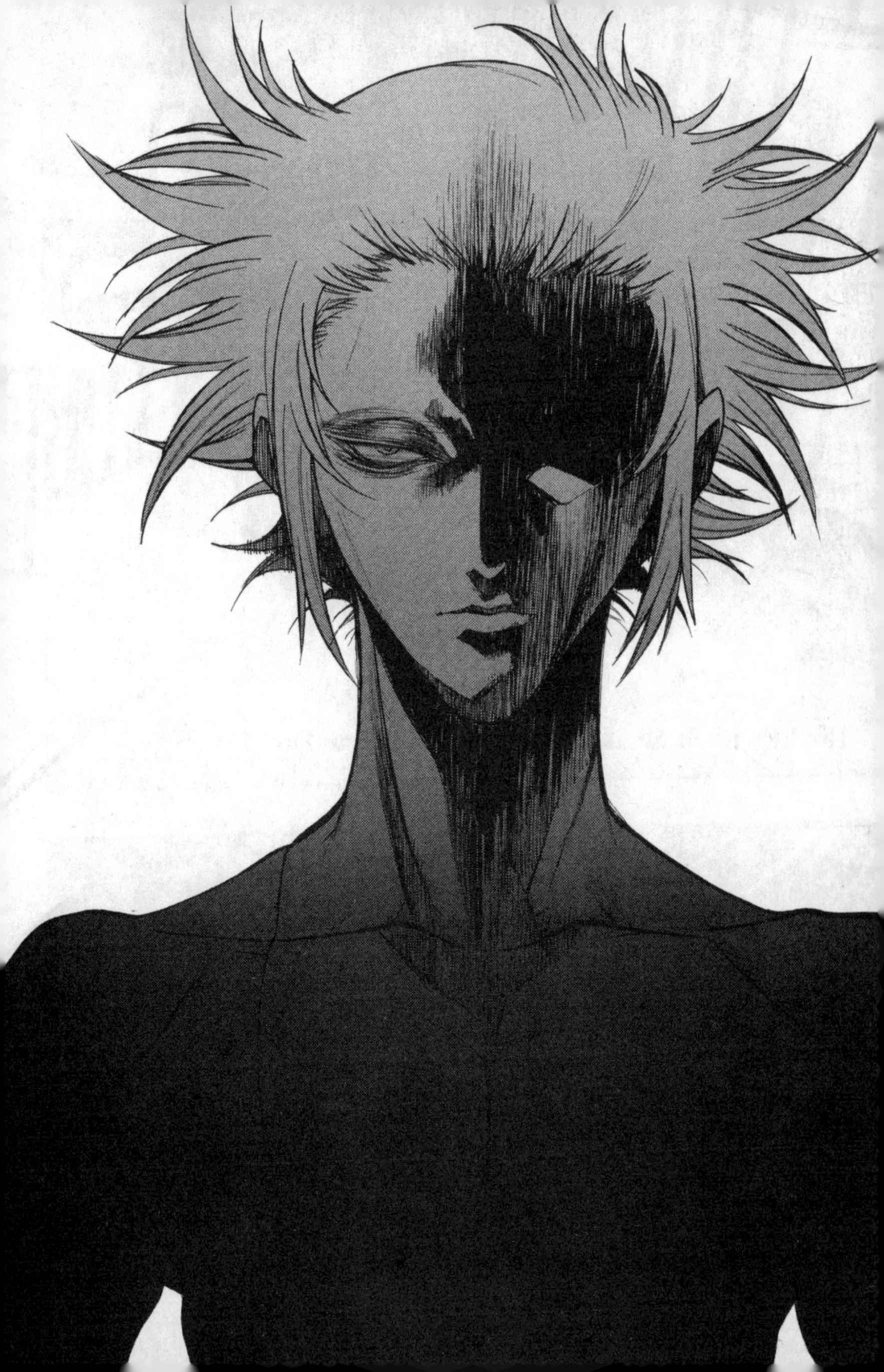

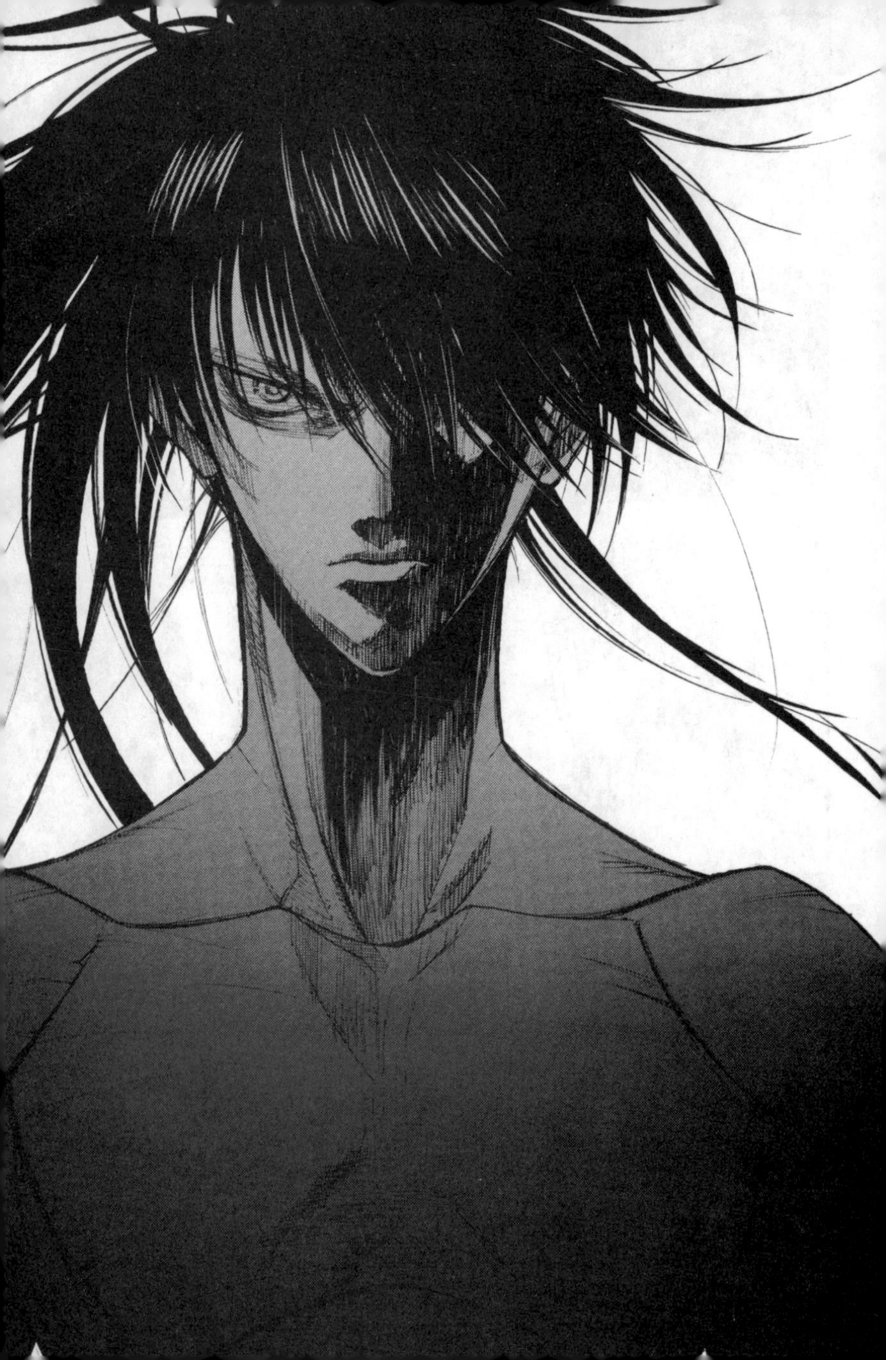

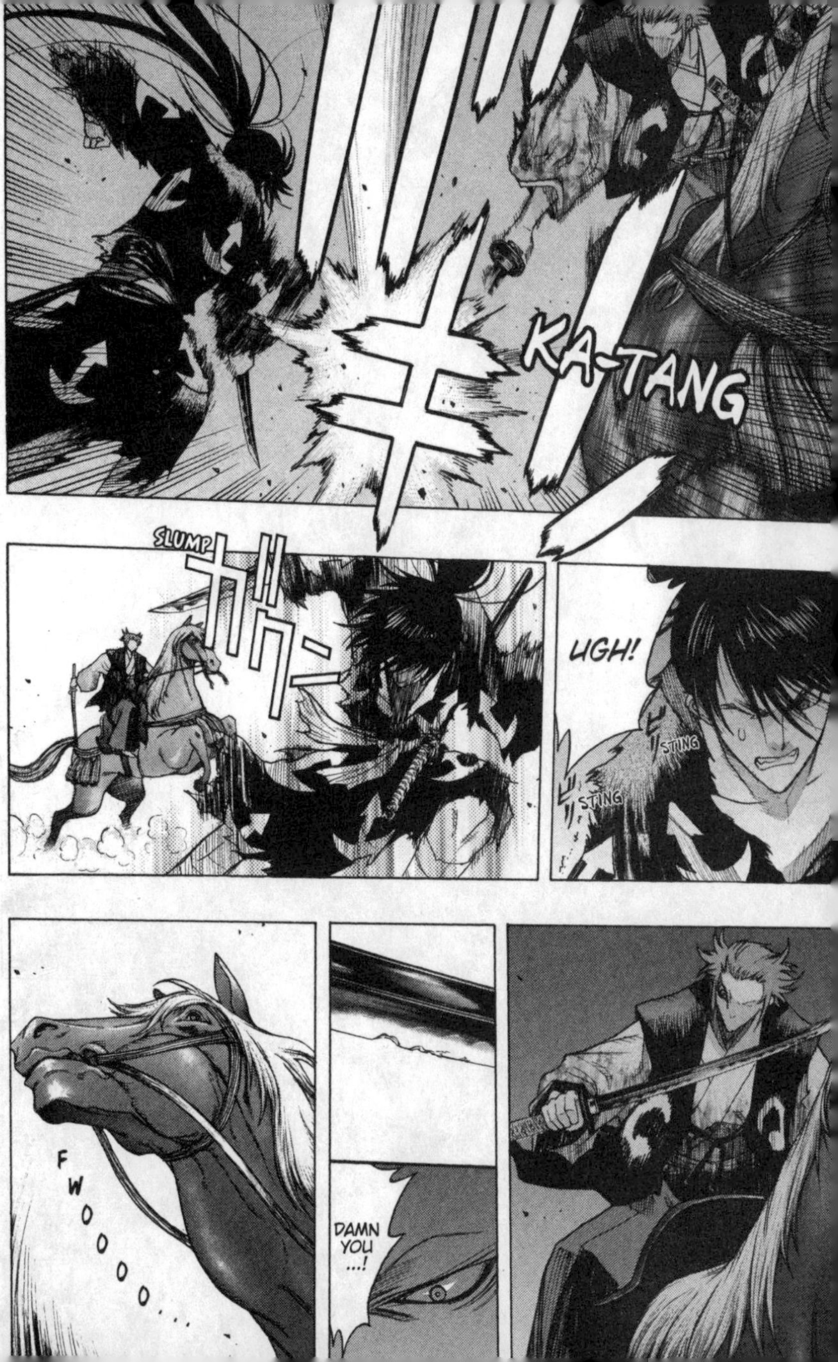
KA-TANG
UGH!
STING
STING
SLUMP
DAMN YOU ...!
FWOOOO...

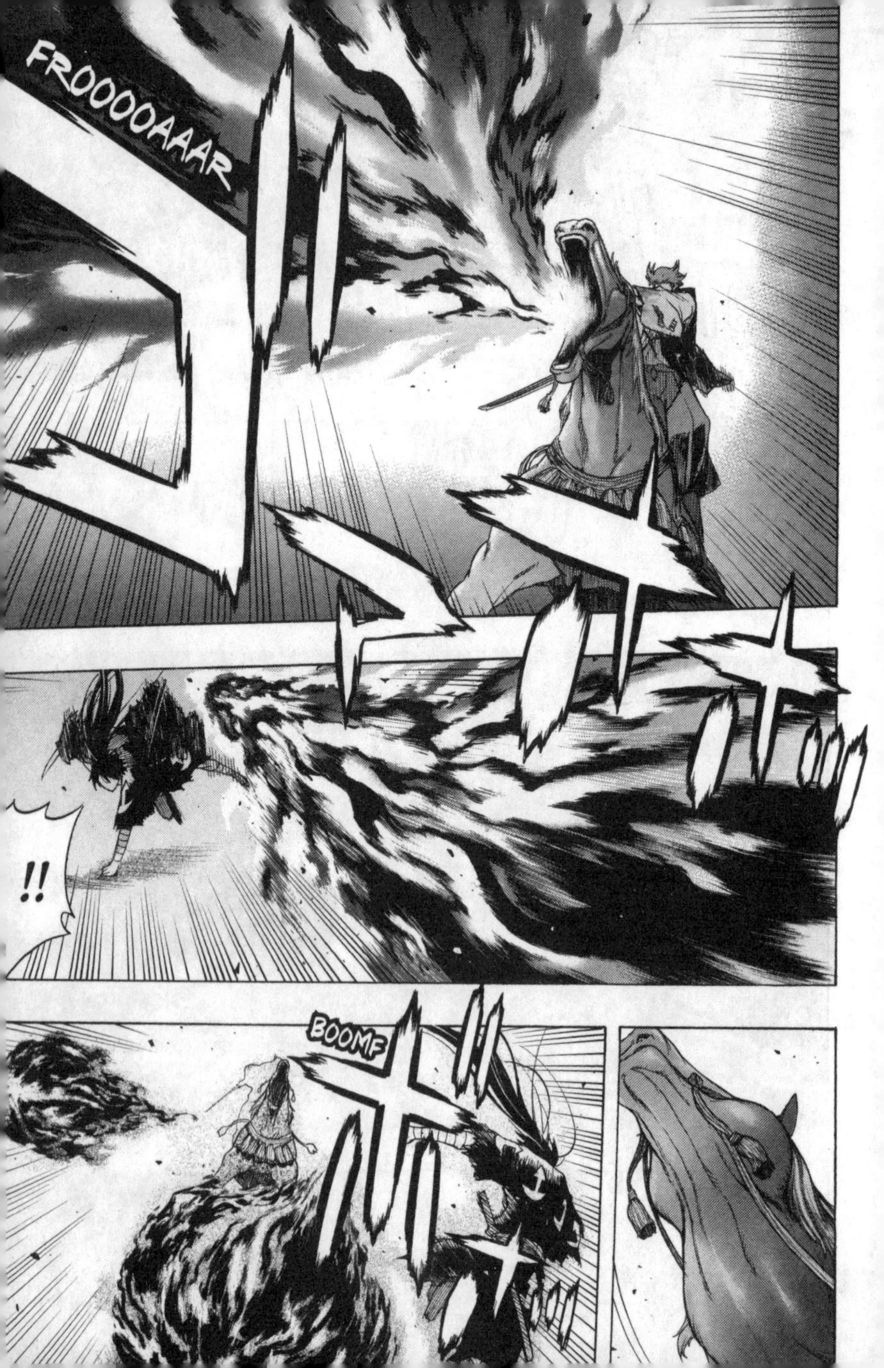
FROOOOAAAR
!!
BOOMF

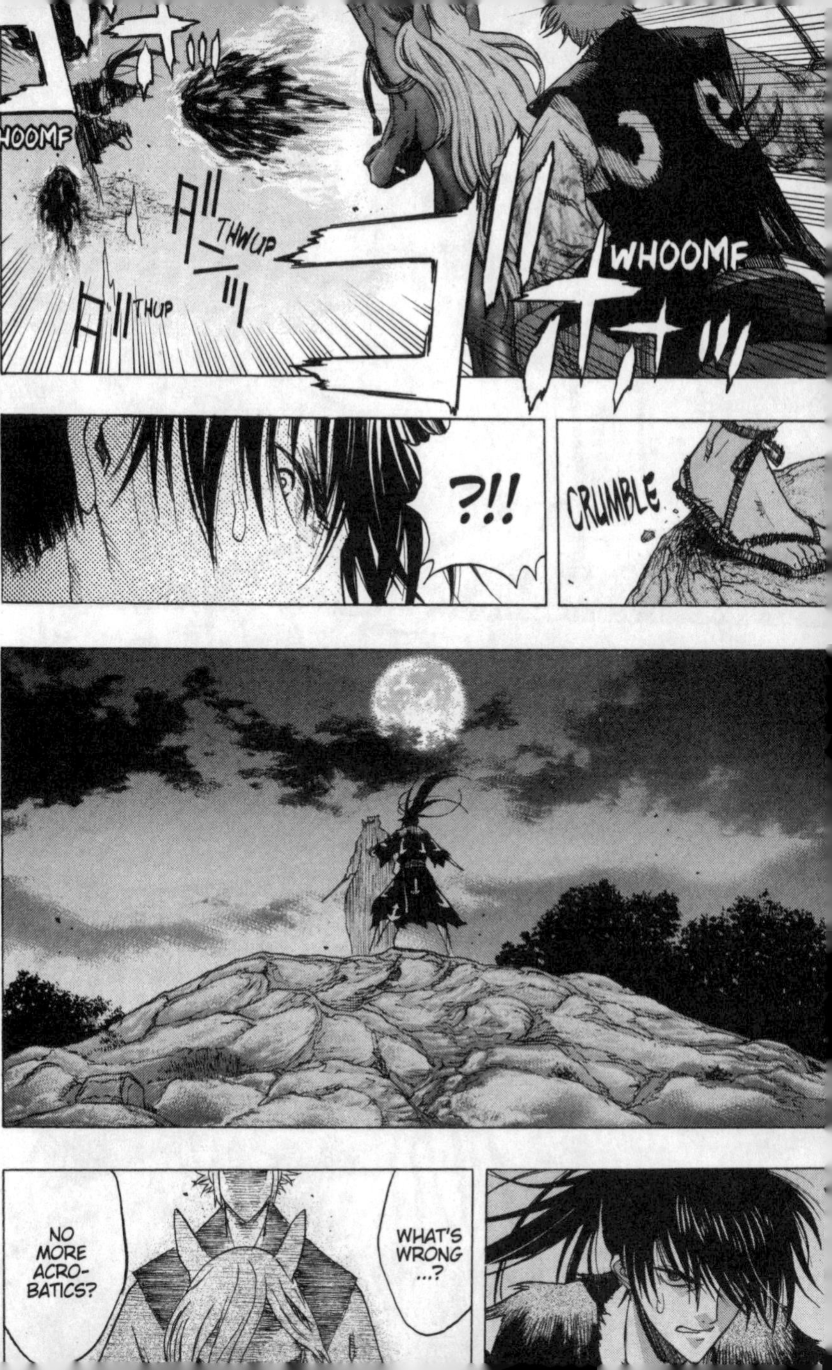
WHOOMF
THWUP
THUP
WHOOMF
CRUMBLE
?!!
WHAT'S WRONG ...?
NO MORE ACRO-BATICS?

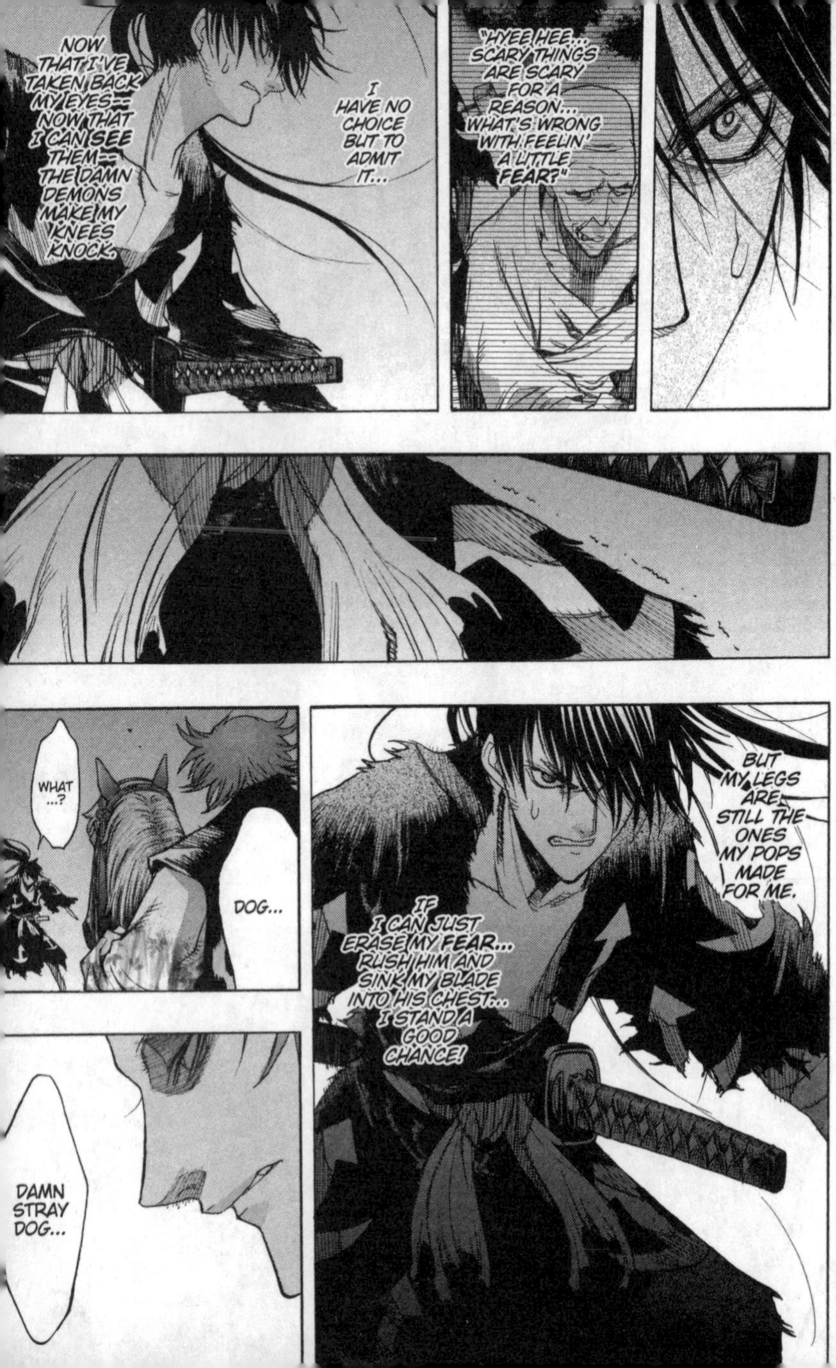
"HYEE HEE... SCARY THINGS ARE SCARY FOR A REASON... WHAT'S WRONG WITH FEELIN' A LITTLE FEAR?"
I HAVE NO CHOICE BUT TO ADMIT IT...
NOW THAT I'VE TAKEN BACK MY EYES-- NOW THAT I CAN SEE THEM-- THE DAMN DEMONS MAKE MY KNEES KNOCK.
BUT MY LEGS ARE STILL THE ONES MY POPS MADE FOR ME.
IF I CAN JUST ERASE MY FEAR... RUSH HIM AND SINK MY BLADE INTO HIS CHEST... I STAND A GOOD CHANCE!
WHAT ...?
DOG...
DAMN STRAY DOG...

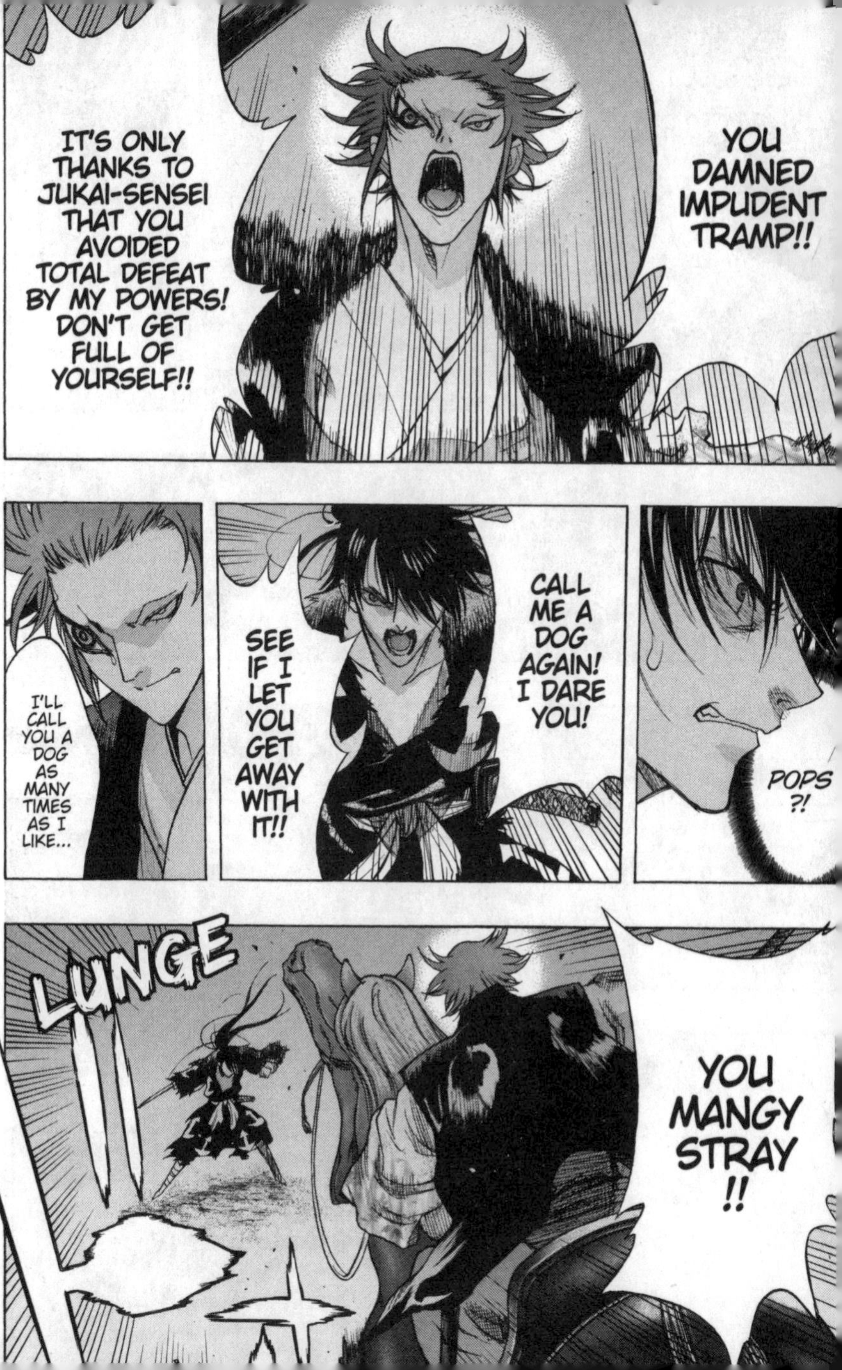
YOU DAMNED IMPUDENT TRAMP!!
IT'S ONLY THANKS TO JUKAI-SENSEI THAT YOU AVOIDED TOTAL DEFEAT BY MY POWERS! DON'T GET FULL OF YOURSELF!!
POPS ?!
CALL ME A DOG AGAIN! I DARE YOU!
SEE IF I LET YOU GET AWAY WITH IT!!
I'LL CALL YOU A DOG AS MANY TIMES AS I LIKE...
YOU MANGY STRAY !!
LUNGE

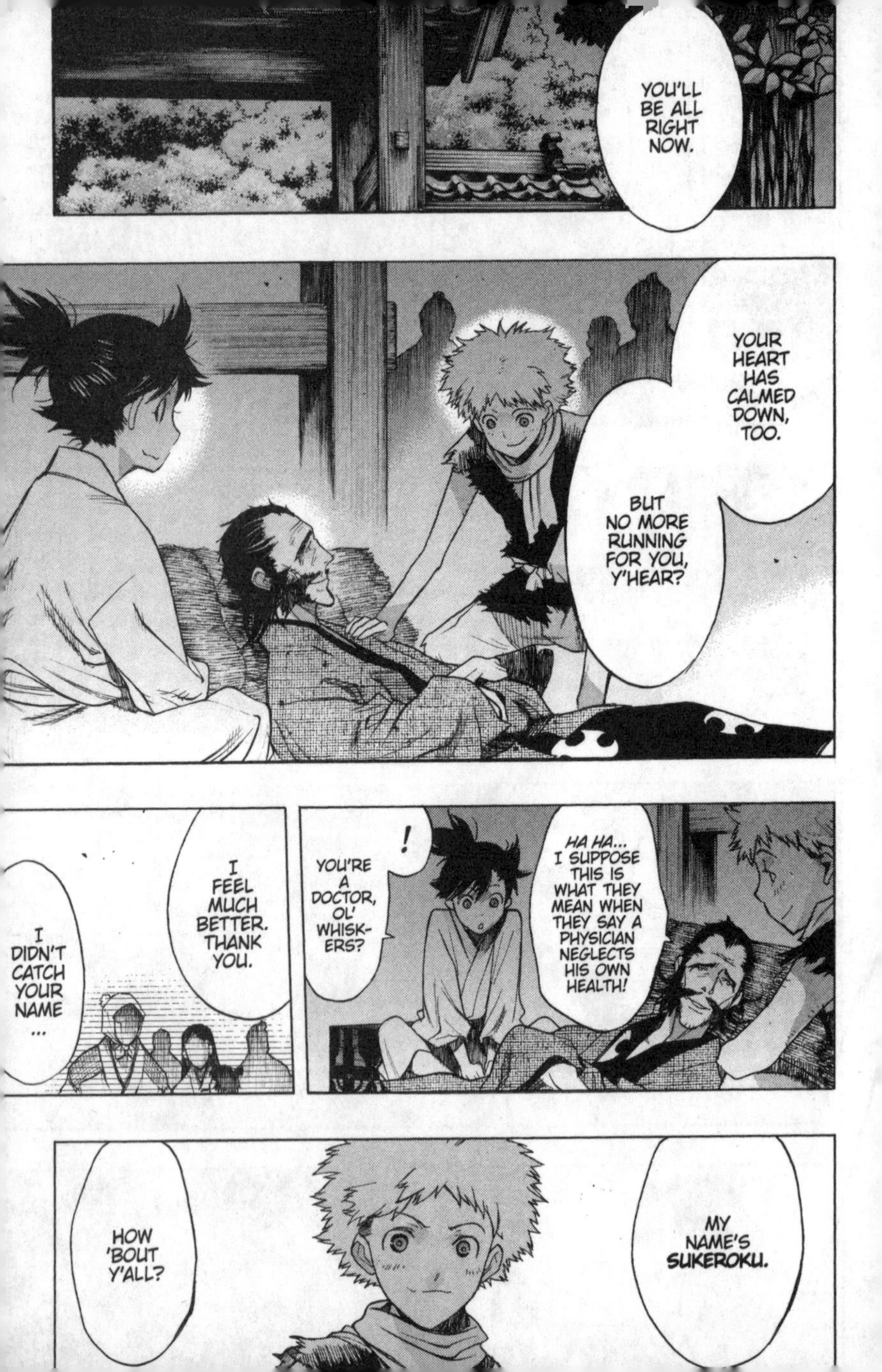
YOU'LL BE ALL RIGHT NOW.
YOUR HEART HAS CALMED DOWN, TOO.
BUT NO MORE RUNNING FOR YOU, Y'HEAR?
HA HA... I SUPPOSE THIS IS WHAT THEY MEAN WHEN THEY SAY A PHYSICIAN NEGLECTS HIS OWN HEALTH!
!
YOU'RE A DOCTOR, OL' WHISK-ERS?
I FEEL MUCH BETTER. THANK YOU.
I DIDN'T CATCH YOUR NAME ...
MY NAME'S SUKEROKU.
HOW 'BOUT Y'ALL?

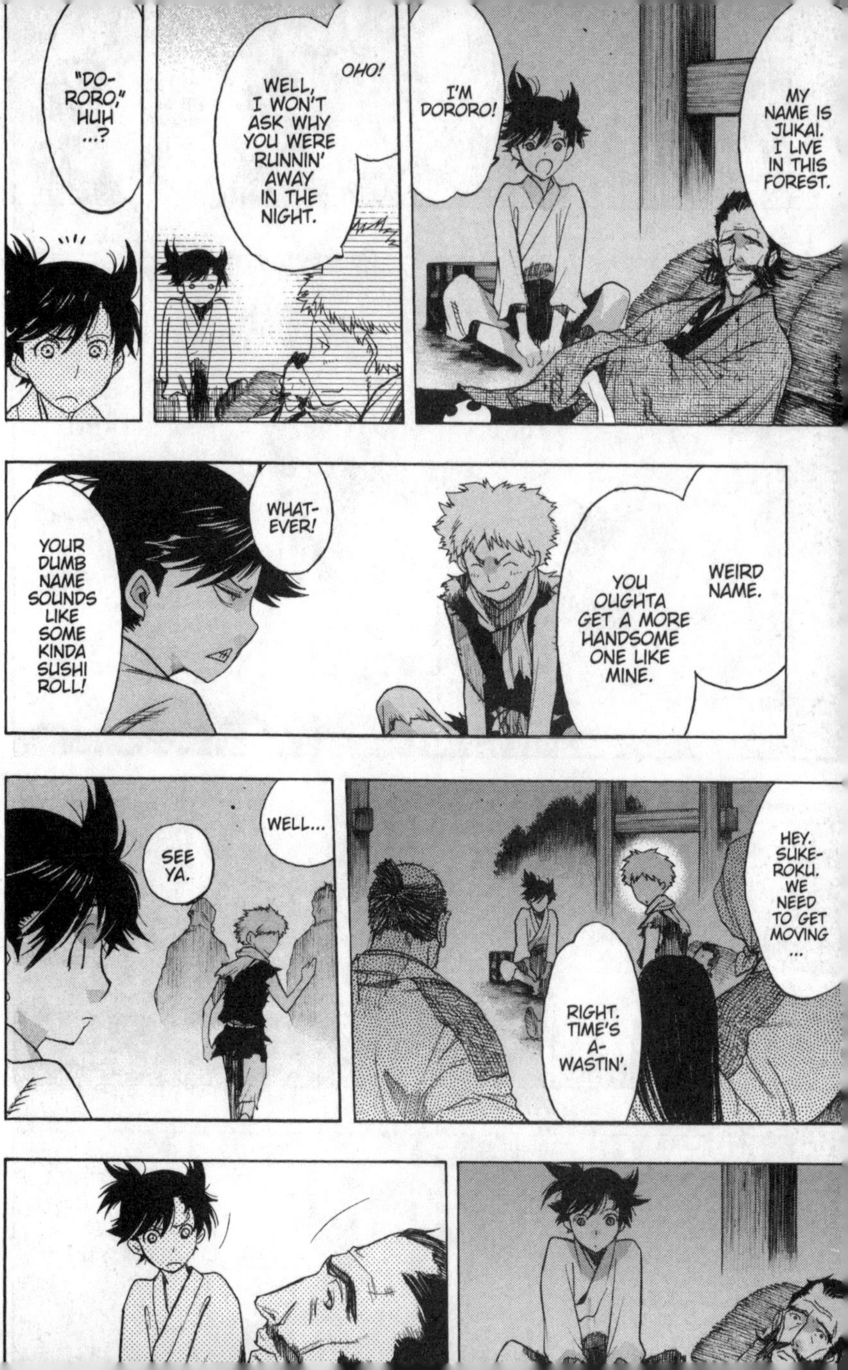
MY NAME IS JUKAI. I LIVE IN THIS FOREST.
I'M DORORO!
OHO!
WELL, I WON'T ASK WHY YOU WERE RUNNIN' AWAY IN THE NIGHT.
"DO-RORO," HUH ...?
WEIRD NAME.
YOU OUGHTA GET A MORE HANDSOME ONE LIKE MINE.
WHAT-EVER!
YOUR DUMB NAME SOUNDS LIKE SOME KINDA SUSHI ROLL!
HEY. SUKE-ROKU. WE NEED TO GET MOVING ...
RIGHT. TIME'S A-WASTIN'.
WELL...
SEE YA.

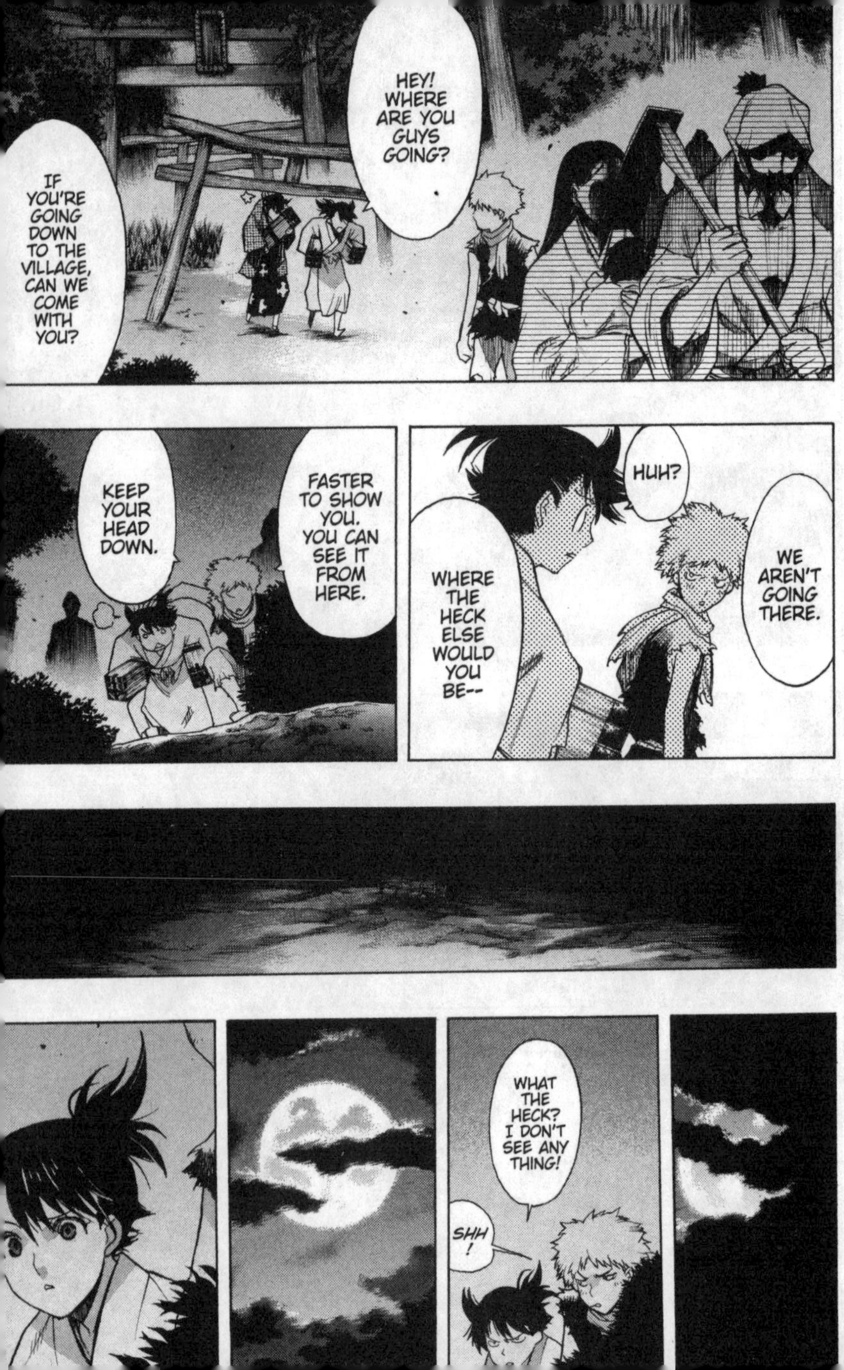
HEY! WHERE ARE YOU GUYS GOING?
IF YOU'RE GOING DOWN TO THE VILLAGE, CAN WE COME WITH YOU?
HUH?
WE AREN'T GOING THERE.
WHERE THE HECK ELSE WOULD YOU BE--
FASTER TO SHOW YOU. YOU CAN SEE IT FROM HERE.
KEEP YOUR HEAD DOWN.
WHAT THE HECK? I DON'T SEE ANY THING!
SHH!

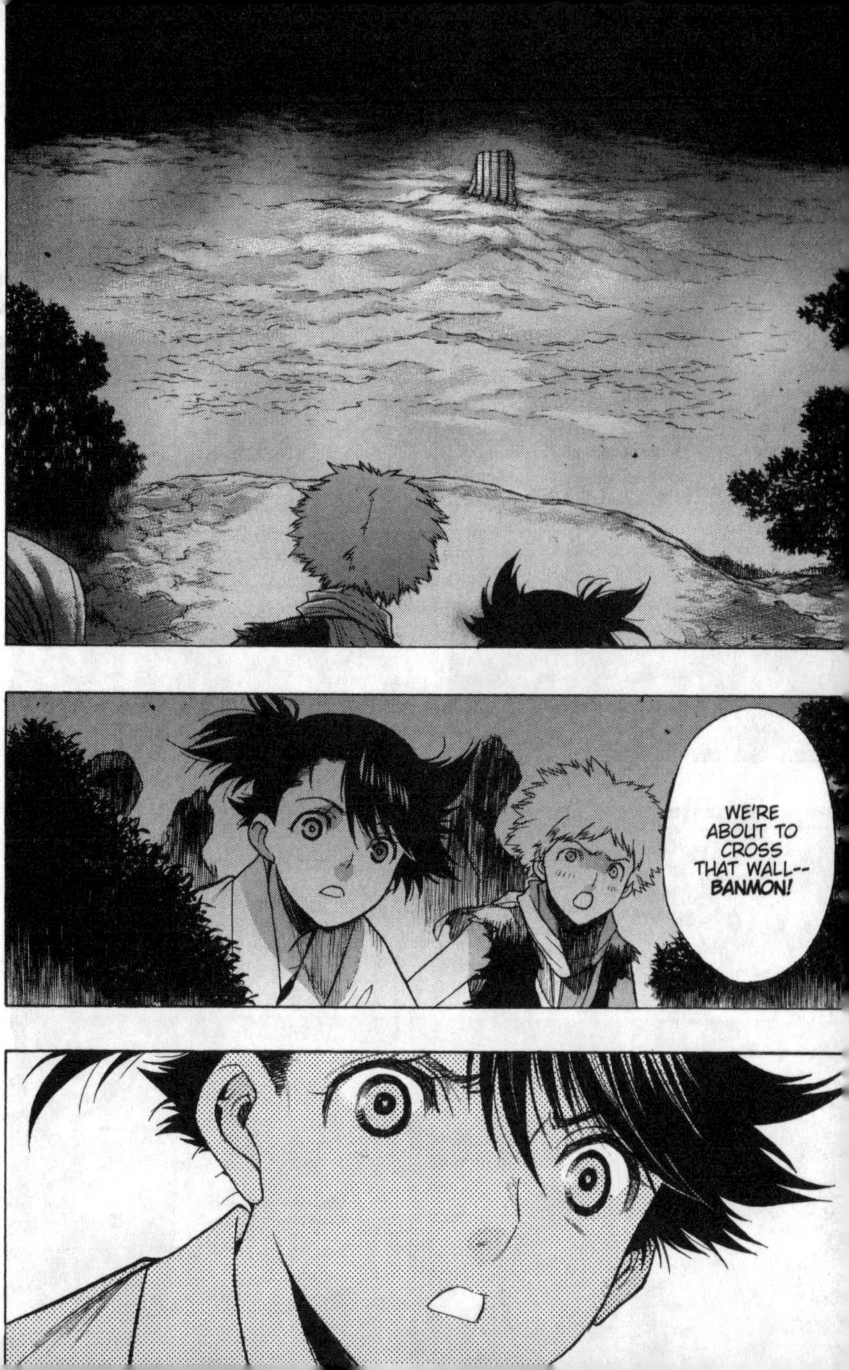
WE'RE ABOUT TO CROSS THAT WALL-- BANMON!

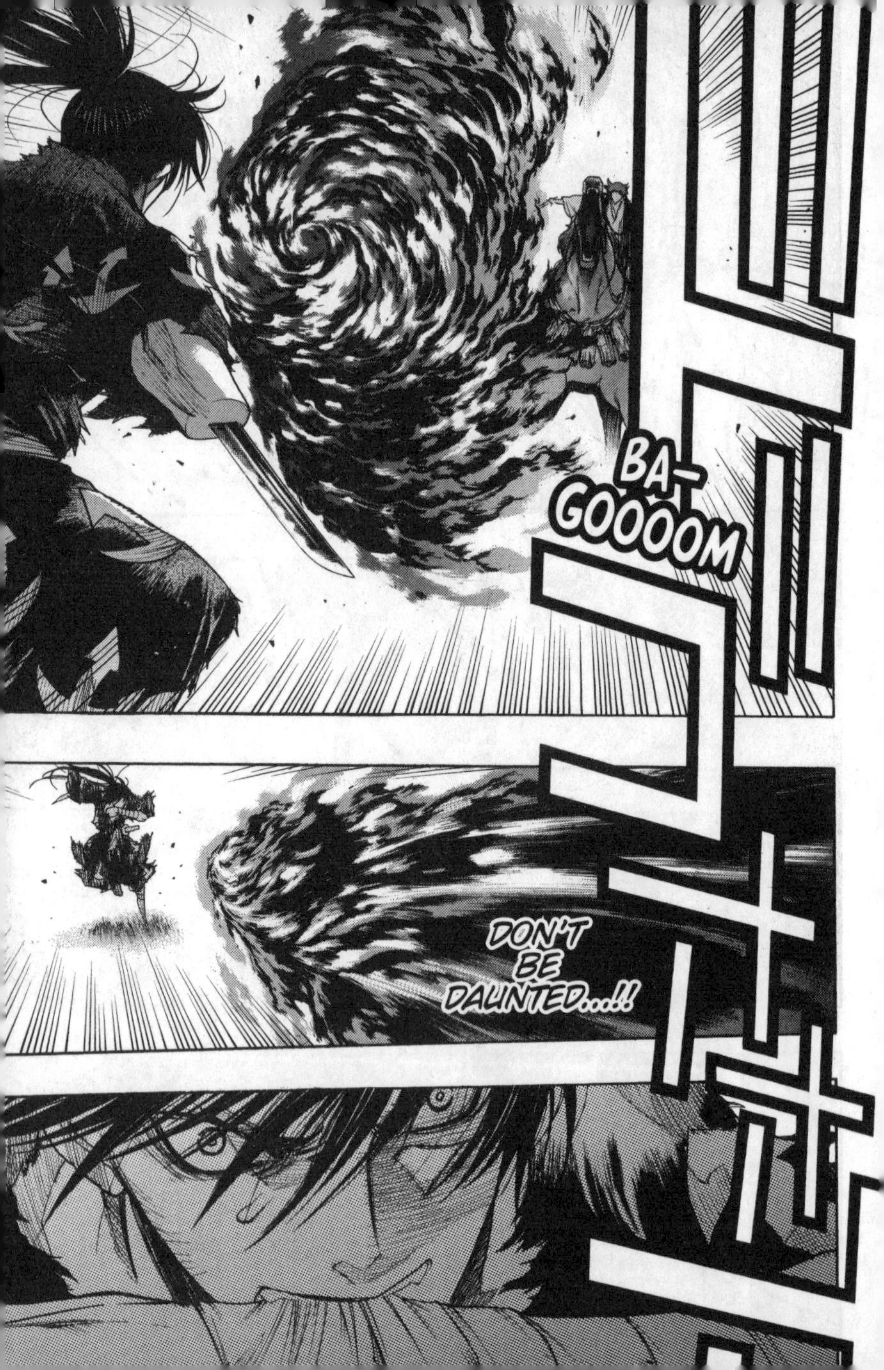
BA-GOOOOM
DON'T BE DAUNTED...!!

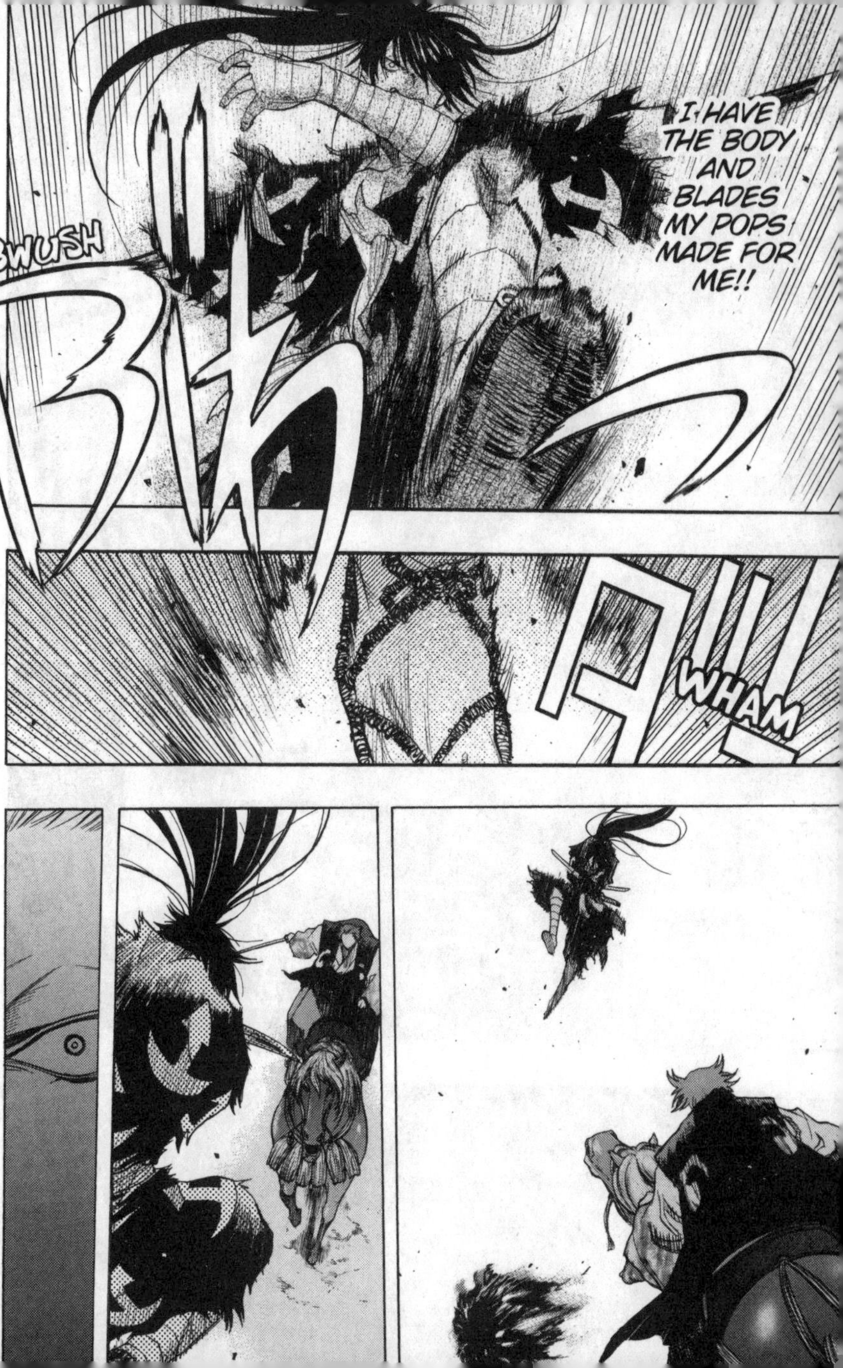
I HAVE THE BODY AND BLADES MY POPS MADE FOR ME!!
BWUSH
WHAM

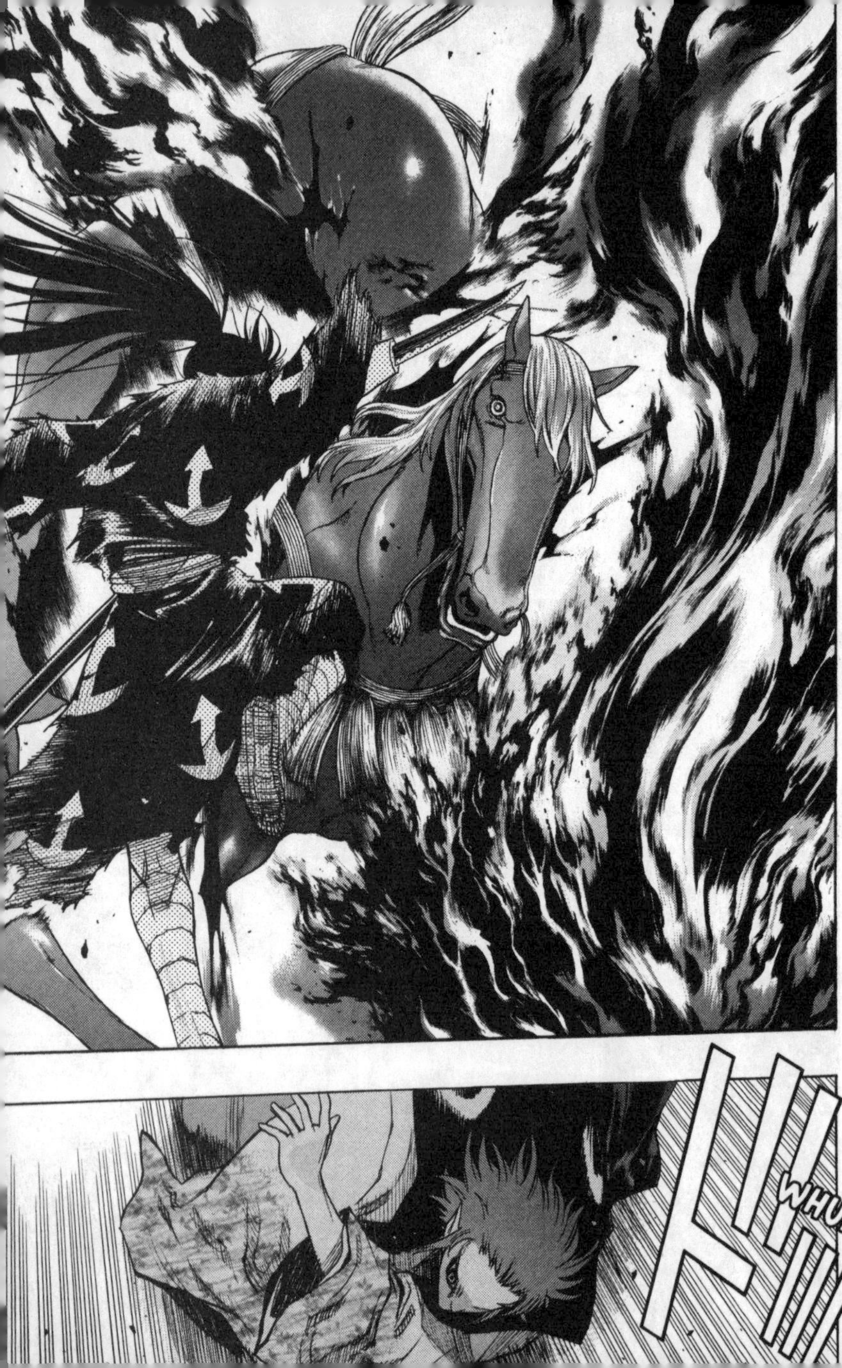
WHUM

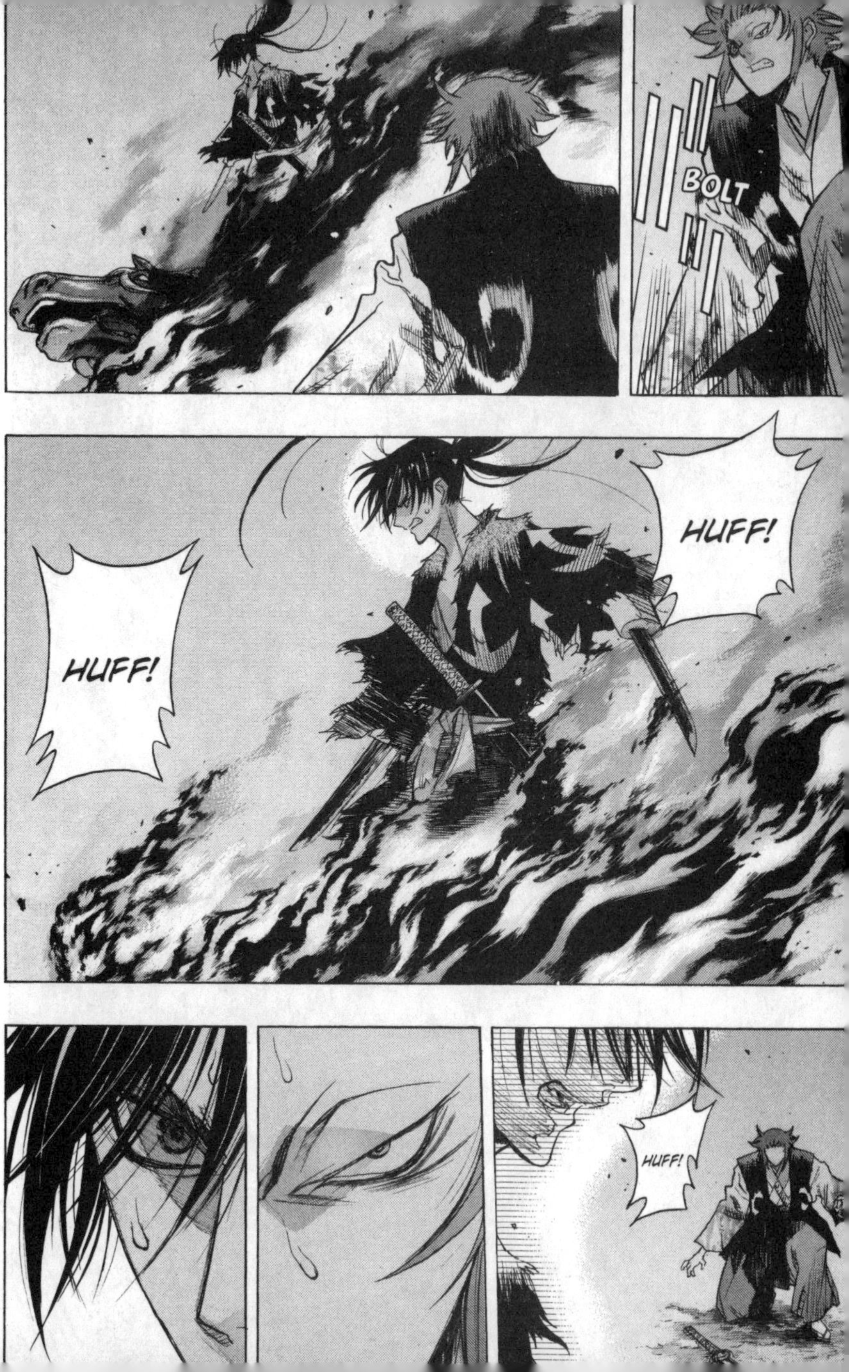
BOLT
HUFF!
HUFF!
HUFF!

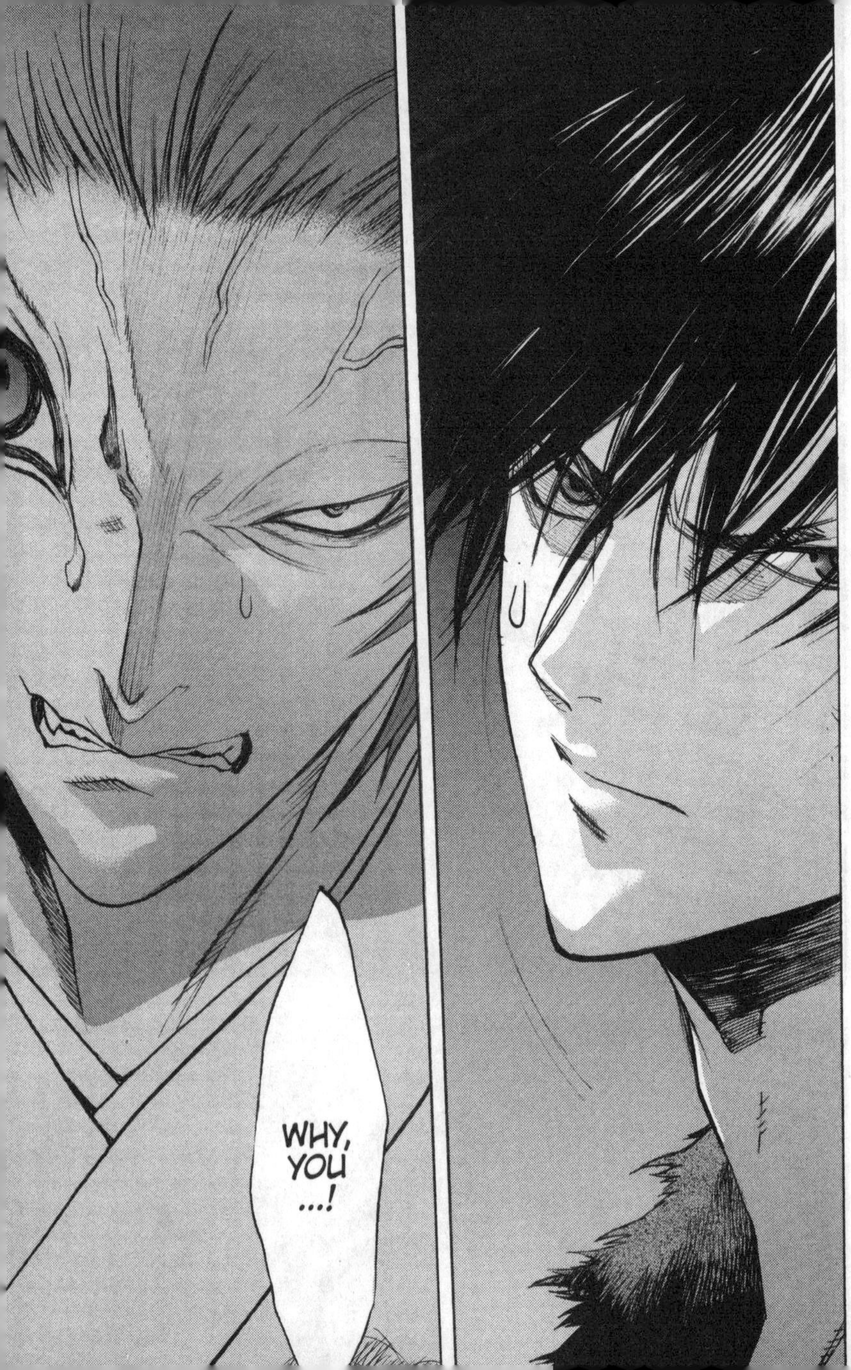
WHY, YOU ...!

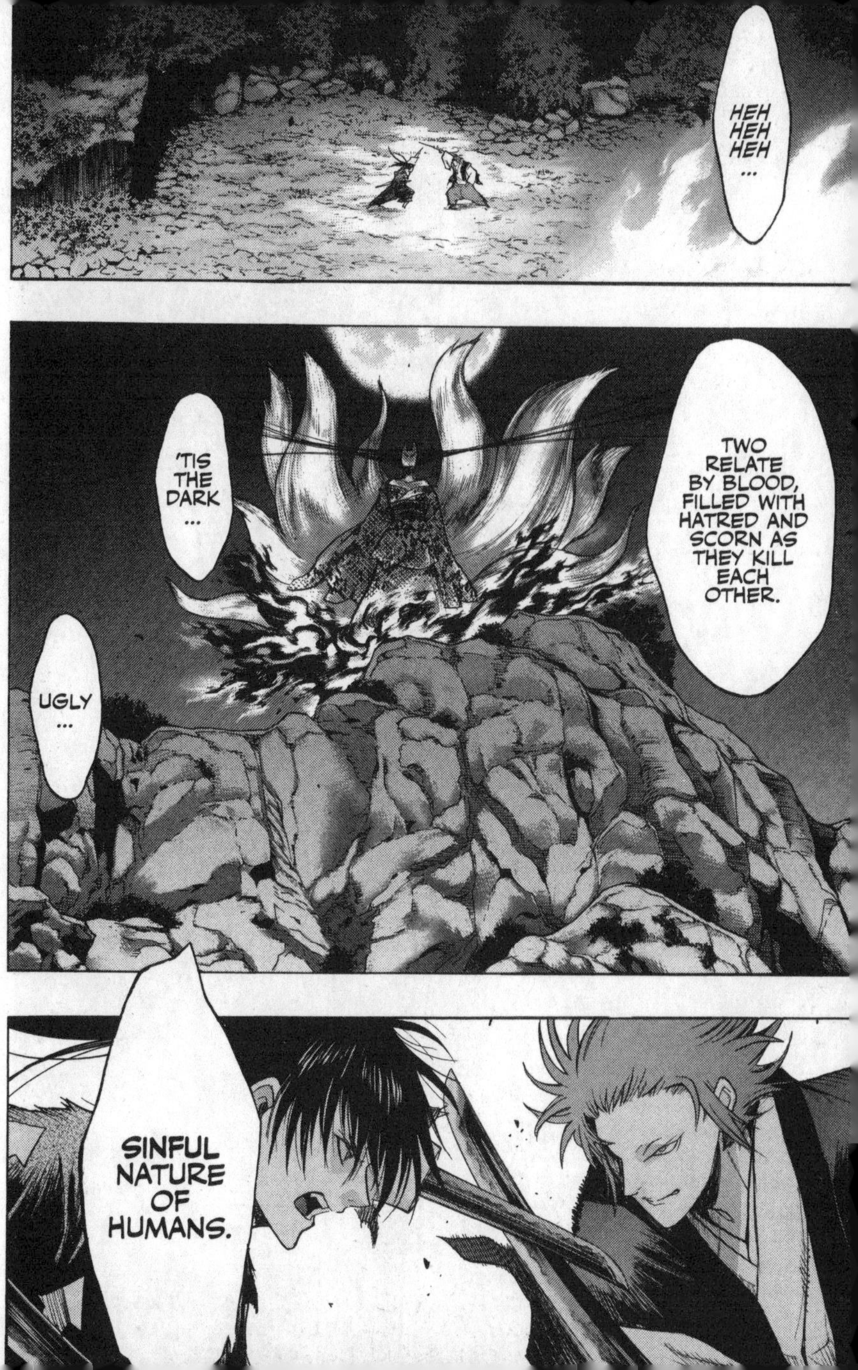
HEH HEH HEH ...
TWO RELATE BY BLOOD, FILLED WITH HATRED AND SCORN AS THEY KILL EACH OTHER.
'TIS THE DARK ...
UGLY ...
SINFUL NATURE OF HUMANS.

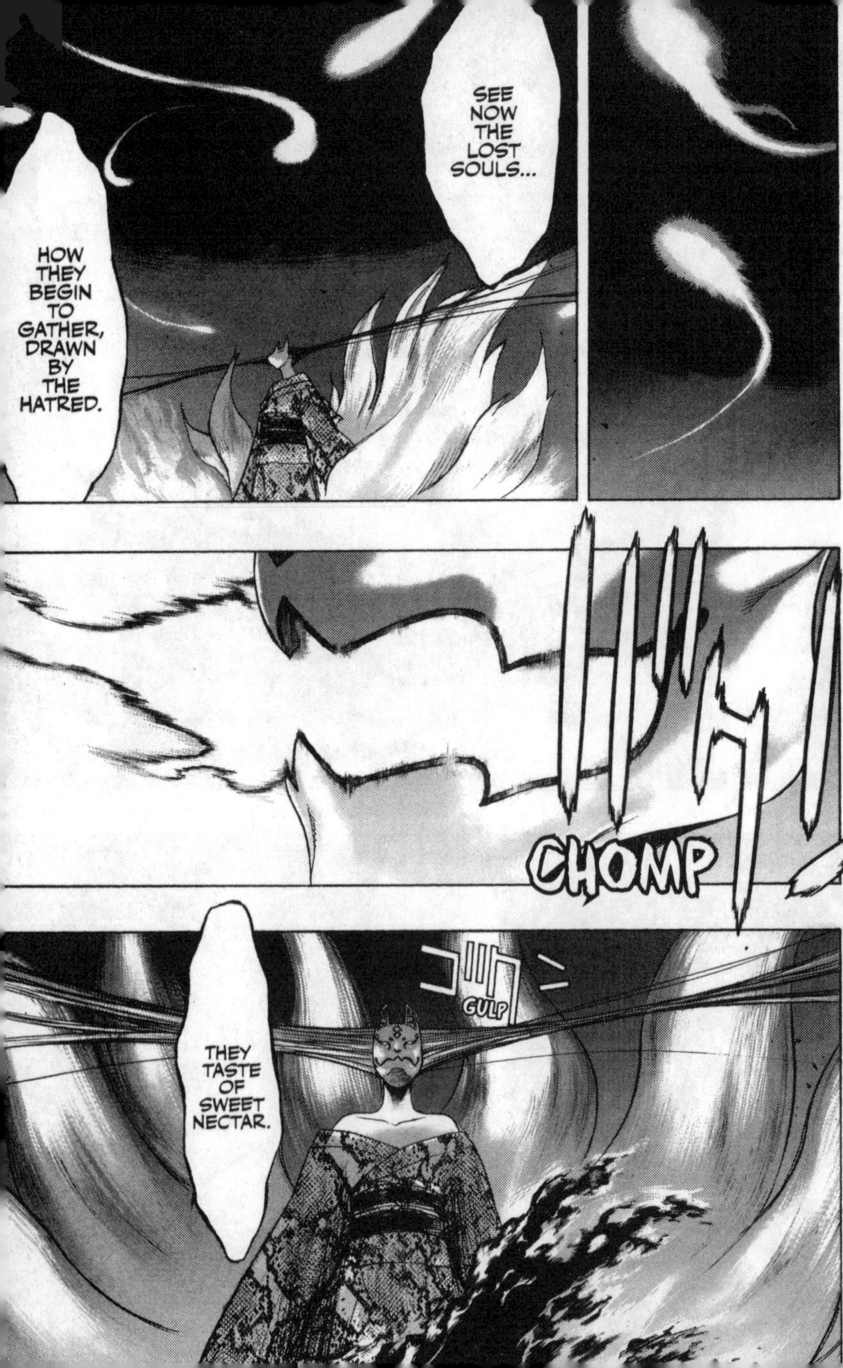
SEE NOW THE LOST SOULS...
HOW THEY BEGIN TO GATHER, DRAWN BY THE HATRED.
CHOMP
GULP
THEY TASTE OF SWEET NECTAR.

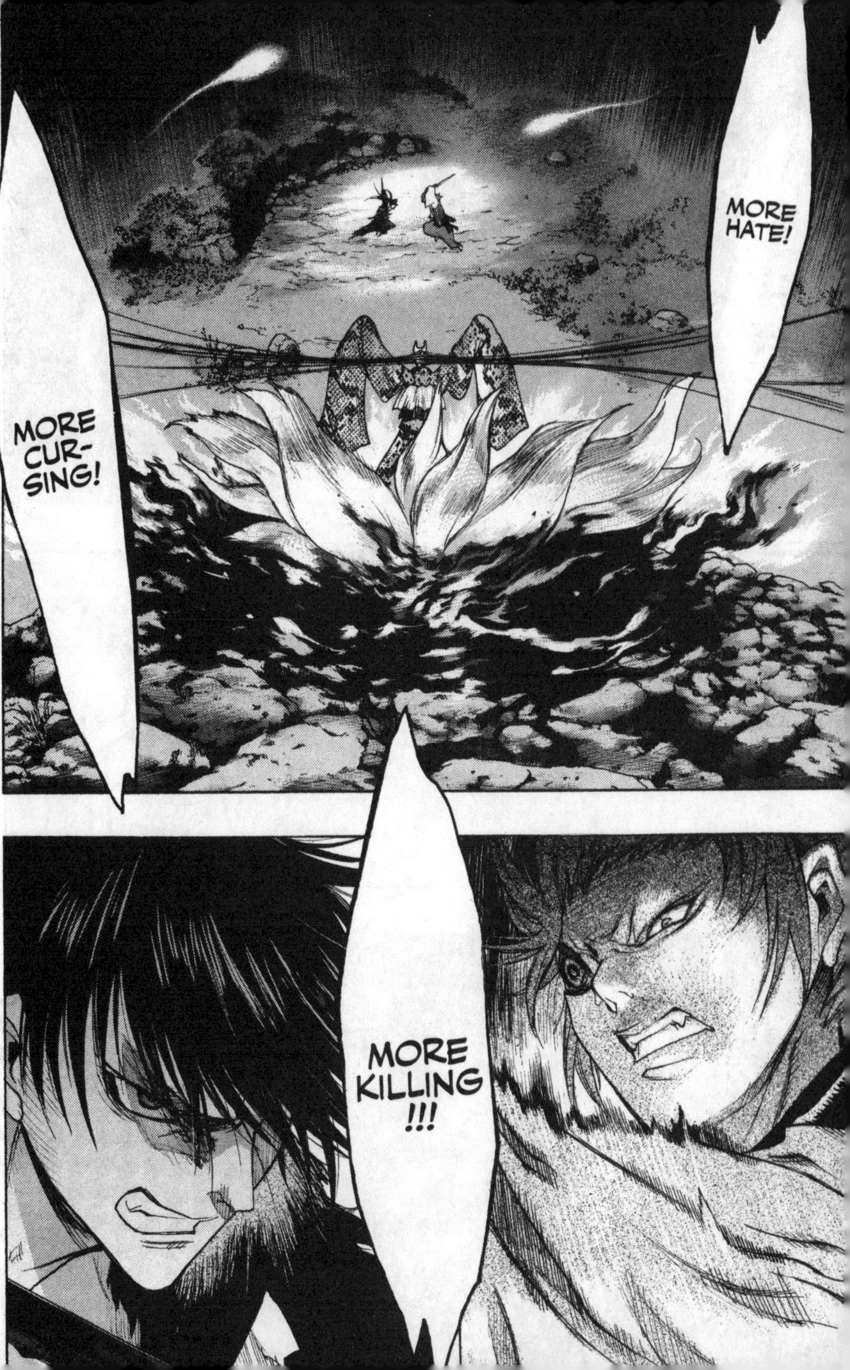
MORE HATE!
MORE CUR-SING!
MORE KILLING!!!

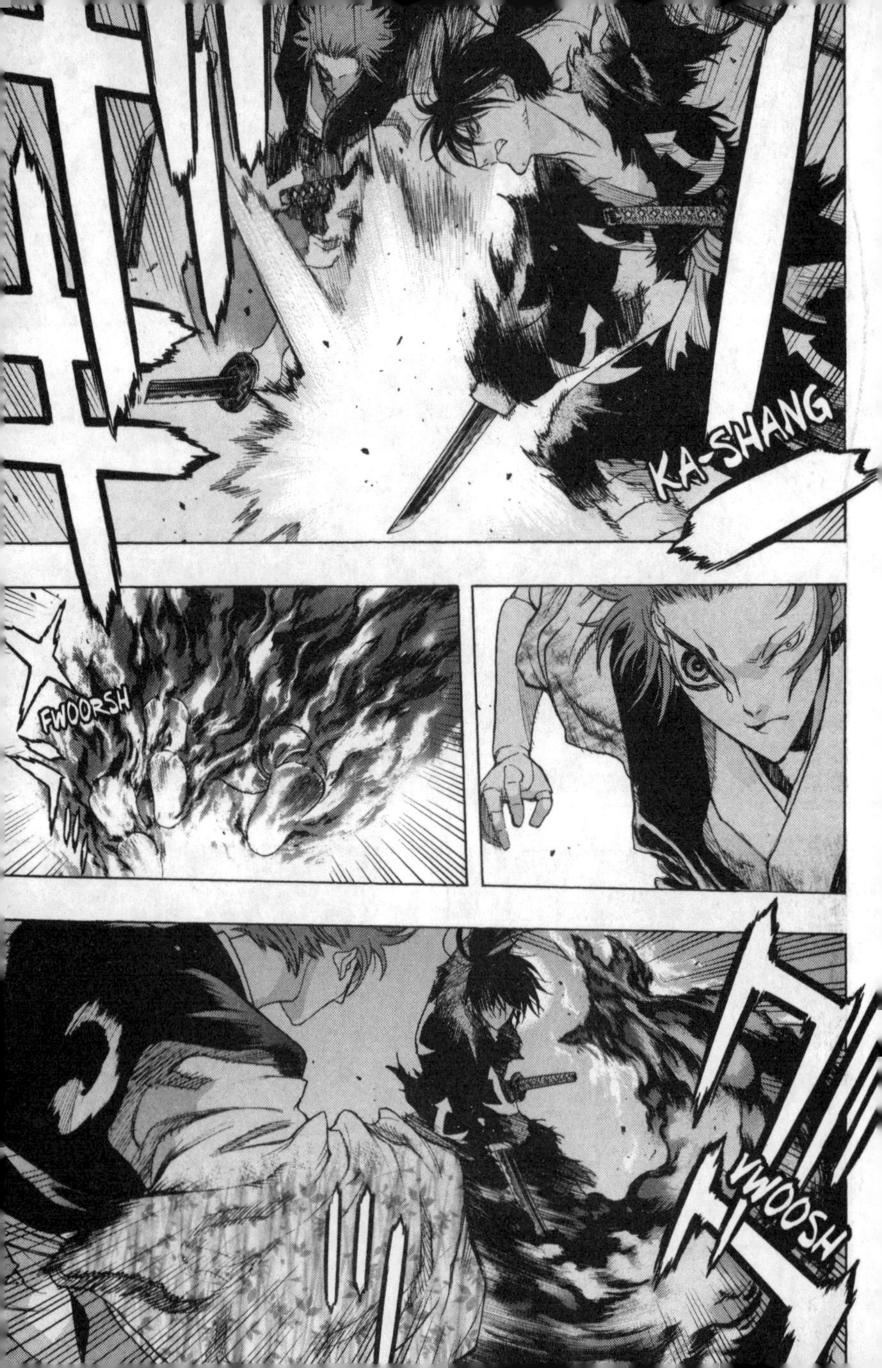
KA-SHANG
FWOORSH
VWOOSH

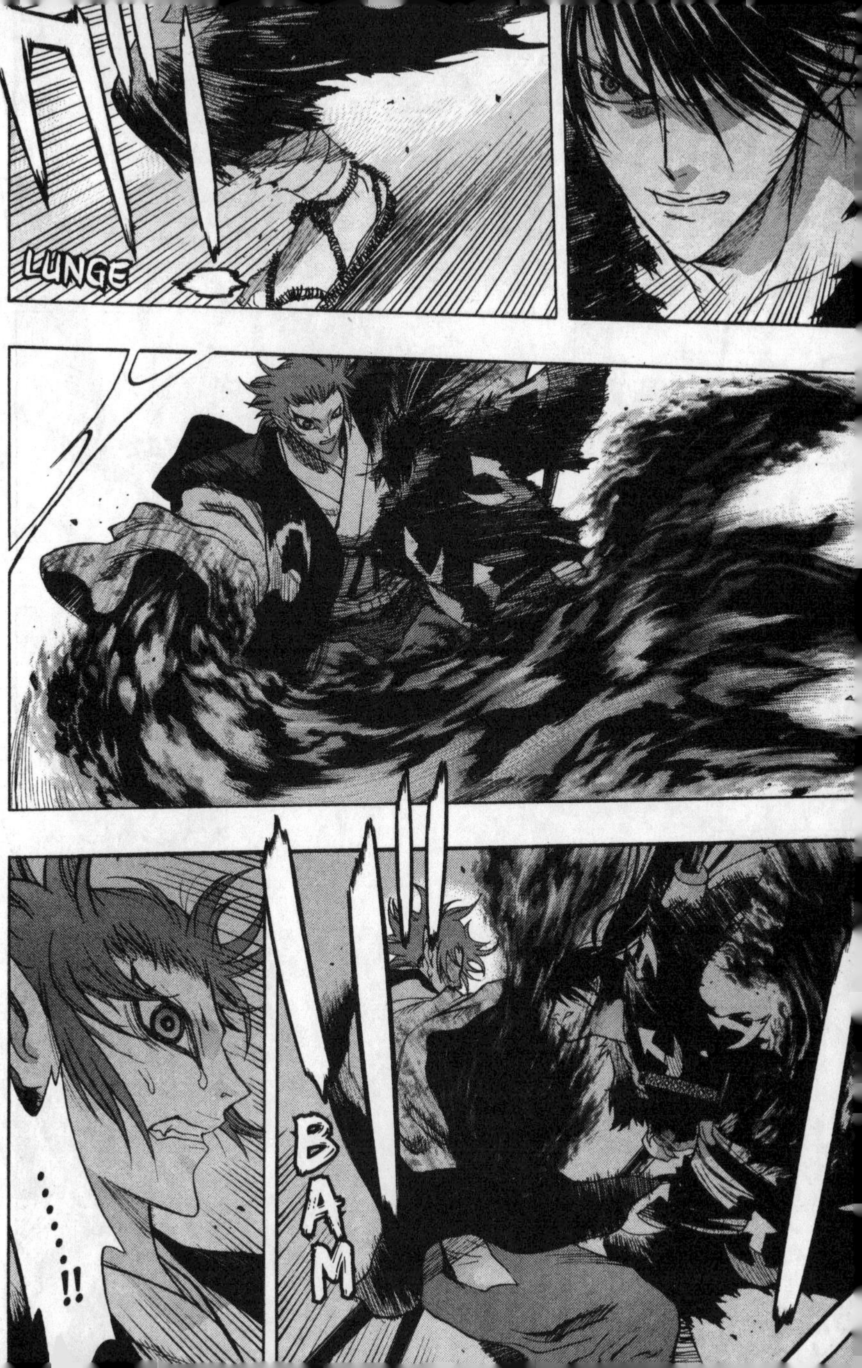
LUNGE
BAM
......!!

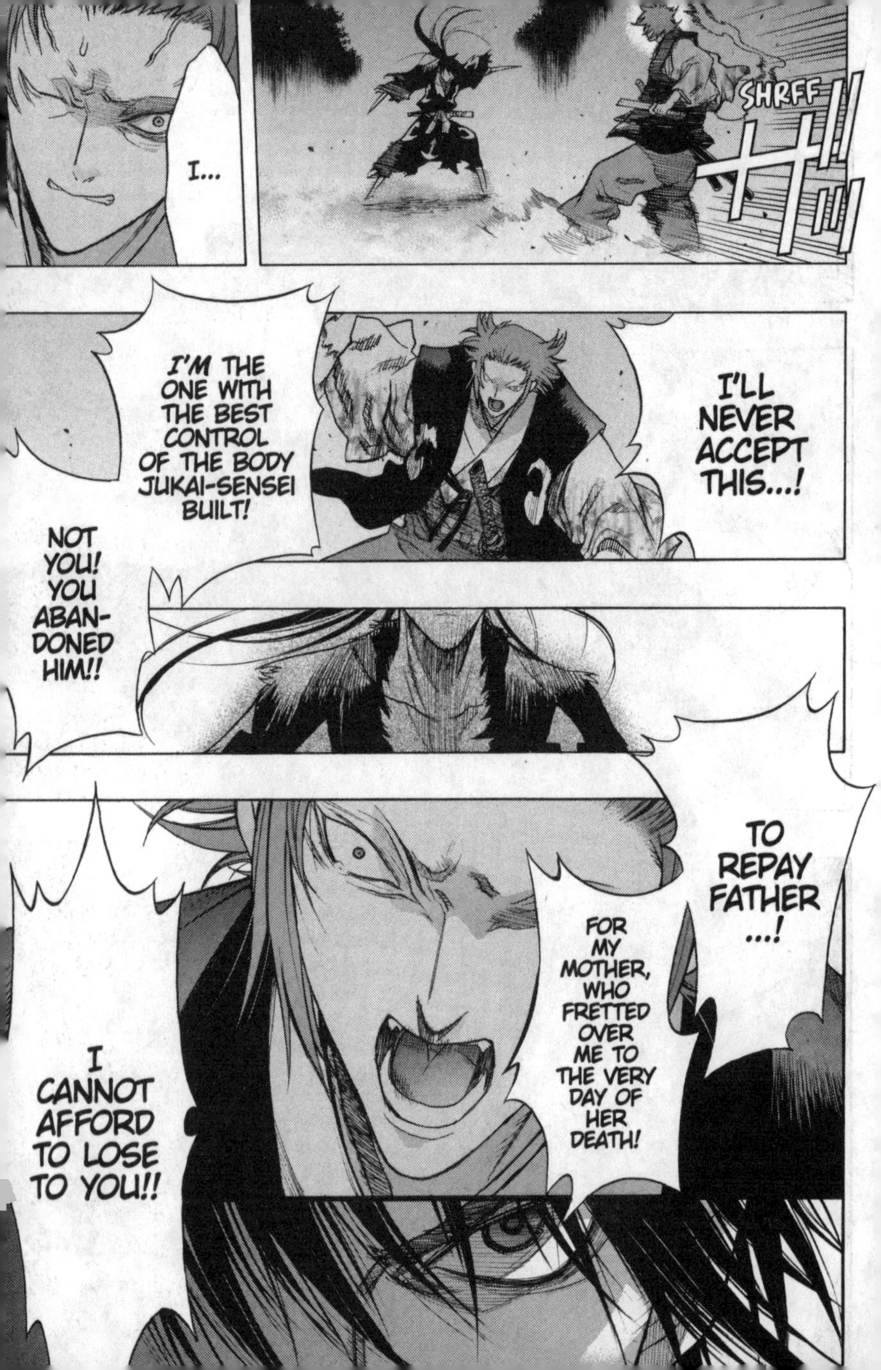
SHRFF
I...
I'LL NEVER ACCEPT THIS...!
I'M THE ONE WITH THE BEST CONTROL OF THE BODY JUKAI-SENSEI BUILT!
NOT YOU! YOU ABAN-DONED HIM!!
TO REPAY FATHER ...!
FOR MY MOTHER, WHO FRETTED OVER ME TO THE VERY DAY OF HER DEATH!
I CANNOT AFFORD TO LOSE TO YOU!!

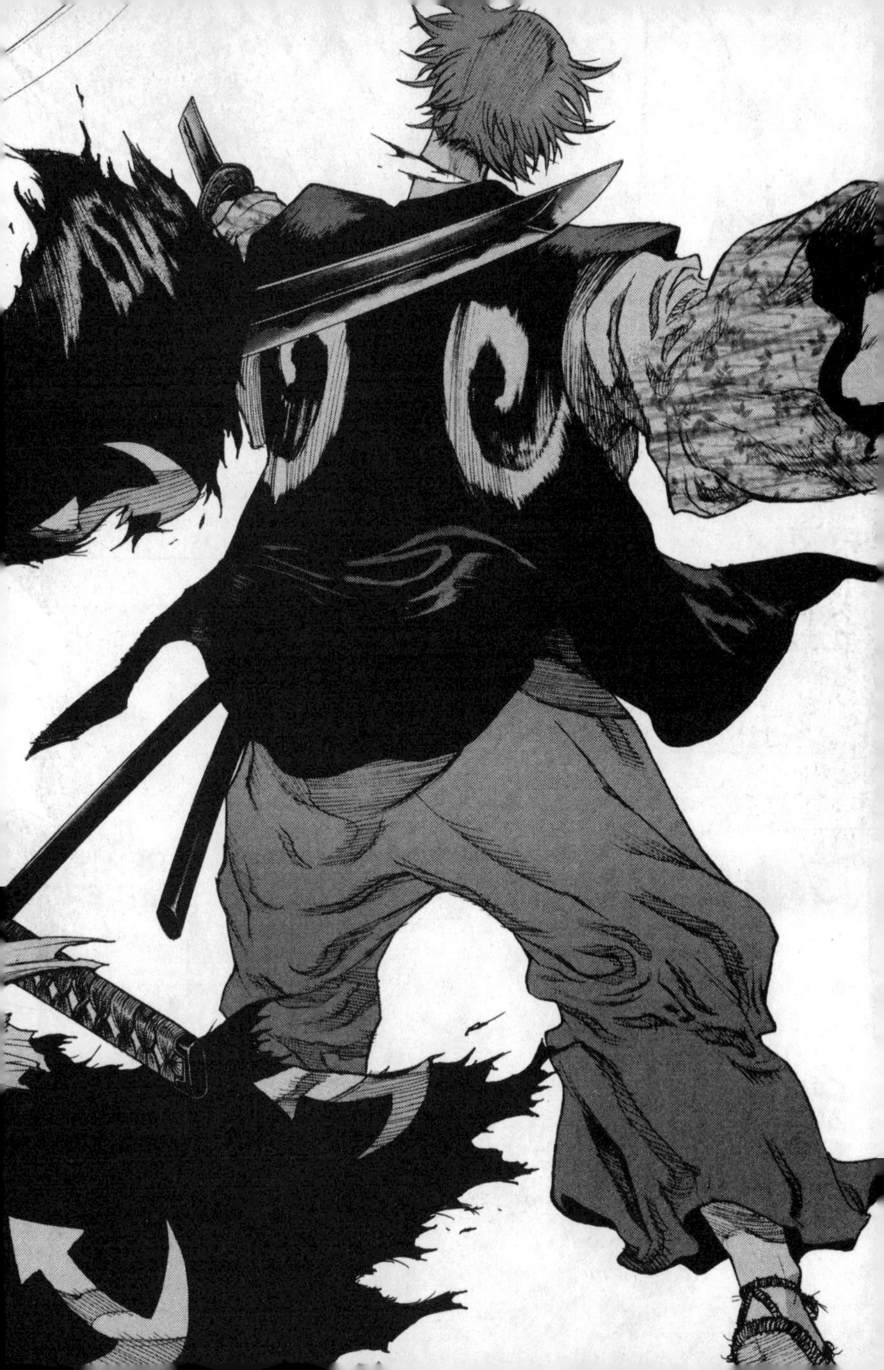

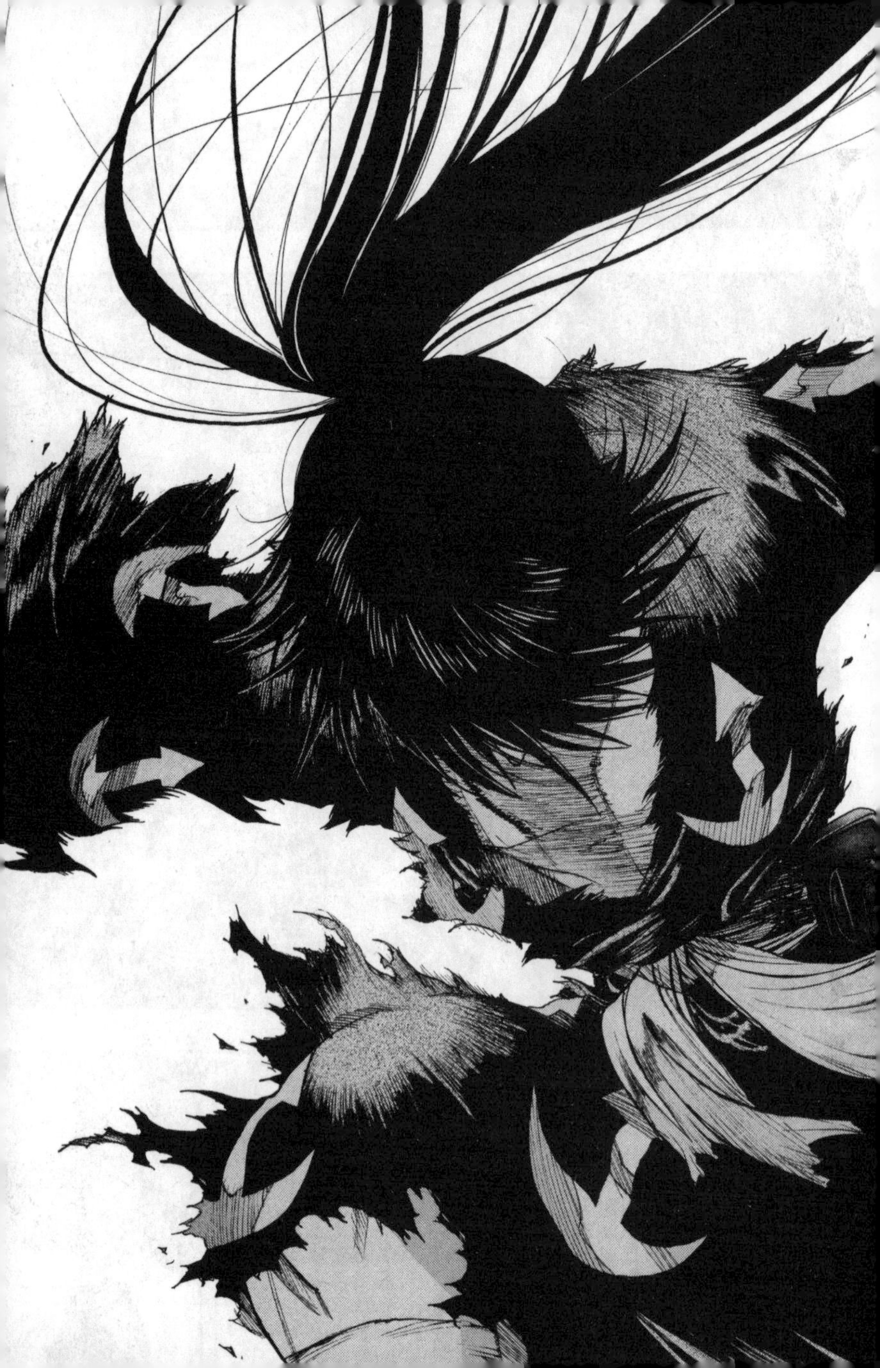

TILT...

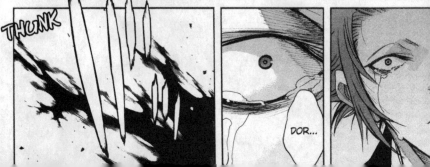

THUNK

DOR...

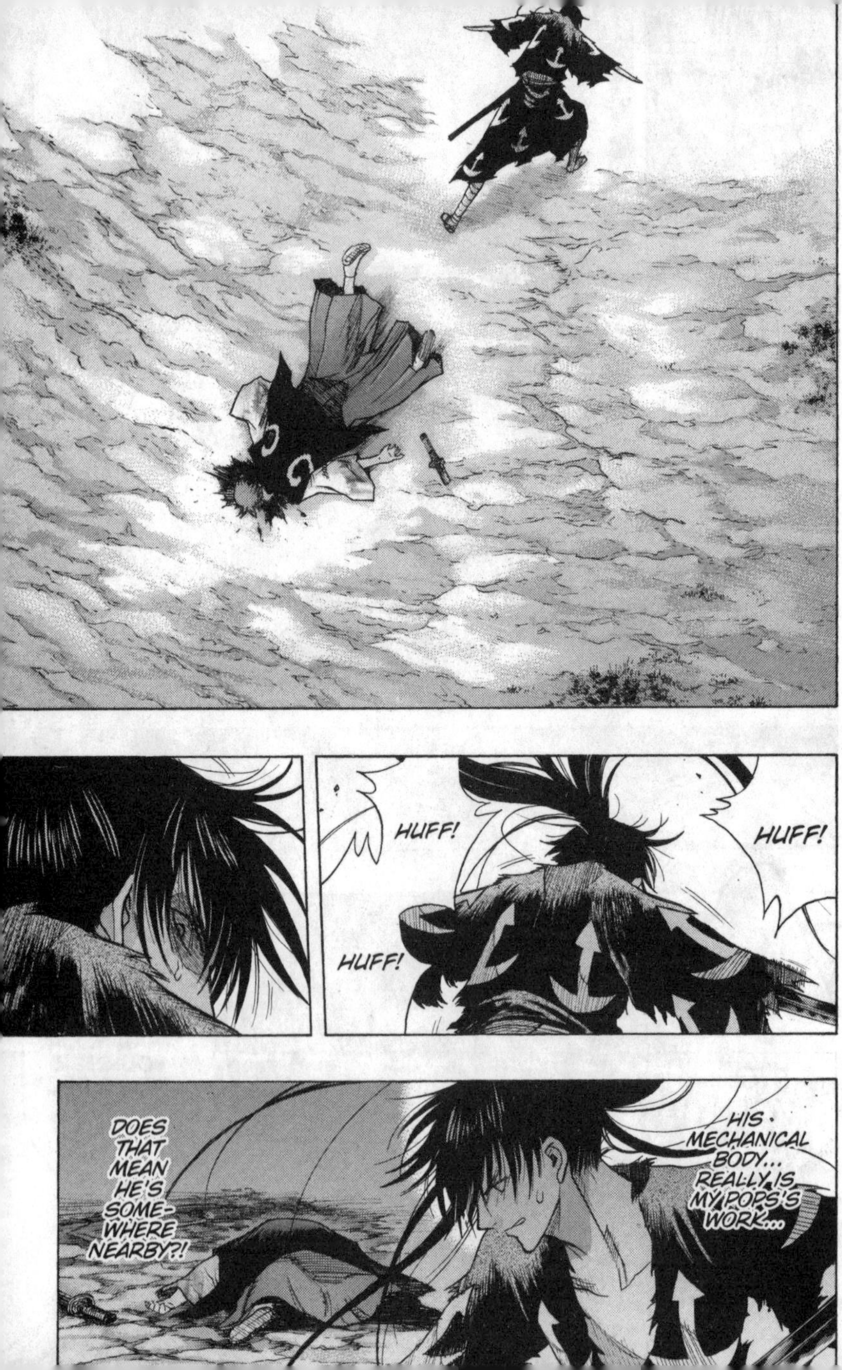
HUFF!
HUFF!
HUFF!
HIS MECHANICAL BODY... REALLY IS MY POPS'S WORK...
DOES THAT MEAN HE'S SOME-WHERE NEARBY?!

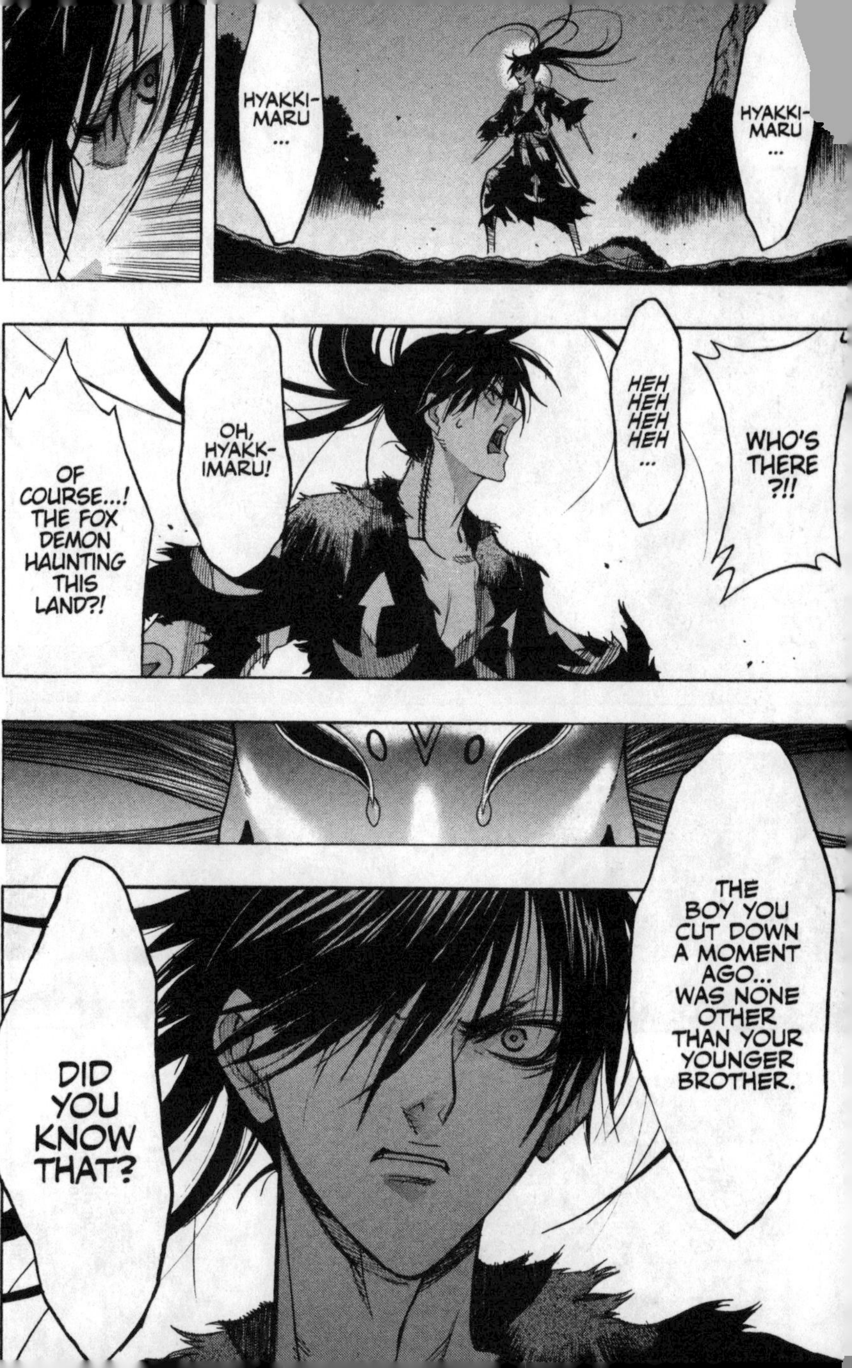
HYAKKI-MARU ...
HYAKKI-MARU ...
WHO'S THERE ?!!
HEH HEH HEH HEH ...
OH, HYAKK-IMARU!
OF COURSE...! THE FOX DEMON HAUNTING THIS LAND?!
THE BOY YOU CUT DOWN A MOMENT AGO... WAS NONE OTHER THAN YOUR YOUNGER BROTHER.
DID YOU KNOW THAT?

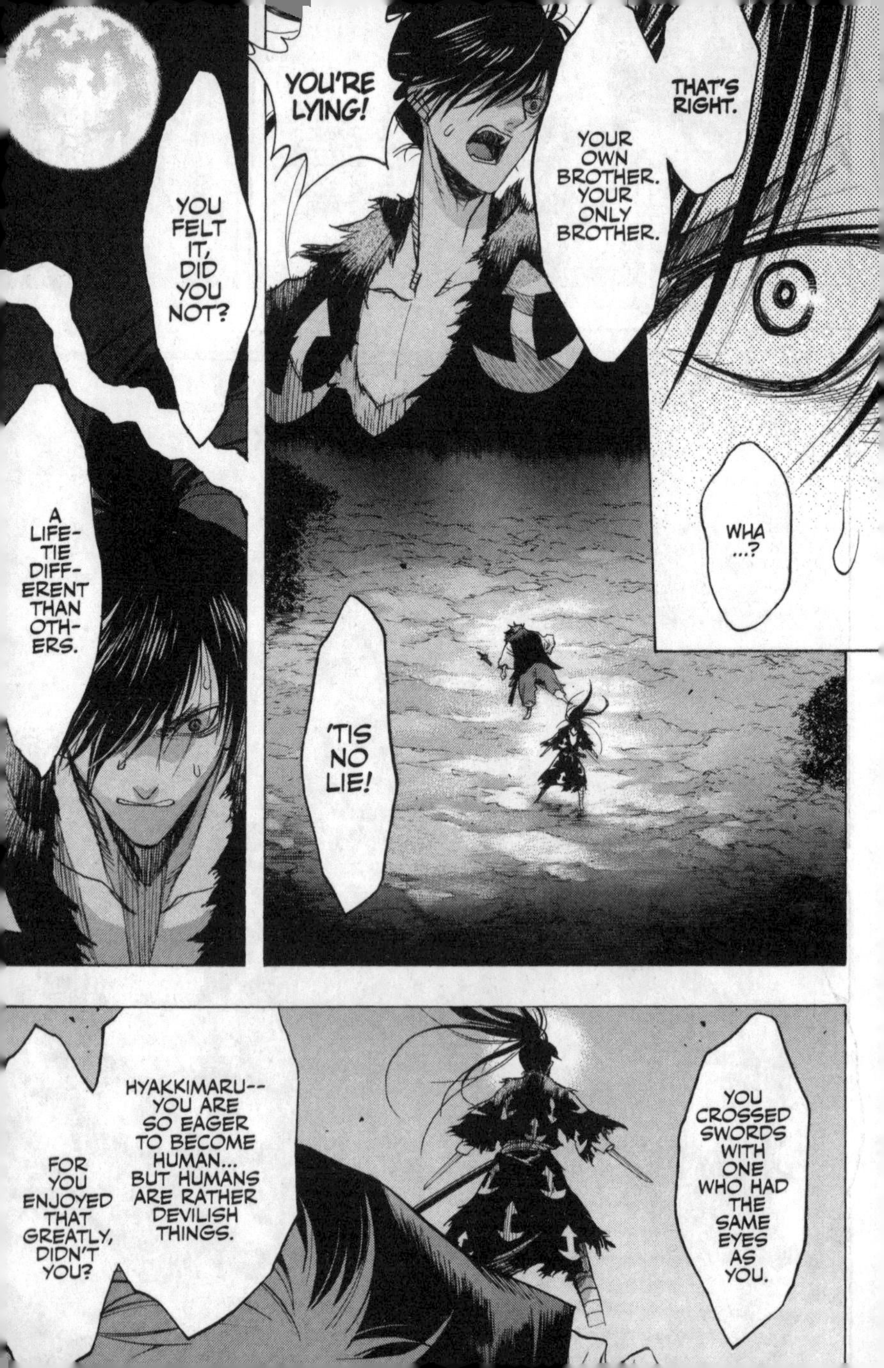
THAT'S RIGHT.
YOUR OWN BROTHER. YOUR ONLY BROTHER.
WHA ...?
YOU'RE LYING!
'TIS NO LIE!
YOU FELT IT, DID YOU NOT?
A LIFE-TIE DIFF-ERENT THAN OTH-ERS.
YOU CROSSED SWORDS WITH ONE WHO HAD THE SAME EYES AS YOU.
HYAKKIMARU-- YOU ARE SO EAGER TO BECOME HUMAN... BUT HUMANS ARE RATHER DEVILISH THINGS.
FOR YOU ENJOYED THAT GREATLY, DIDN'T YOU?

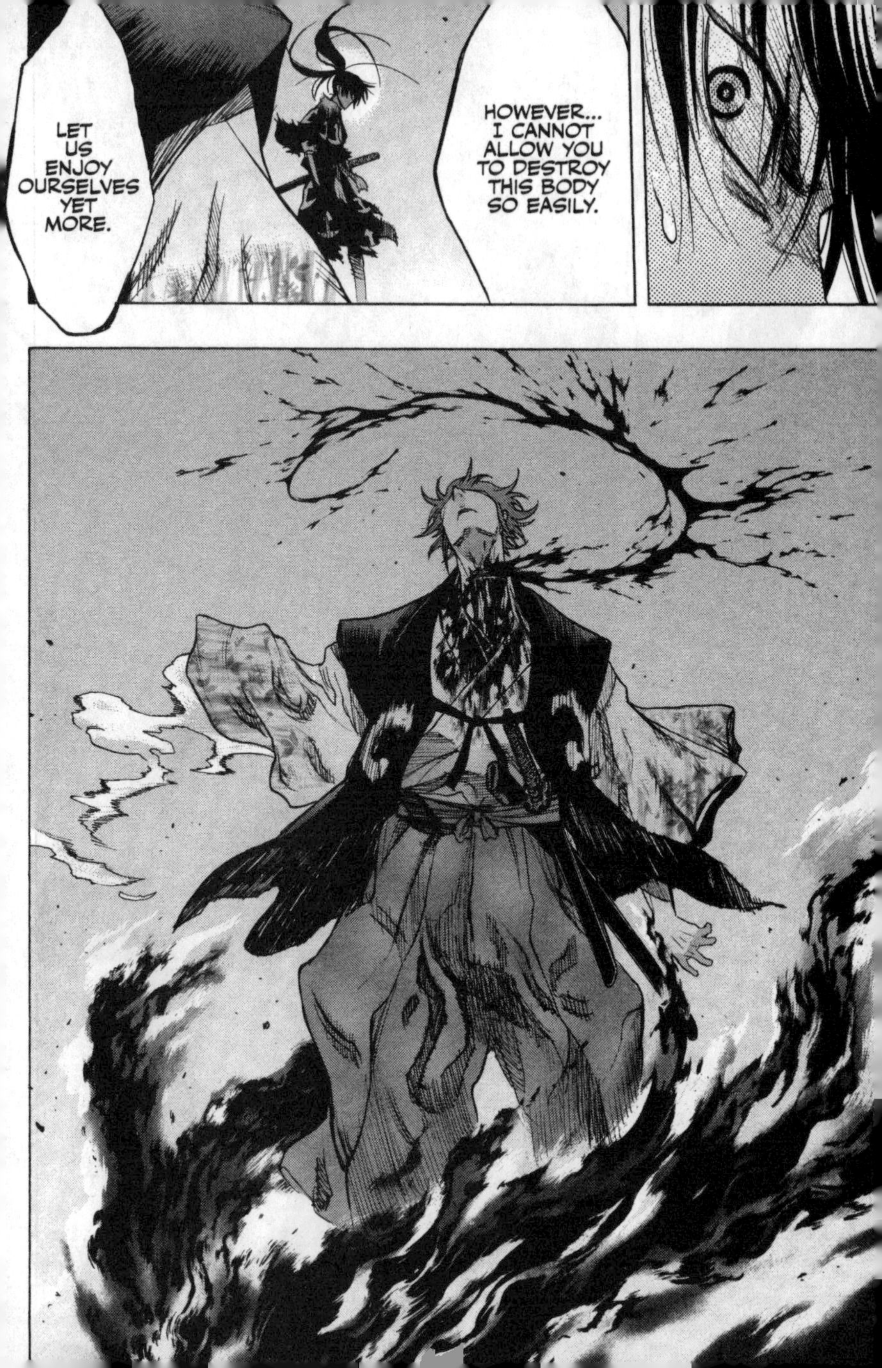
HOWEVER... I CANNOT ALLOW YOU TO DESTROY THIS BODY SO EASILY.
LET US ENJOY OURSELVES YET MORE.

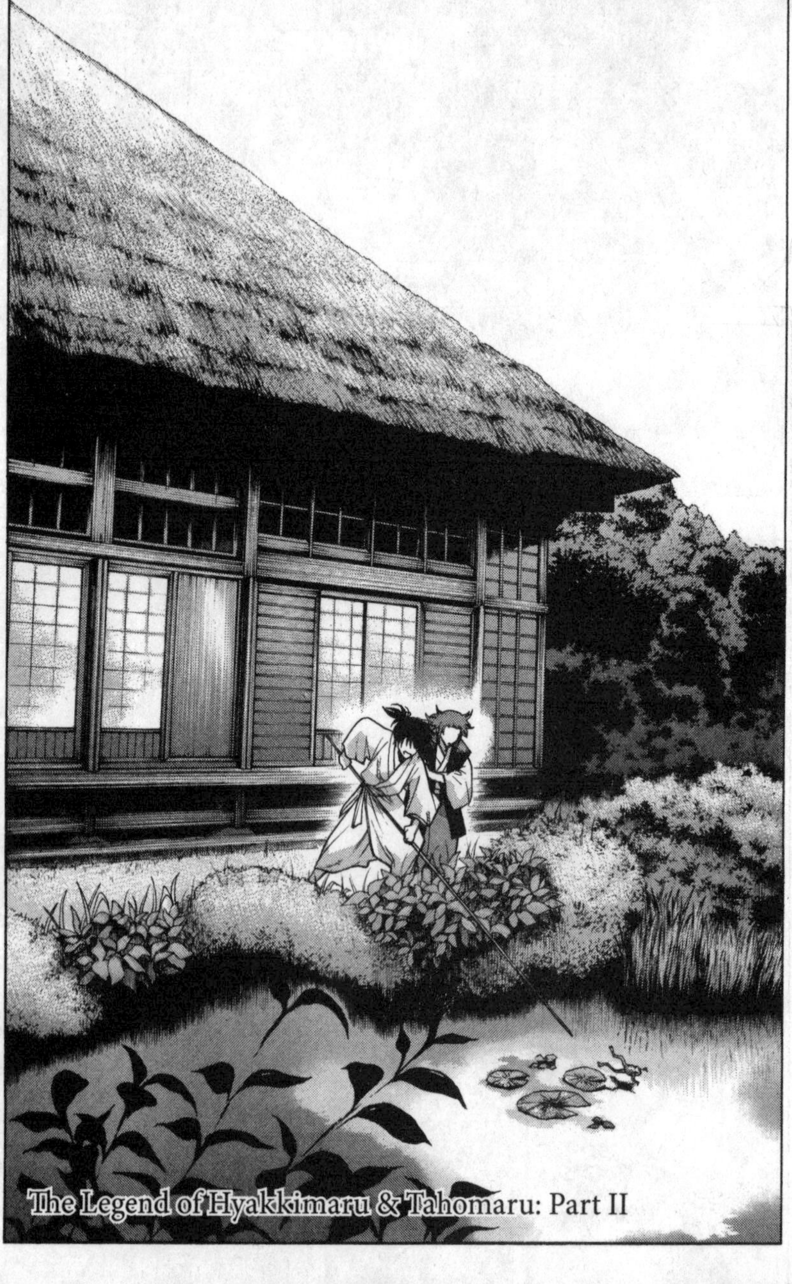
The Legend of Hyakkimaru & Tahomaru: Part II

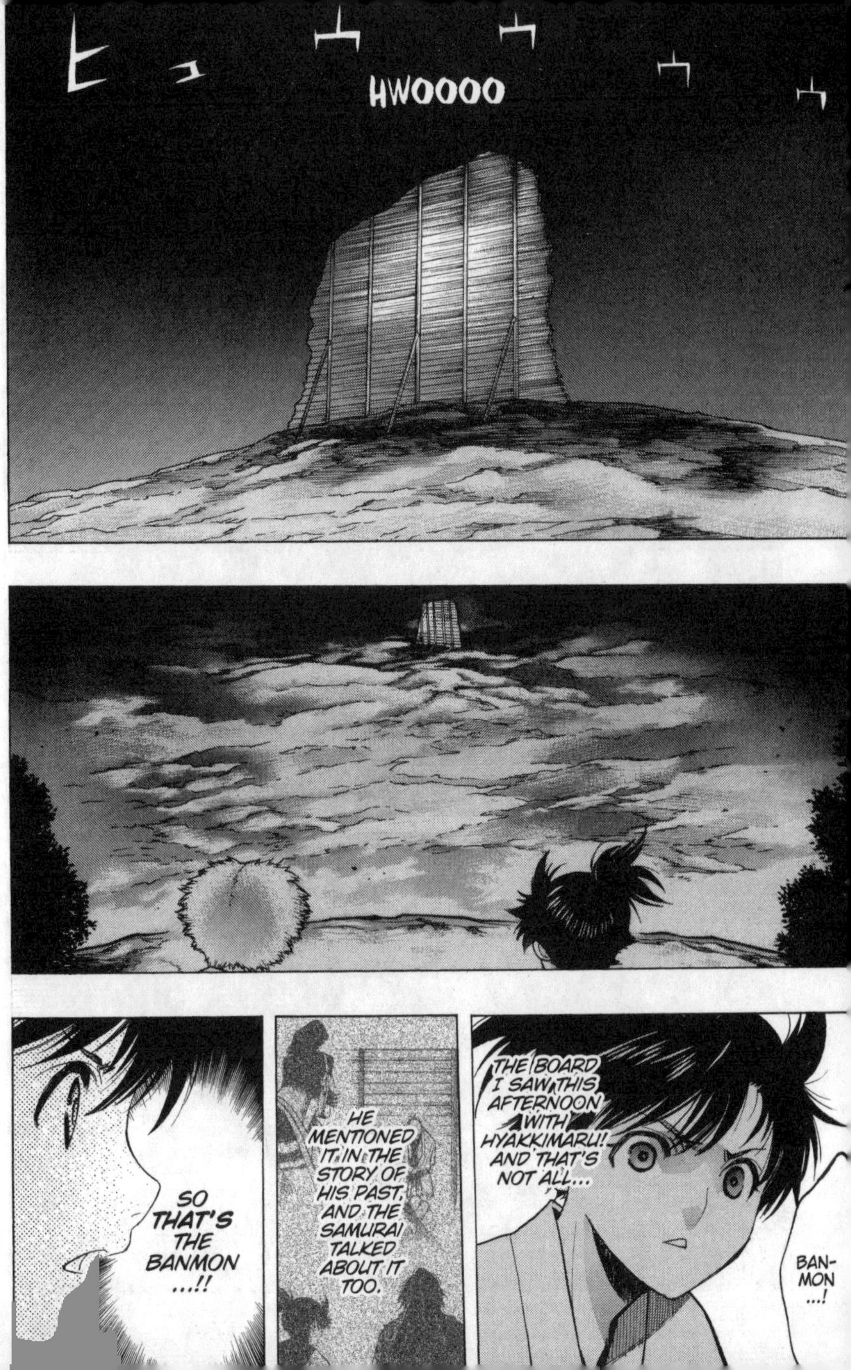
ヒュウウウウ
HWOOOO
BAN-MON ...!
THE BOARD I SAW THIS AFTERNOON WITH HYAKKIMARU! AND THAT'S NOT ALL...
HE MENTIONED IT IN THE STORY OF HIS PAST, AND THE SAMURAI TALKED ABOUT IT TOO.
SO THAT'S THE BANMON ...!!

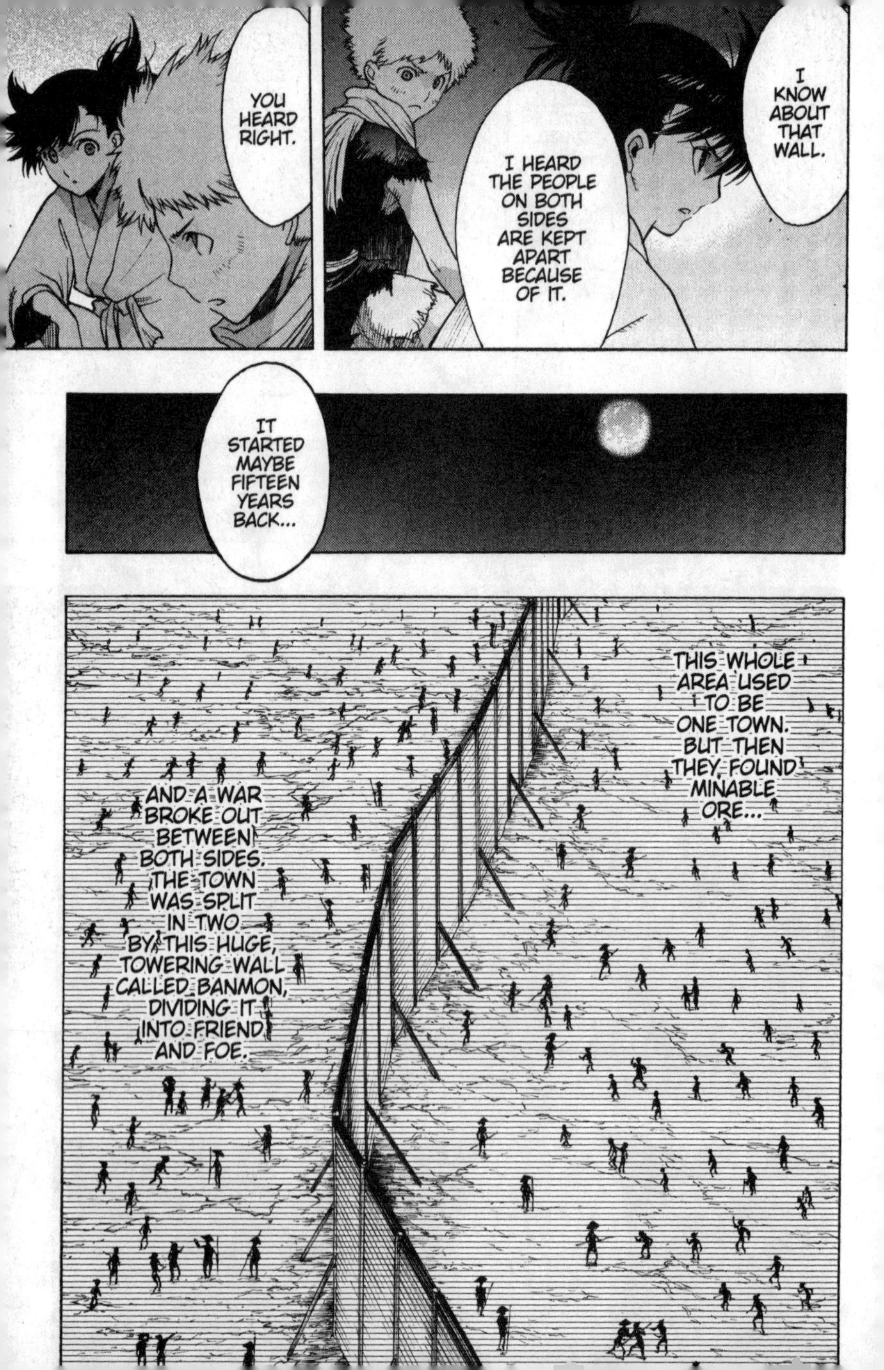
I KNOW ABOUT THAT WALL.
I HEARD THE PEOPLE ON BOTH SIDES ARE KEPT APART BECAUSE OF IT.
YOU HEARD RIGHT.
IT STARTED MAYBE FIFTEEN YEARS BACK...
THIS WHOLE AREA USED TO BE ONE TOWN. BUT THEN THEY FOUND MINABLE ORE...
AND A WAR BROKE OUT BETWEEN BOTH SIDES. THE TOWN WAS SPLIT IN TWO BY THIS HUGE, TOWERING WALL CALLED BANMON, DIVIDING IT INTO FRIEND AND FOE.

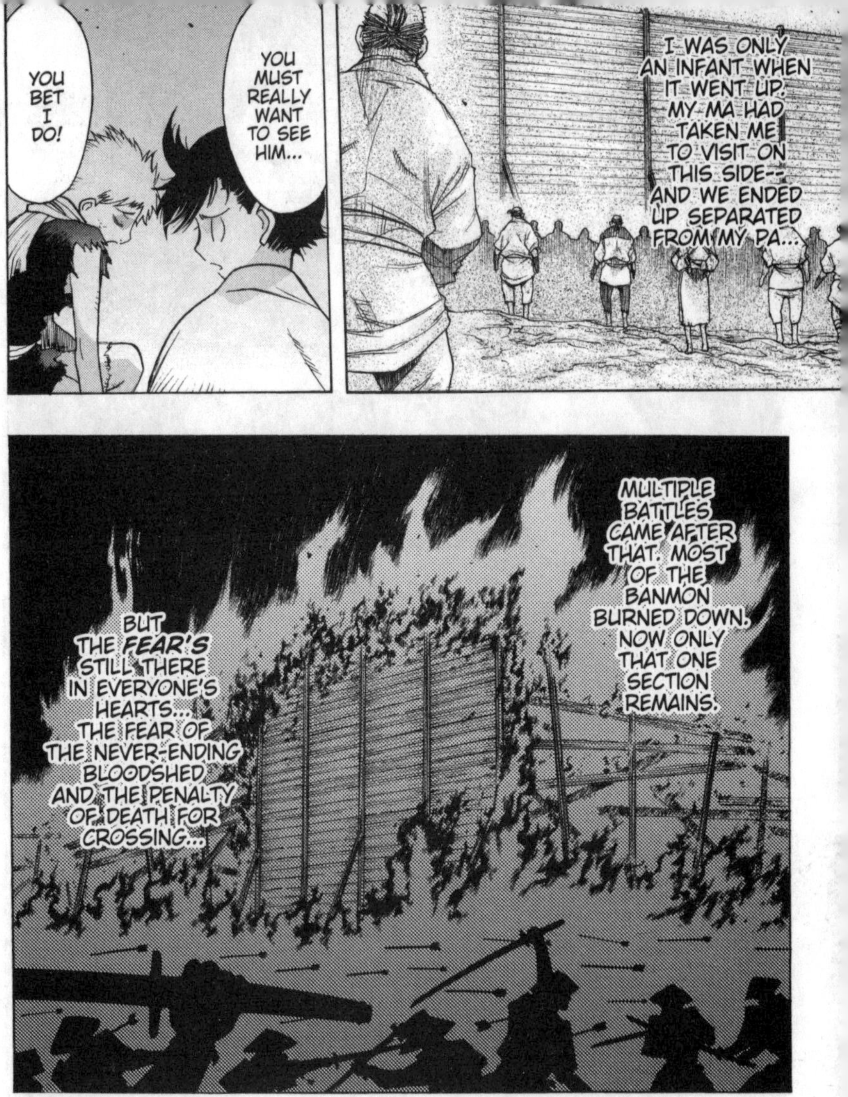
I WAS ONLY AN INFANT WHEN IT WENT UP. MY MA HAD TAKEN ME TO VISIT ON THIS SIDE-- AND WE ENDED UP SEPARATED FROM MY PA...
YOU MUST REALLY WANT TO SEE HIM...
YOU BET I DO!
MULTIPLE BATTLES CAME AFTER THAT. MOST OF THE BANMON BURNED DOWN. NOW ONLY THAT ONE SECTION REMAINS.
BUT THE FEAR'S STILL THERE IN EVERYONE'S HEARTS... THE FEAR OF THE NEVER-ENDING BLOODSHED AND THE PENALTY OF DEATH FOR CROSSING...

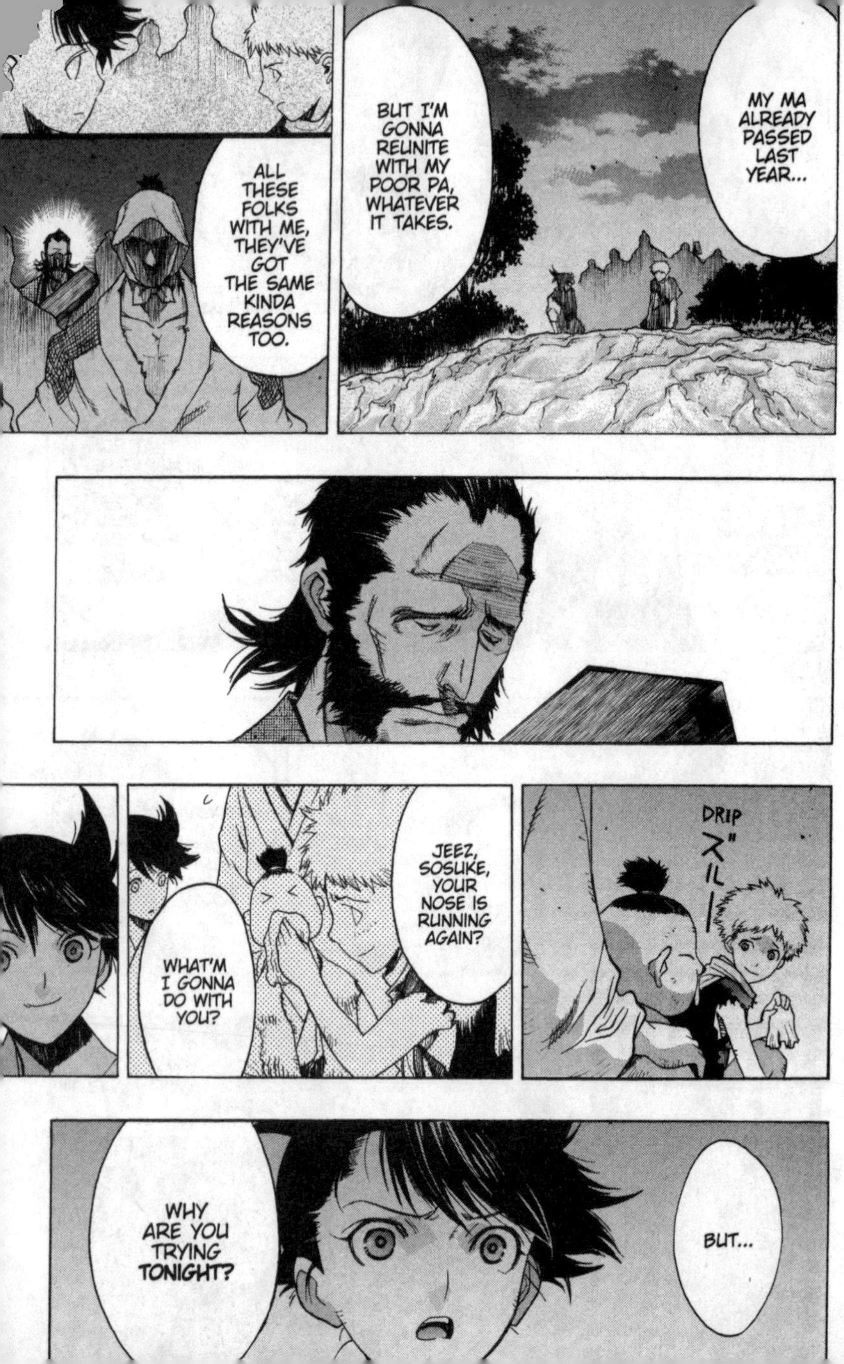
MY MA ALREADY PASSED LAST YEAR...
BUT I'M GONNA REUNITE WITH MY POOR PA, WHATEVER IT TAKES.
ALL THESE FOLKS WITH ME, THEY'VE GOT THE SAME KINDA REASONS TOO.
DRIP
ズルー
JEEZ, SOSUKE, YOUR NOSE IS RUNNING AGAIN?
WHAT'M I GONNA DO WITH YOU?
BUT...
WHY ARE YOU TRYING TONIGHT?

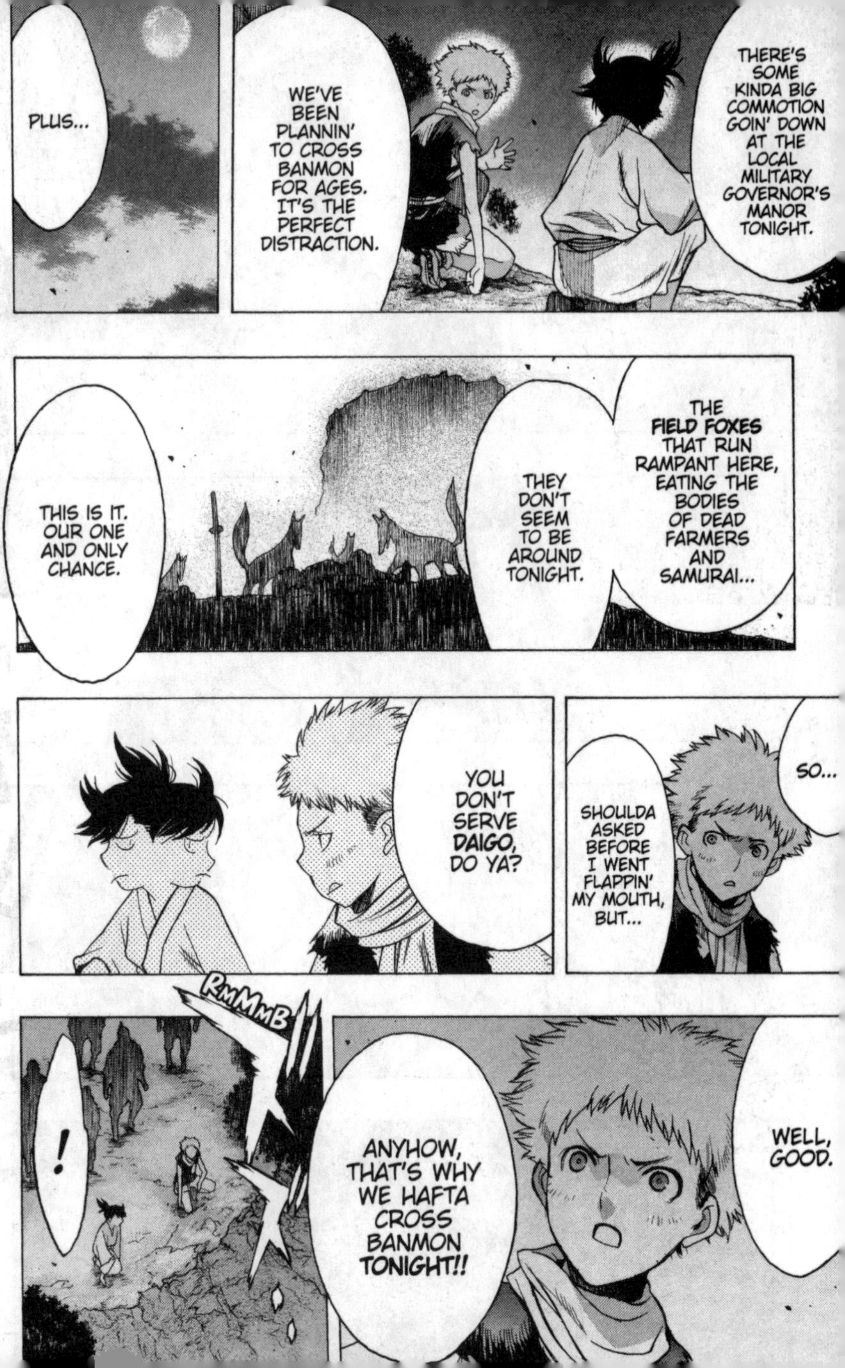
THERE'S SOME KINDA BIG COMMOTION GOIN' DOWN AT THE LOCAL MILITARY GOVERNOR'S MANOR TONIGHT.
WE'VE BEEN PLANNIN' TO CROSS BANMON FOR AGES. IT'S THE PERFECT DISTRACTION.
PLUS...
THE **FIELD FOXES** THAT RUN RAMPANT HERE, EATING THE BODIES OF DEAD FARMERS AND SAMURAI...
THEY DON'T SEEM TO BE AROUND TONIGHT.
THIS IS IT. OUR ONE AND ONLY CHANCE.
SO...
SHOULDA ASKED BEFORE I WENT FLAPPIN' MY MOUTH, BUT...
YOU DON'T SERVE **DAIGO**, DO YA?
WELL, GOOD.
ANYHOW, THAT'S WHY WE HAFTA CROSS BANMON **TONIGHT!!**
RMMMB
!

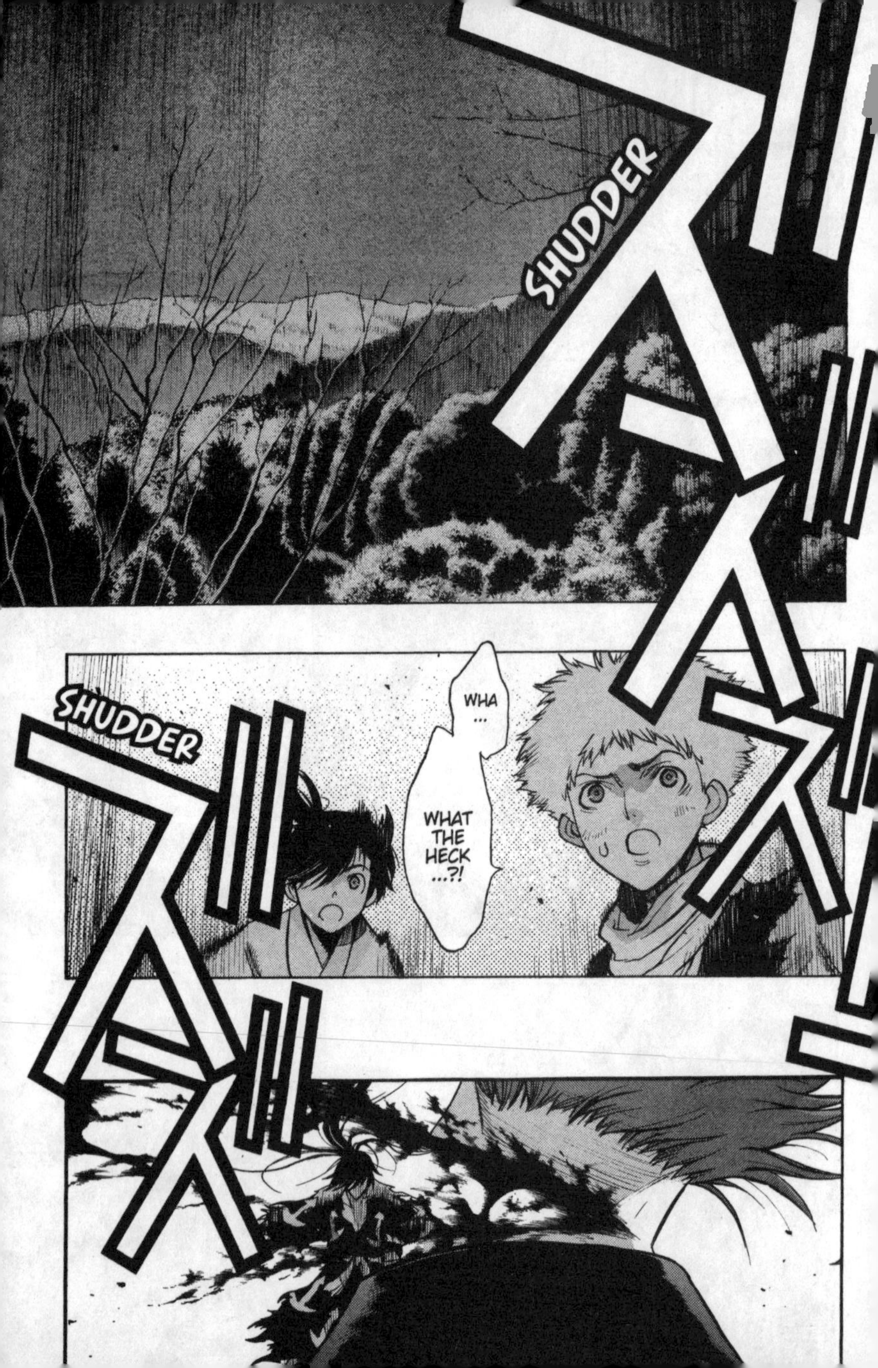
SHUDDER
SHUDDER
WHA ... WHAT THE HECK ...?!

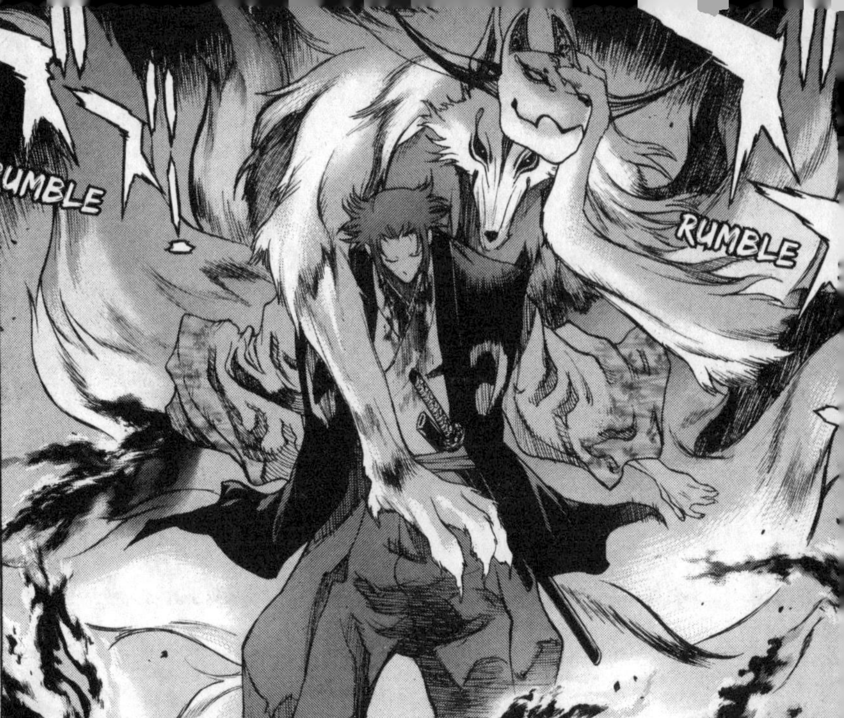
RUMBLE
RUMBLE
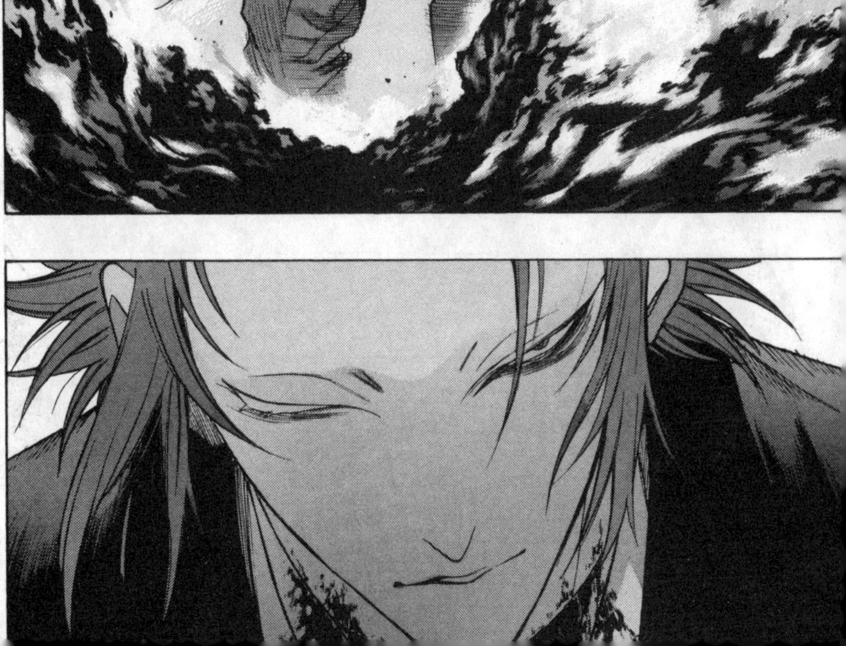

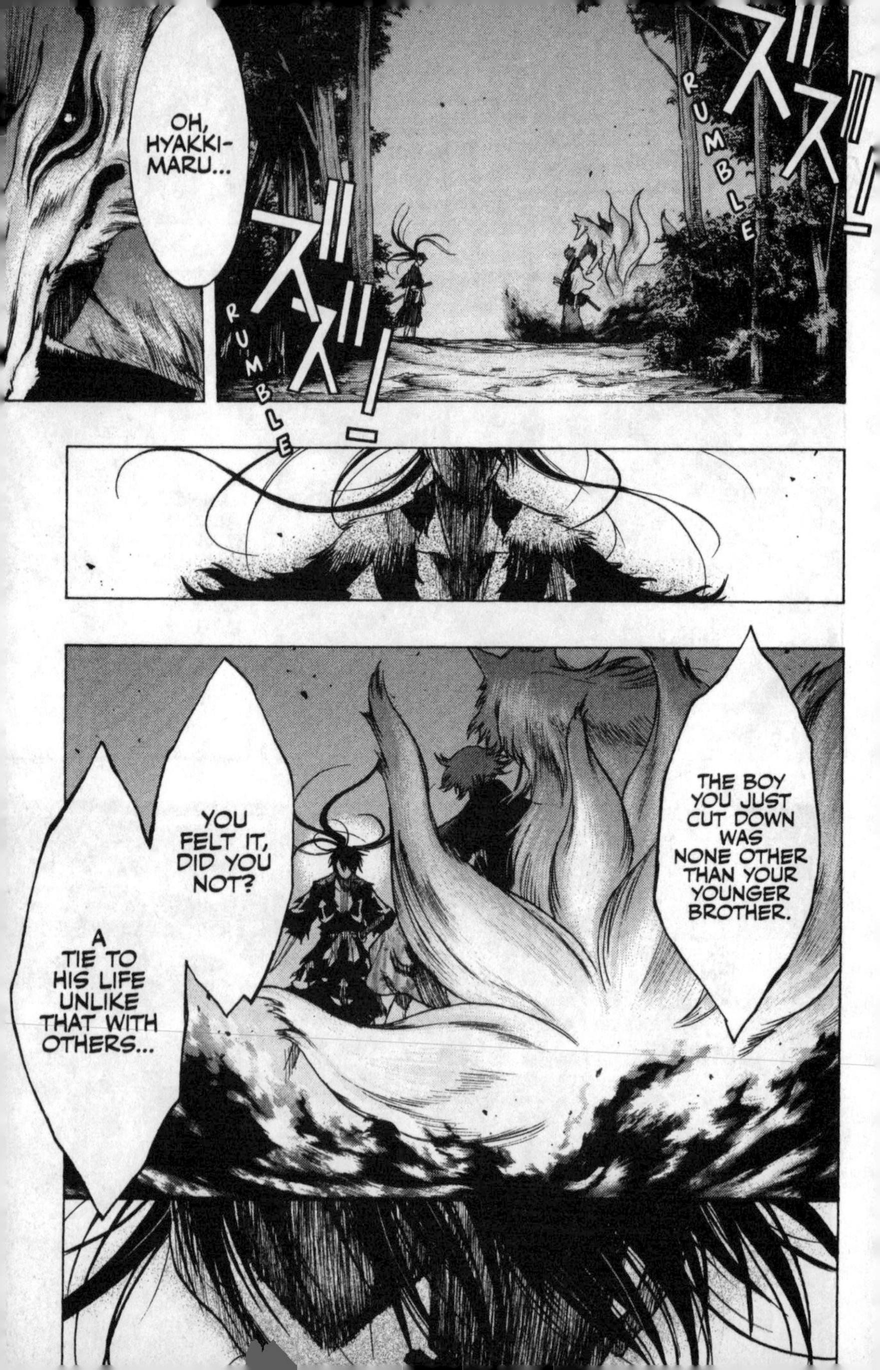

ズズー
RUMBLE
ズズー
RUMBLE
OH, HYAKKI-MARU...
THE BOY YOU JUST CUT DOWN WAS NONE OTHER THAN YOUR YOUNGER BROTHER.
YOU FELT IT, DID YOU NOT?
A TIE TO HIS LIFE UNLIKE THAT WITH OTHERS...

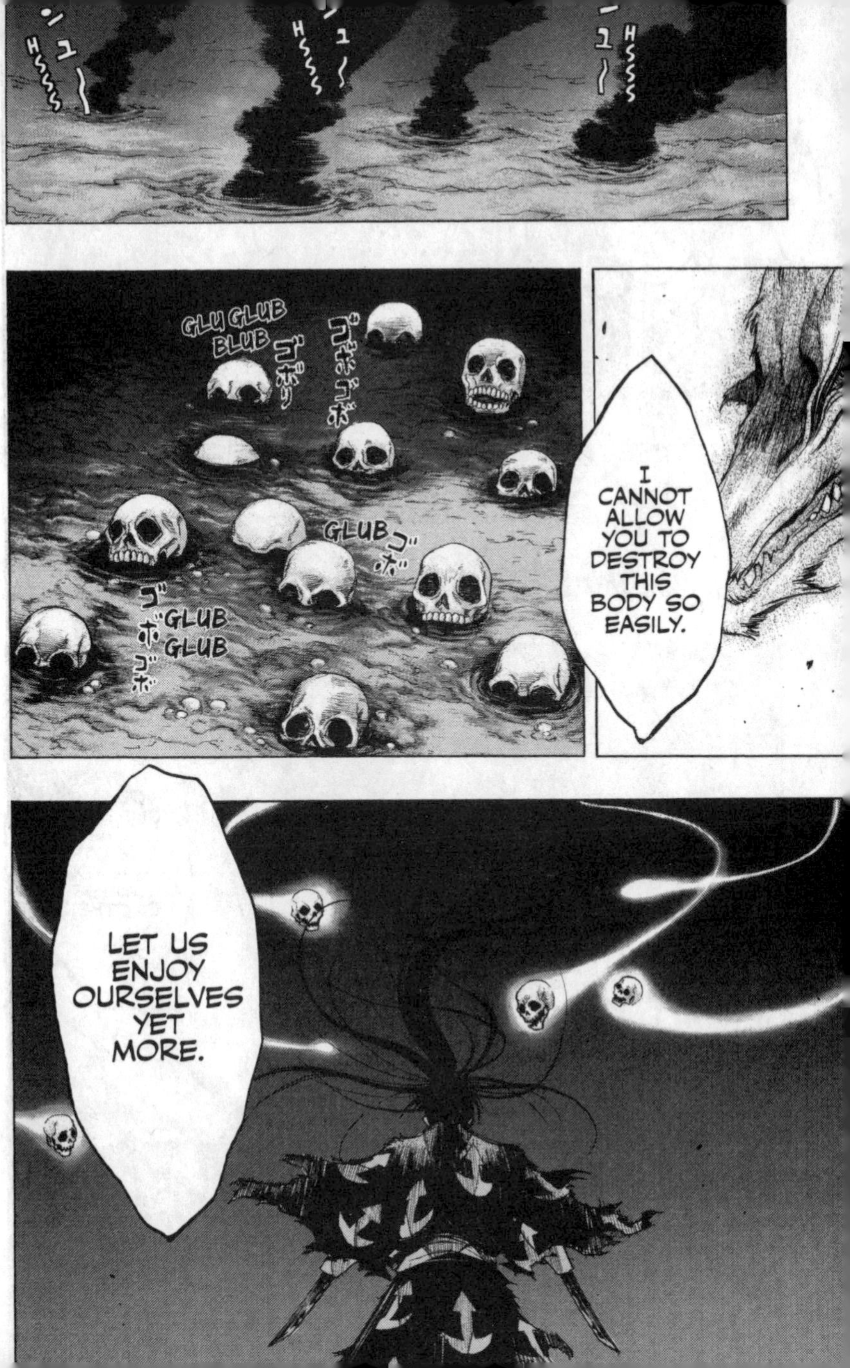
HSSSS
HSSSS
HSSSS
I CANNOT ALLOW YOU TO DESTROY THIS BODY SO EASILY.
ゴボゴボ
GLU GLUB BLUB
ゴボリ
GLUB
ゴボ
GLUB GLUB
ゴボゴボ
LET US ENJOY OURSELVES YET MORE.

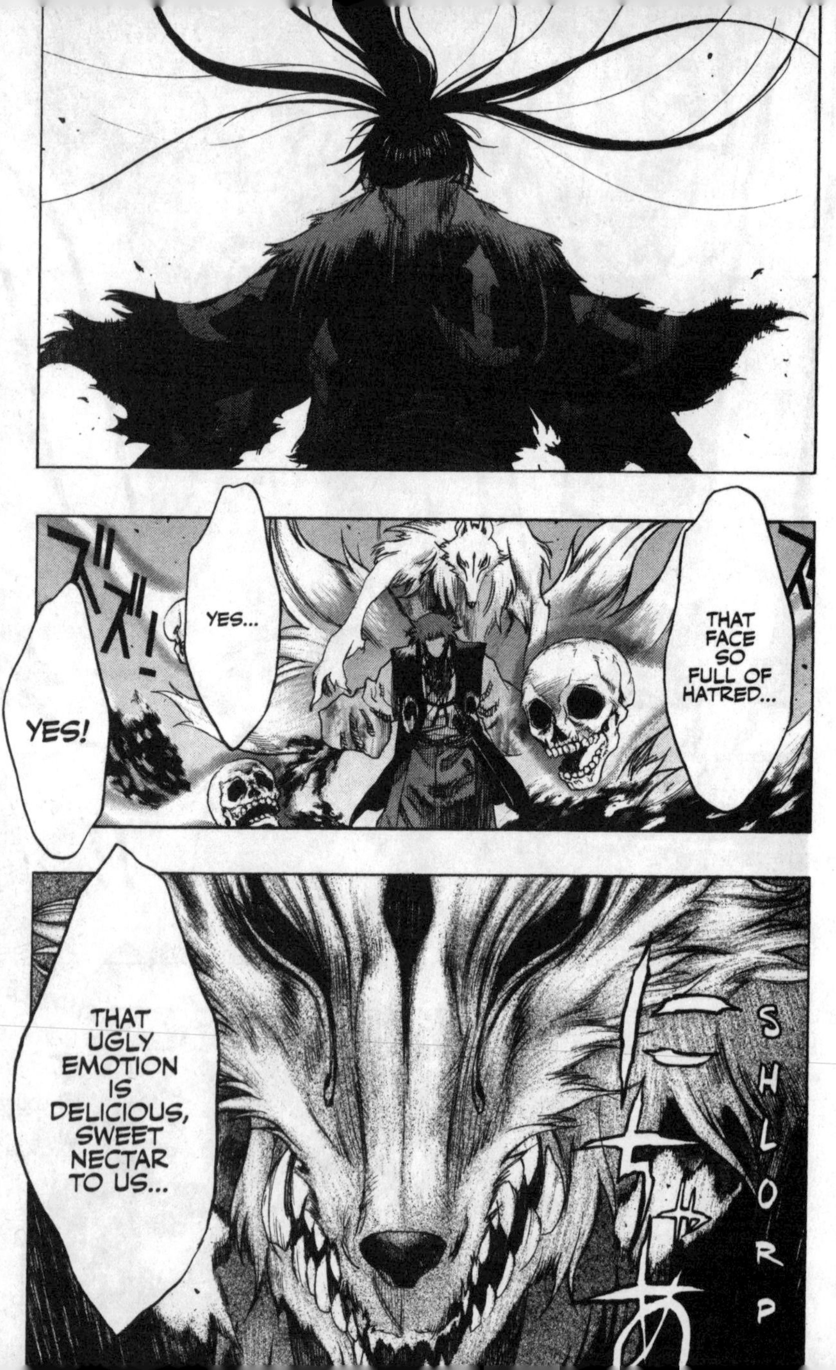
THAT FACE SO FULL OF HATRED...
YES...
YES!
SHLORP
THAT UGLY EMOTION IS DELICIOUS, SWEET NECTAR TO US...

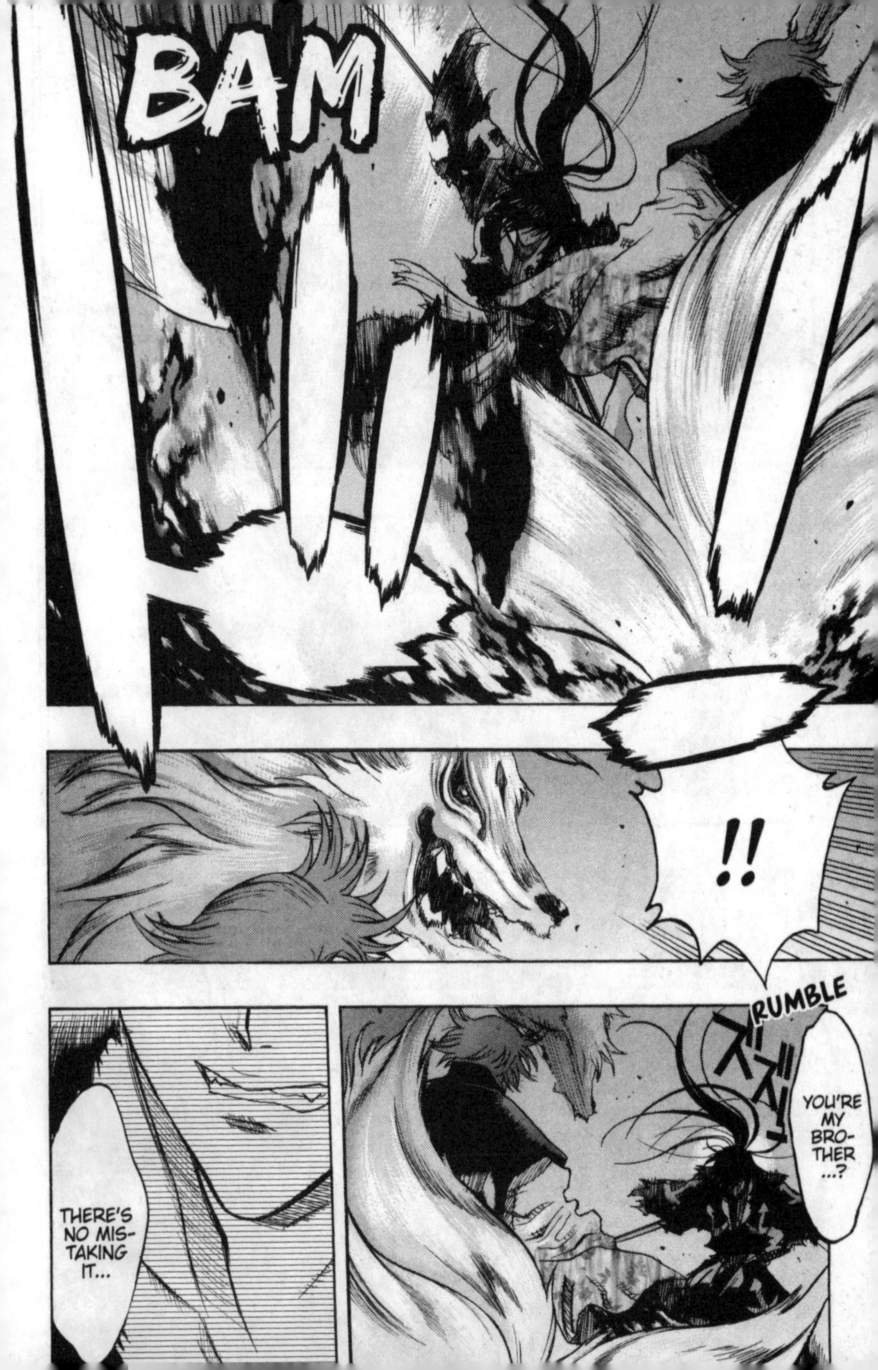
BAM
!!
RUMBLE
YOU'RE MY BRO-THER ...?
THERE'S NO MIS-TAKING IT...

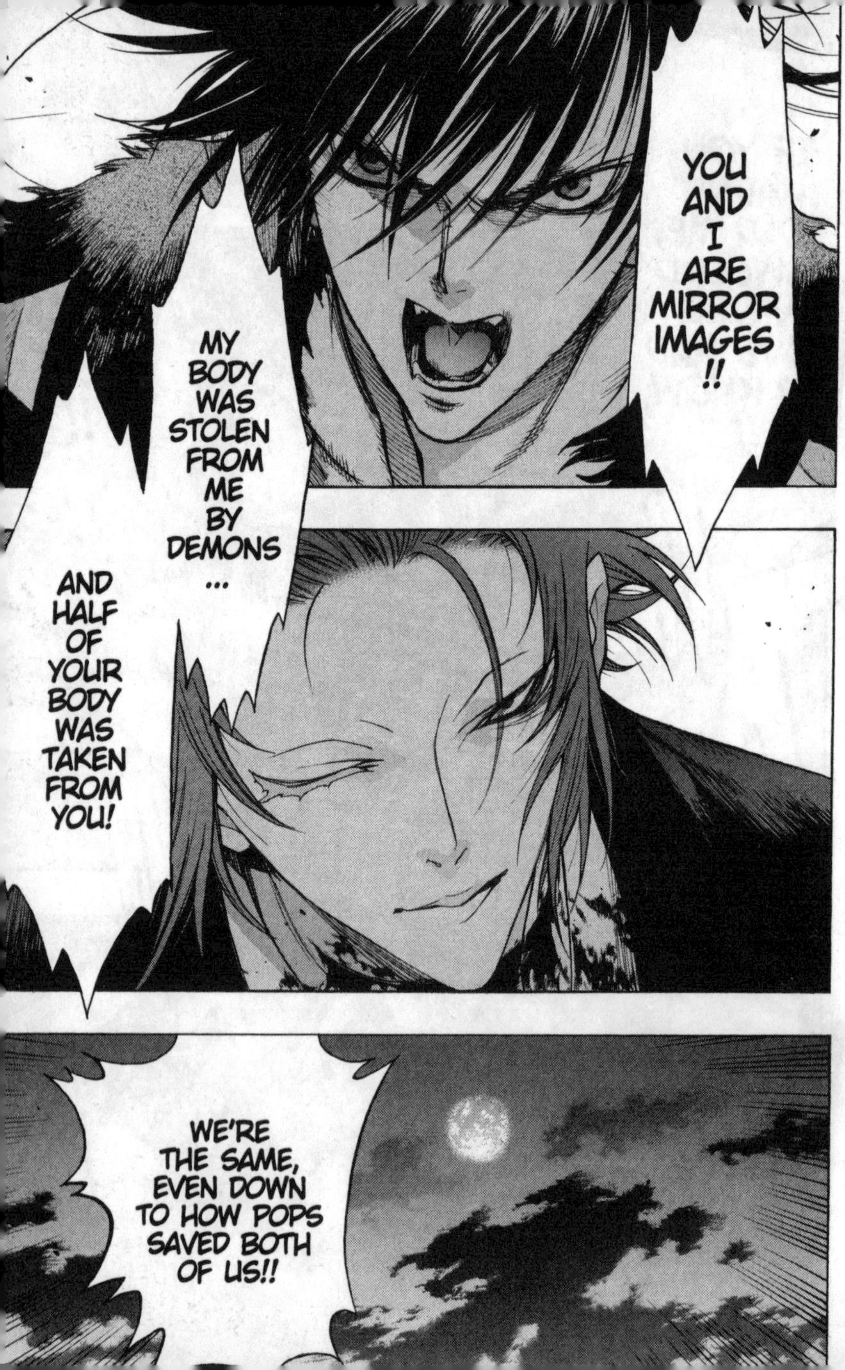
YOU AND I ARE MIRROR IMAGES!!
MY BODY WAS STOLEN FROM ME BY DEMONS...
AND HALF OF YOUR BODY WAS TAKEN FROM YOU!
WE'RE THE SAME, EVEN DOWN TO HOW POPS SAVED BOTH OF US!!

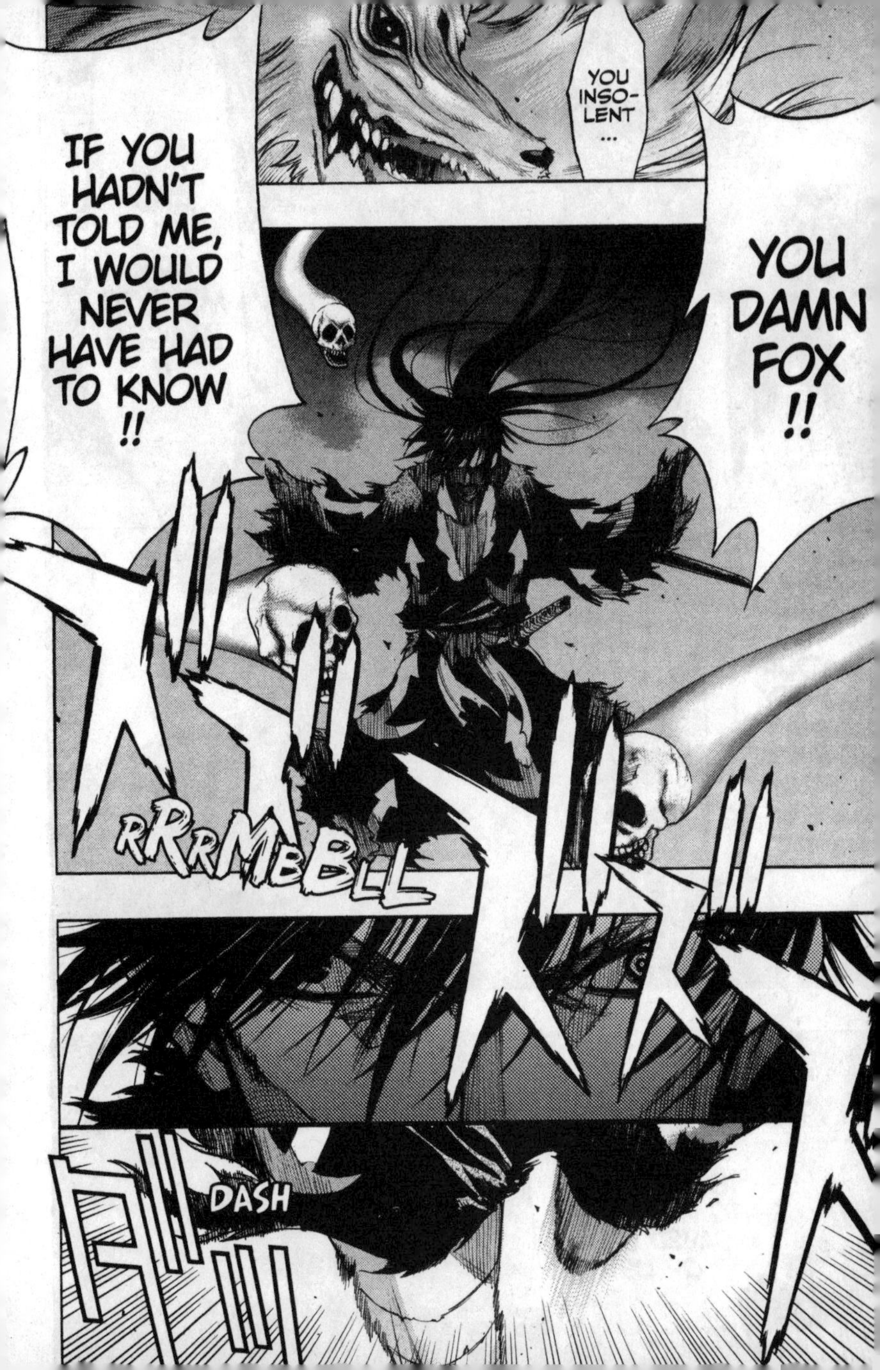
YOU INSO-LENT ...
YOU DAMN FOX !!
IF YOU HADN'T TOLD ME, I WOULD NEVER HAVE HAD TO KNOW !!
RRRMBBLL
DASH

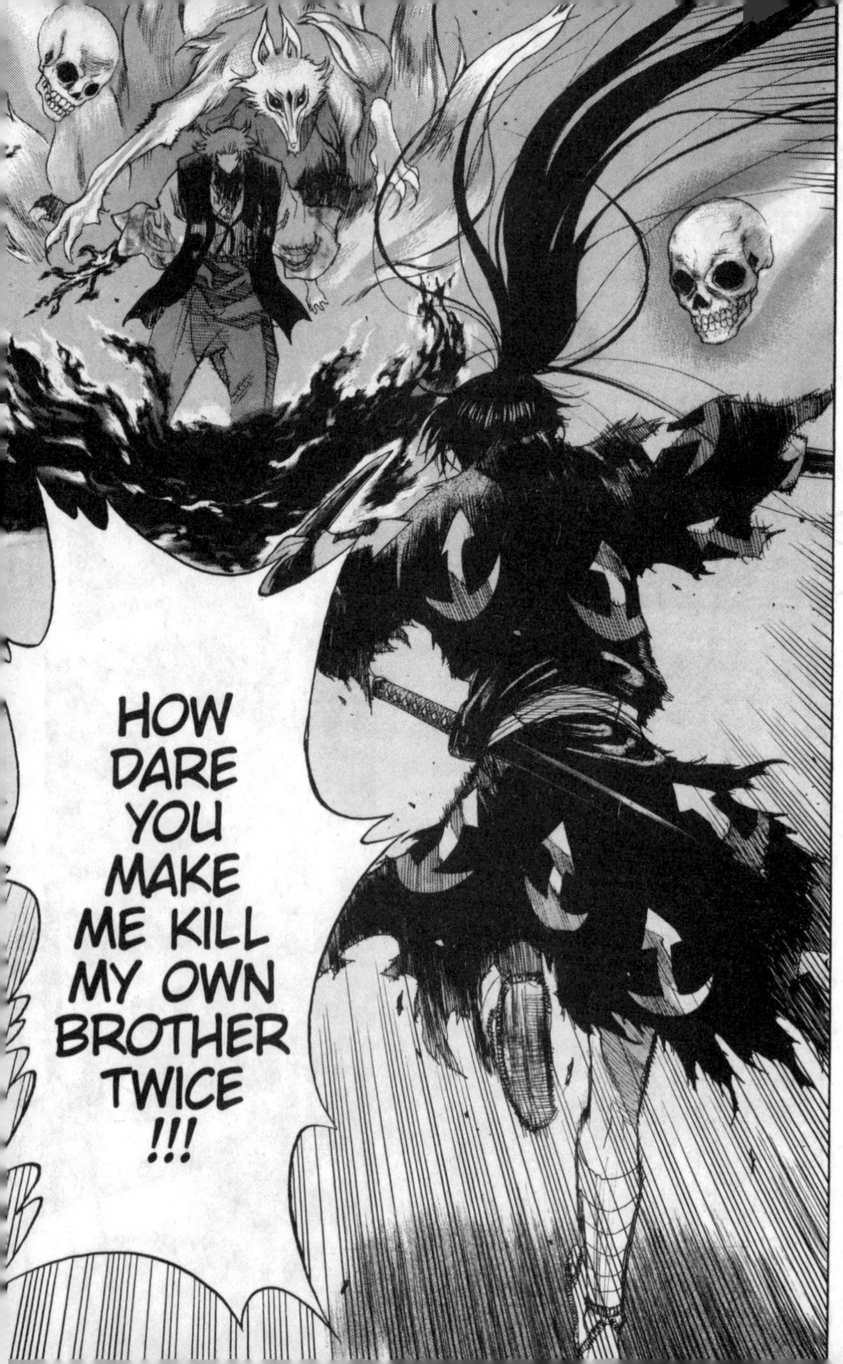
HOW DARE YOU MAKE ME KILL MY OWN BROTHER TWICE !!!

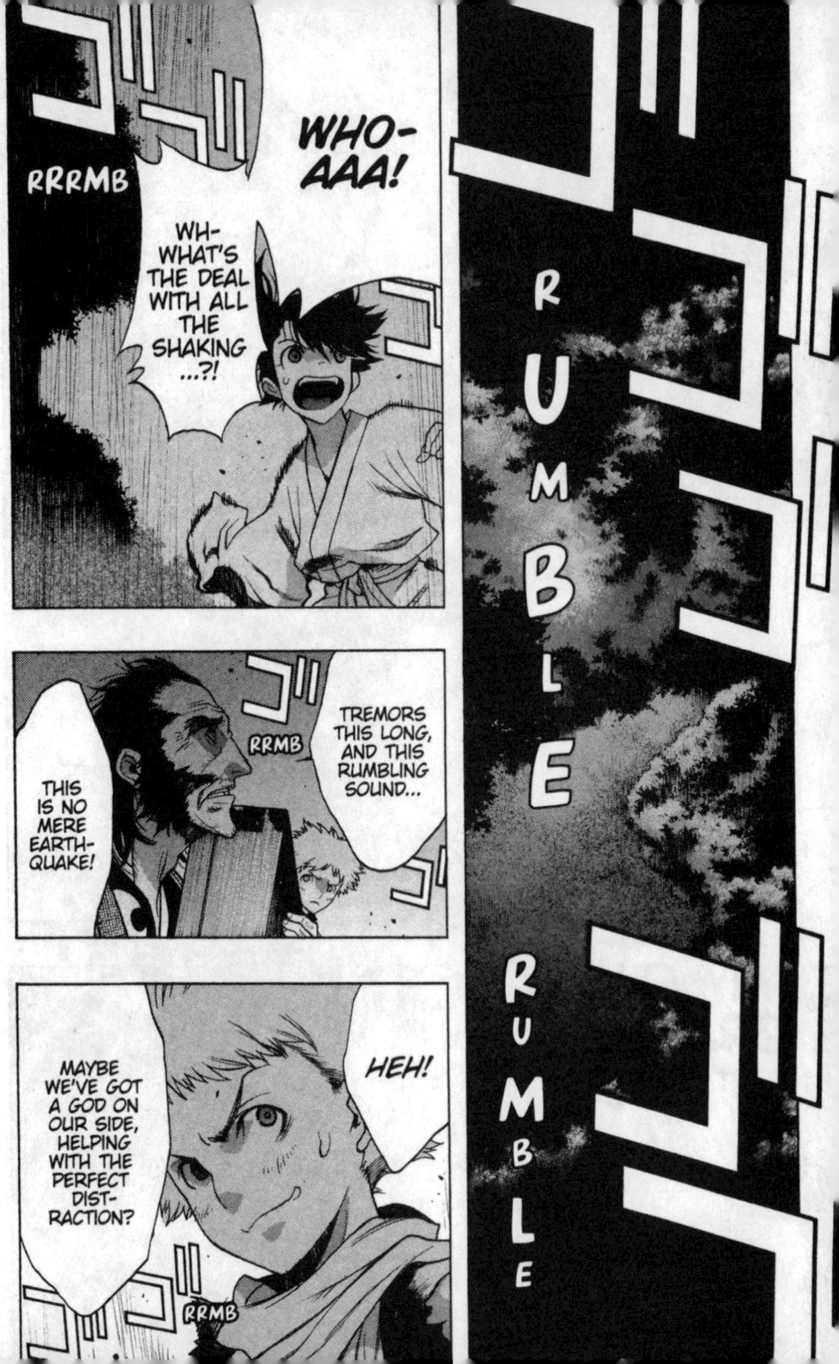
RUMBLE
RUMBLE
WHO-AAA!
RRRMB
WH-WHAT'S THE DEAL WITH ALL THE SHAKING ...?!
TREMORS THIS LONG, AND THIS RUMBLING SOUND...
RRMB
THIS IS NO MERE EARTHQUAKE!
HEH!
MAYBE WE'VE GOT A GOD ON OUR SIDE, HELPING WITH THE PERFECT DISTRACTION?
RRMB

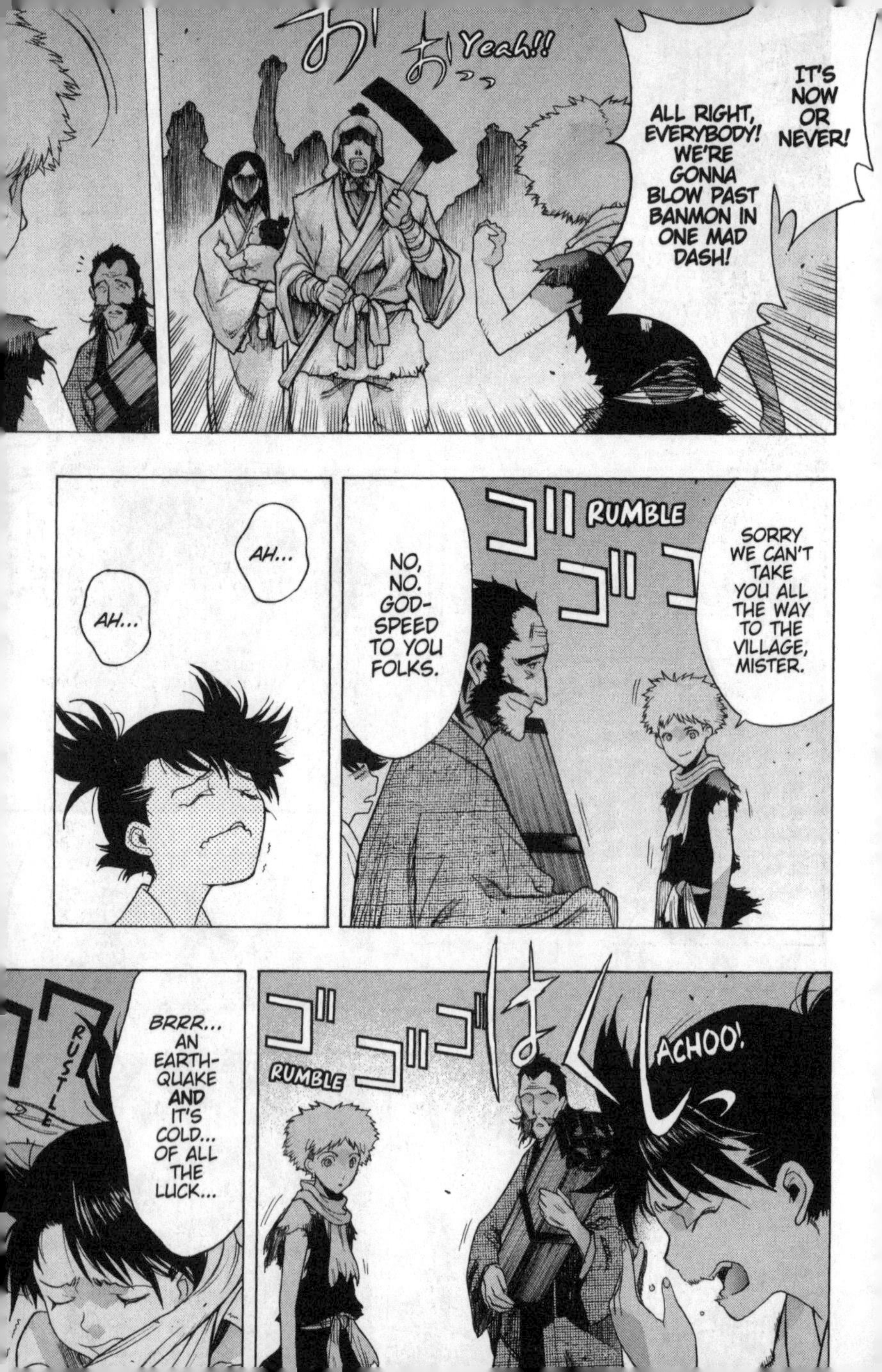
IT'S NOW OR NEVER!
ALL RIGHT, EVERYBODY! WE'RE GONNA BLOW PAST BANMON IN ONE MAD DASH!
Yeah!!
SORRY WE CAN'T TAKE YOU ALL THE WAY TO THE VILLAGE, MISTER.
RUMBLE
NO, NO. GOD-SPEED TO YOU FOLKS.
AH...
AH...
ACHOO!
RUMBLE
BRRR... AN EARTH-QUAKE AND IT'S COLD... OF ALL THE LUCK...
RUSTLE

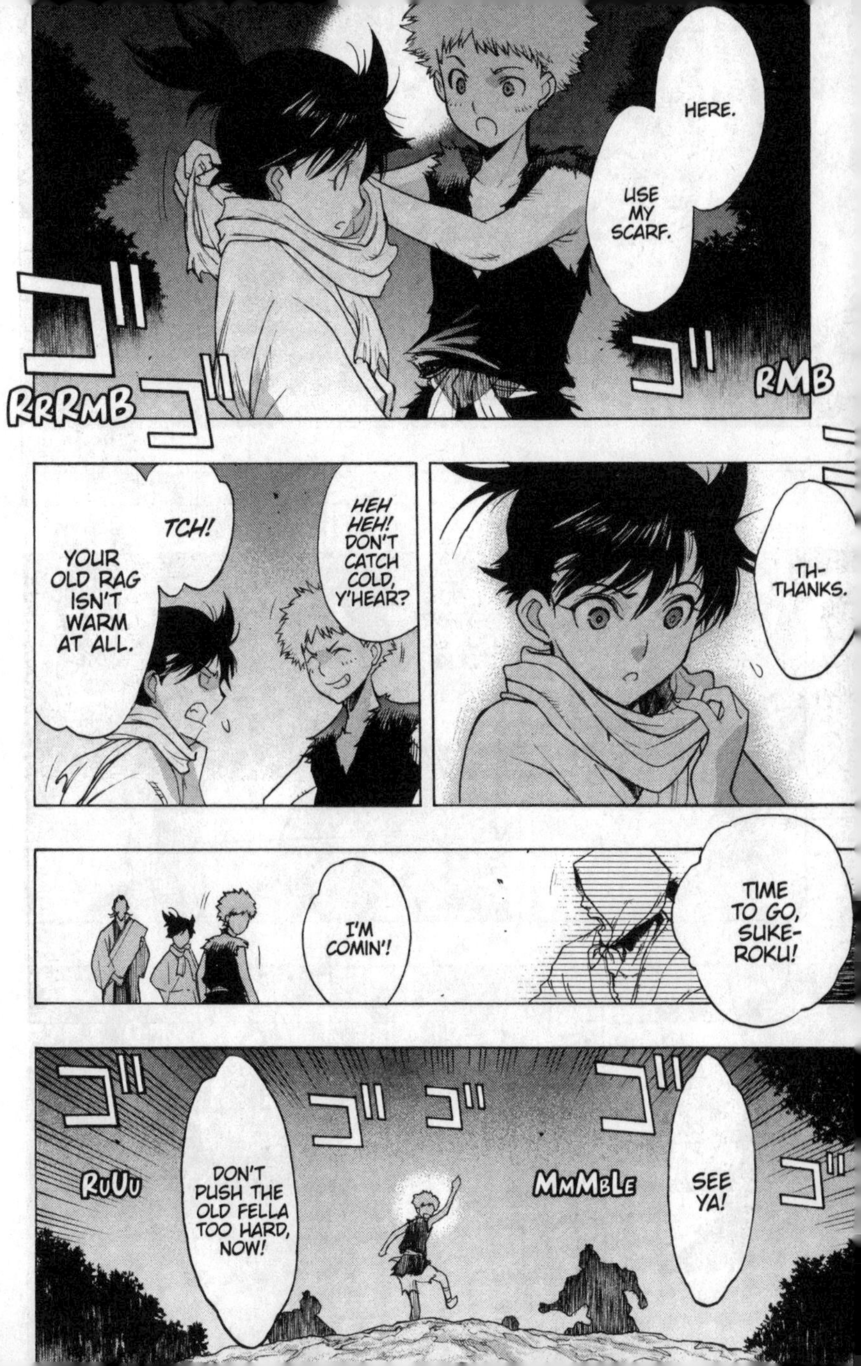
HERE.
USE MY SCARF.
RMB
RRRMB
TH- THANKS.
HEH HEH! DON'T CATCH COLD, Y'HEAR?
TCH! YOUR OLD RAG ISN'T WARM AT ALL.
TIME TO GO, SUKE-ROKU!
I'M COMIN'!
SEE YA!
MMMBLE
DON'T PUSH THE OLD FELLA TOO HARD, NOW!
RUUU

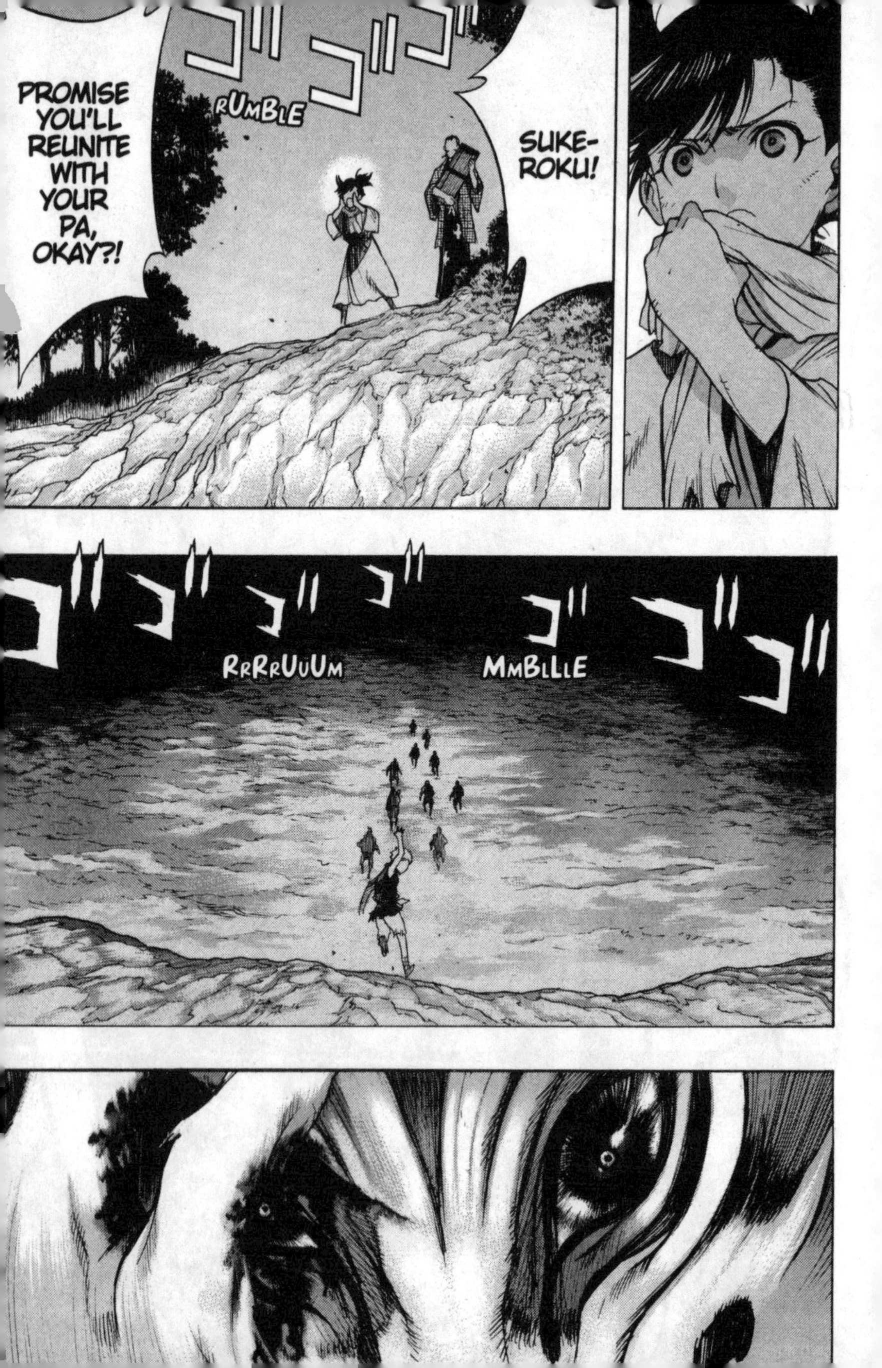
SUKE-ROKU!
RUMBLE
PROMISE YOU'LL REUNITE WITH YOUR PA, OKAY?!
RRRRUUUM
MMBLLLE

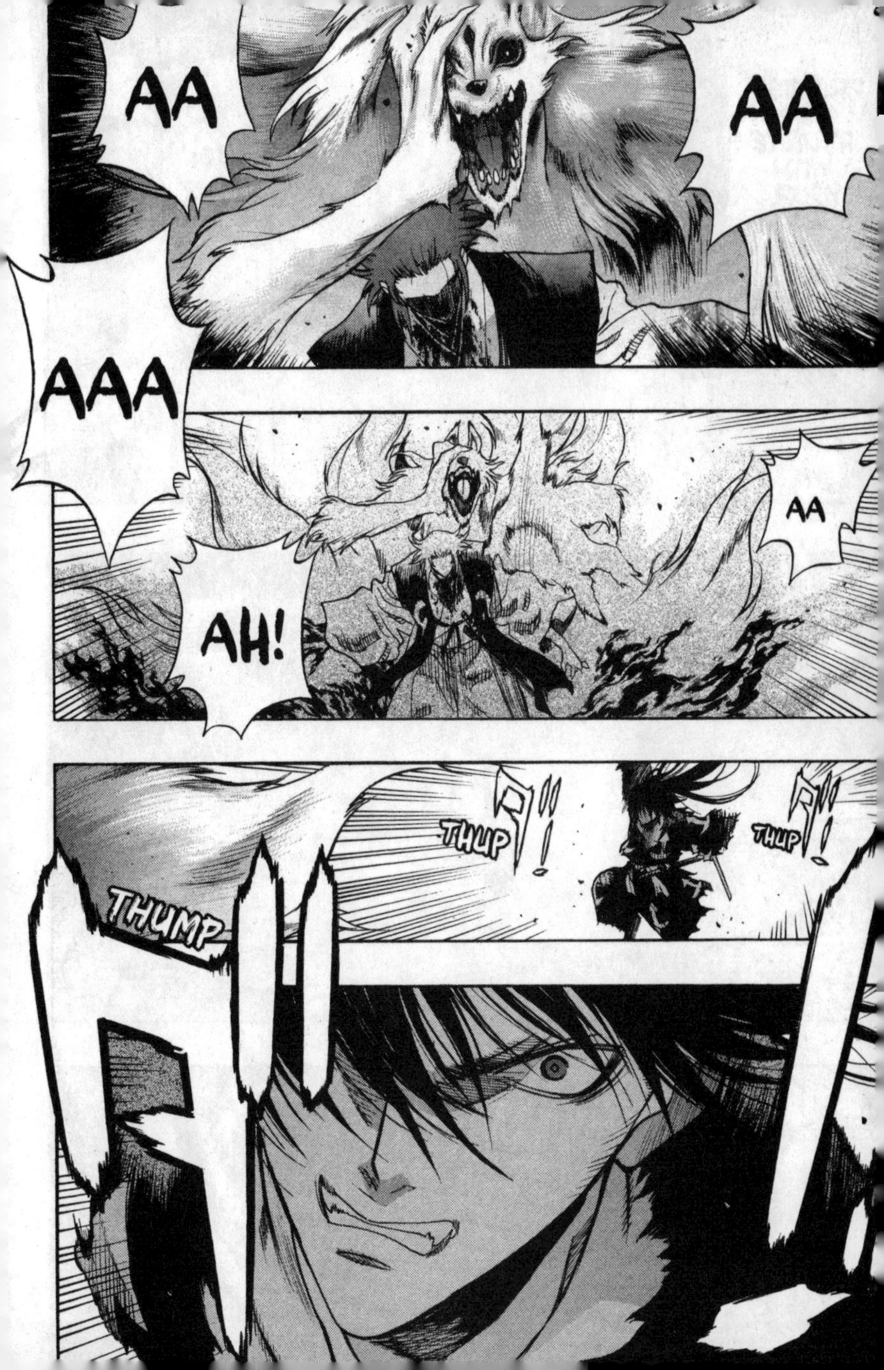
AA
AA
AAA
AA
AH!
THUP
THUP
THUMP

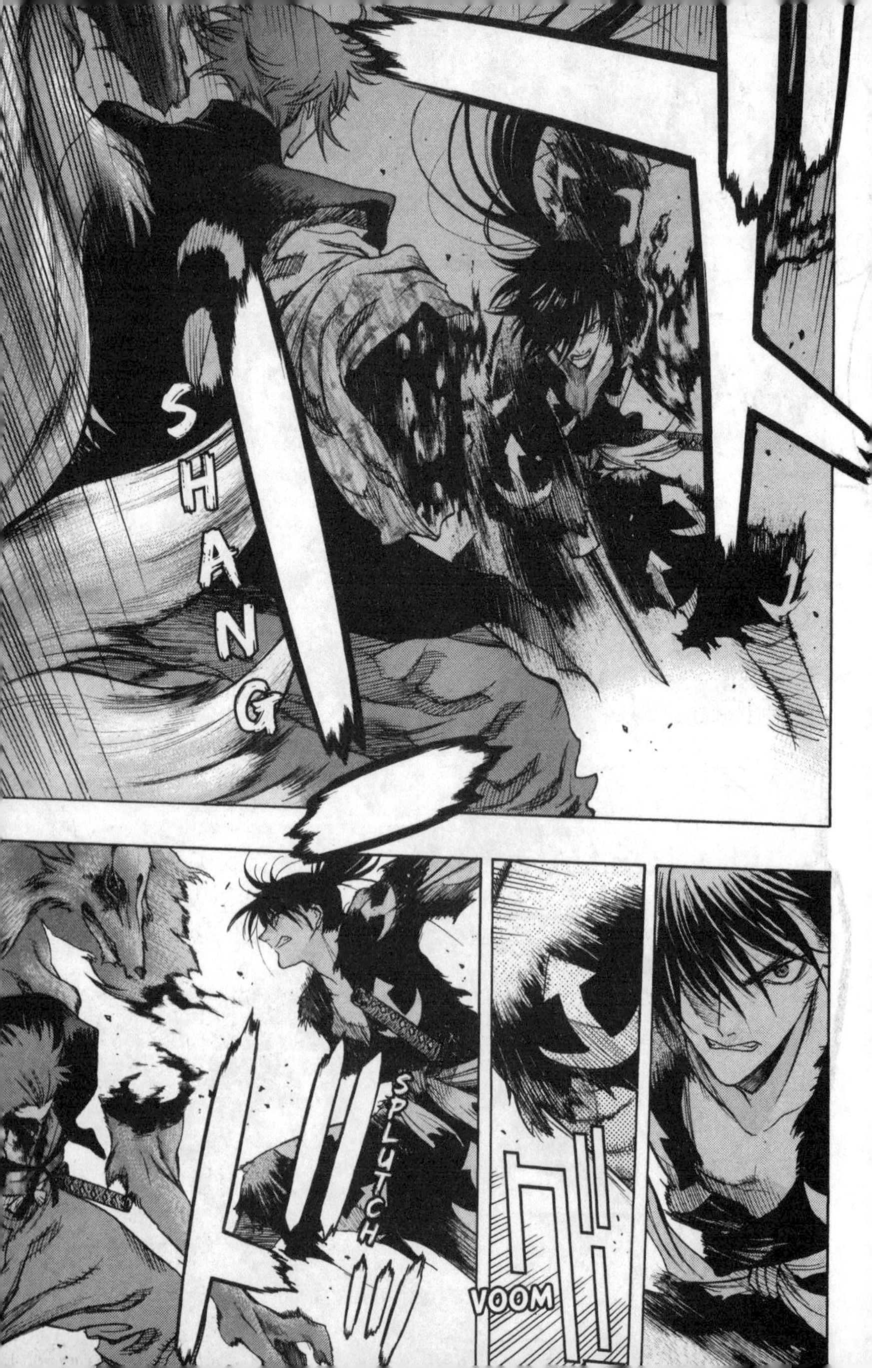
SHANG
VOOM
SPLUTCH

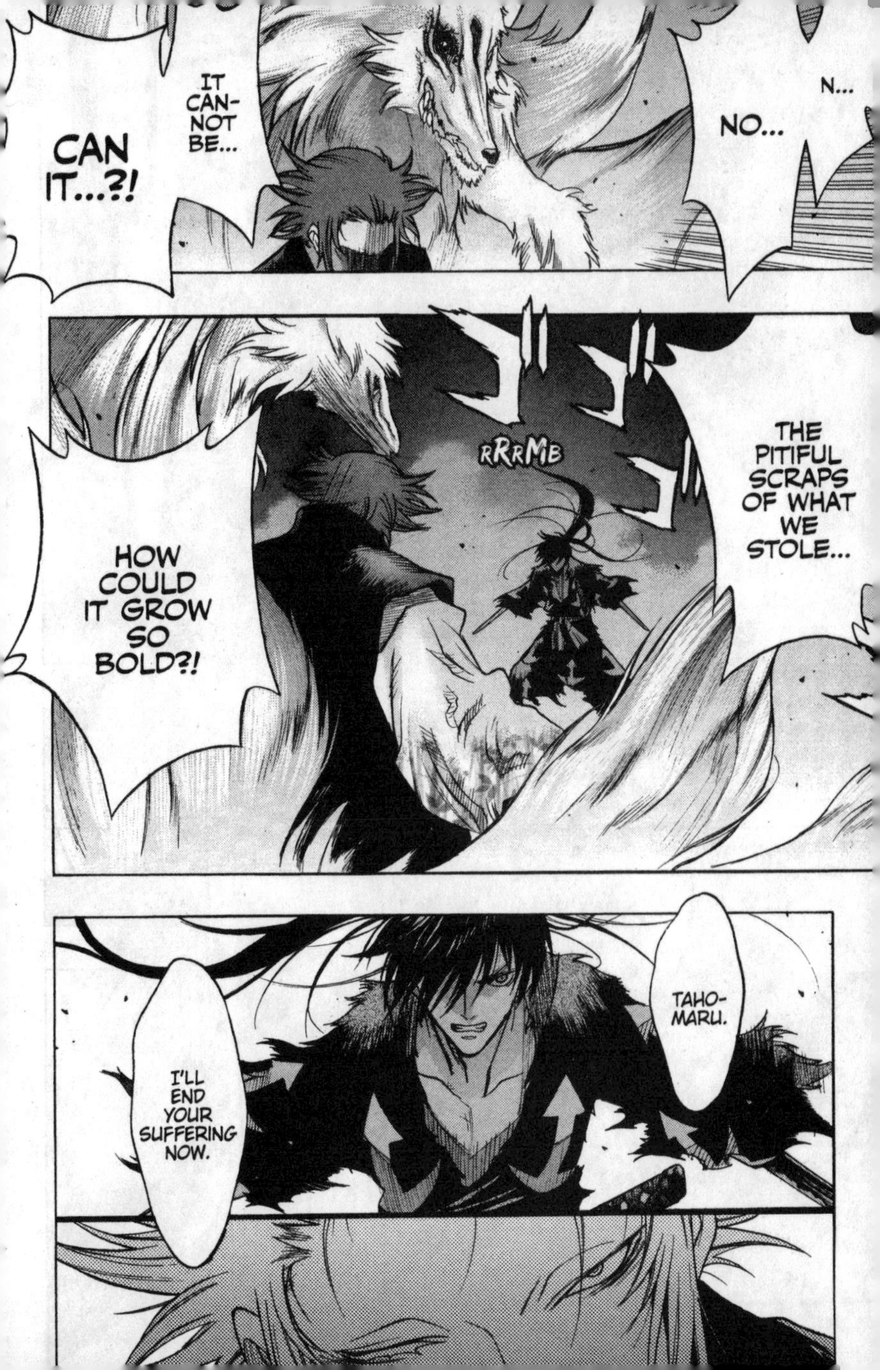
N...
NO...
IT CAN-NOT BE...
CAN IT...?!
THE PITIFUL SCRAPS OF WHAT WE STOLE...
RRRMB
HOW COULD IT GROW SO BOLD?!
TAHO-MARU.
I'LL END YOUR SUFFERING NOW.

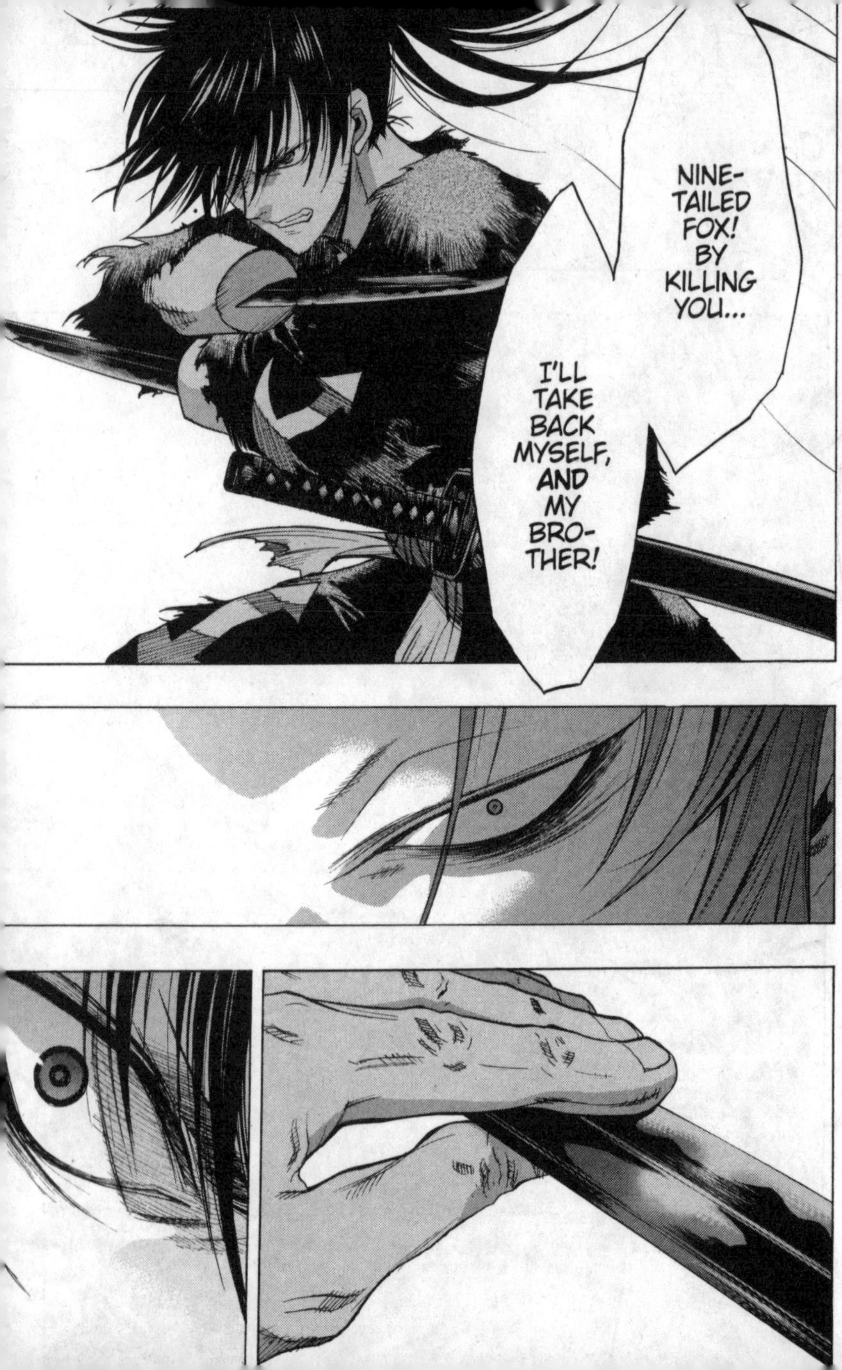
NINE-TAILED FOX! BY KILLING YOU...
I'LL TAKE BACK MYSELF, AND MY BROTHER!

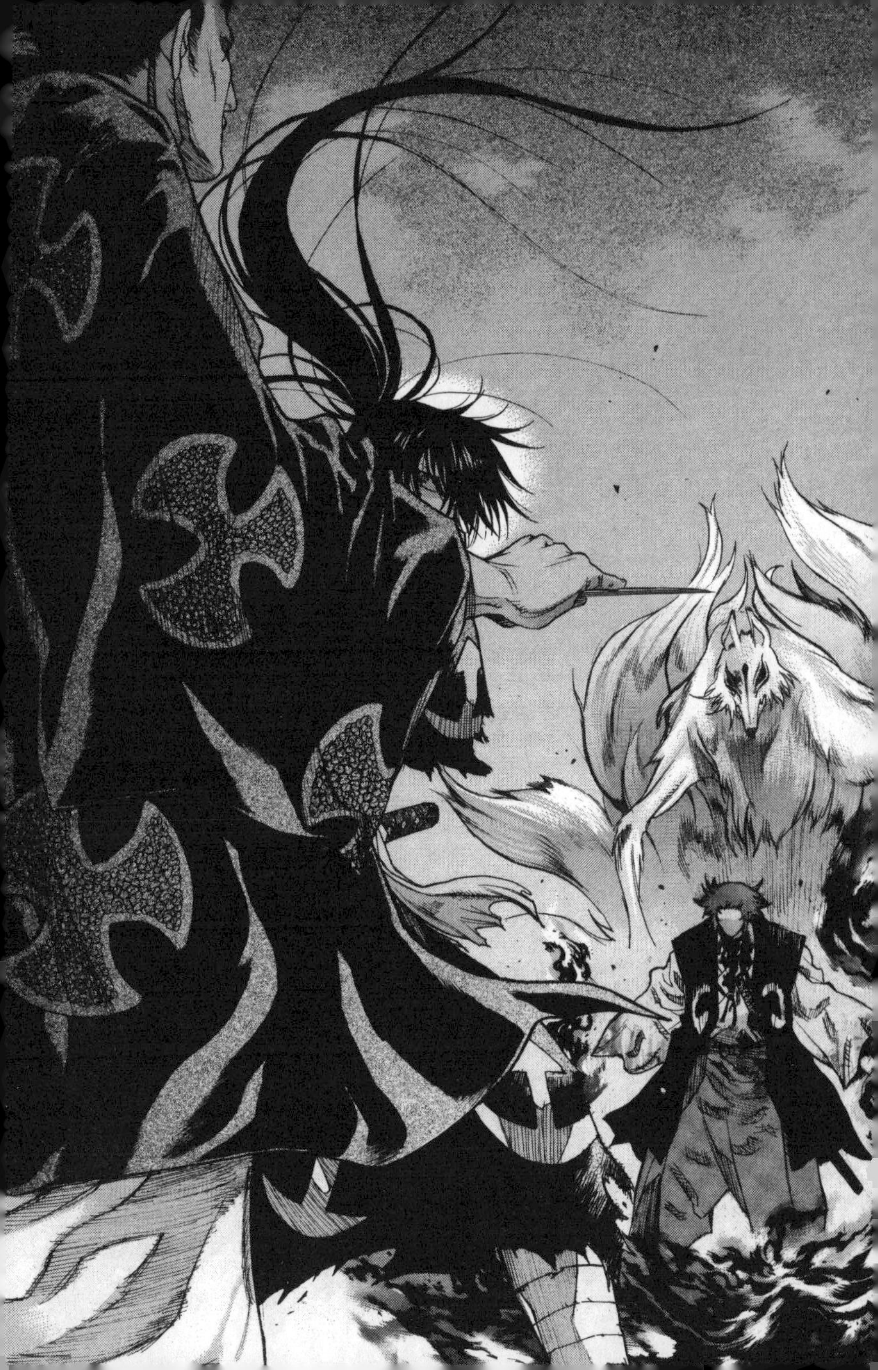

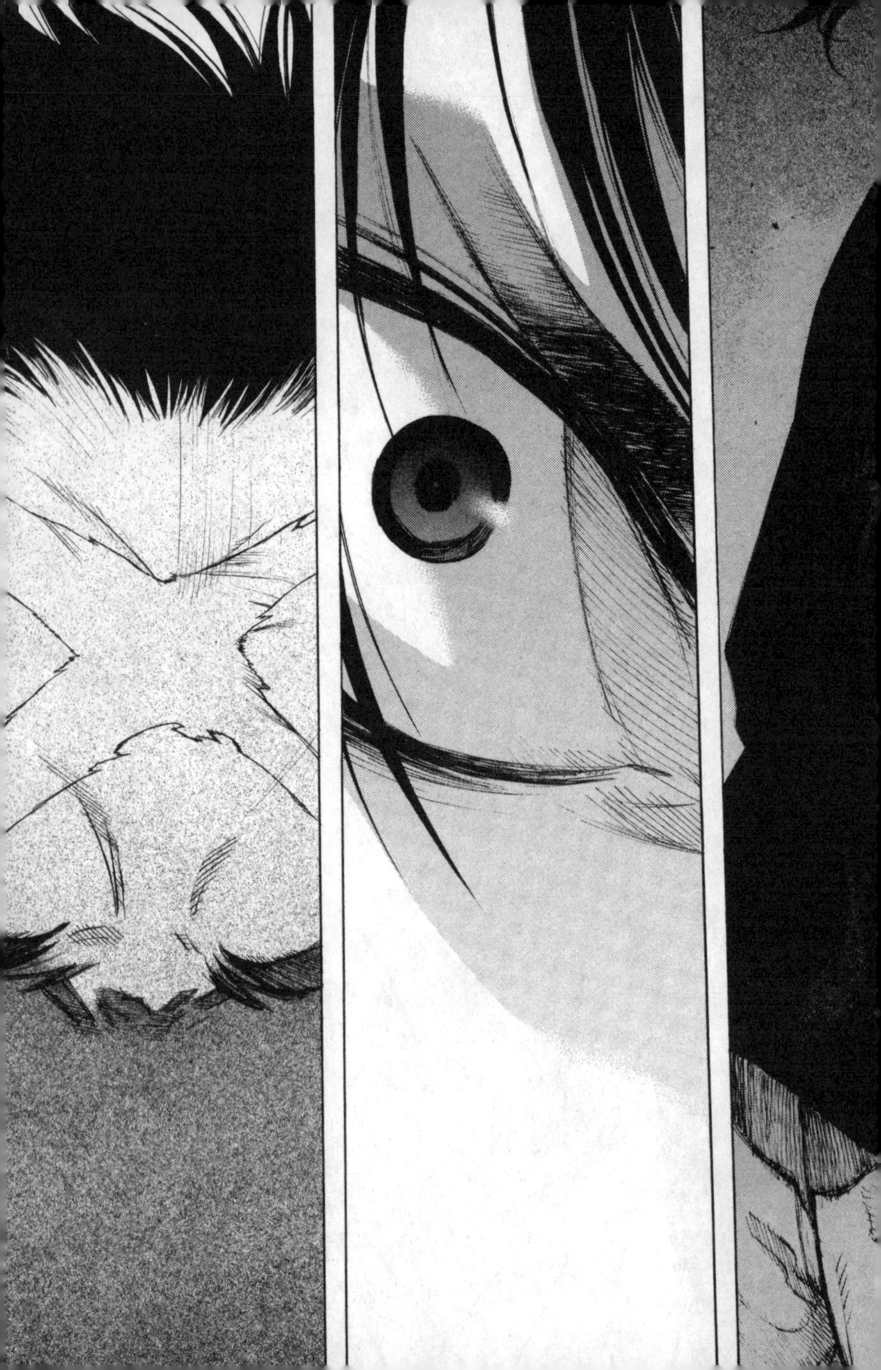

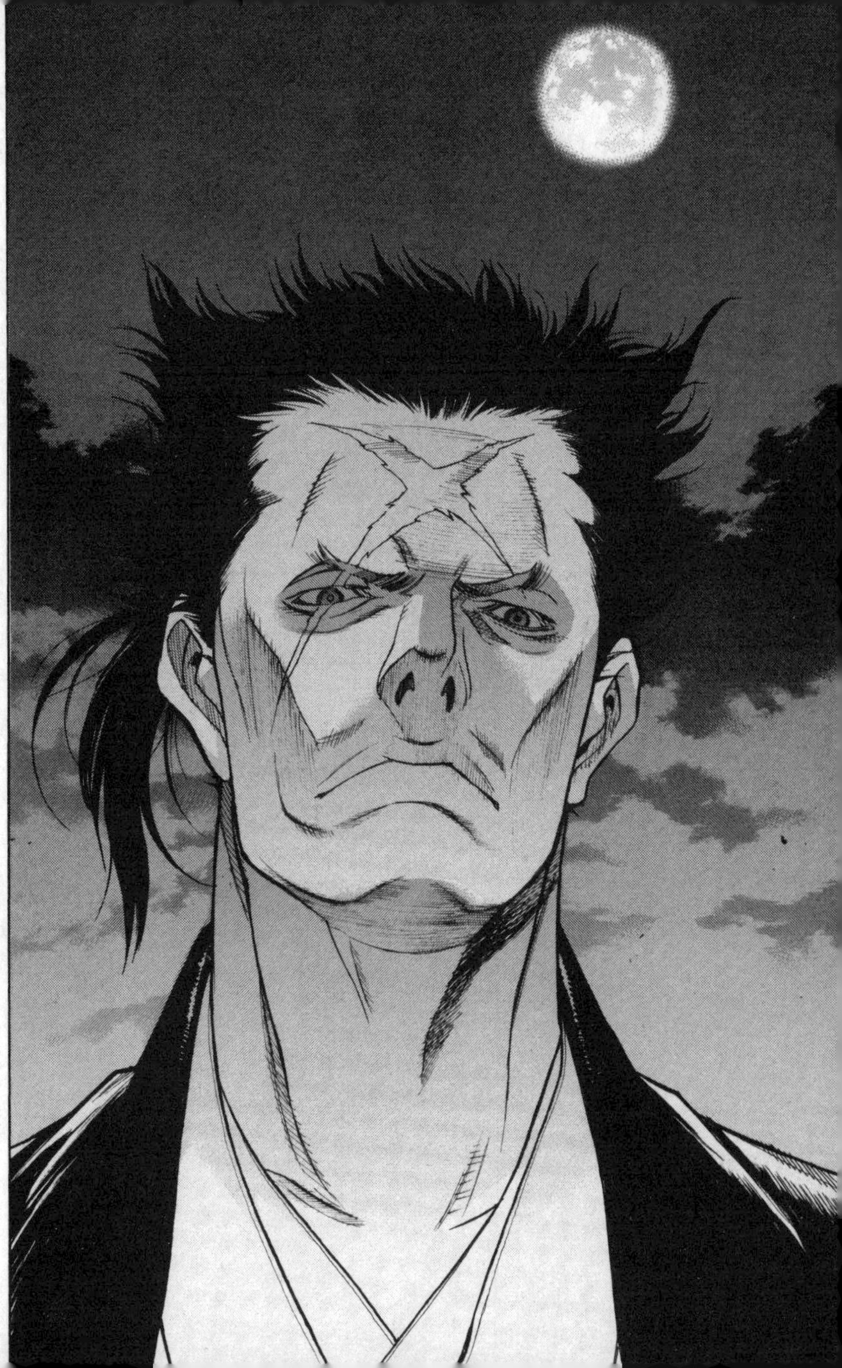

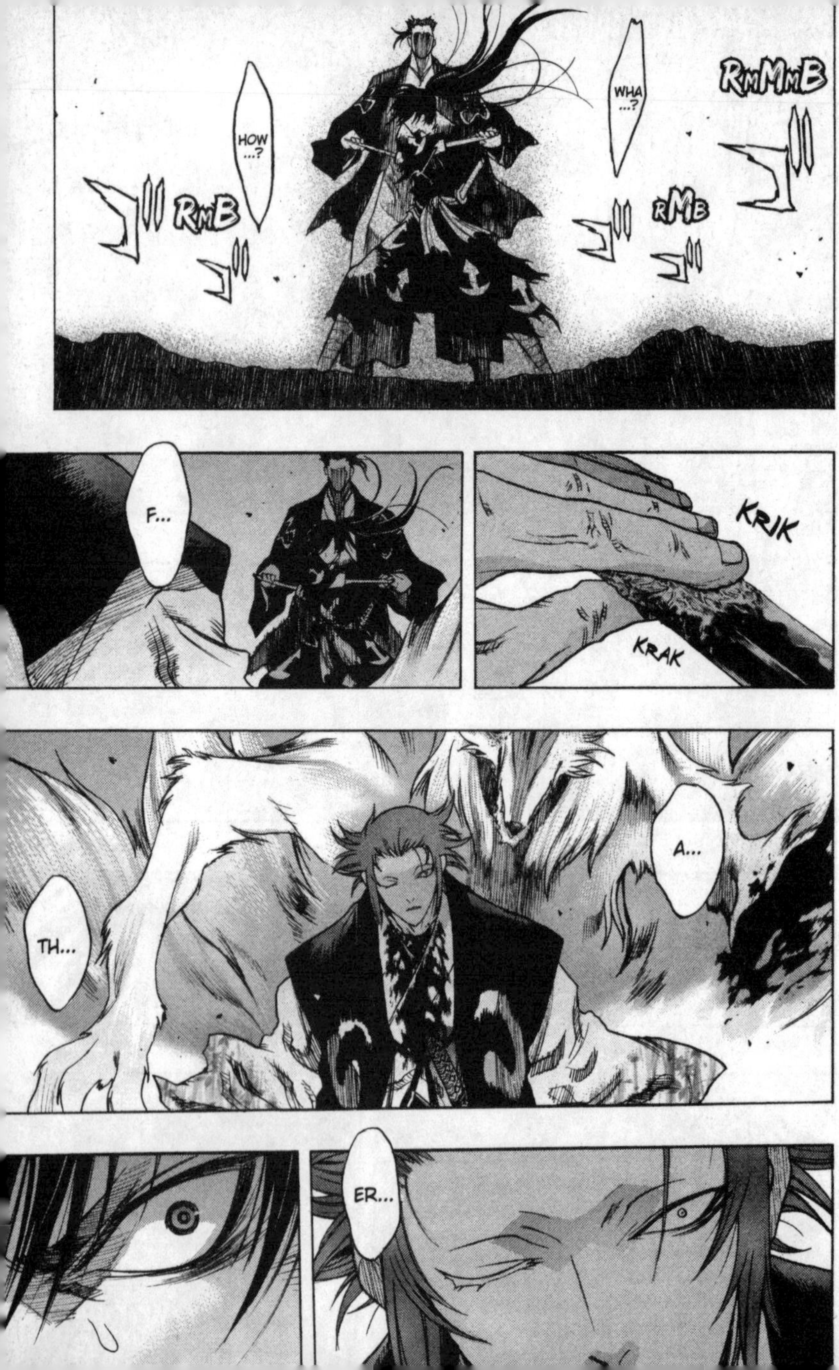
RMMMB
WHA ...?
RMB
HOW ...?
RMB
KRIK
KRAK
F...
A...
TH...
ER...

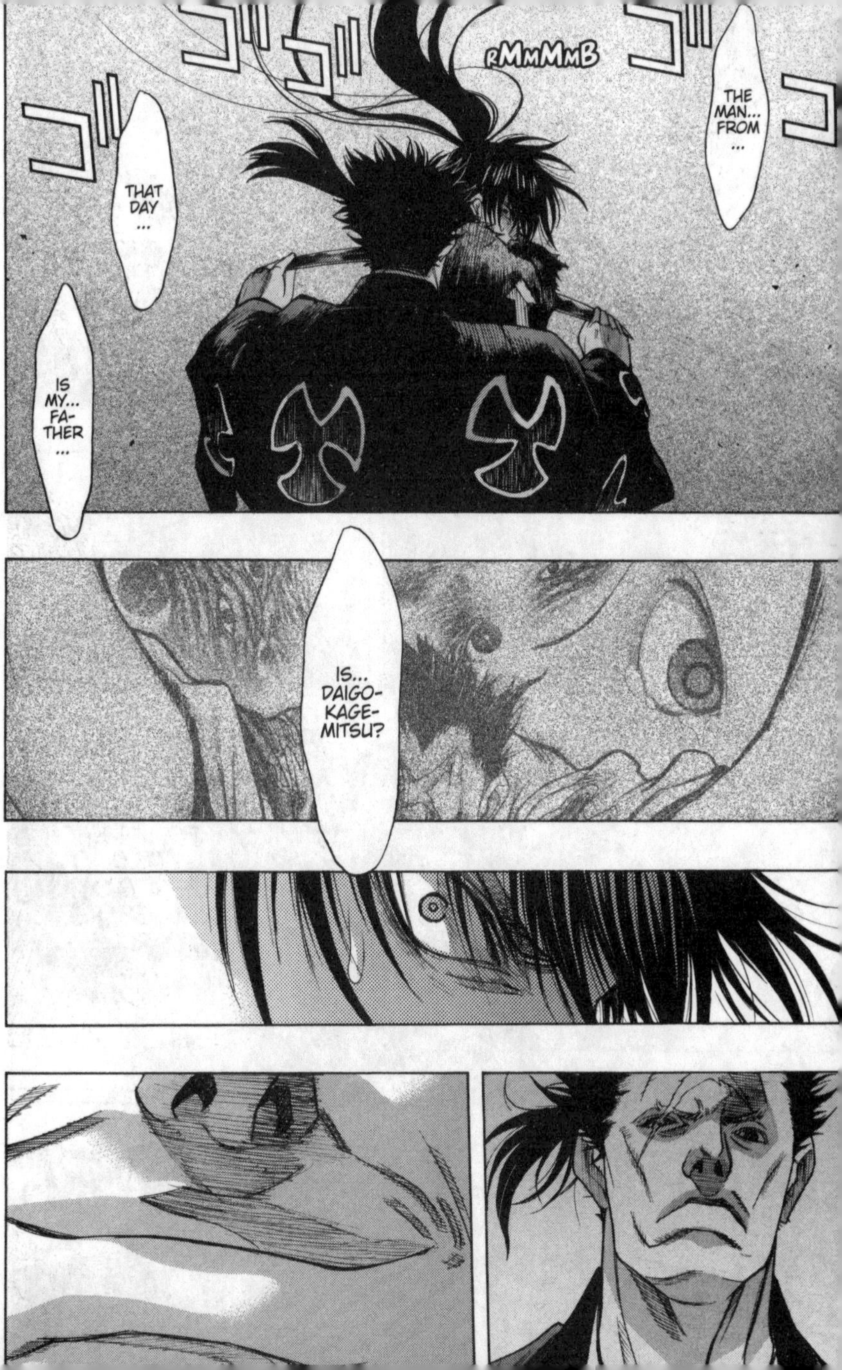
rMMMMB
THE MAN... FROM ...
THAT DAY ...
IS MY... FA-THER ...
IS... DAIGO-KAGE-MITSU?

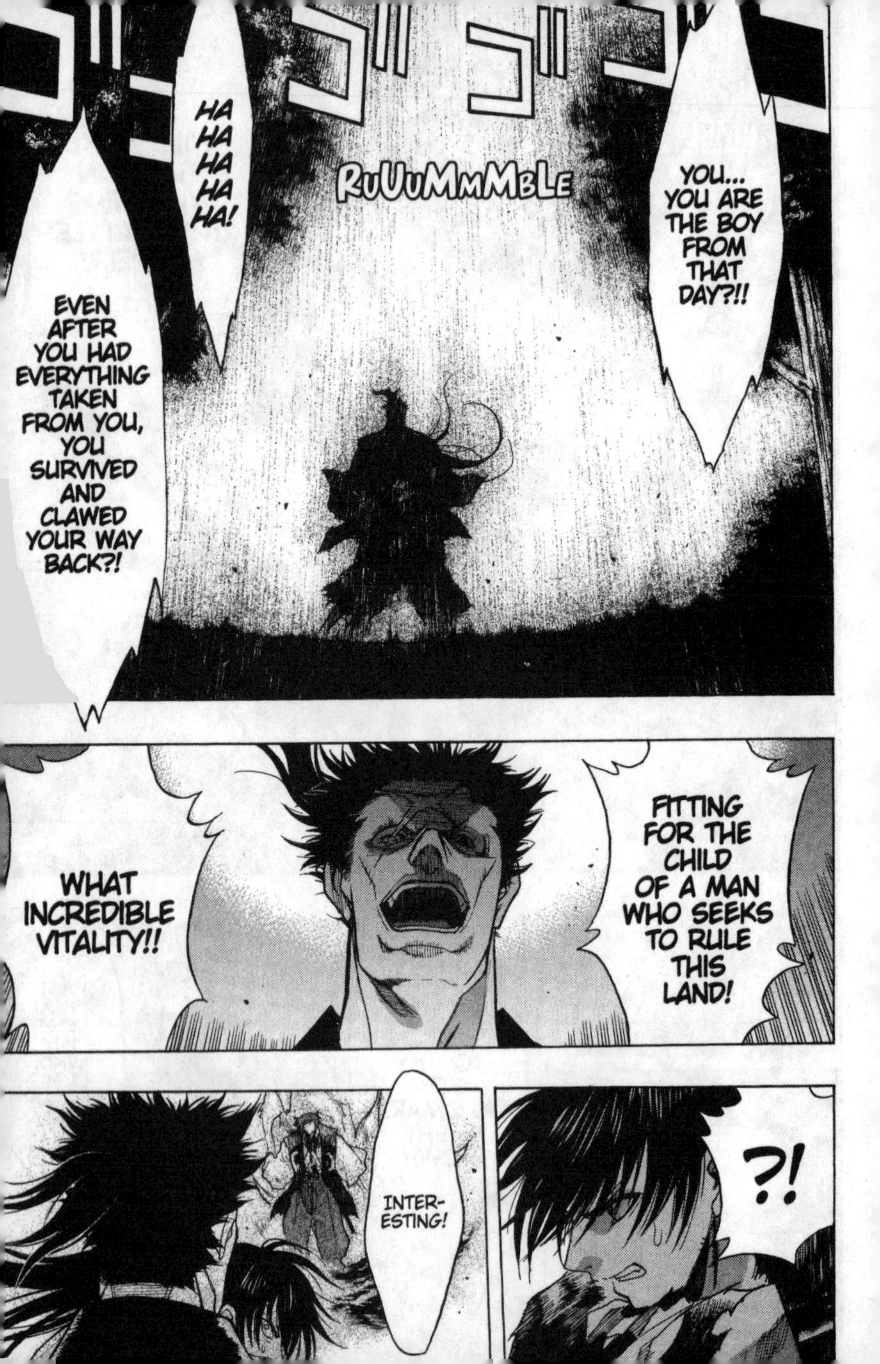
YOU... YOU ARE THE BOY FROM THAT DAY?!!
HA HA HA HA HA!
RUUUMMMBLE
EVEN AFTER YOU HAD EVERYTHING TAKEN FROM YOU, YOU SURVIVED AND CLAWED YOUR WAY BACK?!
FITTING FOR THE CHILD OF A MAN WHO SEEKS TO RULE THIS LAND!
WHAT INCREDIBLE VITALITY!!
?!
INTER-ESTING!

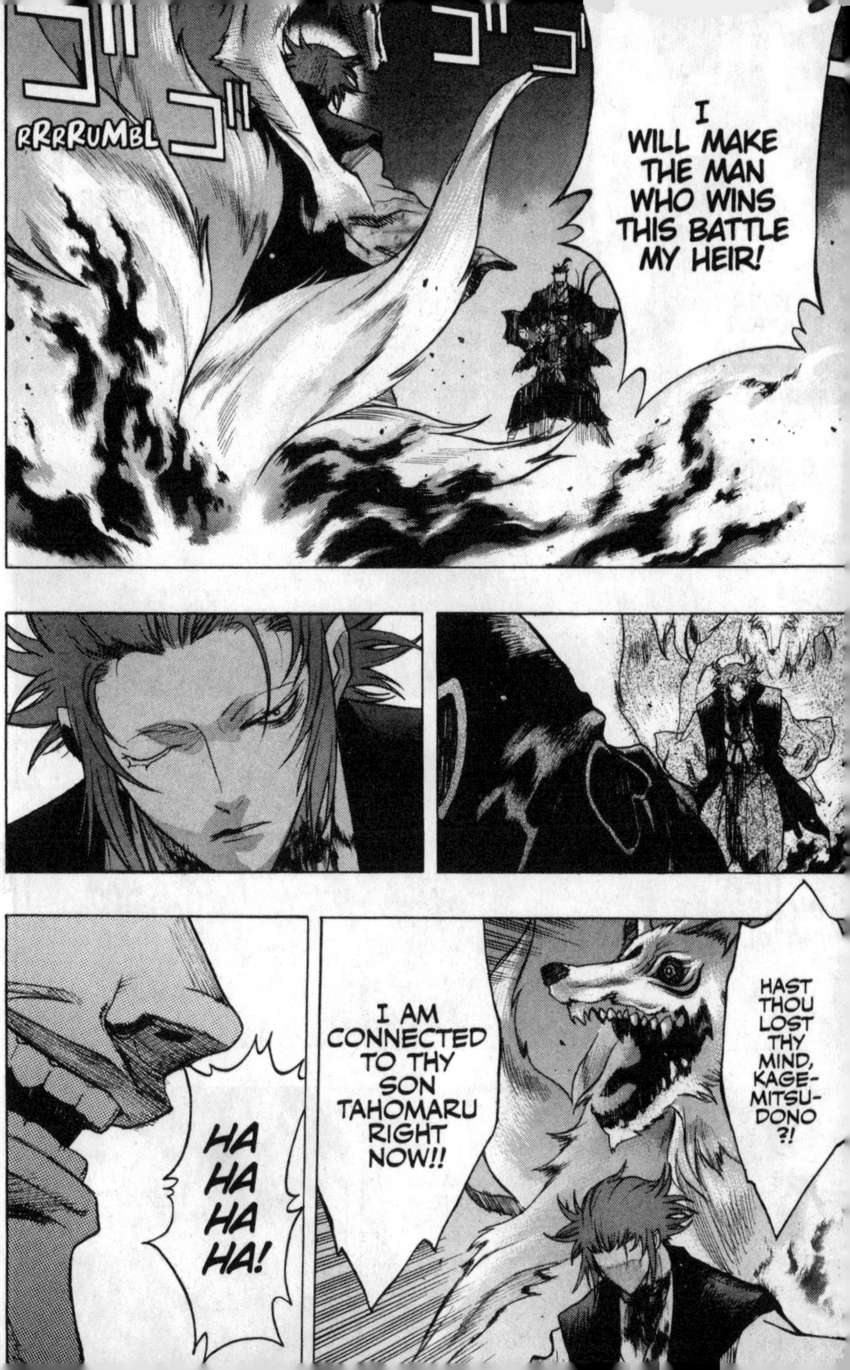
I WILL MAKE THE MAN WHO WINS THIS BATTLE MY HEIR!
RRRRUMBL
HAST THOU LOST THY MIND, KAGE-MITSU-DONO?!
I AM CONNECTED TO THY SON TAHOMARU RIGHT NOW!!
HA HA HA HA!

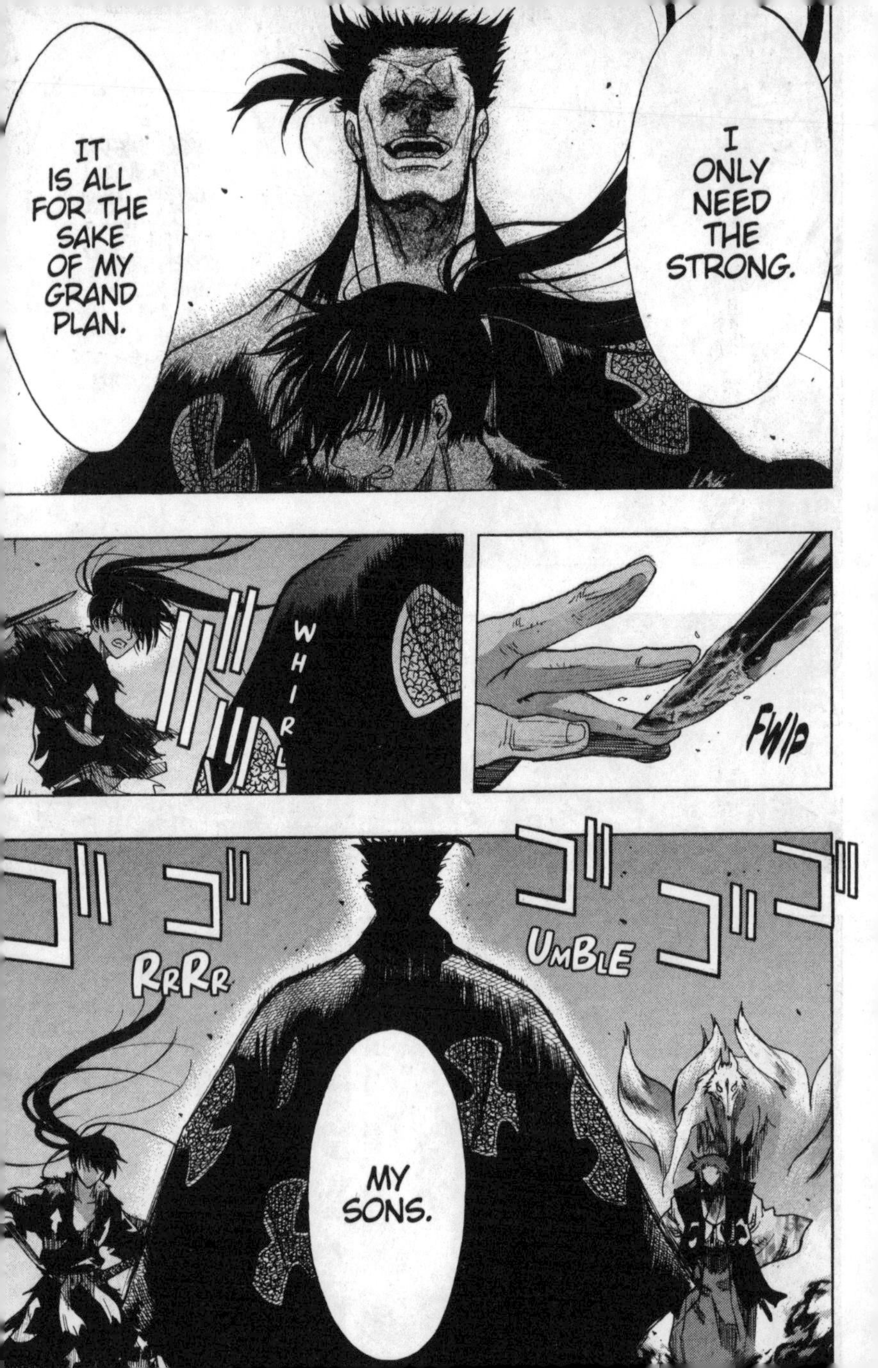
I ONLY NEED THE STRONG.
IT IS ALL FOR THE SAKE OF MY GRAND PLAN.
FWIP
WHIRL
ゴゴゴ
UMBLE
ゴゴ
RRRR
MY SONS.

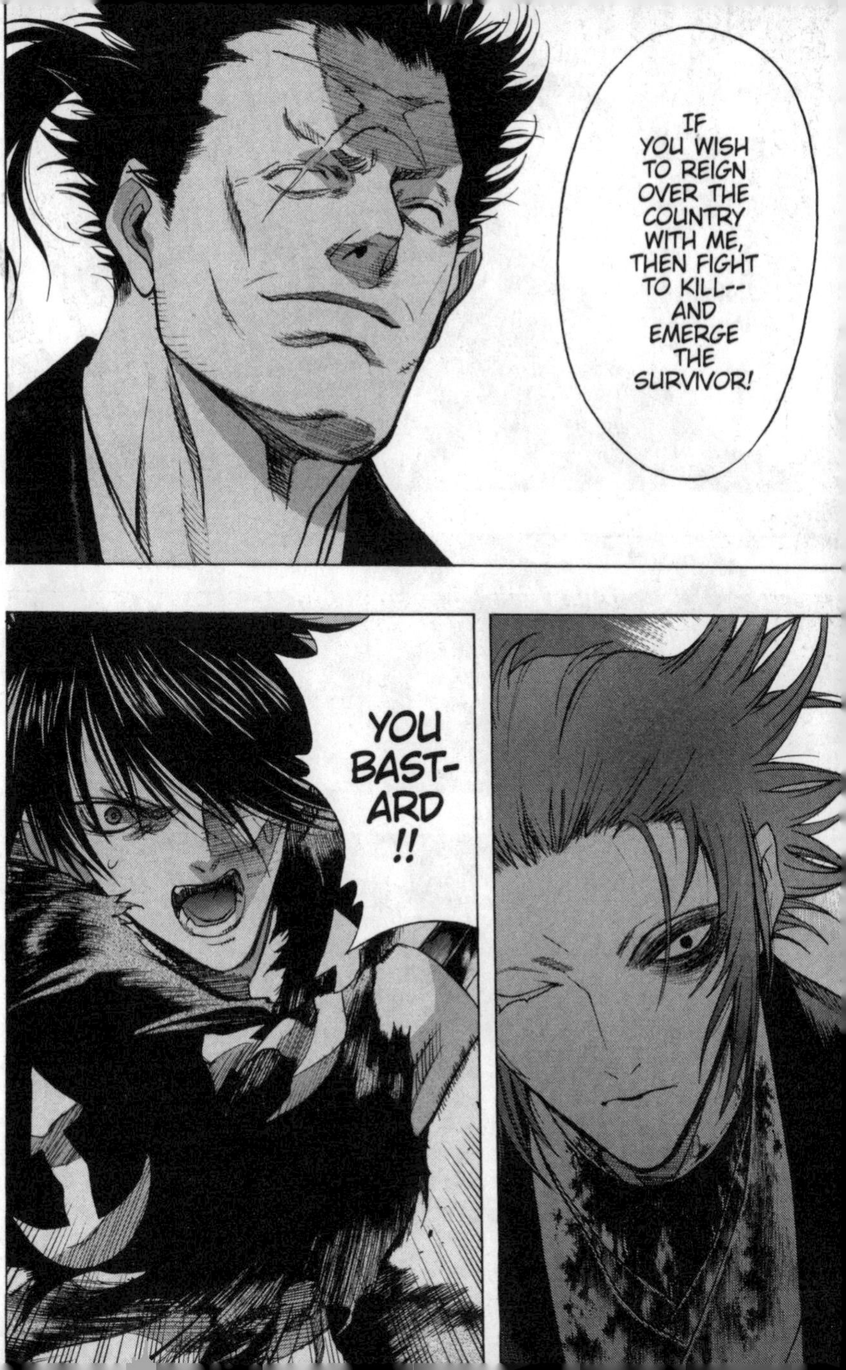
IF YOU WISH TO REIGN OVER THE COUNTRY WITH ME, THEN FIGHT TO KILL--AND EMERGE THE SURVIVOR!
YOU BAST-ARD!!

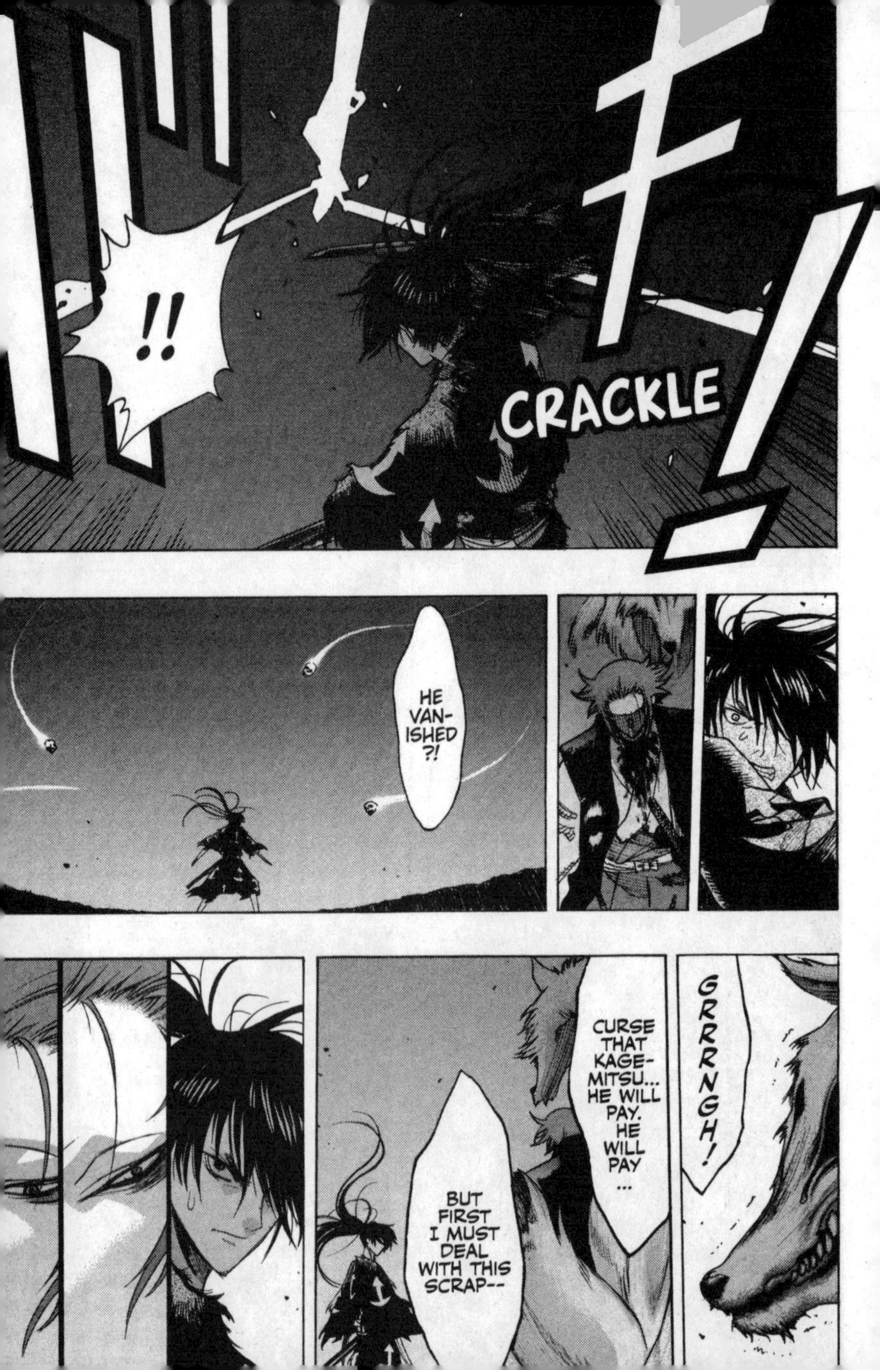
!!
CRACKLE
HE VAN-ISHED ?!
GRRRNGH!
CURSE THAT KAGE-MITSU... HE WILL PAY. HE WILL PAY ...
BUT FIRST I MUST DEAL WITH THIS SCRAP--

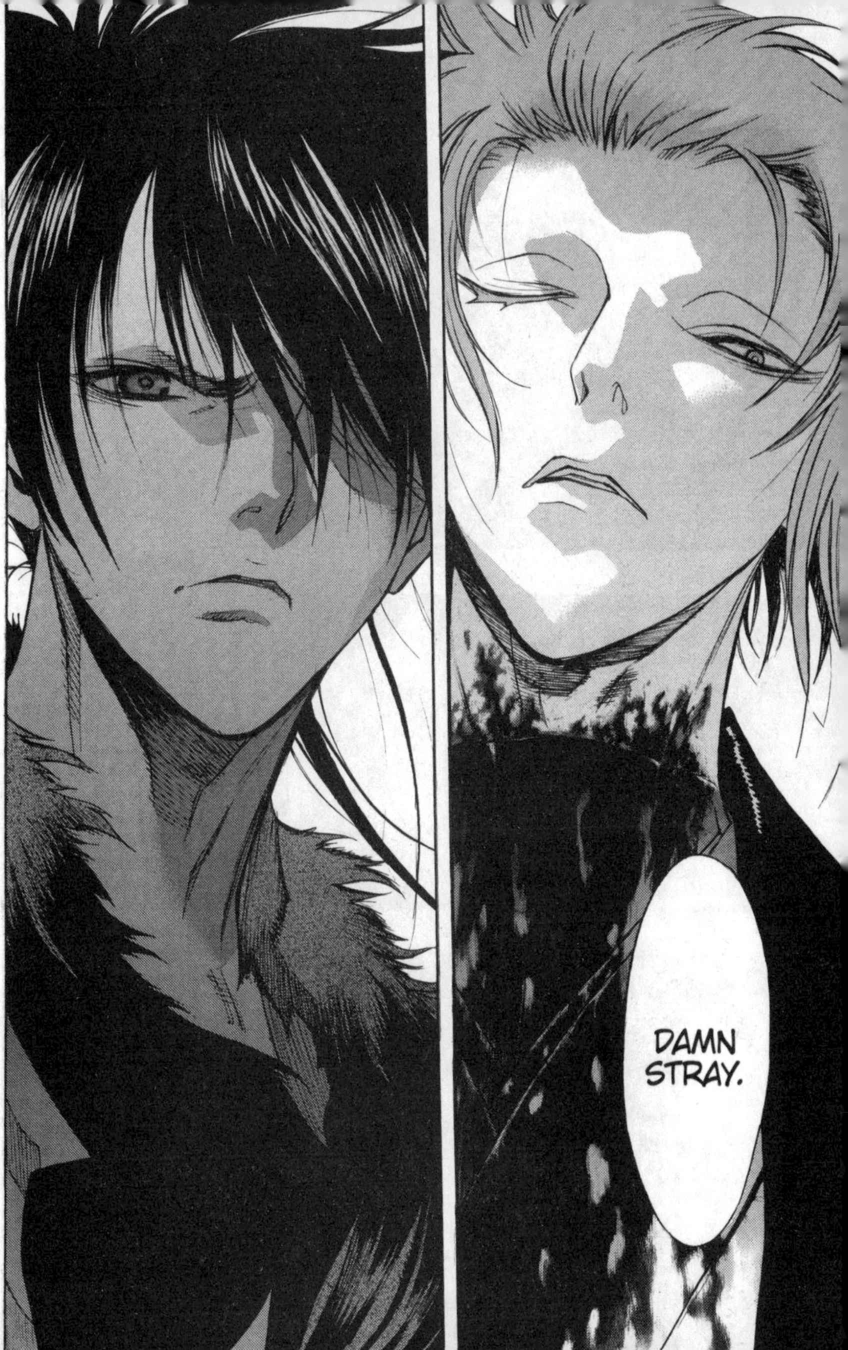
DAMN STRAY.

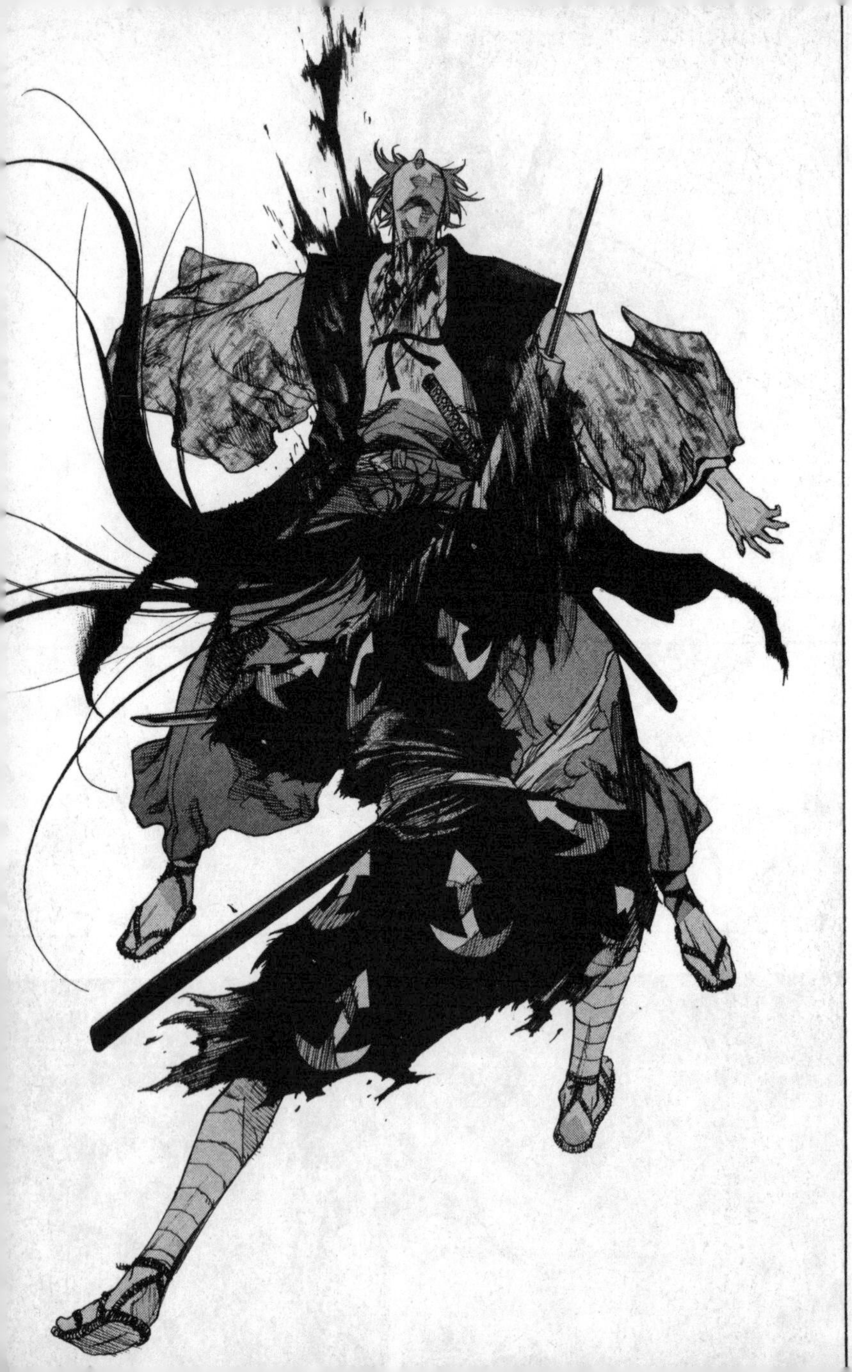

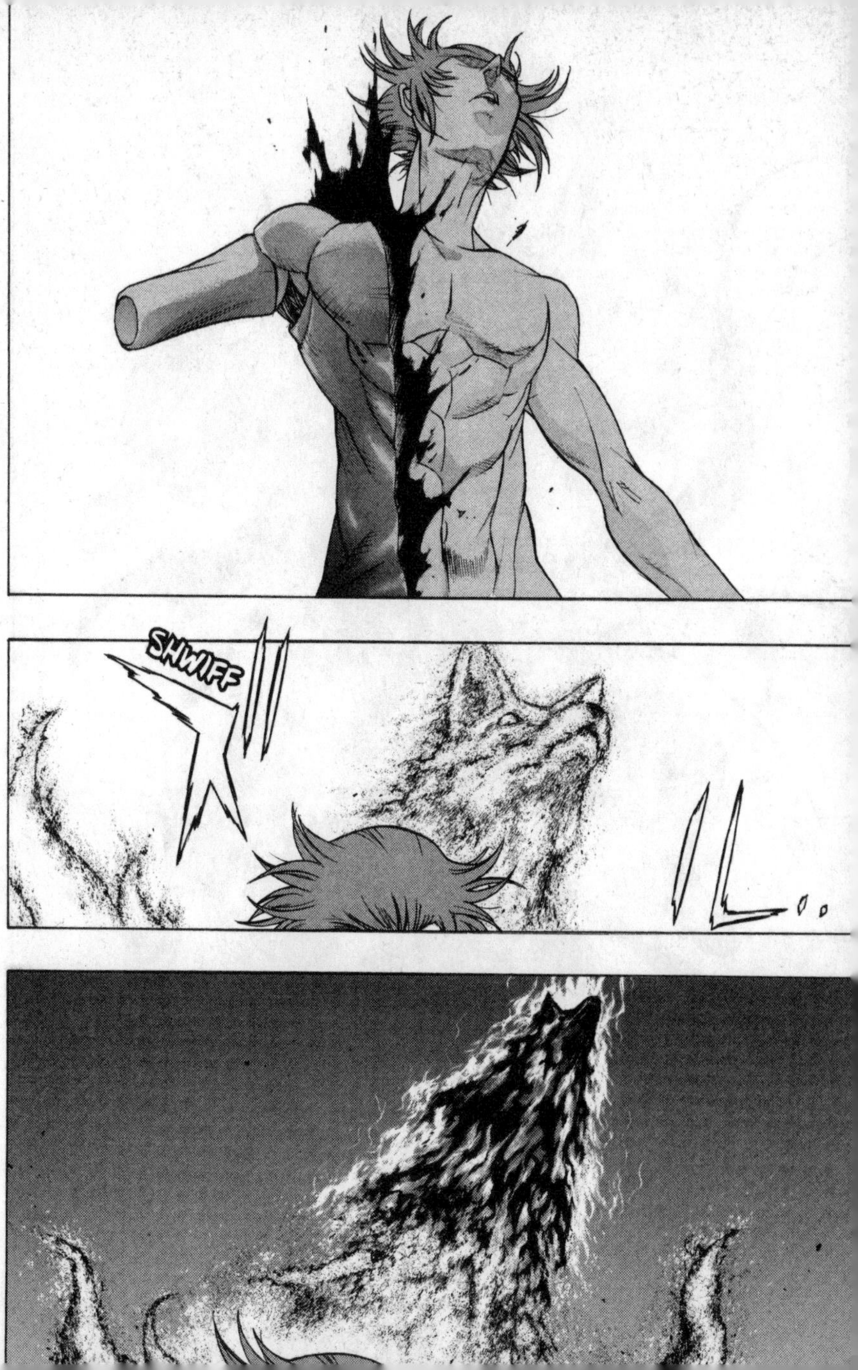
SHWIFF

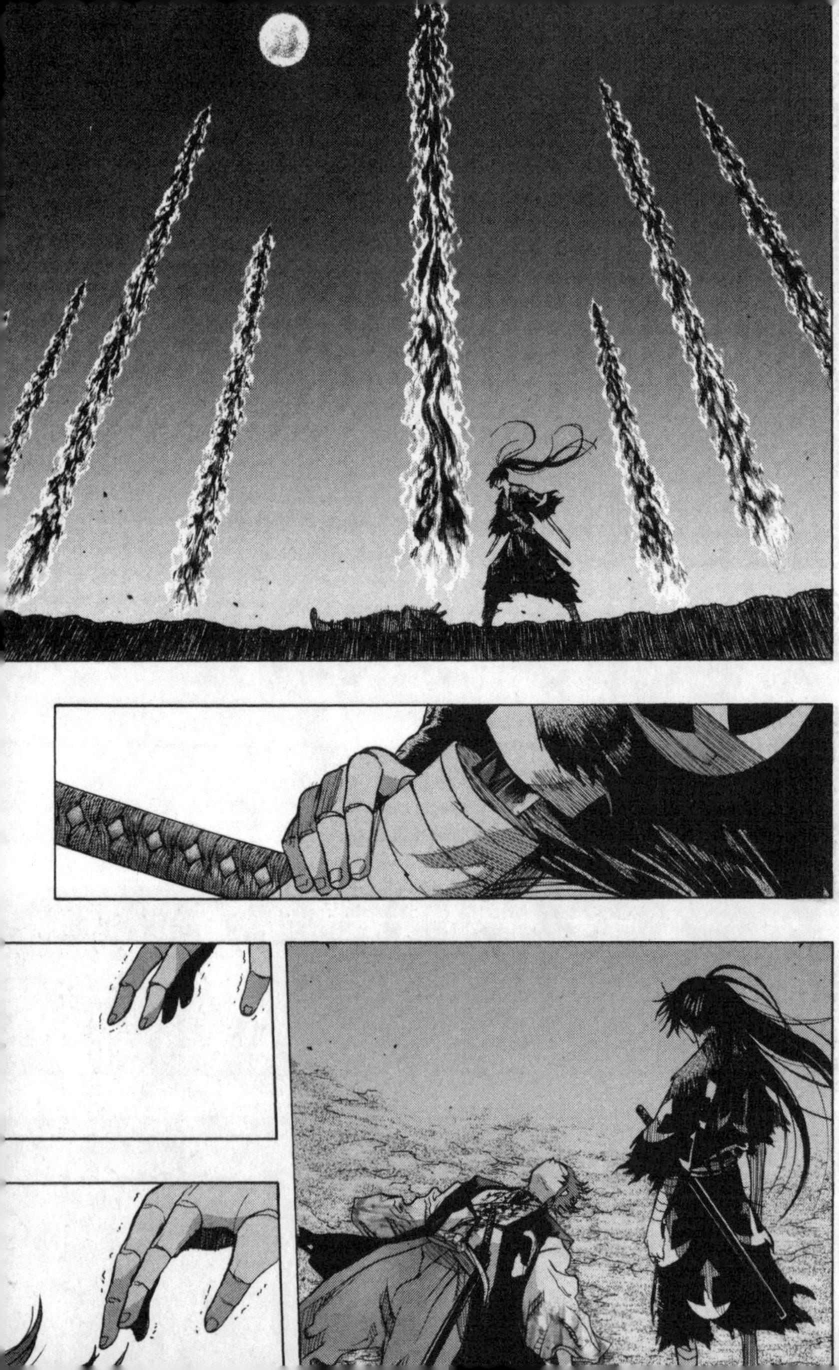

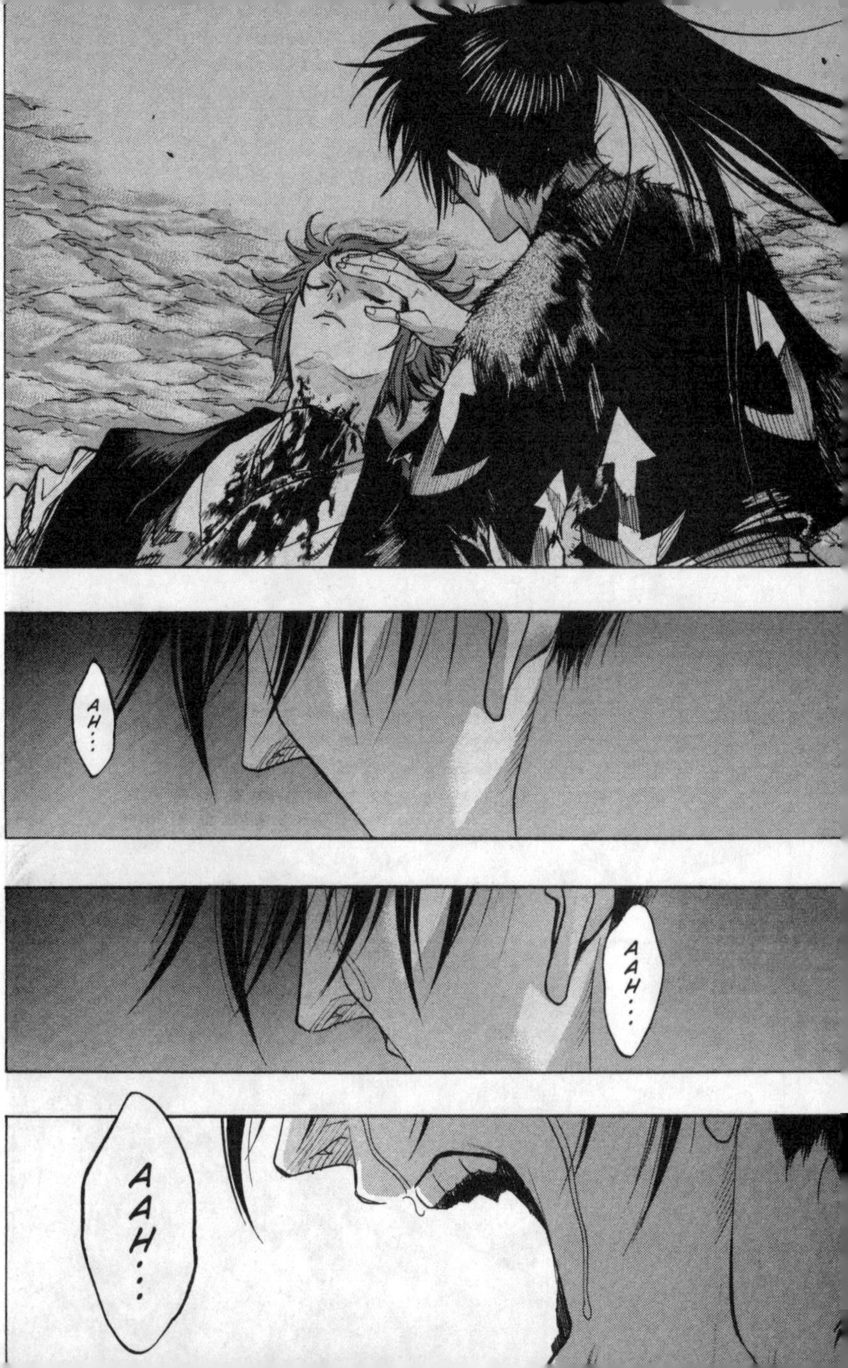
AH...
AAH...
AAH...

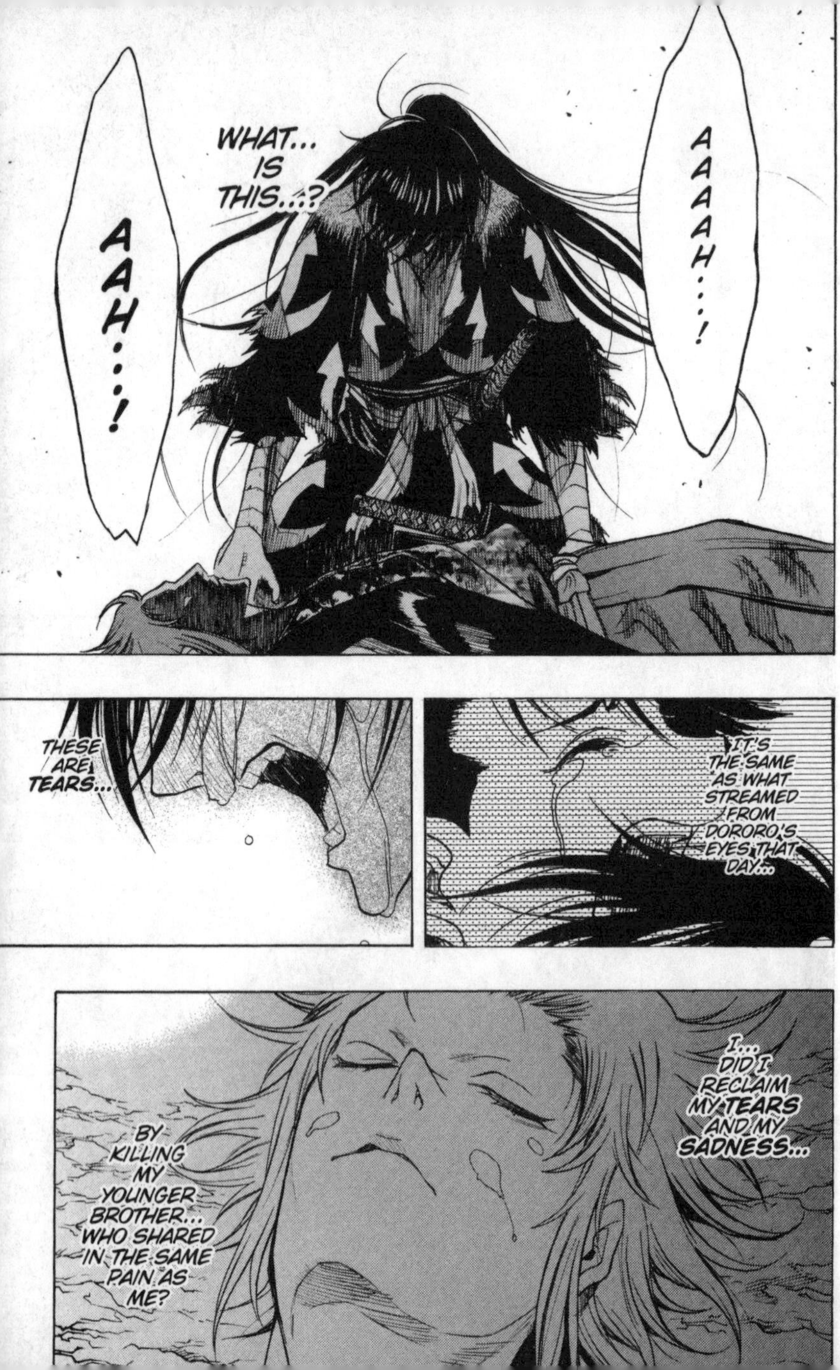
AAAAAH...!
WHAT... IS THIS...?
AAH...!
IT'S THE SAME AS WHAT STREAMED FROM DORORO'S EYES THAT DAY...
THESE ARE TEARS...
I... DID I RECLAIM MY TEARS AND MY SADNESS...
BY KILLING MY YOUNGER BROTHER... WHO SHARED IN THE SAME PAIN AS ME?

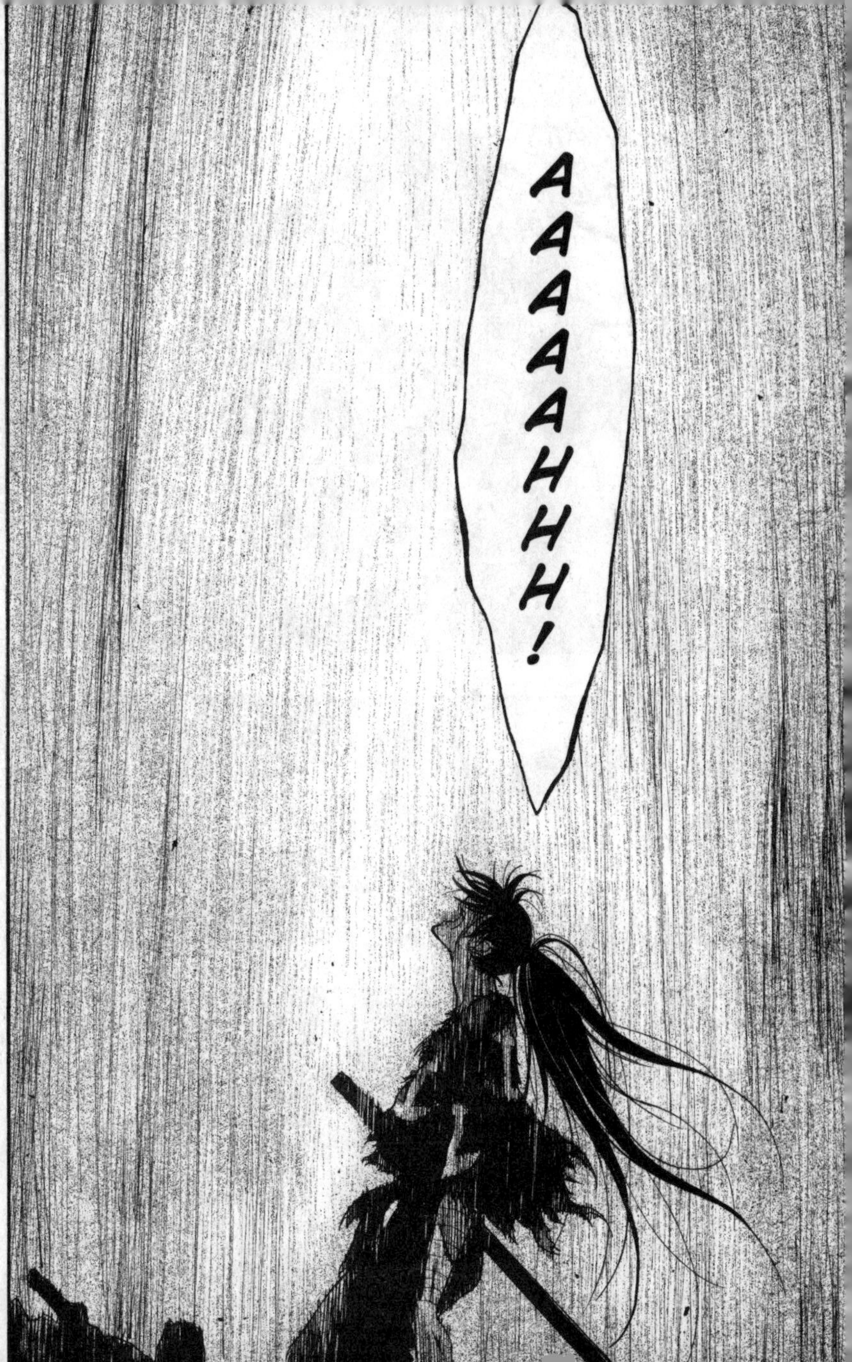
AAAAAAHHH!

どろろと
百鬼丸伝

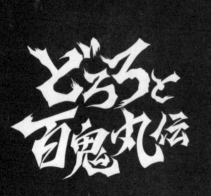

THE LEGEND OF
DORORO AND **HYAKKIMARU**

The Legend of Hyakkimaru and Tahomaru: Part III

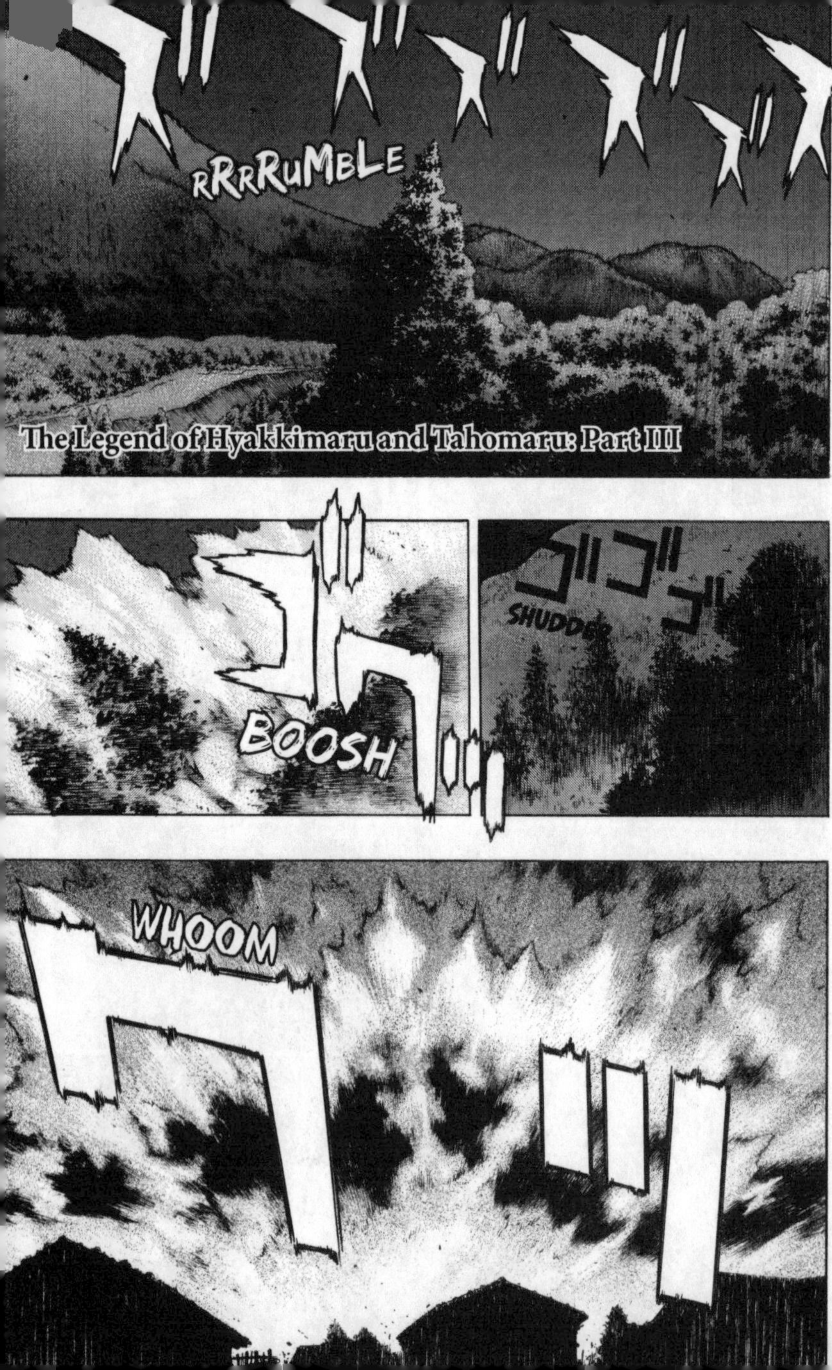
RRRRUMBLE
SHUDD
BOOSH
WHOOM

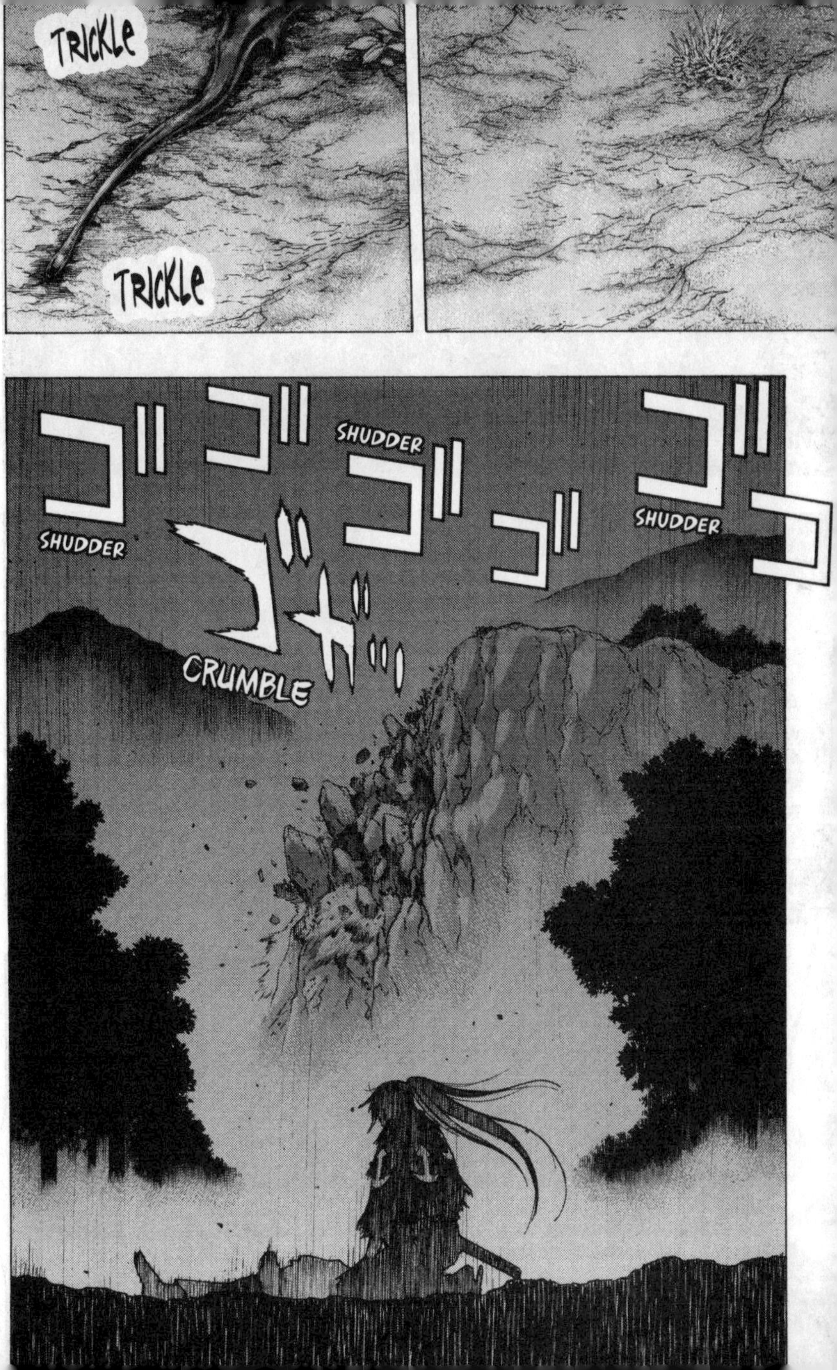
TRICKLE
TRICKLE
SHUDDER
SHUDDER
SHUDDER
CRUMBLE

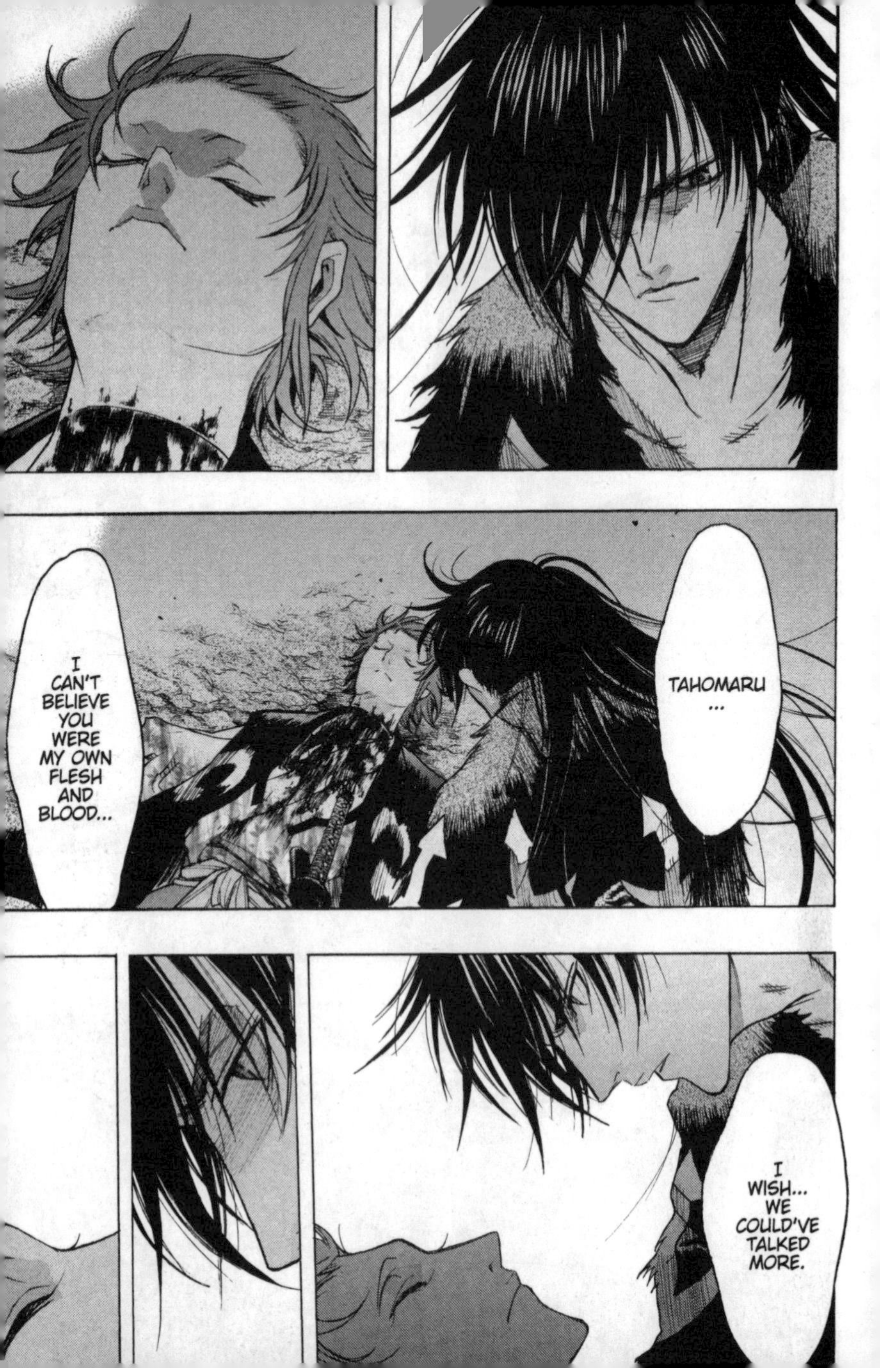
TAHOMARU ...
I CAN'T BELIEVE YOU WERE MY OWN FLESH AND BLOOD...
I WISH... WE COULD'VE TALKED MORE.

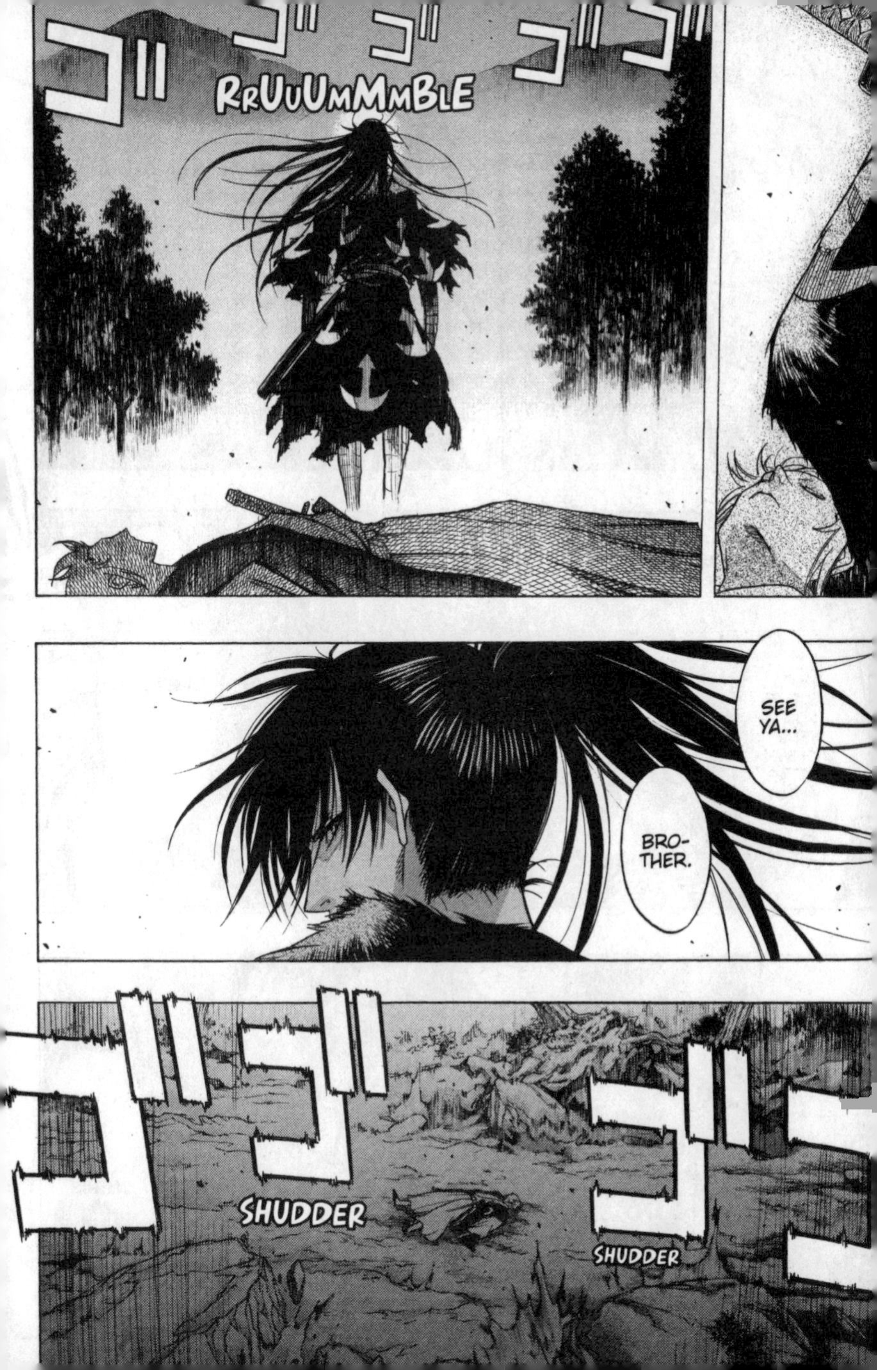
RRUUUMMMBLE
SEE YA...
BRO-THER.
SHUDDER
SHUDDER

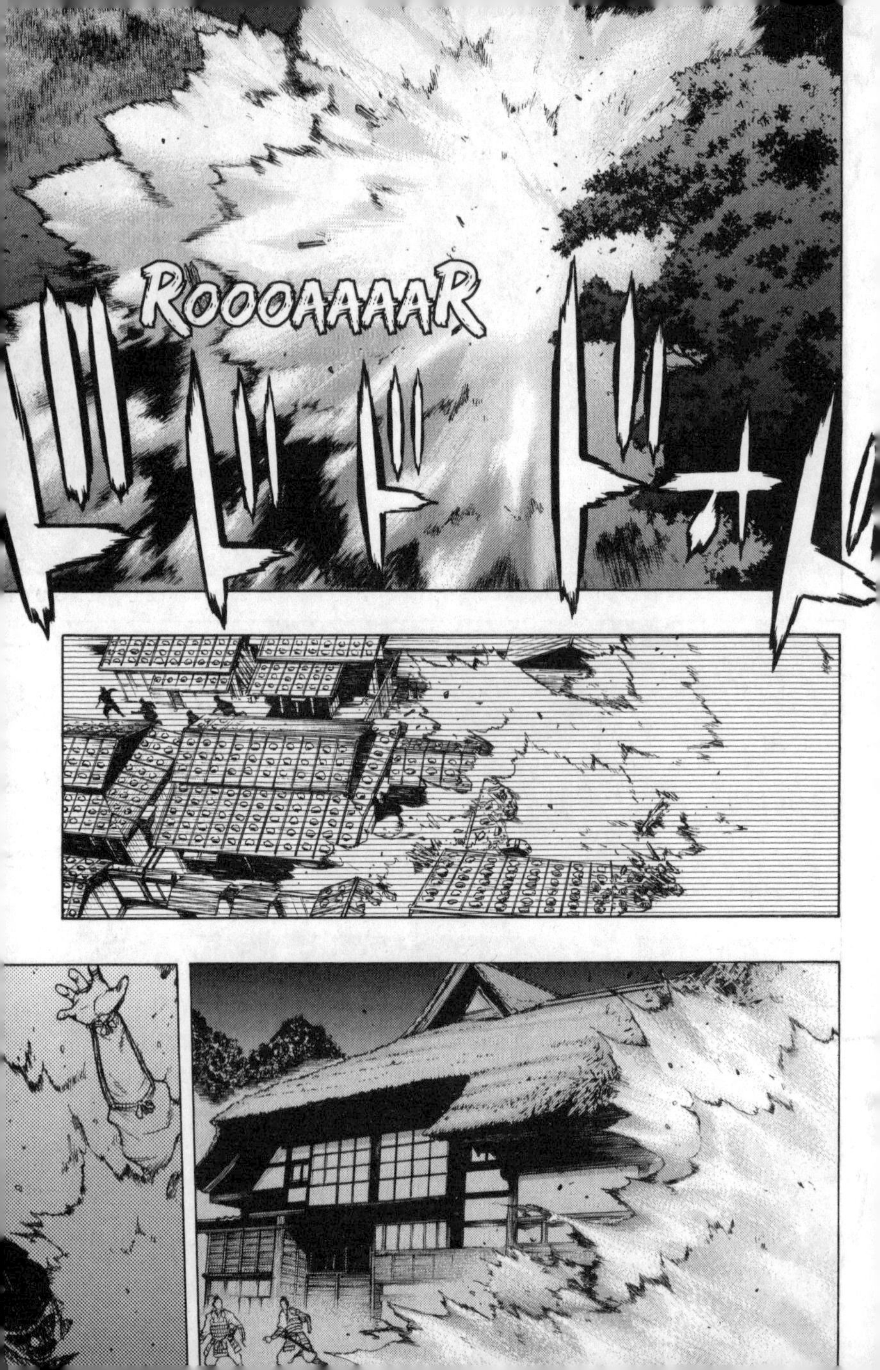
ROOOAAAAR

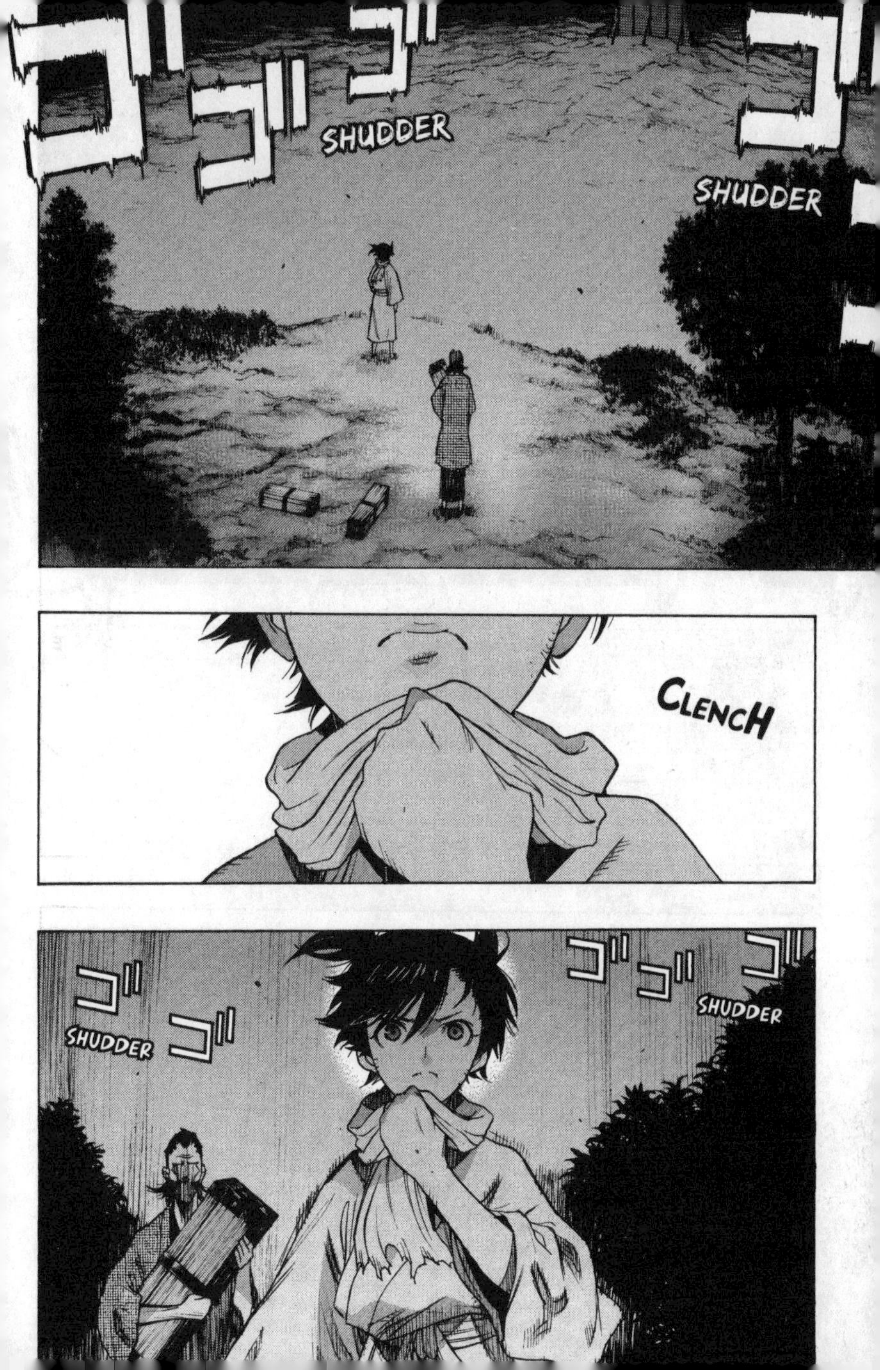

ゴ
SHUDDER
ゴゴゴ
SHUDDER
CLENCH
ゴゴゴ
SHUDDER
ゴゴ
SHUDDER

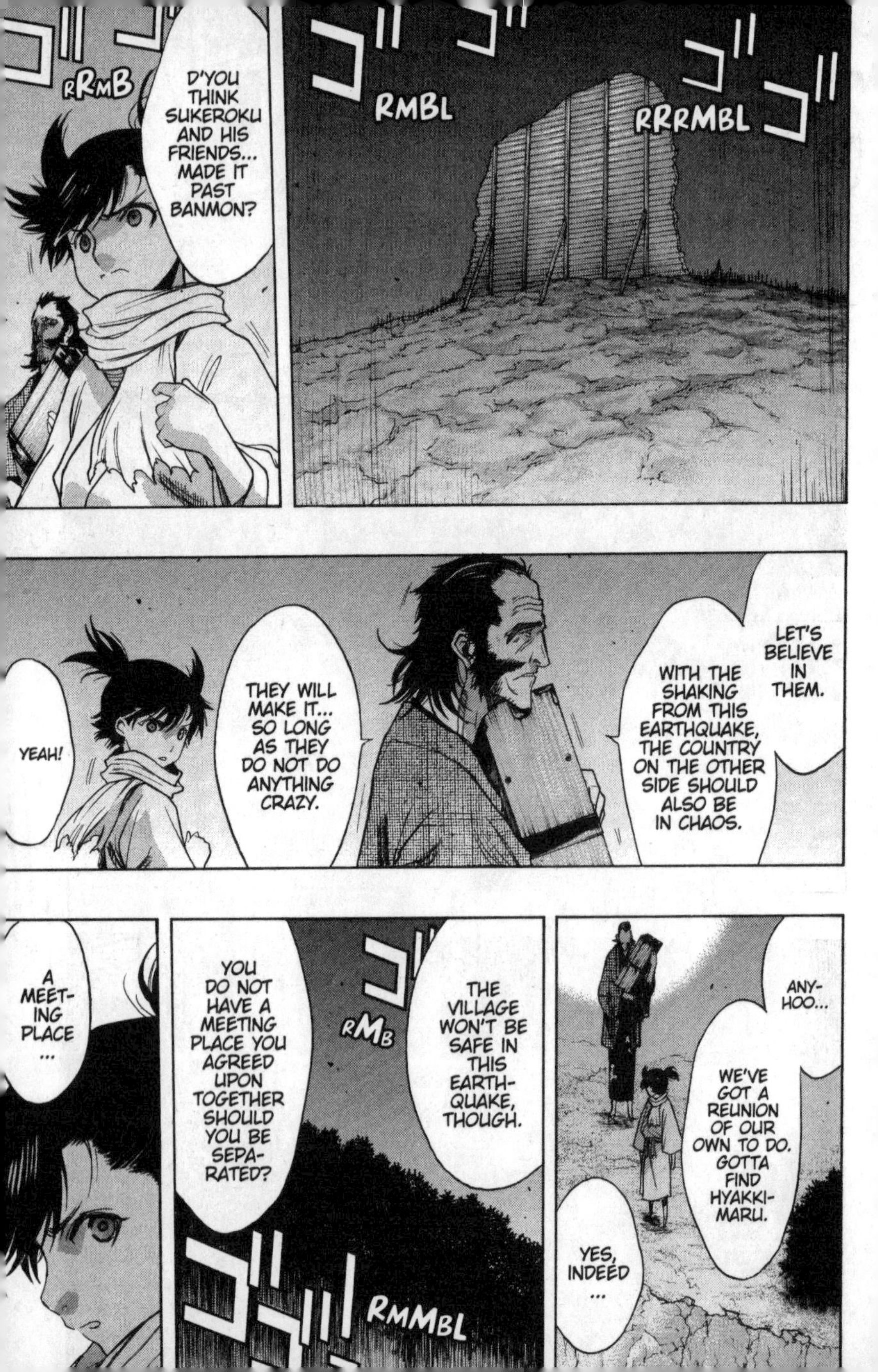
RRRMBL
RMBL
D'YOU THINK SUKEROKU AND HIS FRIENDS... MADE IT PAST BANMON?
RRMB
LET'S BELIEVE IN THEM.
WITH THE SHAKING FROM THIS EARTHQUAKE, THE COUNTRY ON THE OTHER SIDE SHOULD ALSO BE IN CHAOS.
THEY WILL MAKE IT... SO LONG AS THEY DO NOT DO ANYTHING CRAZY.
YEAH!
ANY-HOO...
WE'VE GOT A REUNION OF OUR OWN TO DO. GOTTA FIND HYAKKI-MARU.
YES, INDEED...
THE VILLAGE WON'T BE SAFE IN THIS EARTH-QUAKE, THOUGH.
RMB
YOU DO NOT HAVE A MEETING PLACE YOU AGREED UPON TOGETHER SHOULD YOU BE SEPA-RATED?
RMMBL
A MEET-ING PLACE...

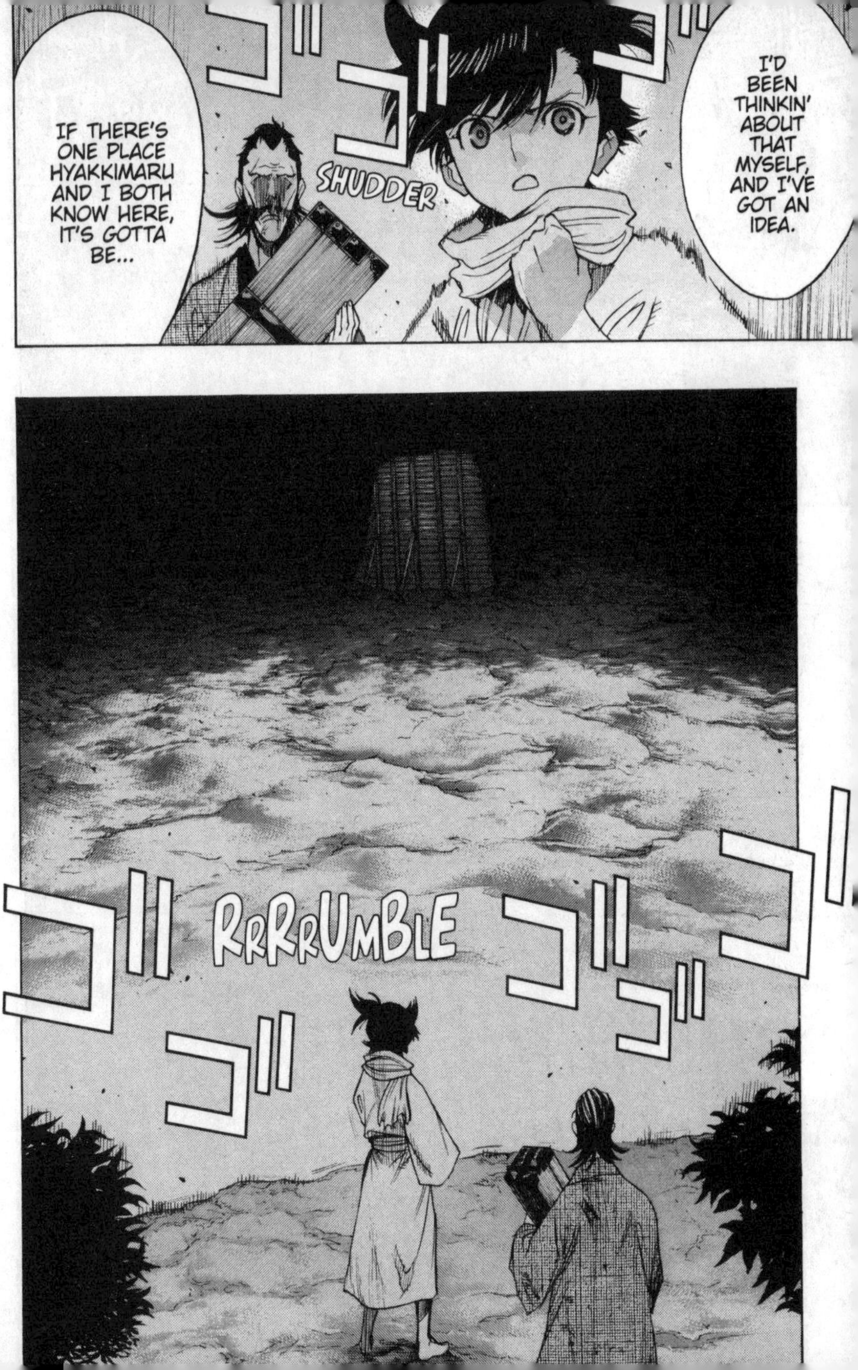
ゴゴゴ
I'D BEEN THINKIN' ABOUT THAT MYSELF, AND I'VE GOT AN IDEA.
SHUDDER
IF THERE'S ONE PLACE HYAKKIMARU AND I BOTH KNOW HERE, IT'S GOTTA BE...
ゴゴゴゴ
RRRRUMBLE

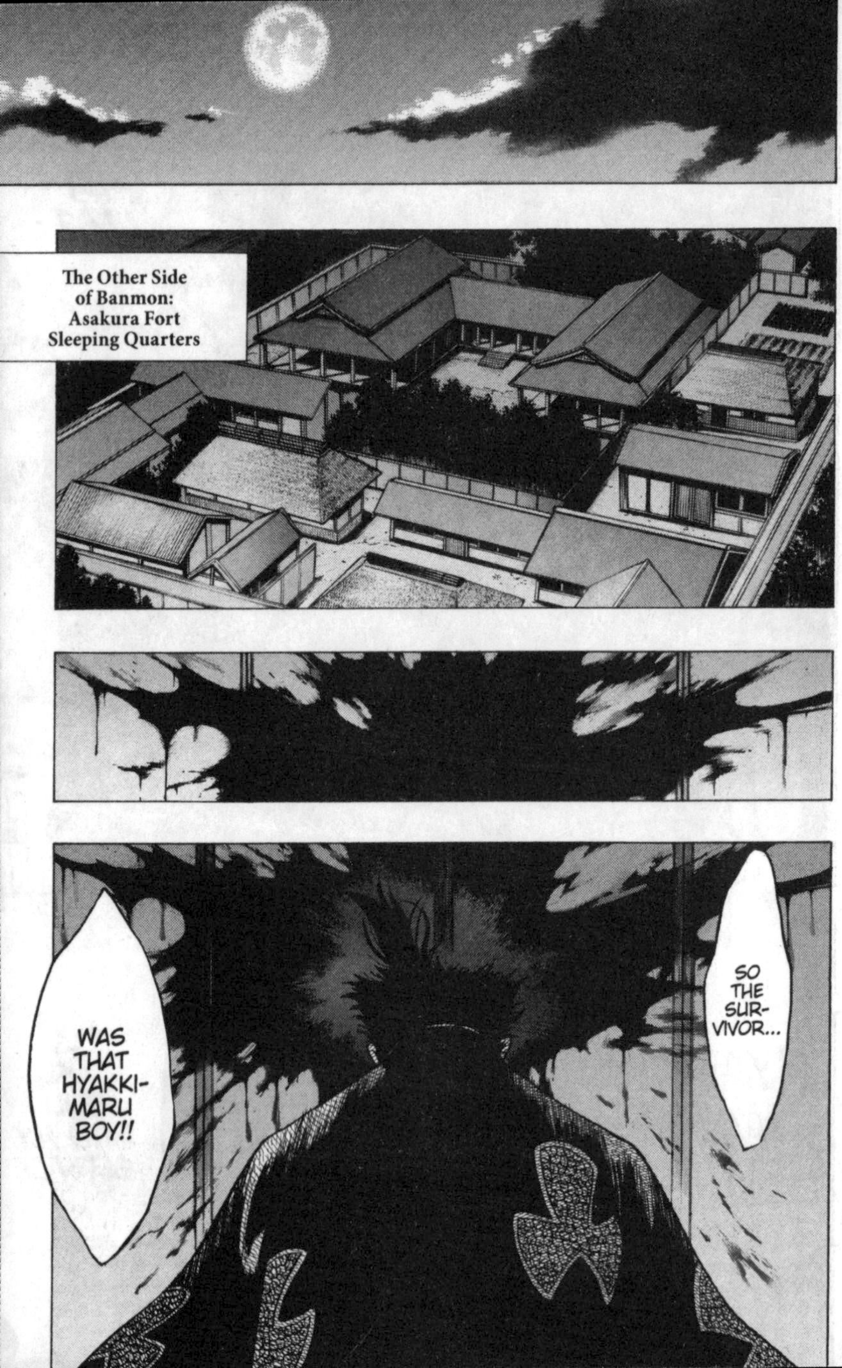
The Other Side of Banmon: Asakura Fort Sleeping Quarters
SO THE SURVIVOR...
WAS THAT HYAKKIMARU BOY!!

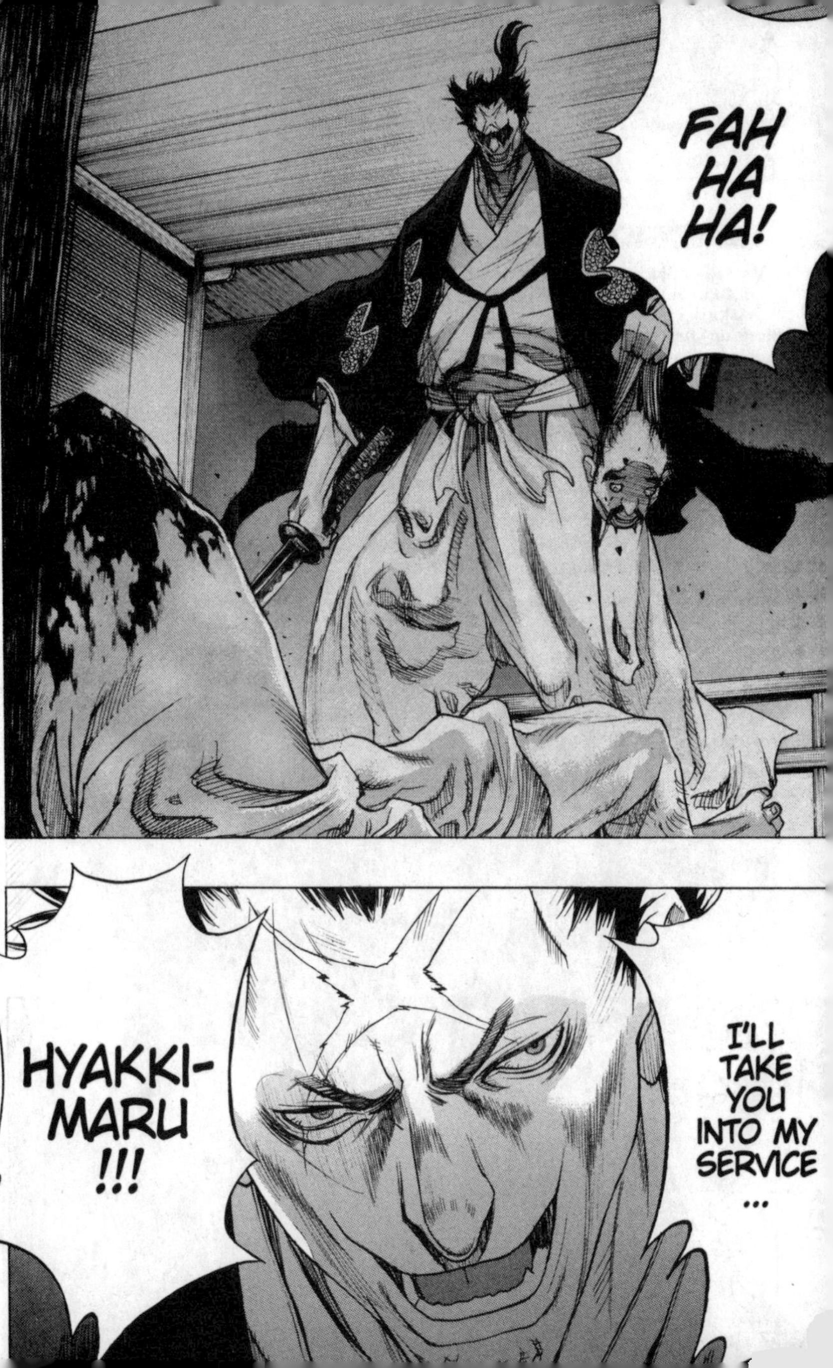
FAH HA HA!
I'LL TAKE YOU INTO MY SERVICE ...
HYAKKI-MARU !!!

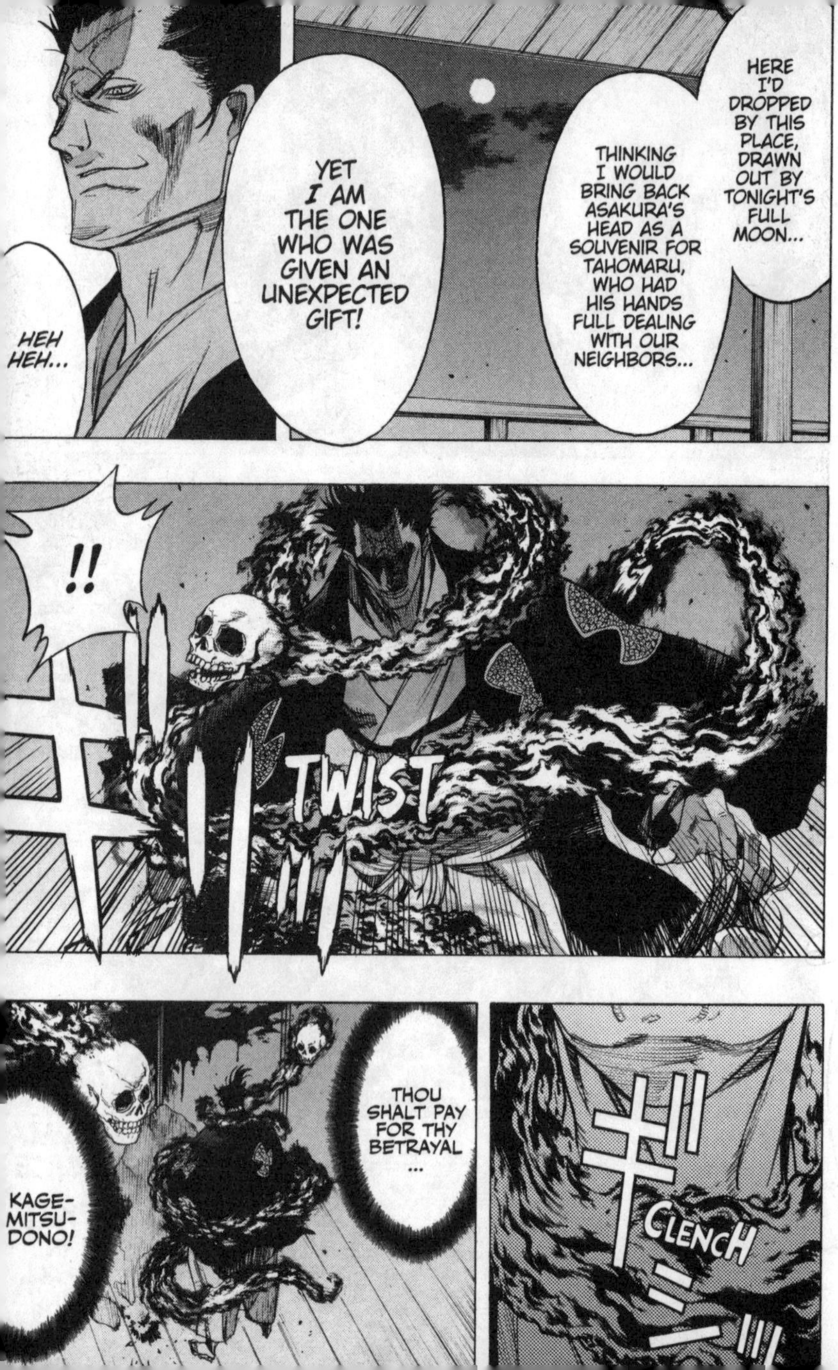
HERE I'D DROPPED BY THIS PLACE, DRAWN OUT BY TONIGHT'S FULL MOON...
THINKING I WOULD BRING BACK ASAKURA'S HEAD AS A SOUVENIR FOR TAHOMARU, WHO HAD HIS HANDS FULL DEALING WITH OUR NEIGHBORS...
YET *I* AM THE ONE WHO WAS GIVEN AN UNEXPECTED GIFT!
HEH HEH...
!!
TWIST
CLENCH
THOU SHALT PAY FOR THY BETRAYAL ...
KAGE-MITSU-DONO!

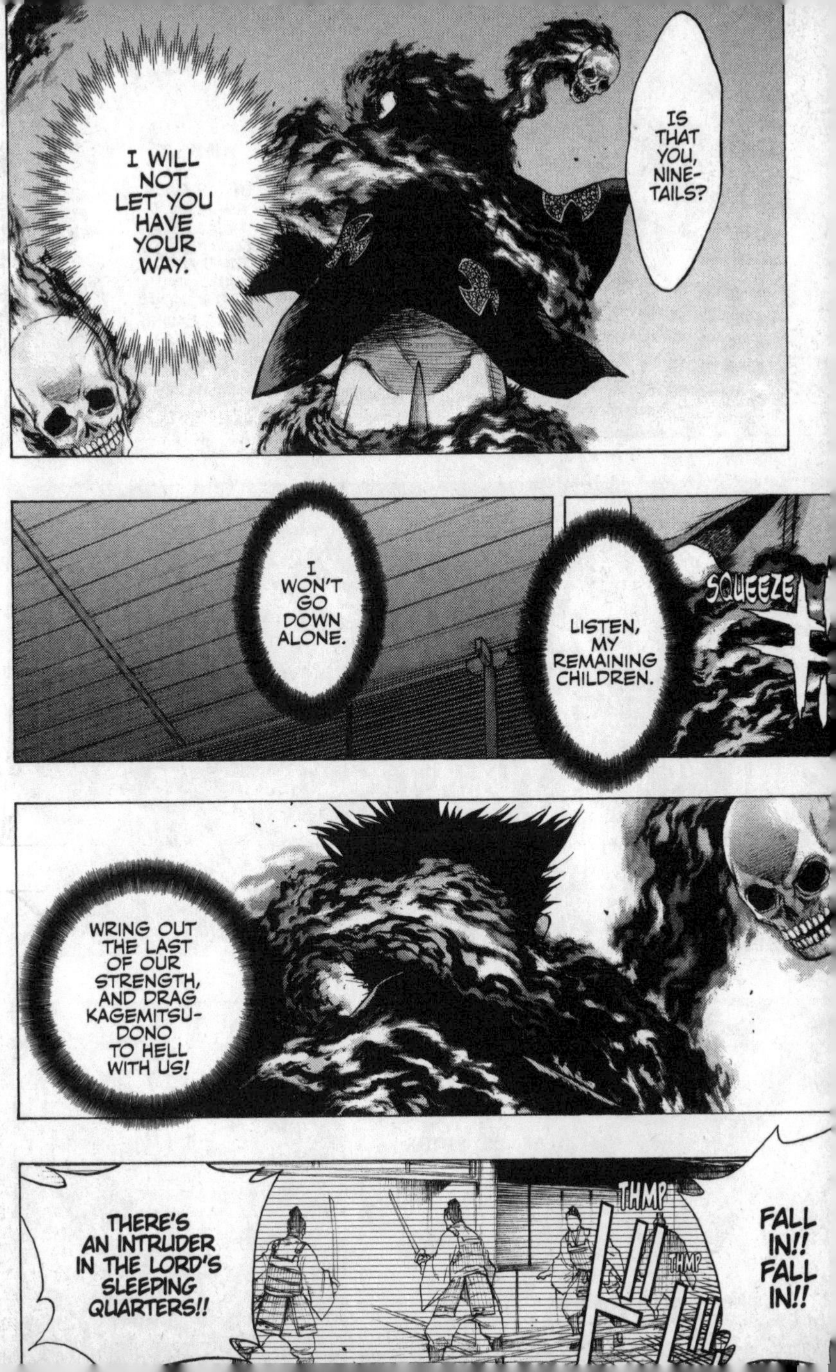
IS THAT YOU, NINE-TAILS?
I WILL NOT LET YOU HAVE YOUR WAY.
SQUEEZE
LISTEN, MY REMAINING CHILDREN.
I WON'T GO DOWN ALONE.
WRING OUT THE LAST OF OUR STRENGTH, AND DRAG KAGEMITSU-DONO TO HELL WITH US!
FALL IN!! FALL IN!!
THMP
THMP
THERE'S AN INTRUDER IN THE LORD'S SLEEPING QUARTERS!!

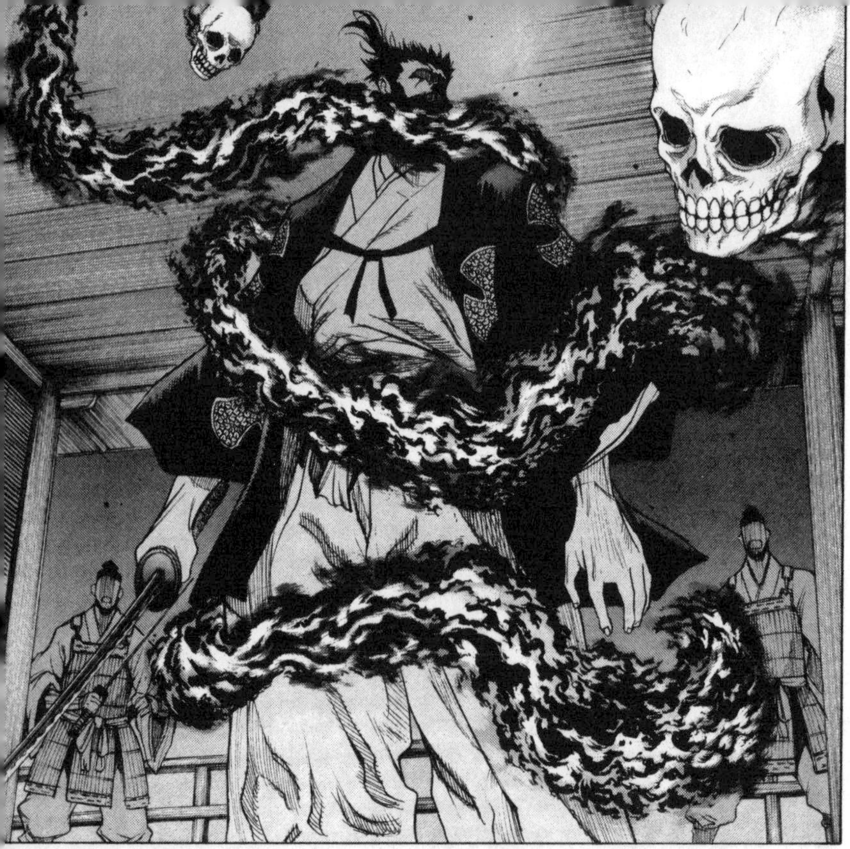
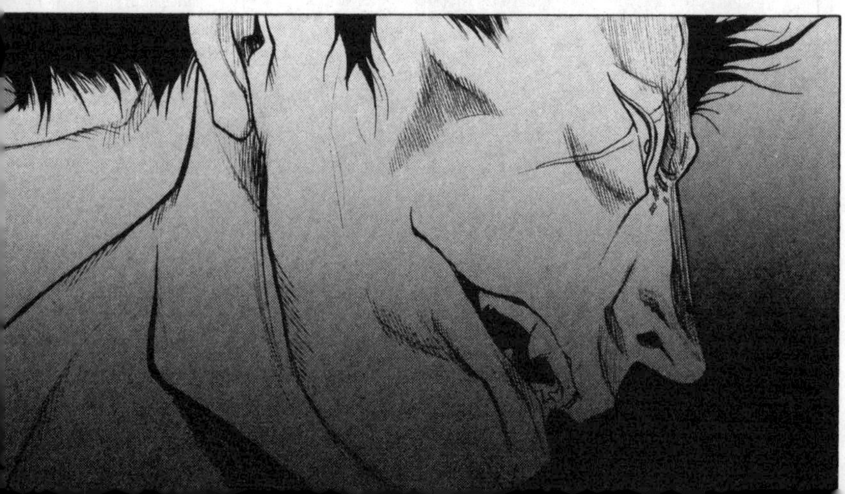

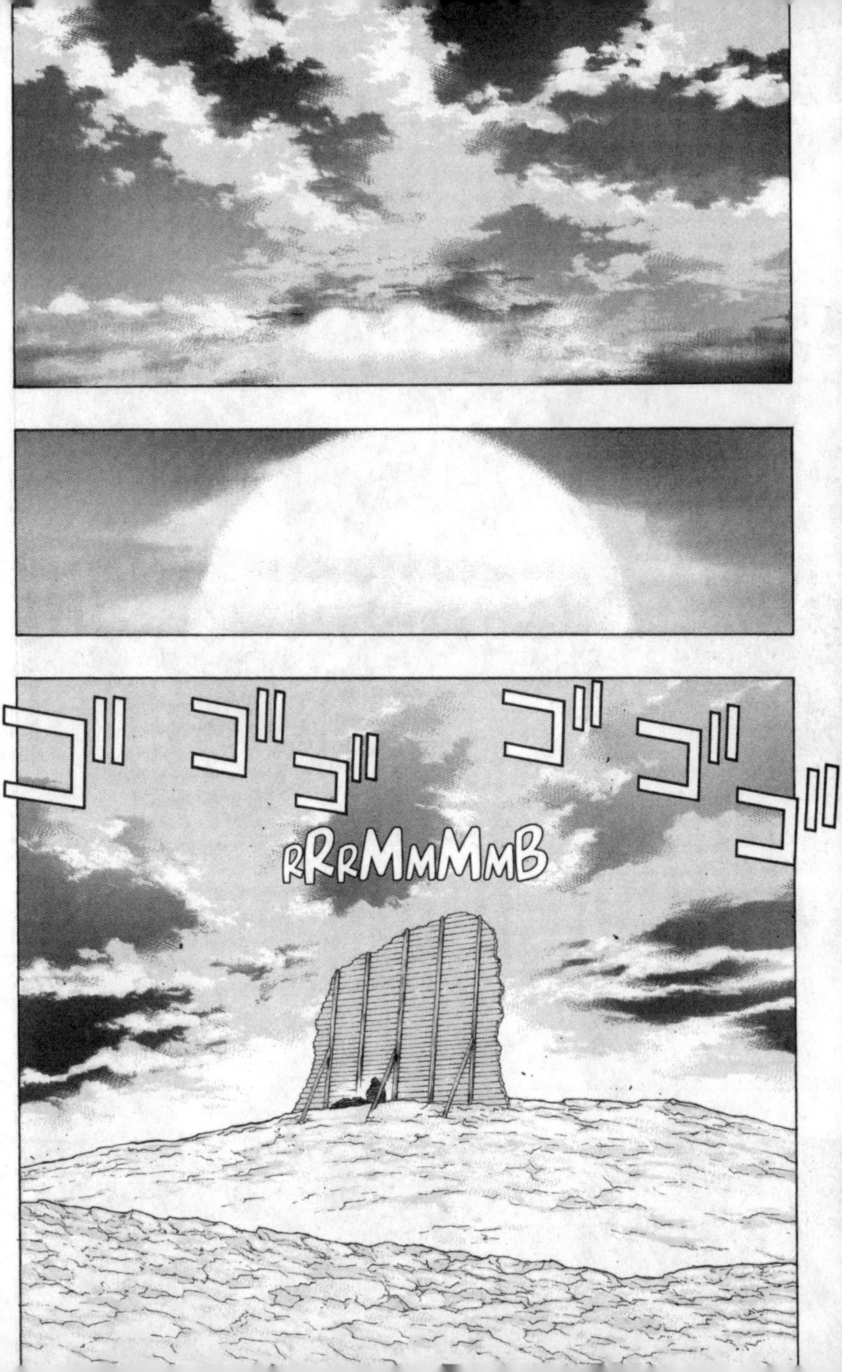
ゴゴゴ
ゴゴゴ
RRRMMMMMB

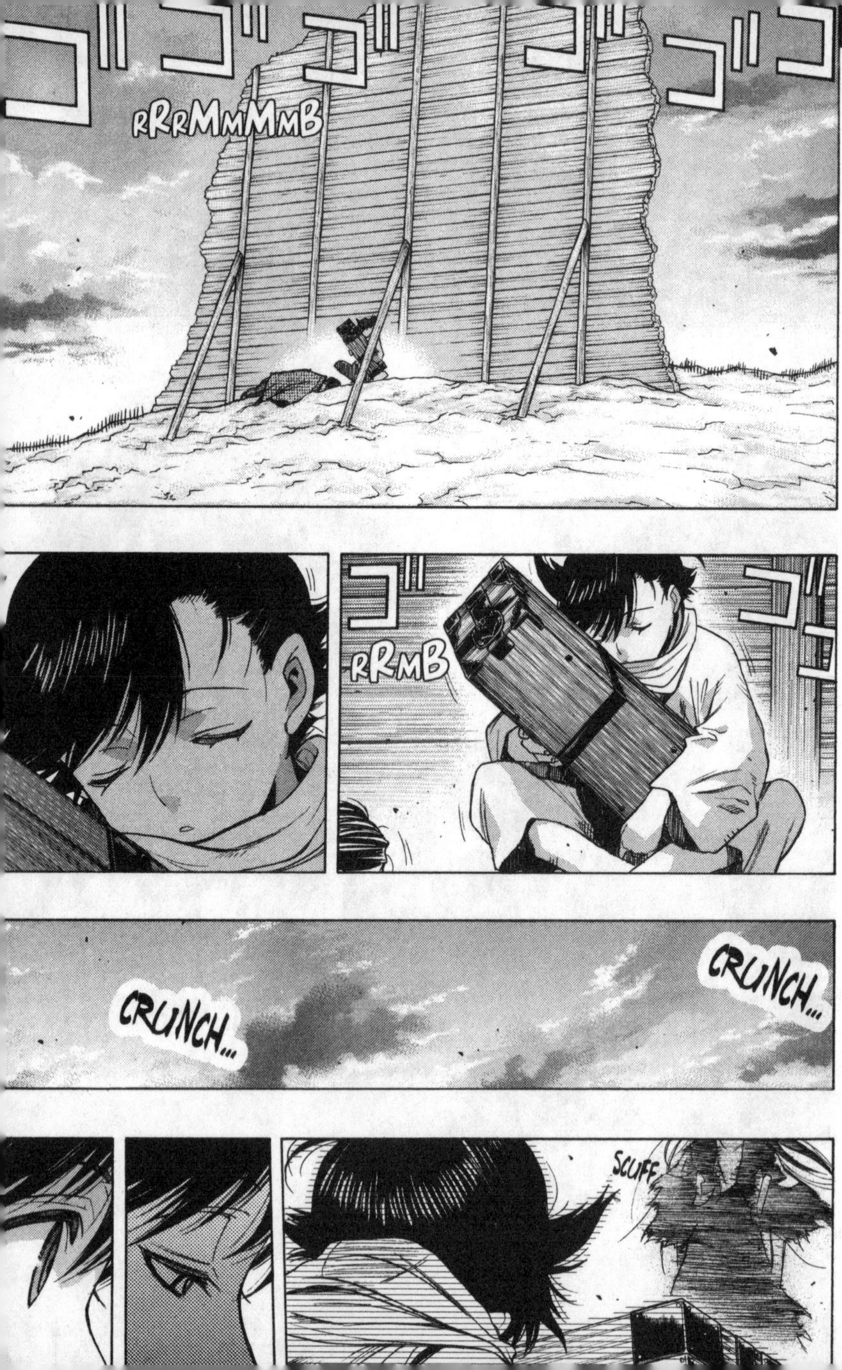
ゴゴゴゴゴゴ
RRRMMMMMB
ゴゴ
RRMB
ゴ
CRUNCH...
CRUNCH...
SCUFF

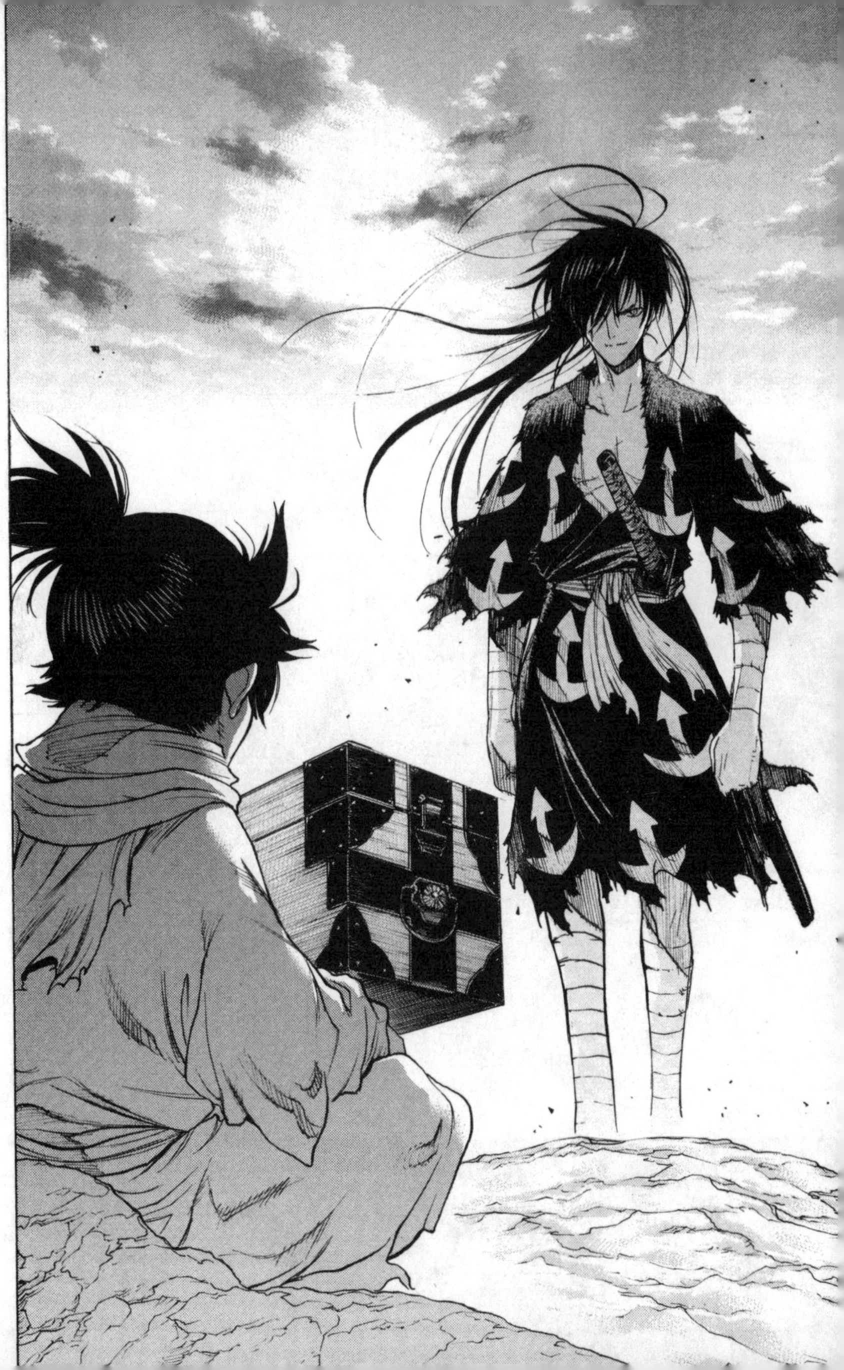

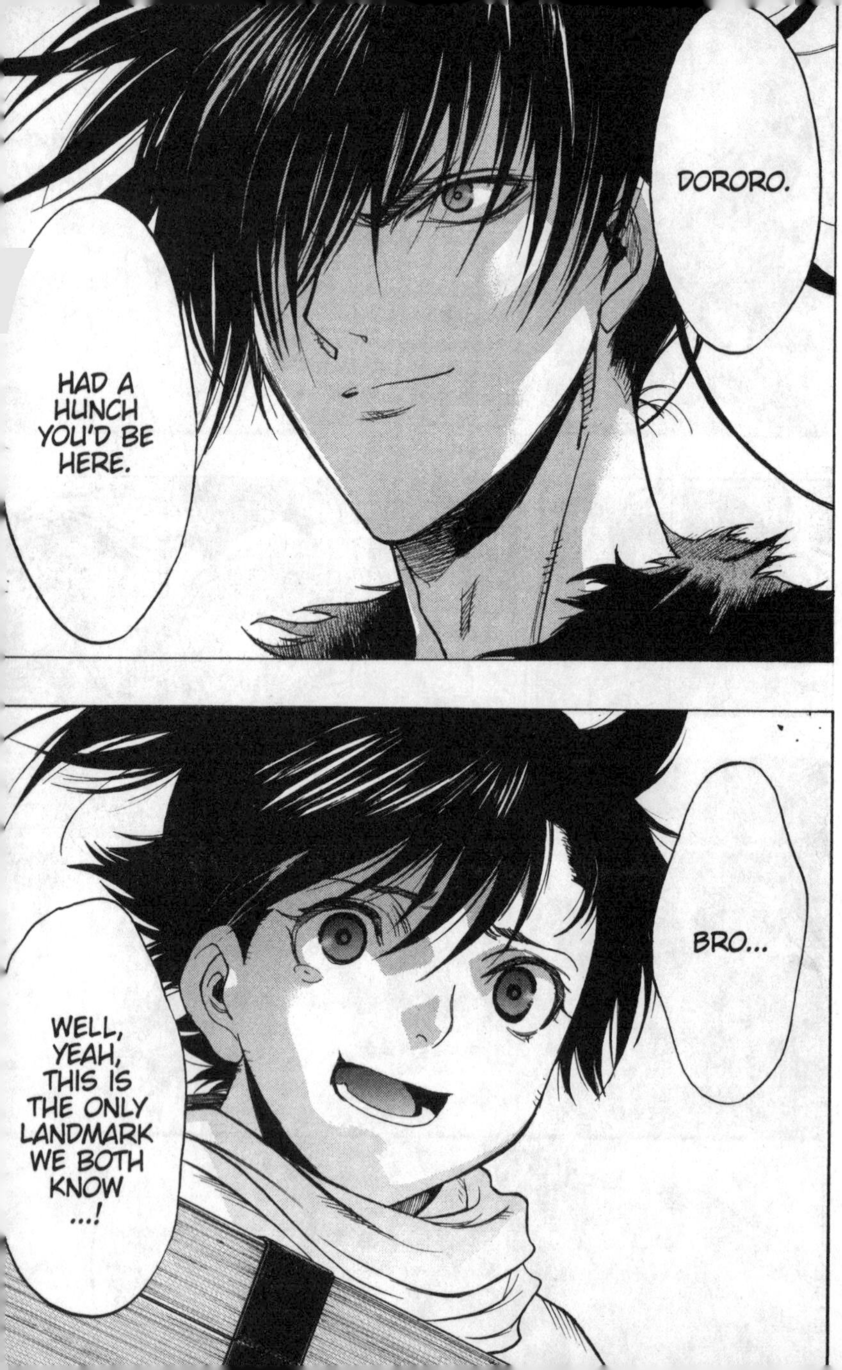
DORORO.
HAD A HUNCH YOU'D BE HERE.
BRO...
WELL, YEAH, THIS IS THE ONLY LANDMARK WE BOTH KNOW ...!

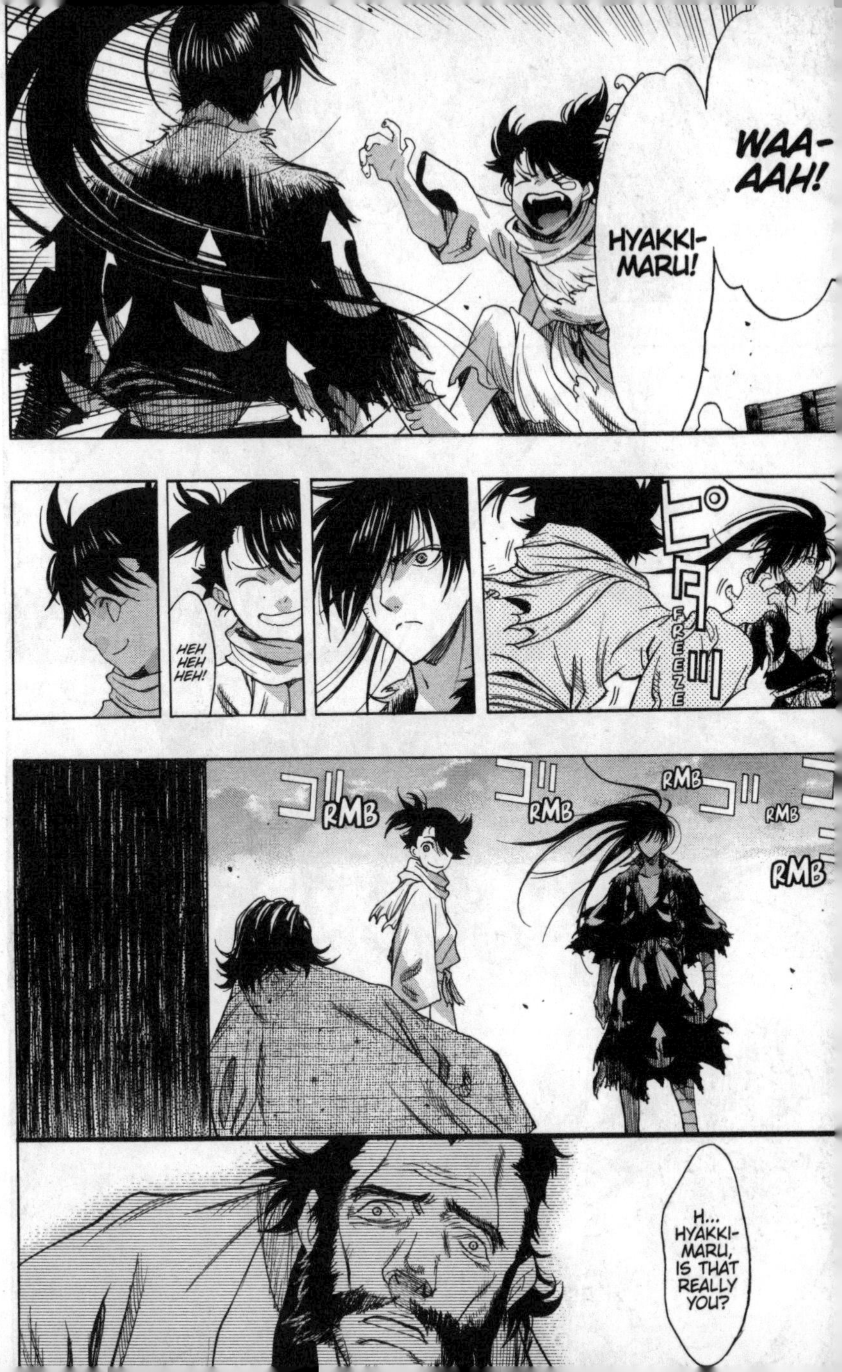
WAA-AAH!
HYAKKI-MARU!
ピタ
FREEZE
HEH HEH HEH!
RMB
RMB
RMB
RMB
RMB
H... HYAKKI-MARU, IS THAT REALLY YOU?

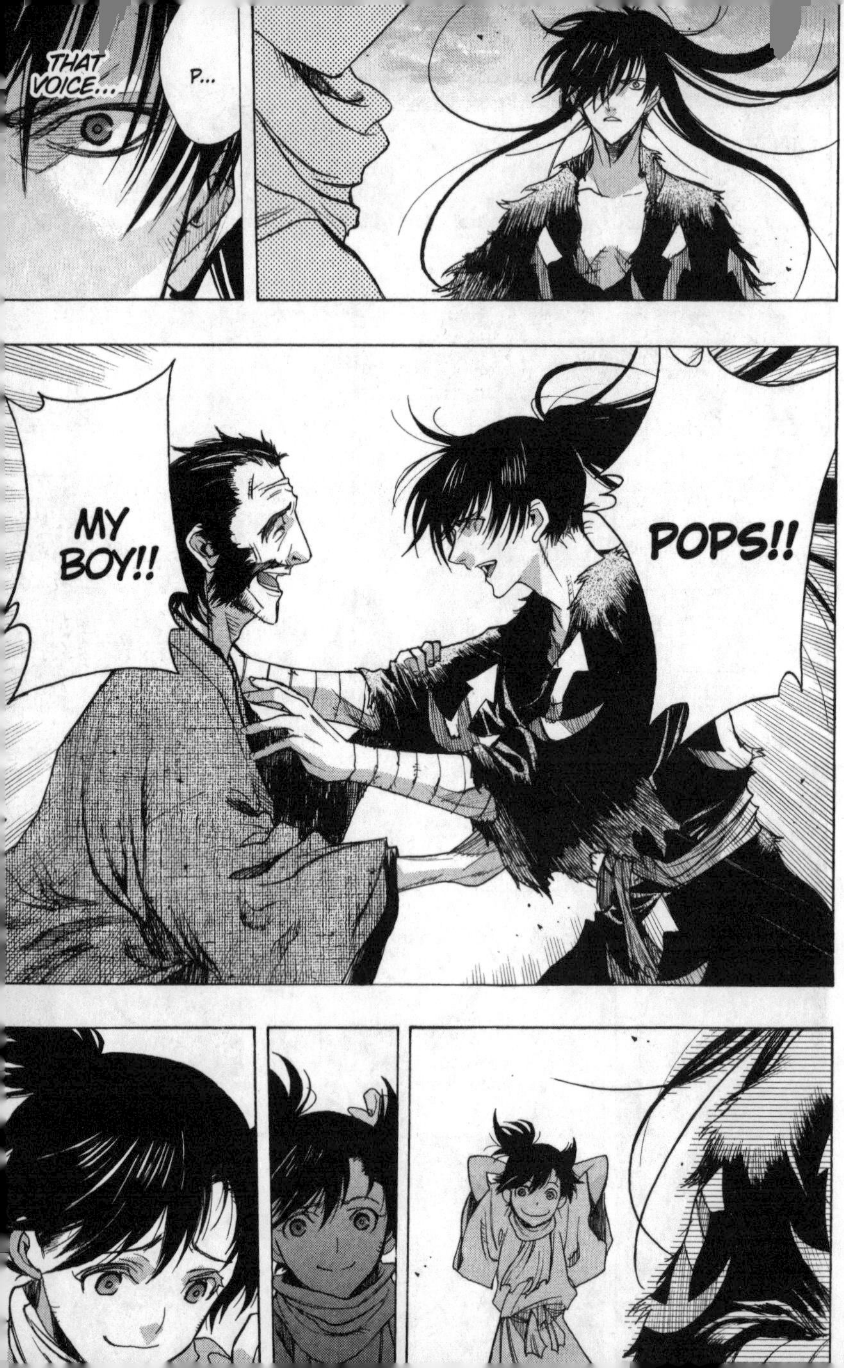
P...
THAT VOICE...
POPS!!
MY BOY!!

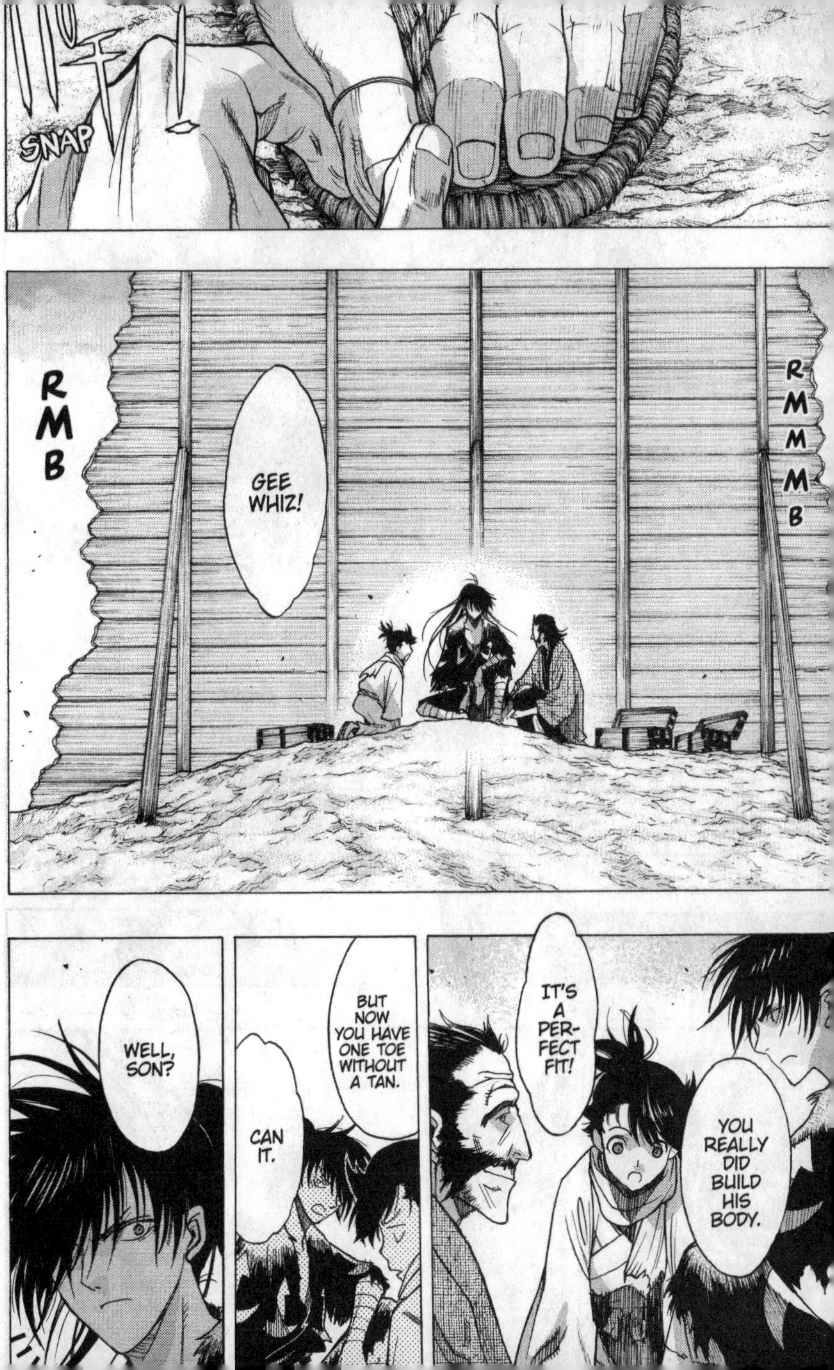
SNAP
RMMMMB
GEE WHIZ!
RMB
IT'S A PER-FECT FIT!
YOU REALLY DID BUILD HIS BODY.
BUT NOW YOU HAVE ONE TOE WITHOUT A TAN.
CAN IT.
WELL, SON?

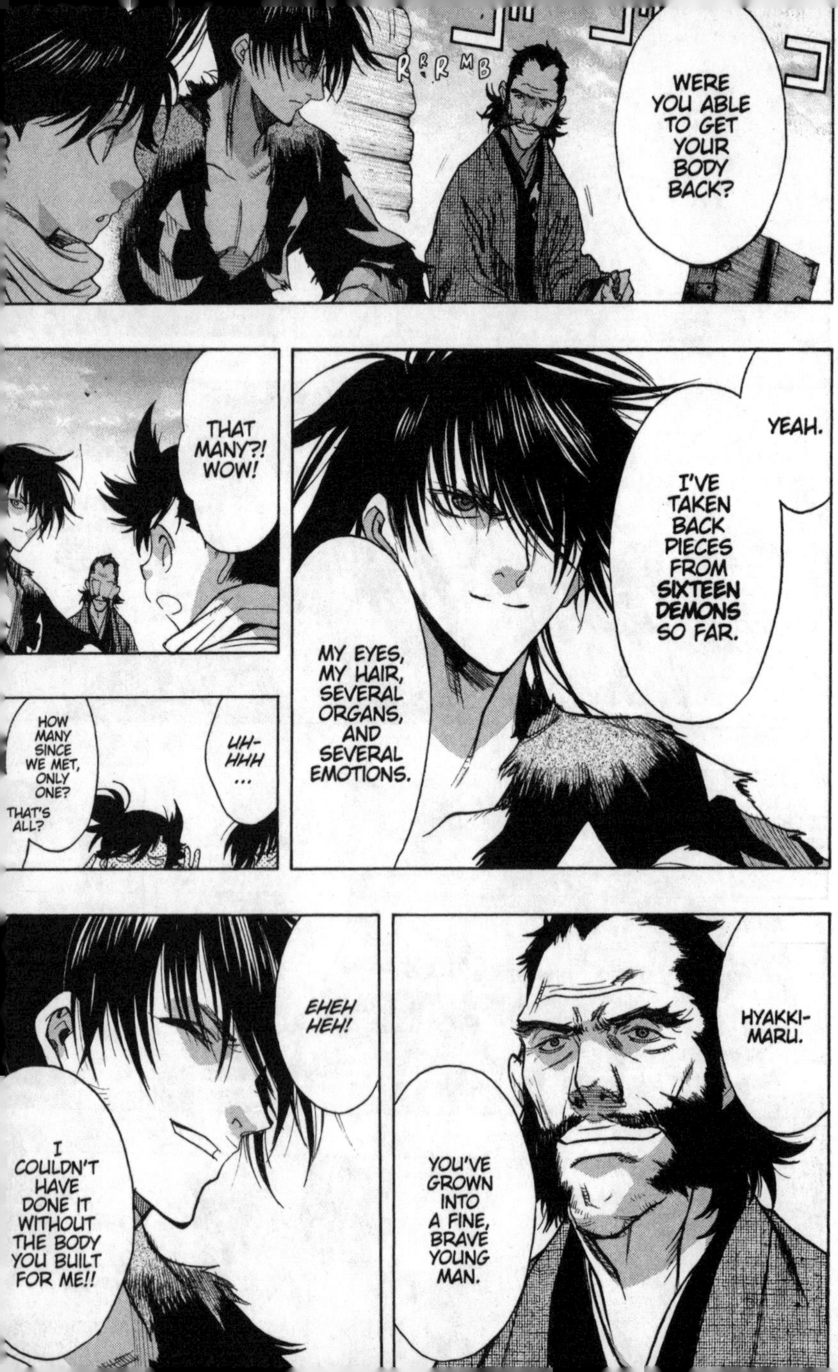
RRRMB
WERE YOU ABLE TO GET YOUR BODY BACK?
YEAH.
I'VE TAKEN BACK PIECES FROM SIXTEEN DEMONS SO FAR.
MY EYES, MY HAIR, SEVERAL ORGANS, AND SEVERAL EMOTIONS.
THAT MANY?! WOW!
UH-HHH ...
HOW MANY SINCE WE MET, ONLY ONE? THAT'S ALL?
HYAKKI-MARU.
YOU'VE GROWN INTO A FINE, BRAVE YOUNG MAN.
EHEH HEH!
I COULDN'T HAVE DONE IT WITHOUT THE BODY YOU BUILT FOR ME!!

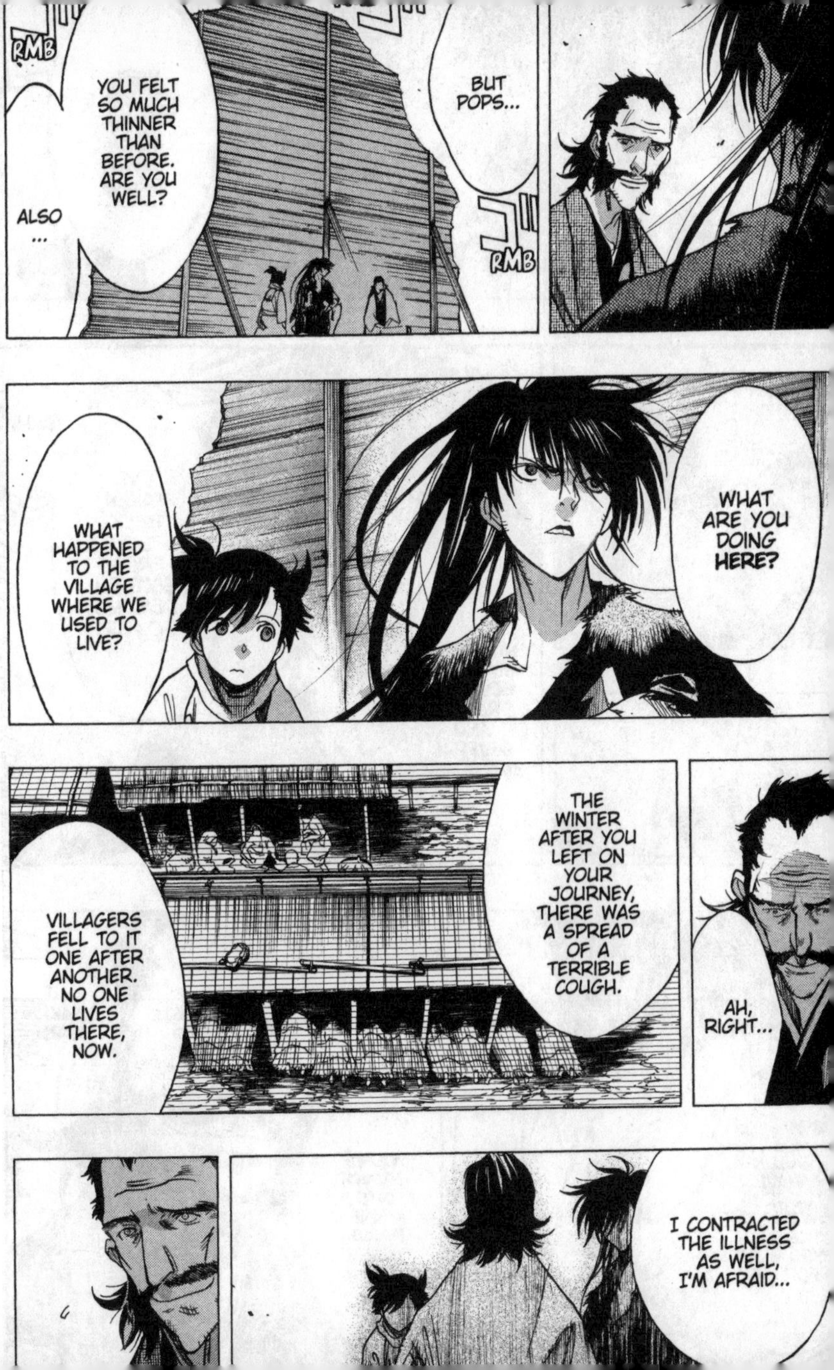
BUT POPS...
RMB
RMB
YOU FELT SO MUCH THINNER THAN BEFORE. ARE YOU WELL?
ALSO ...
WHAT ARE YOU DOING HERE?
WHAT HAPPENED TO THE VILLAGE WHERE WE USED TO LIVE?
AH, RIGHT...
THE WINTER AFTER YOU LEFT ON YOUR JOURNEY, THERE WAS A SPREAD OF A TERRIBLE COUGH.
VILLAGERS FELL TO IT ONE AFTER ANOTHER. NO ONE LIVES THERE, NOW.
I CONTRACTED THE ILLNESS AS WELL, I'M AFRAID...

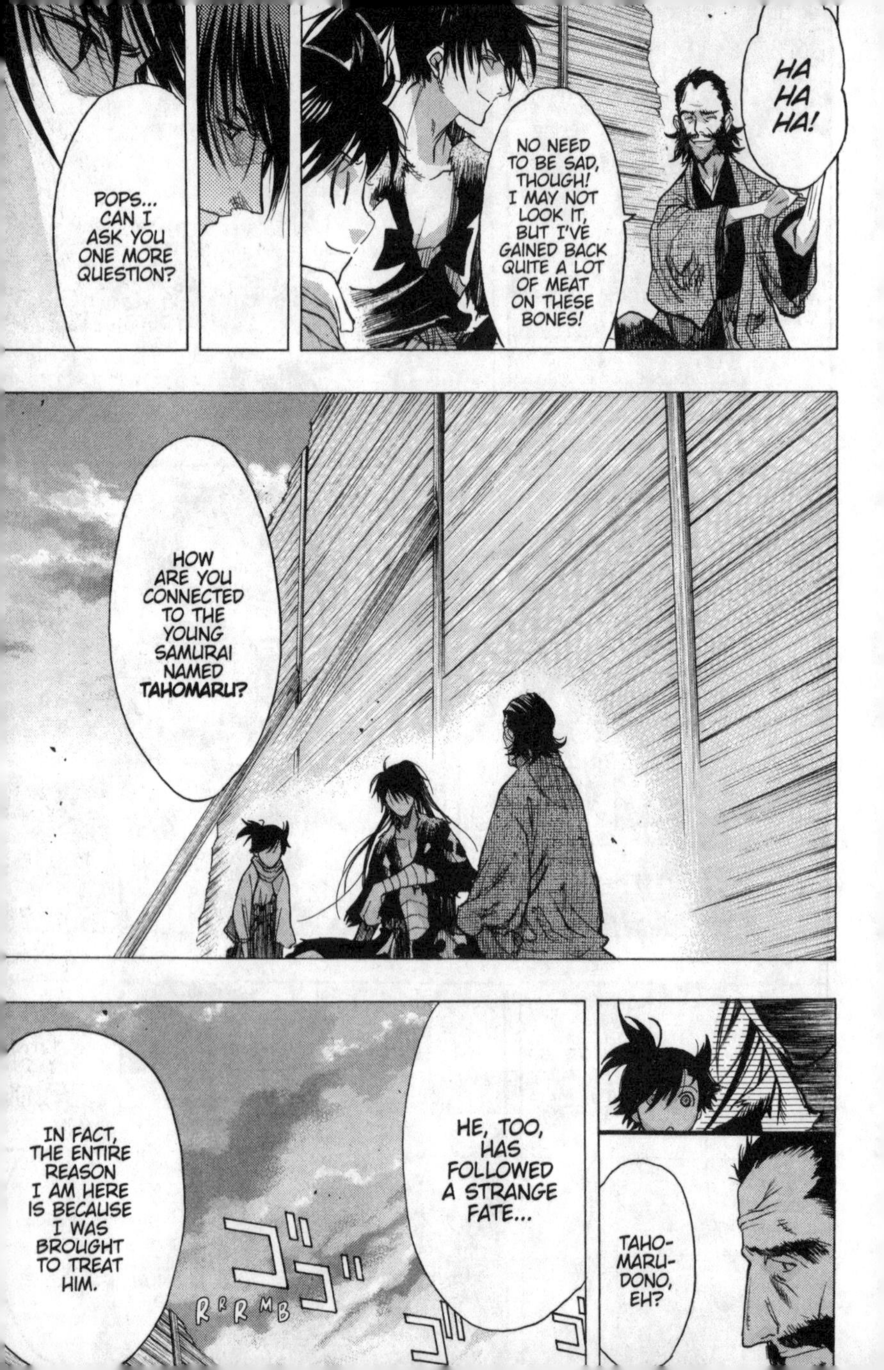
HA HA HA!
NO NEED TO BE SAD, THOUGH! I MAY NOT LOOK IT, BUT I'VE GAINED BACK QUITE A LOT OF MEAT ON THESE BONES!
POPS... CAN I ASK YOU ONE MORE QUESTION?
HOW ARE YOU CONNECTED TO THE YOUNG SAMURAI NAMED TAHOMARU?
TAHO-MARU-DONO, EH?
HE, TOO, HAS FOLLOWED A STRANGE FATE...
IN FACT, THE ENTIRE REASON I AM HERE IS BECAUSE I WAS BROUGHT TO TREAT HIM.
ゴゴ
RRRMB

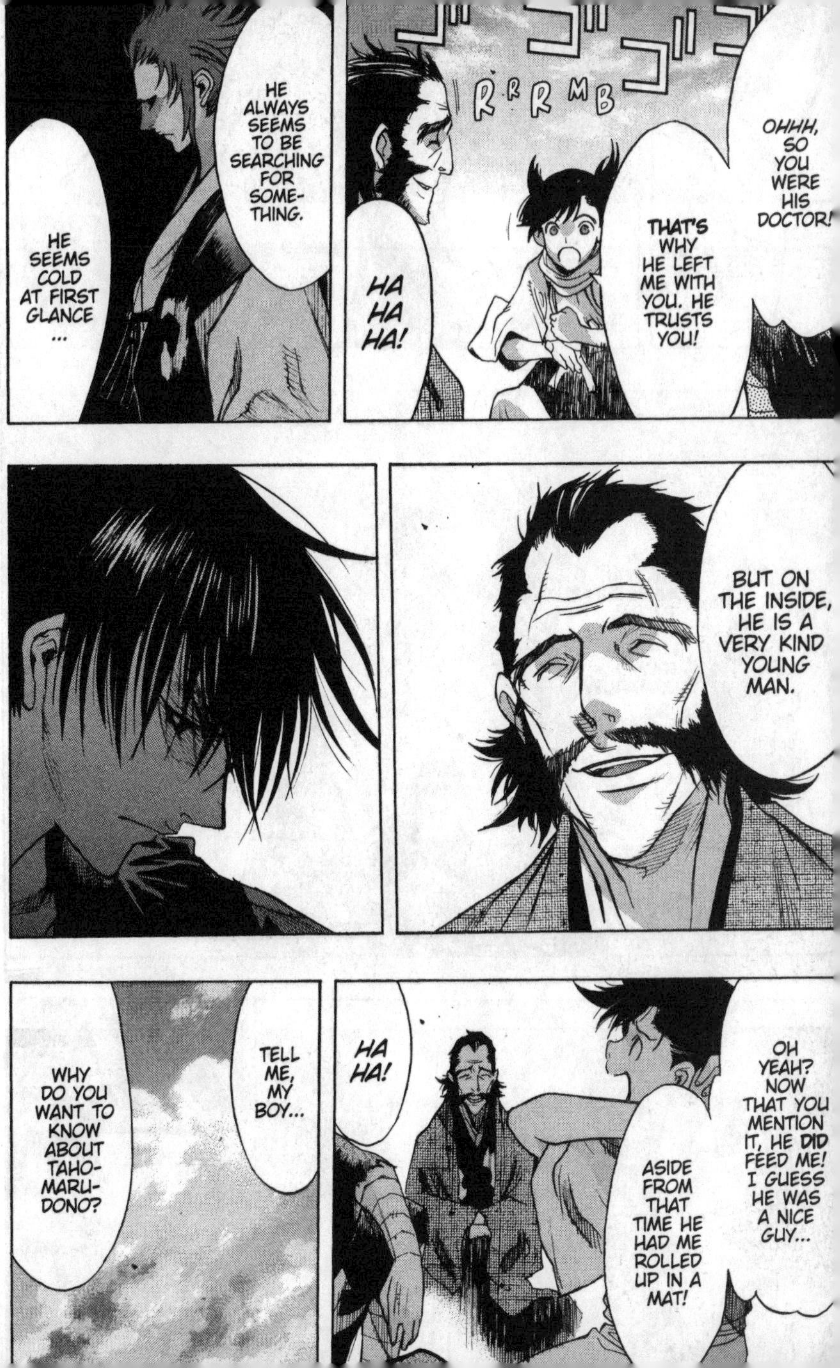
RRRMB
OHHH, SO YOU WERE HIS DOCTOR!
THAT'S WHY HE LEFT ME WITH YOU. HE TRUSTS YOU!
HA HA HA!
HE ALWAYS SEEMS TO BE SEARCHING FOR SOME-THING.
HE SEEMS COLD AT FIRST GLANCE ...
BUT ON THE INSIDE, HE IS A VERY KIND YOUNG MAN.
OH YEAH? NOW THAT YOU MENTION IT, HE DID FEED ME! I GUESS HE WAS A NICE GUY...
ASIDE FROM THAT TIME HE HAD ME ROLLED UP IN A MAT!
HA HA!
TELL ME, MY BOY...
WHY DO YOU WANT TO KNOW ABOUT TAHO-MARU-DONO?

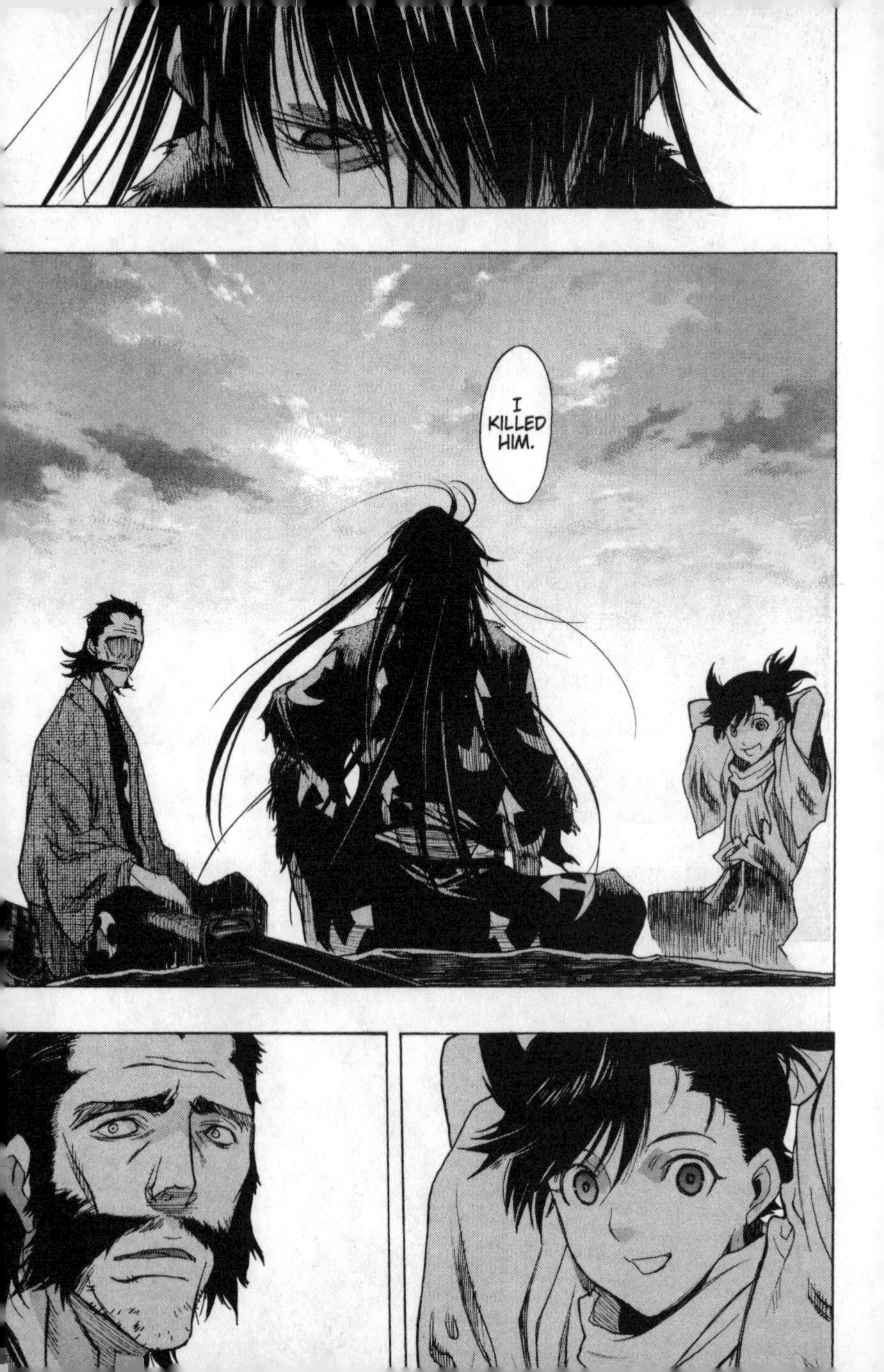
I KILLED HIM.

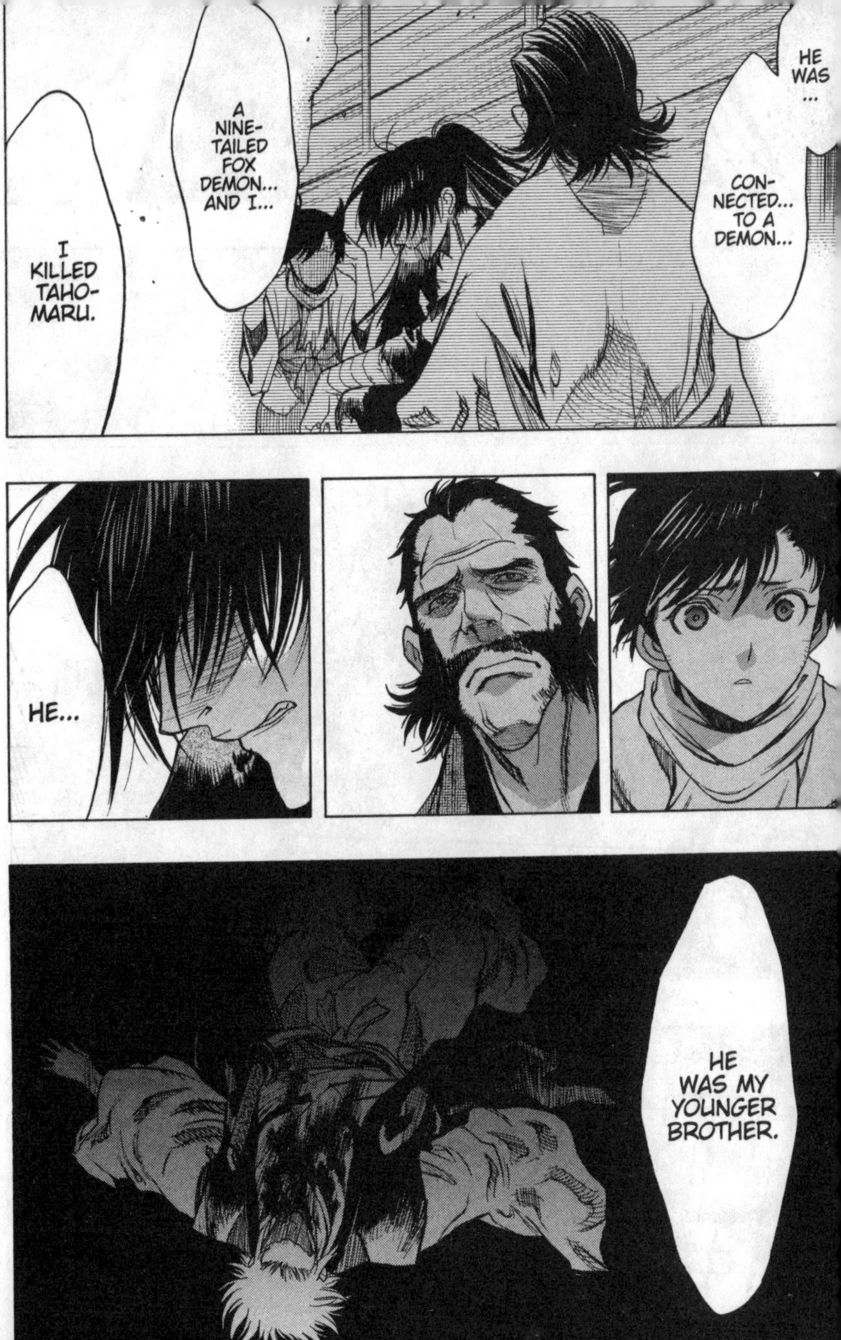
HE WAS ...
CON-NECTED... TO A DEMON...
A NINE-TAILED FOX DEMON... AND I...
I KILLED TAHO-MARU.
HE...
HE WAS MY YOUNGER BROTHER.

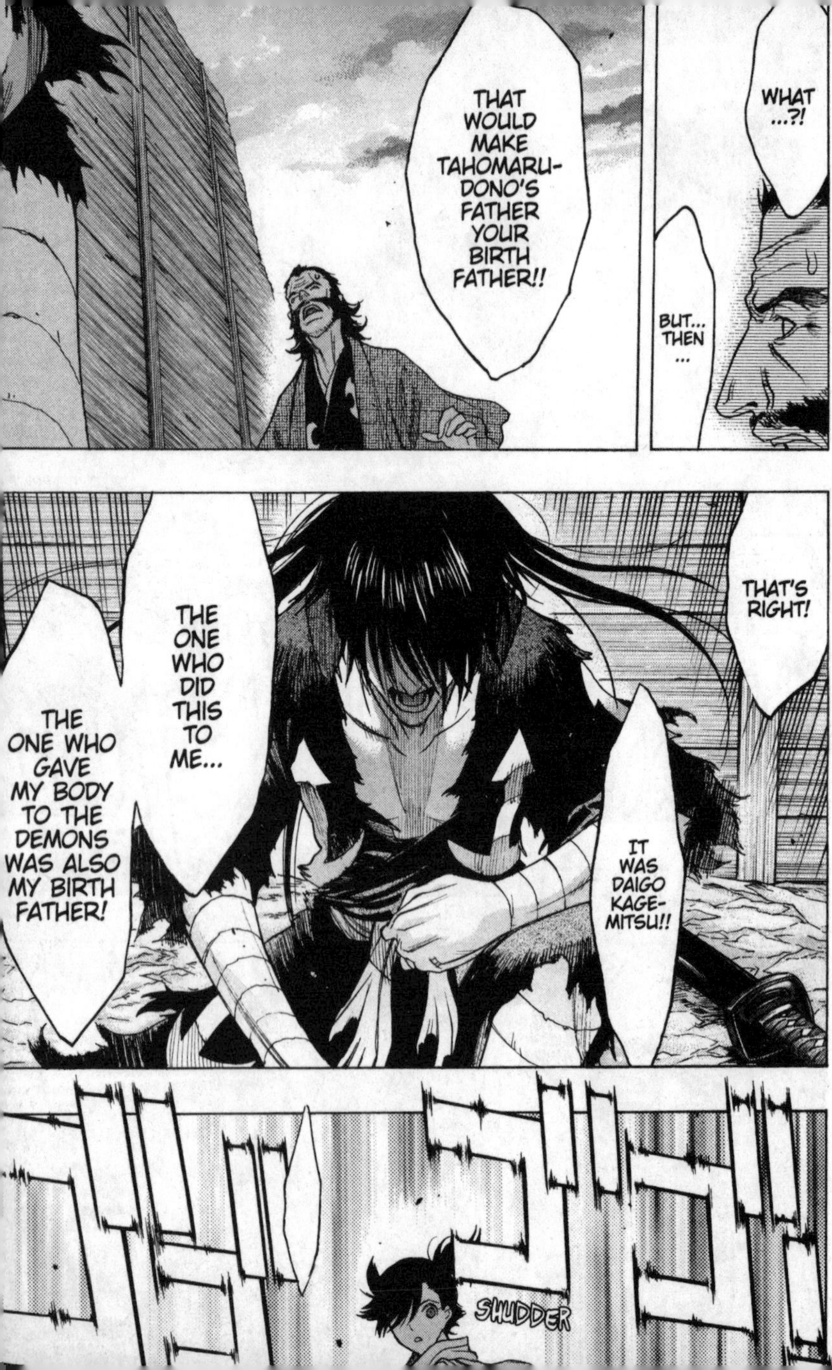
WHAT ...?!
BUT... THEN ...
THAT WOULD MAKE TAHOMARU-DONO'S FATHER YOUR BIRTH FATHER!!
THAT'S RIGHT!
IT WAS DAIGO KAGE-MITSU!!
THE ONE WHO DID THIS TO ME...
THE ONE WHO GAVE MY BODY TO THE DEMONS WAS ALSO MY BIRTH FATHER!
SHUDDER

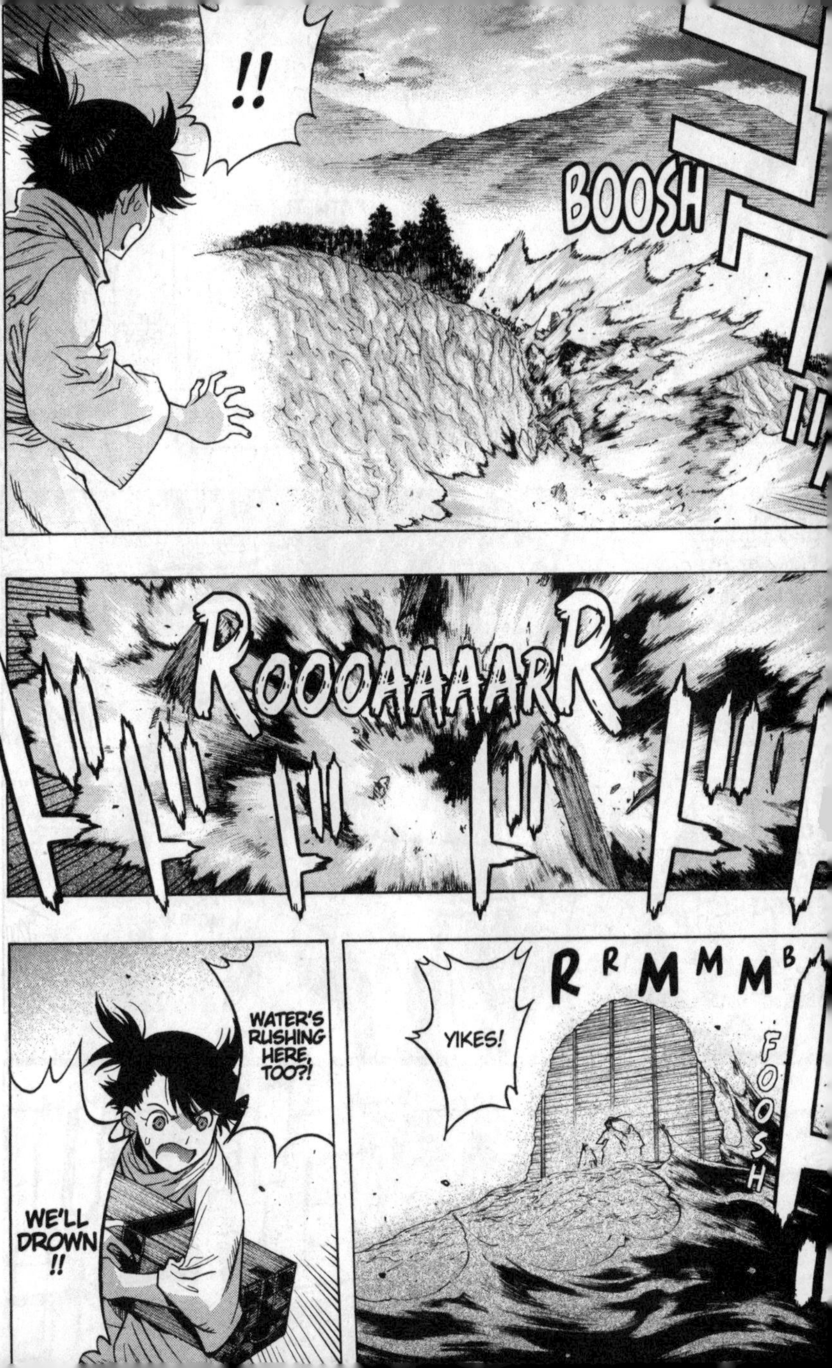
!!
BOOSH
ROOOAAAARR
RRMMMB
YIKES!
FOOSH
WATER'S RUSHING HERE, TOO?!
WE'LL DROWN !!

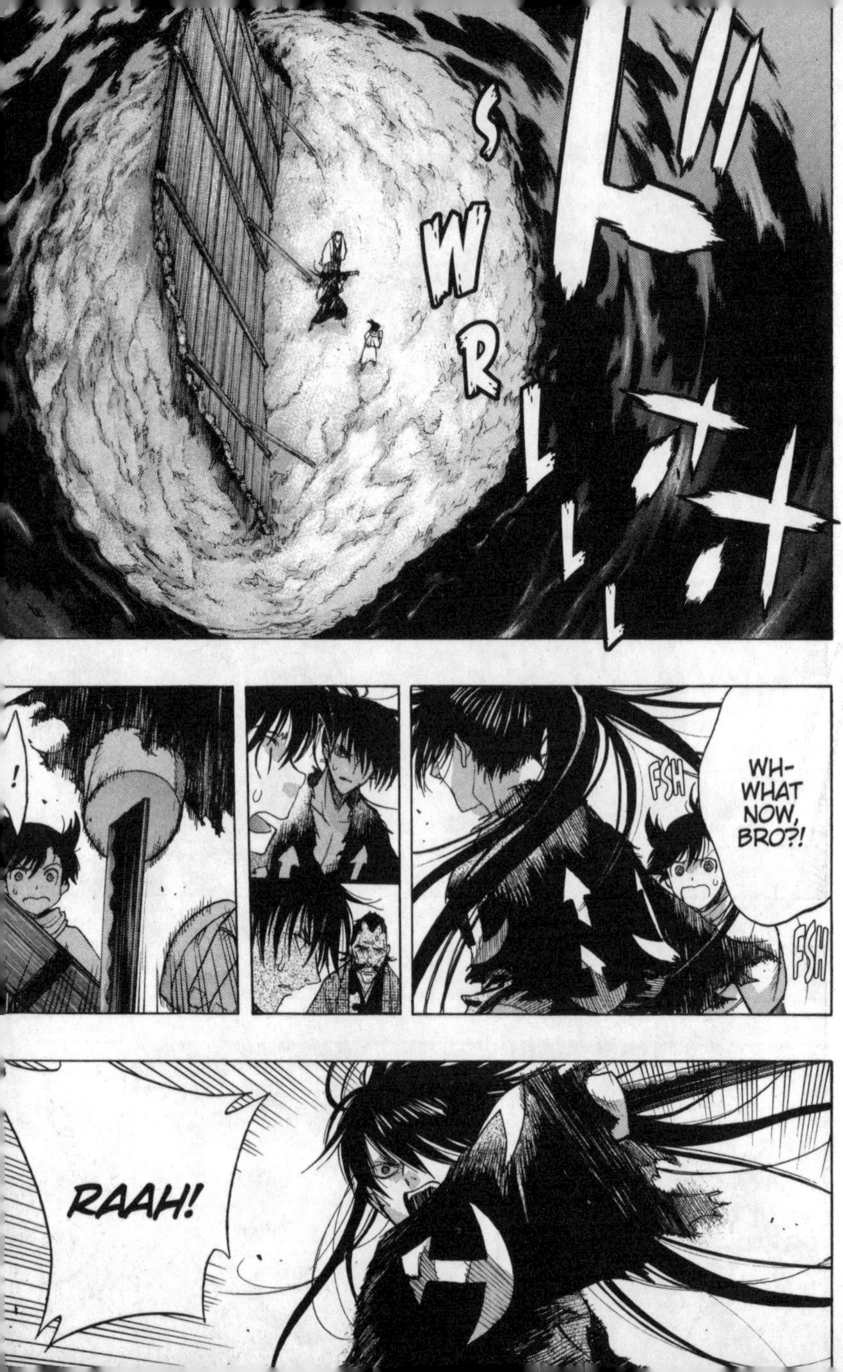
SWRLLLL
FSH
WH-
WHAT
NOW,
BRO?!
FSH
!
RAAH!

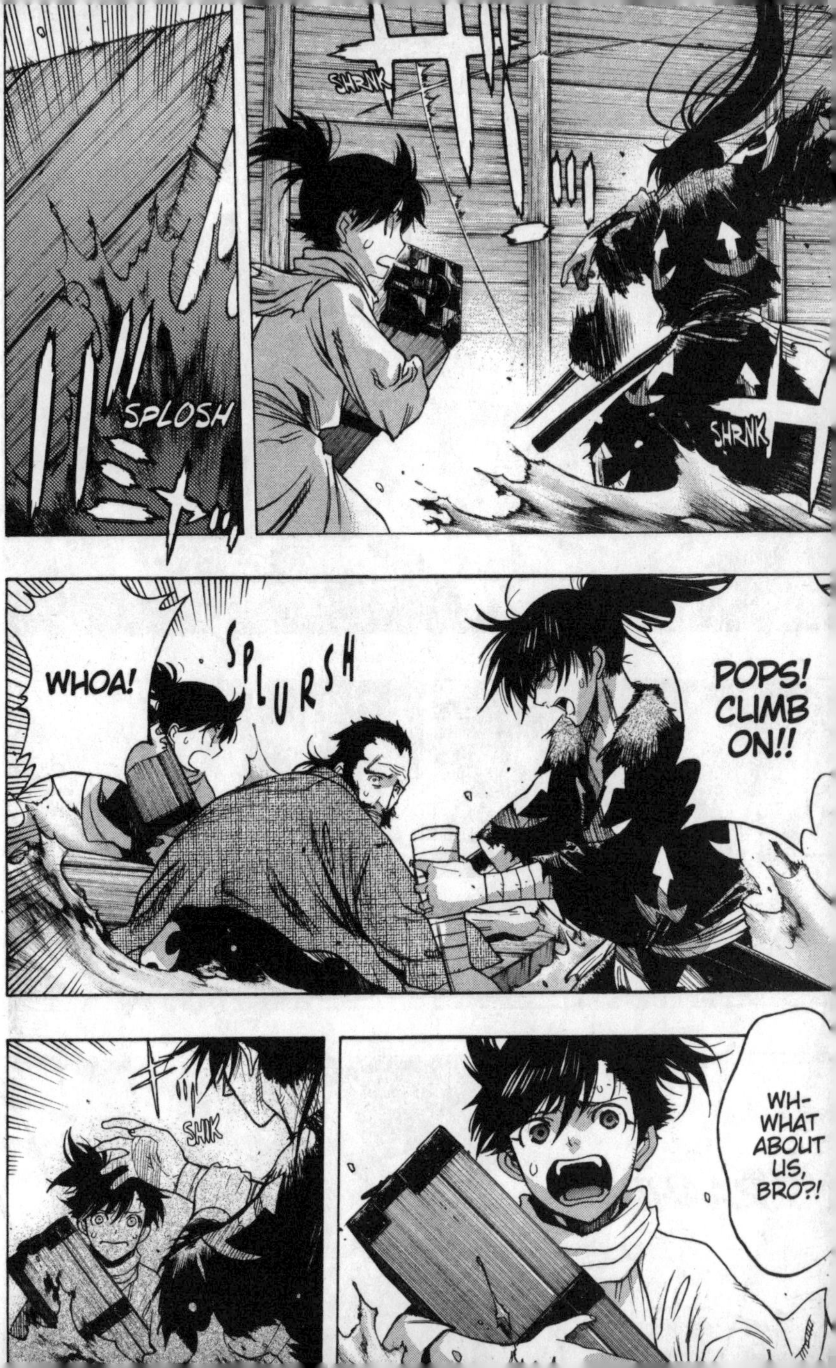
SHRNK
SHRNK
SPLOSH
POPS! CLIMB ON!!
SPLURSH
WHOA!
WH-WHAT ABOUT US, BRO?!
SHIK

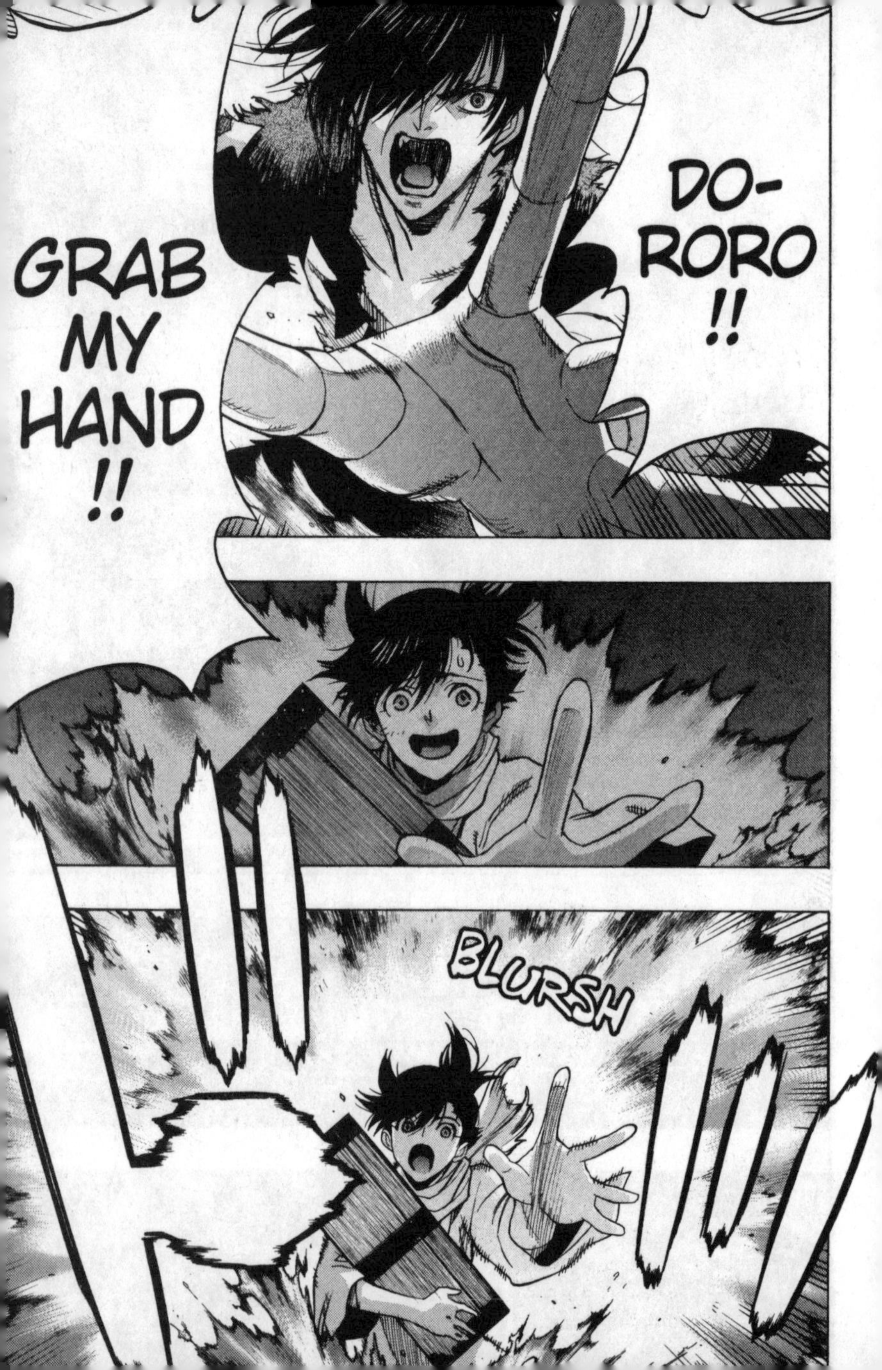
DO-RORO!!
GRAB MY HAND!!
BLURSH

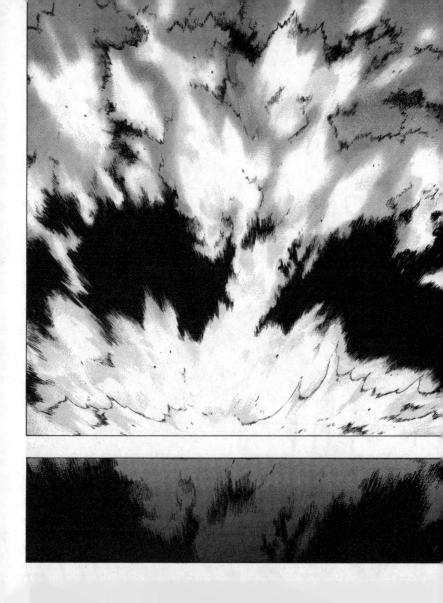

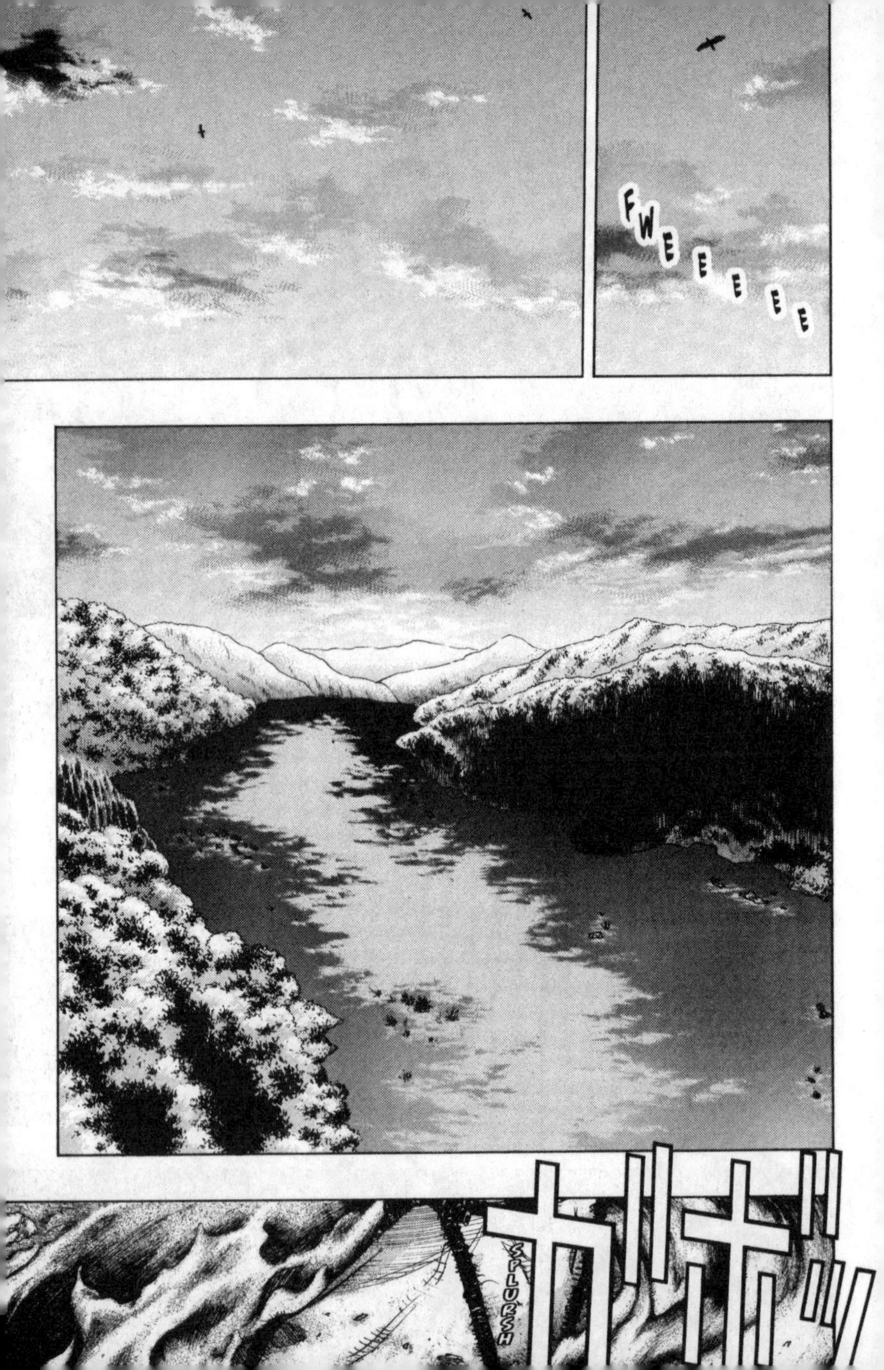
FWEEEEE
ガボッ
SPLURSH

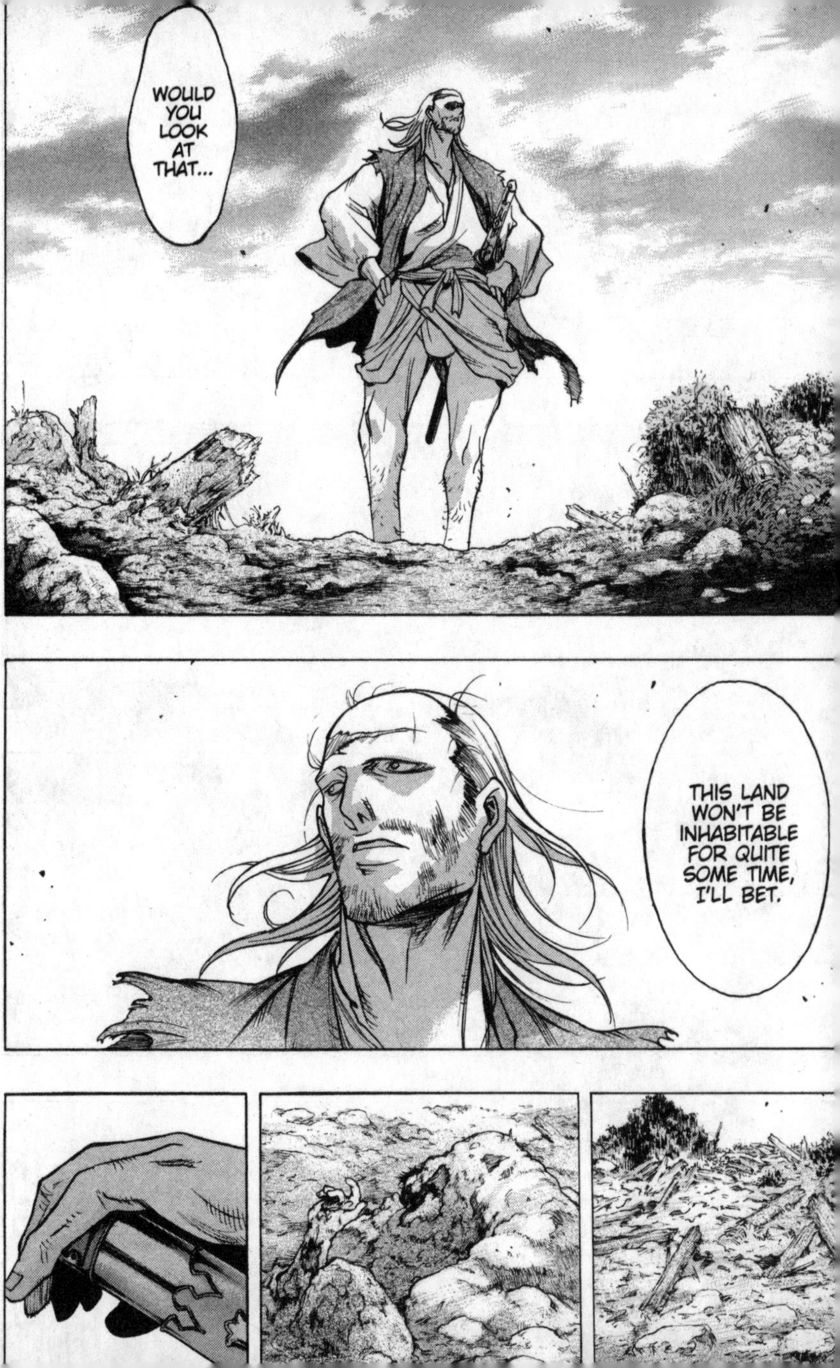
WOULD YOU LOOK AT THAT...
THIS LAND WON'T BE INHABITABLE FOR QUITE SOME TIME, I'LL BET.

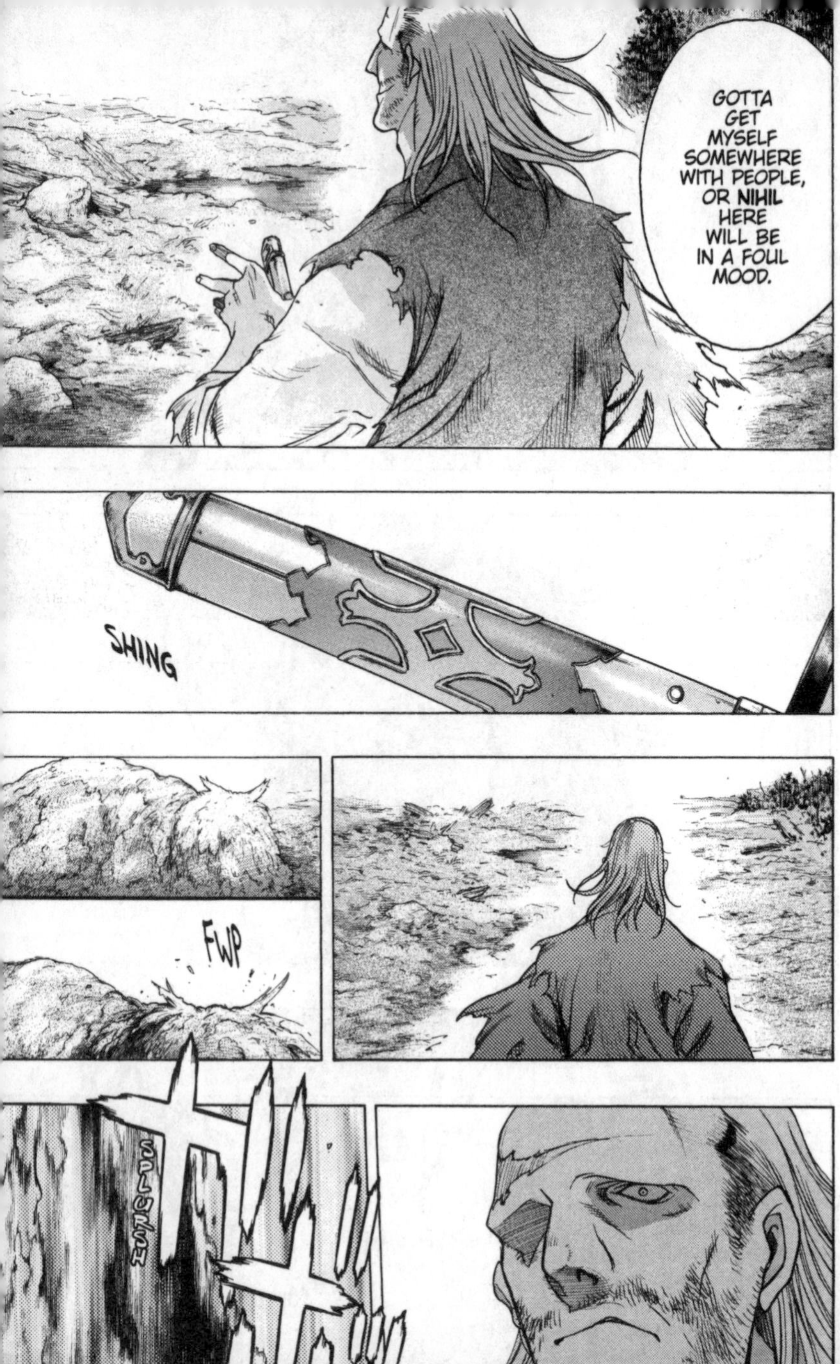
GOTTA GET MYSELF SOMEWHERE WITH PEOPLE, OR NIHIL HERE WILL BE IN A FOUL MOOD.
SHING
FWP
SPLURSH

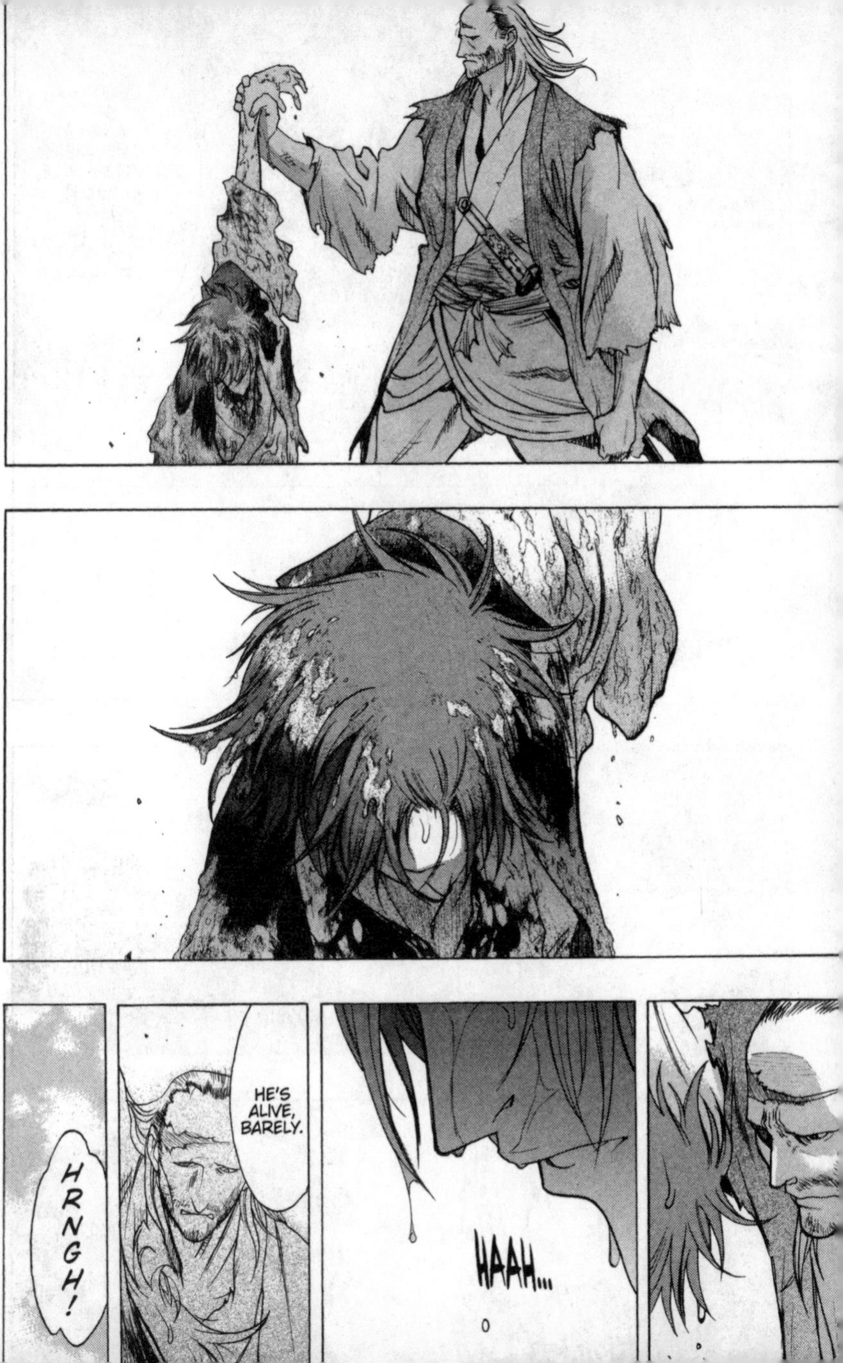
HAAH...
HE'S ALIVE, BARELY.
HRNGH!

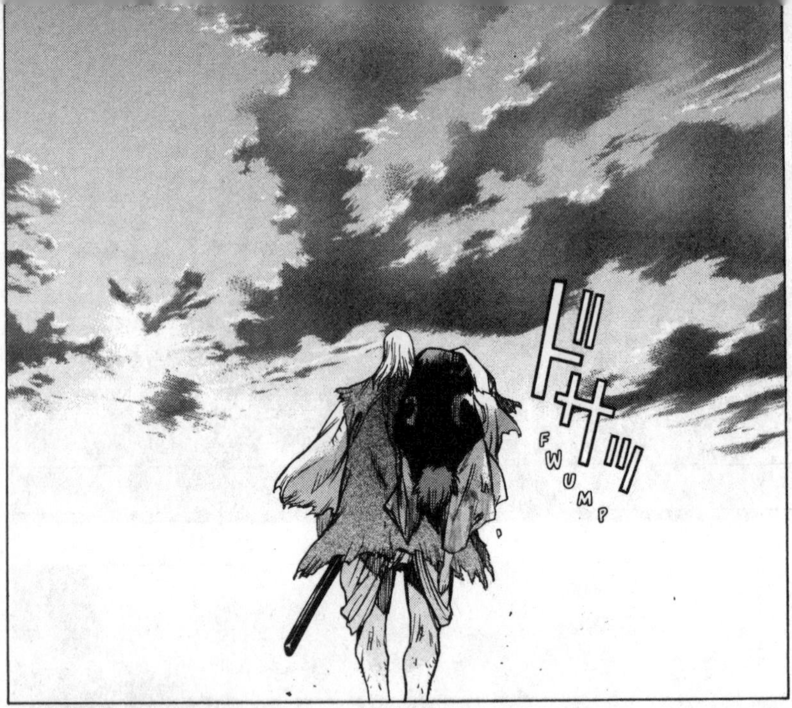
ドサッ
FWUMP
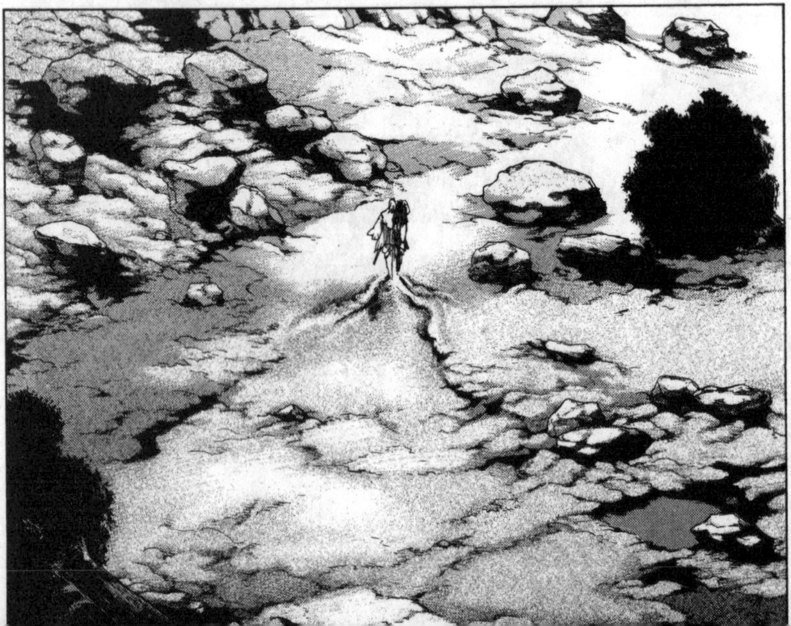

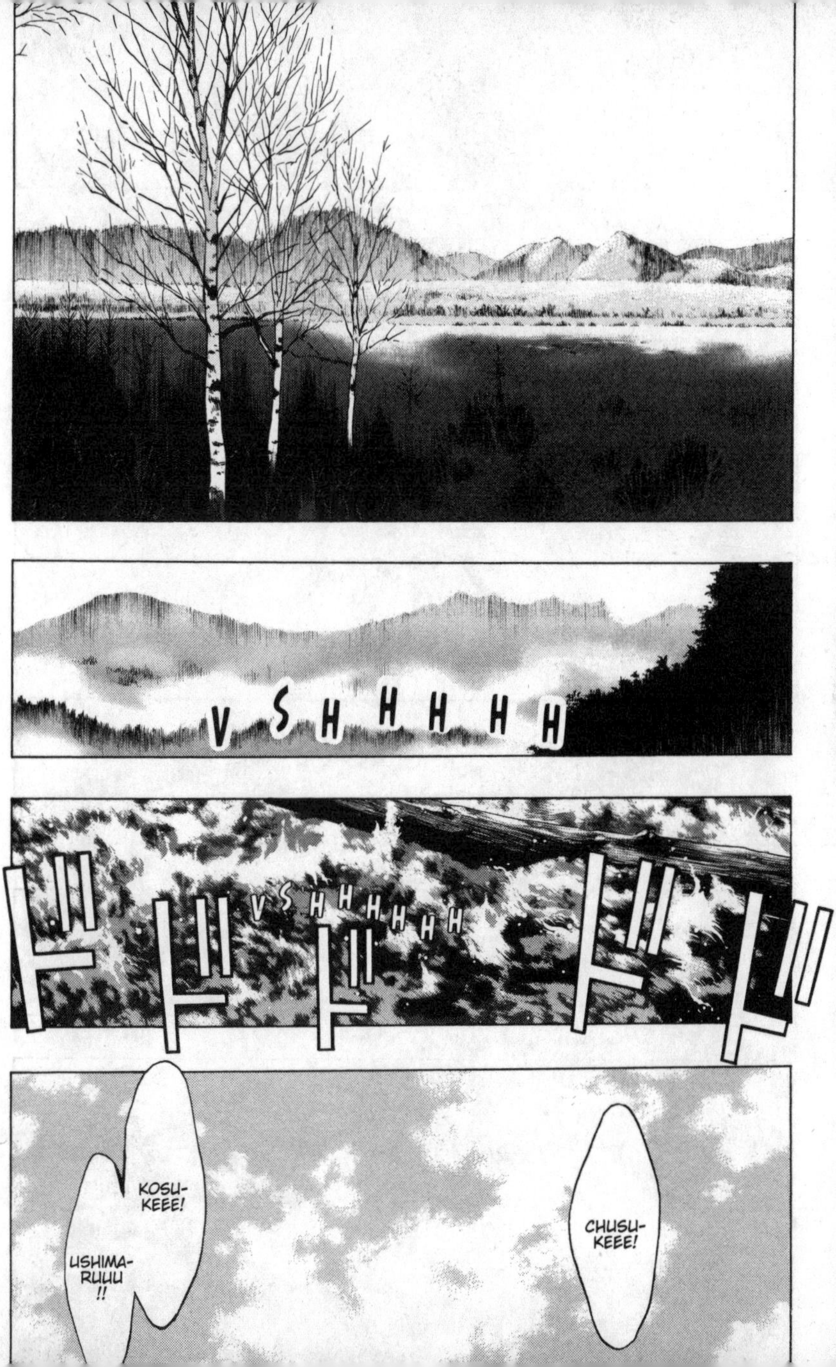
VSHHHHH
ドドドドド
VSHHHHHH
CHUSU-KEEE!
KOSU-KEEE!
USHIMA-RUUU!!

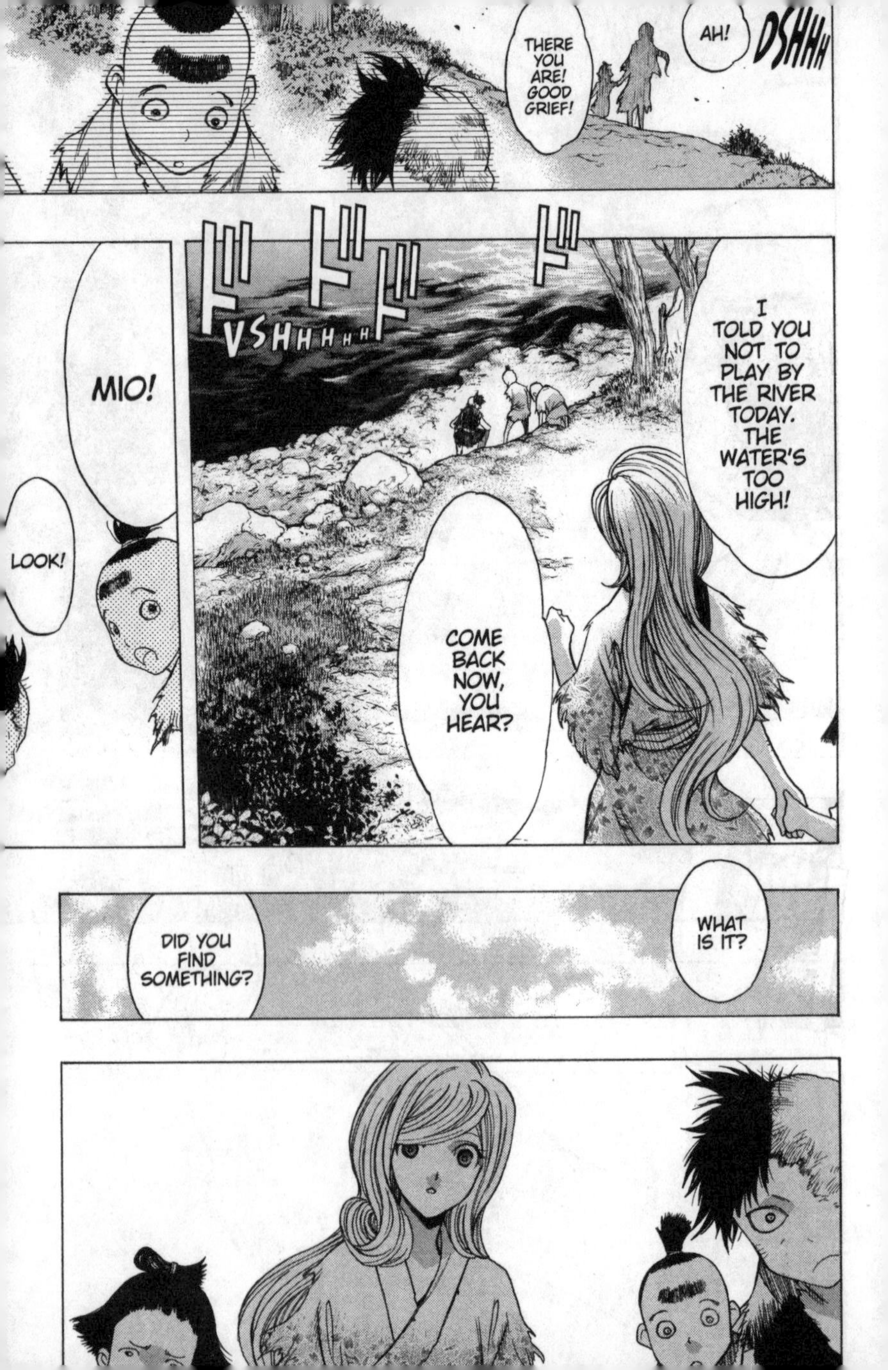
AH!
DSHHH
THERE YOU ARE! GOOD GRIEF!
I TOLD YOU NOT TO PLAY BY THE RIVER TODAY. THE WATER'S TOO HIGH!
ドドドドド
VSHHHHH
COME BACK NOW, YOU HEAR?
MIO!
LOOK!
WHAT IS IT?
DID YOU FIND SOMETHING?

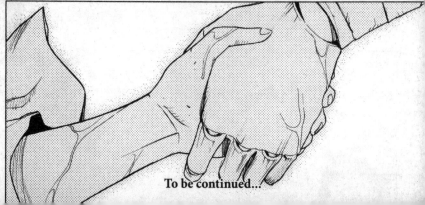

To be continued...

どろろと百鬼丸伝

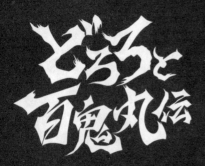

SEVEN SEAS ENTERTAIN[MENT]

THE LEGEND OF
DORORO AND H[YAKKIMARU]

story and art by **SATOSHI SHIKI**   original story by **OSAMU TEZUKA**

TRANSLATION
Amanda Haley

LETTERING AND RETOUCH
Sean Bishop

COVER DESIGN
Nicky Lim
(LOGO) **Kris Aubin**

PROOFREADER
Dawn Davis

EDITOR
J.P. Sullivan

PREPRESS TECHNICIAN
Rhiannon Rasmussen-Silverstein

PRODUCTION MANAGER
Lissa Pattillo

MANAGING EDITOR
Julie Davis

ASSOCIATE PUBLISHER
Adam Arnold

PUBLISHER
Jason DeAngelis

DORORO TO HYAKKIMARU-DEN Volume 3
©Tezuka Productions / Satoshi Shiki 2020
Originally published in Japan in 2020 by Akita Publishing Co., Ltd.
English translation rights arranged with Akita Publishing Co., Ltd.
through TOHAN CORPORATION, Tokyo.

Seven Seas press and purchase enquiries can be sent to Marketing Manager
Lianne Sentar at press@gomanga.com. Information regarding the distribution
and purchase of digital editions is available from Digital Manager CK Russell
at digital@gomanga.com.

Seven Seas and the Seven Seas logo are trademarks of
Seven Seas Entertainment. All rights reserved.

ISBN: 978-1-64827-100-7

Printed in Canada

First Printing: April 2021

10 9 8 7 6 5 4 3 2 1

FOLLOW US ONLINE: *www.sevenseasentertainment.com*

READING DIRECTIONS

This book reads from **right to left**, Japanese style.
If this is your first time reading manga, you start
reading from the top right panel on each page and
take it from there. If you get lost, just follow the
numbered diagram here. It may seem backwards at
first, but you'll get the hang of it! Have fun!!

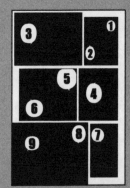